SO-BEA-665

Money and the Economy

THE HARBRACE SERIES IN BUSINESS AND ECONOMICS

JOHN J. KLEIN
Fordham University

*Money
and the Economy*

Under the General Editorship of
WILLIAM J. BAUMOL *Princeton University*

HARCOURT, BRACE & WORLD, INC.
NEW YORK / CHICAGO / BURLINGAME

To Sylvia and Leslie

Library of Congress Catalog Card Number: 65-17744

PRINTED IN THE UNITED STATES OF AMERICA

Editor's Foreword

By its nature monetary policy is most successful when the need for it is least apparent. On this criterion, the performance of monetary policy has been mixed in recent years. We have had no cataclysmic depressions, and price levels have been relatively stable. At the same time, however, unemployment has remained distressingly high, economic growth has fallen short of what some would like to see us achieve, and our balance of payments has often given us cause for concern.

Unfortunately, the interrelationships among monetary problems are of such complexity that relatively untutored common sense can provide little understanding of their workings. For one thing, these problems cannot be treated effectively by monetary measures alone, and the relationship between monetary policy and other governmental activities is difficult to measure. Moreover, most monetary policy actions themselves produce a mixture of salutary and deleterious consequences. Most monetary measures that are designed to stimulate employment, for example, are also likely to increase inflationary pressures and to aggravate the payments imbalance.

Money and the Economy is an analysis of the role of money in the economy. Although the emphasis is largely on monetary policy throughout, Professor Klein devotes nearly half of his text to a lucid, concise explanation of the workings of our private institutions and the operations of the Federal Reserve System. In addition he presents a fairly extensive historical critique of monetary controls. He then develops his own model of income determination, which leads the student in easy stages to a relatively sophisticated understanding of monetary theory. Having presented this solid background, Professor Klein then proceeds to discuss in detail the problems that currently face us in monetary, fiscal, and international economic policy.

In *Money and the Economy* Professor Klein has made an important contribution toward helping the student master an important and demanding subject and, in so doing, he has supplied a text that satisfies the most basic objectives of this series.

WILLIAM J. BAUMOL

Princeton, New Jersey
January, 1965

Preface

This textbook is designed to fill the needs of a comprehensive one-semester course in money and banking. It was primarily written for two types of student: the liberal arts student who takes only one course in money and banking, and the business student who studies money and banking in those economics and finance departments that stress money and the economy rather than bank management. For both it attempts to provide a basic but rigorous exposition of banking, theoretical analysis, and economic policy.

I have written this book in the belief that a textbook should be addressed primarily to the student rather than to the professional economist. It should be clear, self-contained, and self-explanatory, and at the same time it should be timely and challenging; this is a hard balance to strike. Furthermore, I think that the student should be able to understand the basic principles of a discipline from a close reading of a text with a minimum of assistance from the instructor. It does not seem to me that the function of the instructor is to teach a textbook. A textbook may serve as a helpful guide to him, but in the final analysis he should teach his own course.

The theme of this book is that money plays an important role in the economy. With historical perspective, the text discusses the operation of the banking system and presents a critical analysis of monetary theory and policy. It is divided into four main parts. Part I, "Money and Private Financial Institutions," examines the private financial institutions that determine the volume and composition of our monetary resources. The commercial banking system is also studied in some detail. Emphasis is placed on financial institutions as potential sources of economic disturbance. Part II, "Money and Government," offers a concise history of central banking in the United States and evaluates federal government attempts over the years to regulate money in order to prevent the extremes of inflation and deflation. Part III, "Money and Aggregate Economic Activity," traces the historical development of monetary theory and posits a contemporary framework of analysis for studying the impact of money supply and demand forces upon economic activity. Finally, Part IV, "Money and Aggregate Economic Policy," uses the analytical framework developed in the preceding section to evaluate various alternative monetary, fiscal, and international economic policies.

It is my hope that the student will emerge from his reading of this book neither with a banker's view of the system, nor with the Federal Reserve's view, nor with the bias of any school of economic theory, but rather with a well-integrated, overall perception of the monetary system and the theory on which it is based.

My gratitude extends to many. I owe an intellectual debt to my past teachers of monetary and fiscal economics, Milton Friedman, Earl J. Hamilton, Lloyd Mints, and Kenyon Poole. Portions of the manuscript have been read by Eugene Lerner, William Partlan, Louis Spadaro, and Charles J. Walsh. William J. Baumol read the manuscript in its entirety, contributing significantly in the process. The Reverend Arthur A. North, S.J., former Dean of the Graduate School of Arts and Sciences at Fordham University, is to be thanked for his encouragement and assistance. My wife Sylvia served as editor at home and helped me to make the volume more readable. I am grateful also to Elaine Haessler, who typed the entire manuscript. My undergraduate students at Fordham University and Manhattanville College worked their way through classroom versions of the manuscript. Among my graduate students at Fordham University who caught errors and challenged me to rethink parts of the analysis are Albert Bookbinder, James Gallagher, Francis McGrath, Ernest Therrien, and Sister Francis Xavier Thiel. Finally, a fellowship from Fordham University during the summer of 1963 helped support some of the research necessary for the second section of the text.

JOHN J. KLEIN

Spring Valley, New York
January, 1965

Contents

tionship Between Y and i. Summary of Forces Affecting IS.

The Demand for Money. The Interaction of the Demand for Money and the Supply of Money. The Relationship Between GNP and the Interest Rate. The Intersection of the IS and LM Schedules. Applications of the Model of Income Determination. The Problem of the Price Level. The Problem of the Productive Capacity of the Economy. The Role of Money.

The Keynesian Position on Money. The Contemporary Quantity Theory Position on Money. The "Competing Financial Asset" Position on Money. Conclusion.

PART IV. MONEY AND AGGREGATE ECONOMIC POLICY

Policy Defined. Choosing Means and Ends. Summary and Preview.

Economic Goals and Federal Reserve Policy. Specific Policy Proposals.

Chapter 1

Introduction

The economist is concerned with how man makes his living. How the individual earns his income, how businesses use resources to produce goods and services, and how the economy as a whole functions are all important aspects of the study of economics. It is for many of us a fascinating and stimulating study, for separate individuals and separate businesses from thousands of political communities somehow manage to work together to produce goods and services that satisfy people's basic wants.

How does the economy accomplish this? Part of the answer lies in the fact that our economy runs on money. Individuals use it to purchase goods and services. Businesses use it to expand production. National governments use it to satisfy social wants.

Money does not always function properly, of course. There are times when businesses, individuals, and governments all feel that there is a shortage of funds. This may happen during periods of either recession or inflation. In periods of recession people with insufficient incomes and monetary resources are forced to reduce their spending. This in turn results in a decreased demand for goods, lower production, and fewer jobs. On the other hand, in periods of inflation almost everyone may be employed and earning apparently adequate incomes, but still feel that their incomes and monetary resources are inadequate in light of rapidly rising prices. How do such paradoxical situations arise? This book will concentrate on problems of this sort.

Part I of this book explains the nature of money and the private financial institutions that create our monetary resources. Particular emphasis is placed on the economic impact of financial institutions, especially their effect on inflation and recession. Part II studies the governmental institutions that determine the size of our monetary base. This section explains how the federal government attempts to regulate monetary resources to prevent inflation and recession. Part III develops a framework within which we can analyze the interdependence and mutual determination of money demand, money supply, interest, prices, employment, and aggregate economic activity. Finally, Part IV introduces various economic policies—monetary, fiscal, and international—that have been suggested as solutions to our current economic problems.

WHAT IS MONEY?

Definitions of money abound. Money is sometimes defined in terms of the job it does. For example, money serves as a medium of exchange, a store of value, a standard of deferred payments, a unit of account, and a means of paying off debt. Money may also be defined according to its physical properties. Sometimes it is coin, paper currency, and checking deposit accounts. It may exist in many other forms, however. In Europe, for example, after World War II, cigarettes were widely used as a medium of exchange, since the supply of currency was so abundant and prices were rising so rapidly that currency had little actual value. In addition, gold, silver, wampum, stone, and even leather coin have been considered money.

For our purposes, the most suitable definition of money focuses on the primary use to which money is put in the American economy, as follows: *money is anything generally acceptable as a means of paying off debt.* In our economy, coin, paper currency, and checking deposit accounts are considered money since nearly everyone will accept these things in payment of debt. It is readily apparent why coin and paper currency are money; it is not so obvious why checking deposit accounts are also considered to be money, however. Checks are money because they function like currency. By far the greater dollar volume of all monetary transactions in the economy involve the use of checks. The extensive utilization of checking deposit accounts (hereafter to be more correctly called demand deposits) is clearly illustrated by the fact that the Federal Reserve banks handle more than a trillion and a third dollars worth of checks a year.[1] Checks are very nearly as liquid as currency. The average man, even when he questions the credit worthiness of a check user, will still be willing to accept a cashier's check from him in lieu of a personal check.

The term "payment of debt" is emphasized in our definition because in most transactions in the economy a debt is created and subsequently extinguished. This occurs because businesses seldom make immediate payment for goods and services. Consequently, for a period of time a debt exists. Similarly, individuals are often not billed for goods and services they have purchased until the end of the month. Here too a debt arises and is subsequently extinguished through the use of either check money or currency. Even when one purchases groceries at a grocery store a momentary debt is created, which is, of course, immediately extinguished by a cash payment to the clerk.

Before any item can function as money it must be generally acceptable, and to retain this quality of acceptability, money must exhibit over time some degree of stability in value. History is full of examples of monies

[1] Board of Governors of the Federal Reserve System, *Annual Report* (1963), p. 226.

that lost their value and were consequently abandoned as a medium of exchange. In order to retain the public's faith money must have stable purchasing power. Consider the effect on the pensioner who is receiving an annual pension of $1,500 when the price level suddenly doubles. The purchasing power of the income from his pension and whatever savings he has are cut in half. The human misery that this entails is not something hypothetical, but very real. Imagine what would have happened to you and your family if you had lived in the Deep South from January of 1861 to January of 1864, when prices rose 27.8 times,[2] or in Germany from August, 1922, to November, 1923, when prices rose 1.02×10^{10}, over ten billion times. After World War II in Hungary from August, 1945, to July, 1946, prices rose by 3.81×10^{27}![3]

How do such tremendous price increases and consequent reductions in the purchasing power of money occur? Several possible solutions to that question will be considered later in this text. For the moment, however, suffice it to say that these price level increases were associated with a money supply that went "out of order." For example, in the Confederacy the money stock increased 11.6 times during the previously mentioned period.[4] In Germany after World War I it increased 7.32×10^9, and in Hungary after World War II 1.19×10^{25}.[5]

On the other hand, do periods of price deflation and accompanying increase in the value of money lead to any lessening of economic distress? Apparently not, since unemployment and a drop in production have usually accompanied price decline in the modern world. For example, in the United States from 1929 to 1933 the price level dropped some 25 percent.[6] Thus, a dollar spent in 1929 would have been able to buy $1.33 worth of goods in 1933, yet unemployment rose from a yearly average of 1,550,000 to 12,830,000 in that period.[7] This was accompanied by a 27 percent drop in the money stock and a 30 percent drop in the real output.[8]

Thus, we can see that money does not always have stable purchasing power. The ability of money to command goods and services decreases with inflation and increases with deflation. This change in the purchasing power of money is accompanied by employment and output changes. In our everyday experience a dollar can buy tomorrow about as much as it can buy today, but over longer periods of time its value may change signifi-

---

[2] Eugene M. Lerner, "Money, Prices, and Wages in the Confederacy, 1861–65," *Journal of Political Economy* (1955), p. 29.

[3] Phillip Cagan, "The Monetary Dynamics of Hyperinflation," *Studies in the Quantity Theory of Money*, Milton Friedman, ed. (Chicago: University of Chicago Press, 1956), p. 26.

[4] Lerner, *op. cit.*, p. 21.

[5] Cagan, *op. cit.*, p. 26.

[6] *Federal Reserve Bulletin*, June, 1964, p. 776.

[7] U.S. Department of Commerce, *Statistical Abstract of the United States*, Washington D.C.

[8] *Federal Reserve Bulletin*, June, 1964, p. 778.

cantly. Consumer prices in the United States in 1929, 1933, 1945, and 1960 were 73, 55, 77, and 126 percent respectively of their 1947–49 average.[9] Thus, the United States, which has had relatively minor price level fluctuation, has nevertheless experienced both price inflation and price deflation at various periods. The behavior of prices in other countries, as previously cited, has been often disastrous by comparison.

Price inflation benefits the debtors in the economy and quite clearly harms the creditors. Who then is harmed by price inflation? The people with large volumes of savings. Who is benefited? Some may imagine that the consuming public benefits because of the large volume of installment debt outstanding. Householders are actually net savers in the economy, however. Businesses and governmental bodies are net debtors. Thus, it is the householder who is hurt by the deterioration in the value of money since his savings during inflation can buy less than formerly. On the other hand the householder benefits from price deflation while debtors are harmed. Similarly, pensioners and those with fixed incomes are benefited by deflation and harmed by inflation.

THE USES OF MONEY

How is money used? Money is used principally in the payment of debts created when goods and services are purchased. Most of us use our productive resources to acquire money and, in turn, use money to purchase goods and services. In reality, then, goods and services are exchanged for goods and services. Money merely facilitates this exchange. For this reason money is often called a *medium of exchange.* Why do we need money? Consider for a moment what this economy would be like without money. How would one exchange goods for goods? Some might answer that there need be no exchange of goods. Let everyone produce what he needs for himself. This would overlook the tremendous advantages of specialization, however. Some people can make shoes better than others; some can produce machines more efficiently; others are very talented in the arts. The total production in an economy will usually be more abundant when everyone is doing that job for which his talents and training best suit him. Civilization depends upon specialization for its very existence.

Imagine, then, a specialized economy with no money. How would goods be exchanged? The producer of shoes who wanted food would have to find a producer of food who wanted shoes. This is known as *double coincidence of wants.* If there were thousands of goods produced and desired, it would be almost impossible to arrange the necessary number of exchanges.

---

[9] *Ibid.,* p. 776.

One would also have to work out innumerable ratios of exchange of one good for another. How many shoes must one give up to acquire guns, stockings, bread, etc., and vice versa? Thus, if there were just 1,000 commodities in the economy, there would have to be almost 500,000 rates of exchange between the goods.[10]

Money eliminates all of these complexities. One need no longer seek out those who have the goods one needs and who also desire the goods that one has produced. Instead, goods may be exchanged for money and money may then be used to buy other goods and services. Much wasted effort in exchanging goods for goods is thus eliminated and the total production of the economy can be substantially increased. All goods now have a price, stated uniformly in terms of money rather than in terms of other goods. Thus, it may also be said that money acts as a *unit of account.* Prices of goods are stated and reckoned in terms of the amount of money that must be given to acquire them. In other words, the price of goods is counted in terms of the monetary unit of account. The dollar, the peso, the lira, the franc, the Deutsche mark, the hwan, the yen, the ruble are all units of account. The things which serve as money—in our economy, currency and demand deposits—are also counted in terms of the unit of account. Thus, in contemporary society the unit of account is simply an abstract measure of value just as the pound or the ounce are abstract measures of weight.

Money also serves as a *store of value.* People want money not only for the goods and services that they can purchase today, but also for the goods and services they will want to buy in the future. Of course, money is only one way of storing up the ability to buy goods and services. Stocks, bonds, and life insurance policies are also means of doing this. These must first be converted into money before goods can actually be purchased, however. Thus, money is sometimes said to be the most liquid of the various types of claims over future goods and services because it is the one thing that can be immediately used to acquire them.

Another function of money is to serve as a *standard of deferred payments.* This role is an outgrowth of the use of money as a means of paying debt and as a unit of account. Contracts are often written providing for future payments to be made in specific sums of money. A bond, for example, is the contractual promise of a corporation to make periodic interest payments to bondholders and to redeem the bond at full face value at some specified time in the future. It is agreed that interest payments plus principal when due on bonds are to be made in the form of money. Thus, money is both the standard by which deferred payments of bond interest are to be reckoned and the means by which these payments are to be made.

---

[10] The formula $n(n-1)/2$, where n refers to the number of goods, may be used to determine the number of different ratios of exchange. This formula is the standard expression for the number of possible combinations of n items taken two at a time.

SUMMARY

This chapter has attempted to (1) give some indication of the importance of money in our economic system, (2) define money, and (3) indicate its uses. Money has been defined in this chapter as anything that serves as a means of paying off debt and is generally acceptable in the community. The basic purpose of money is to facilitate payment of debt and thereby to expedite trade and production in the economy. Money is used to overcome the difficulties of a barter economy. When it is doing its job efficiently, money is able to facilitate trade and stimulate economic activity. It also serves as a store of value, a unit of account, and a standard of deferred payments.

In our modern economy it is important that we regulate money and spending. As our early examples showed, if money is either issued to excess or not issued and spent in sufficient quantities, serious damage may be done to the economy. Thus it is important that money have a stable value, that is, relatively stable purchasing power.

PART I   *Money and Private*
Financial Institutions

Chapter 2

Money and Liquid Wealth
in the United States

Where does money fit within a general scheme of property holding? How does money differ from other forms of wealth and how do other forms of wealth influence money? In this chapter we will try to answer these questions. We will then describe the currency component of our money supply in greater detail. Subsequent chapters will deal intensively with the demand deposit component of the money supply.

WEALTH AND CLAIMS TO WEALTH

The wealth of an individual consists of the total value of his physical goods (*real wealth*) and the total amount of his claims to real wealth (*liquid wealth*). Money is only one of the forms in which an individual may choose to hold his liquid wealth. When held in the form of money, wealth represents generalized purchasing power, the ability to buy goods and services today and in the future. Among the alternatives to money as a form of liquid-wealth holding are claims to wealth such as time and savings deposit accounts in commercial banks, savings deposit accounts in mutual savings banks, savings and loan share accounts, the stocks and bonds of private businesses and governments, and the cash value of life insurance policies.

What determines the distribution of an individual's wealth holdings among these various means of holding liquid wealth? That is difficult to answer. It may be due to individual tastes and preferences, the rate of interest, expectations concerning future prices of goods versus liquid assets, or simply the amount of these items that one already has. For example, a decline in interest rates may very well induce people to hold more money and stocks relative to bonds, other things being equal. If prices are expected to rise, it would be advantageous to reduce one's money holdings and bonds in order to acquire goods now that will shortly cost considerably more. If money holdings have increased relative to other forms of wealth, then one may feel able to purchase additional goods and services. Chapters 19 and 20 will provide a more detailed analysis of the fluctuations in the demand for various forms of wealth.

When speaking of the wealth of a nation, as opposed to the wealth of an individual, it is incorrect to add up the total amount of real wealth and liquid wealth in the economy. *Liquid wealth* in the entire economy represents only a *claim to physical goods*. To add the two together would thus be double counting. The individual can add to his total real wealth by converting his liquid wealth into physical goods. This is impossible for the economy as a whole, however, because if everyone were to convert his claims to wealth into real goods, there would be no more real goods than existed before the conversion. There is only one stock of real goods. The ultimate amount of real wealth in the economy depends not upon the claims to wealth, but rather upon productive resources and technology.

THE LIQUID WEALTH SYSTEM
OF THE UNITED STATES

The liquid wealth of a nation may be classified according to degrees of *moneyness,* by which we mean the relative ability of a liquid asset to be converted into money with rapidity and without loss. Those liquid assets that may be converted into money with great rapidity and with little or no loss are known as *near monies.* Table 2–1 lists the forms of liquid wealth that possess a high degree of moneyness.

Money as a Form of Wealth

The most liquid of these assets is of course money itself, since money can be used immediately without loss to purchase goods and services in our economy. Our total money supply consists of all commercial bank demand deposits and currency that are in circulation and not owned by the Treasury, the Federal Reserve banks, or commercial banks. It is owned and held by private individuals, businesses, state and local governments, and other financial institutions such as savings and loan associations, mutual savings banks, foreign banks, and insurance companies.[1] Table 2–1 shows that the currency holdings of the nonbank public as of March 30, 1964, were $32.1 billion, whereas the total holdings of demand deposits amounted to $118.8 billion.

Demand deposit money is clearly the most important component of our money supply. This type of money is owned by the nonbank public and owed to them by the commercial banks. Thus, the phrase "commercial

---

[1] This listing of those who own money is sometimes called the "nonbank public," sometimes simply the "public."

bank demand deposits" does not mean that the banking system owns these deposits; rather it means that the deposits are "liabilities" of the banking system. Furthermore, as we shall discuss in greater detail in later chapters, the deposits do not exist physically; they are bookkeeping claims of the nonbank public on the banking system.

These claims on the banking system may be transferred from one part of the nonbank public to another by the use of checks. This happens when debt is paid off, when goods and services are purchased with checks. People often demand currency from the banks in exchange for their "demand

TABLE 2–1. MONEY AND NEAR-MONEY HOLDINGS OF THE NONBANK
PUBLIC, MARCH 30, 1964
(IN BILLIONS OF DOLLARS)

FORM OF LIQUID WEALTH		AMOUNT
Currency	$ 32.1	
Demand deposits	118.8	
Total money supply		$150.9
Time deposits in commercial banks	115.8	
Time deposits in mutual savings banks	45.8	
Time deposits in Postal Savings System	0.4	
Total time (savings) deposits		162.0
Marketable and convertible U.S. government securities	113.3	
Savings bonds held by individuals	49.1	
Total U.S. government securities		162.4
Savings and loan shares		93.5
Cash value of life insurance*		114.5
Total money and near-money holdings of the nonbank public		683.3

Source: *Federal Reserve Bulletin*, June, 1964, pp. 735, 748–49, 752–53.
* Estimated at 80 percent of book value of life insurance company assets.

deposits," of course. Since the amount of currency available in the economic system amounts to only a fraction of total demand deposit liabilities, it is fortunate that when some people demand currency, there are usually others who are simultaneously making deposits. Otherwise, as we shall see later, a "cash drain" from the banking system might occur which could cause economic distress. Today, however, it is very unlikely that people in our economy will ever again sustain a loss on their demand deposit holdings. The existence of deposit insurance almost precludes "bank panics" from occurring when too many people attempt to convert their deposits (either demand or time deposits) into currency at the same time. Deposits are insured up to a limit of $10,000 by the Federal Deposit Insurance Corporation. Only $832 million of the demand deposit liabilities of commercial banks are not insured by the FDIC.[2]

---

[2] *Federal Reserve Bulletin*, June, 1964, p. 738.

Savings Deposits as a Form of Wealth

Savings deposits of various sorts are another important part of the non-bank public's total liquid wealth. Savings and loan share accounts, and savings deposits in commercial banks, mutual savings banks, and the Postal Savings System constitute 24 percent of our liquid wealth. Most of these forms of savings are also insured by some agency of the federal government. For example, some 87 percent of mutual savings bank deposits are insured by the FDIC.[3] The Federal Savings and Loan Insurance Corporation insures the share accounts of most savings and loan associations.

How do savings deposits differ from demand deposits? Why cannot savings deposits be included in the money supply? There is usually no possibility of loss on redemption of savings accounts, and they can be quickly used to make payments. There are, however, a number of important differences between savings deposits and checking deposits that should be noted.

First, savings deposits need not be paid on demand. The debtor institutions can legally require the holder of a savings deposit to give thirty days' notice of a withdrawal. For all practical purposes, however, this is not an important distinguishing feature of savings accounts because most financial institutions do redeem these accounts on "demand." Competitive conditions are such that a required thirty-day waiting period could only be enforced if all debtor institutions followed this practice.

Second, interest is paid on savings deposits. There is a legal prohibition against paying interest on checking accounts.

And third, this being the most important difference, savings accounts must *first* be converted into either currency or checking deposits before they can be used as money. They cannot be used directly to purchase goods or services.

There are also a number of differences between the various forms of savings deposits and these differences in form will affect the volume of money and total liquid wealth differently when converted to money. For example, when a savings and loan share account is converted into money there will be no change in the money holdings of the nonbank public, but there will be a reduction in the total volume of liquid wealth. Assume that you have a $1,000 savings account with a savings and loan association. Your ownership of the account means that you have a claim on the assets of the association. Hence your ownership claim is equal in value to a certain percentage of what the association owns. What will happen if you decide to convert that claim into money? The savings and loan association will either give you currency or write a check on its checking account at a commercial bank. There will thus be a transfer of money holdings from one part of the nonbank public, the savings and loan association, to another part, you. The total volume of money in the economy remains the same. On the other hand,

---

[3] *Ibid.*, p. 738.

your claim to the assets of the association will have been reduced. You no longer have a share account. As a result, the total liquid wealth of the economy will have been reduced. This transaction may be formulated in terms of the entire economy as follows: Money + savings and loan shares + other forms of liquid wealth = total liquid wealth.[4] When savings and loan shares are converted into money, the total amount of money remains the same. Total savings and loan shares decrease. Therefore total liquid wealth decreases.

When holders of mutual savings bank "savings deposits" decide to convert their deposits into money, the effects are exactly the same as those just discussed. The effects are entirely different, however, when the holder of a savings deposit account with a commercial bank demands money in place of his savings account. For example, assume a depositor wishes to transfer his account from an interest-earning savings (time) deposit to a demand deposit in the sum of $1,000. The commercial bank simply creates a new checking deposit for him in that amount. It switches his time deposits to demand deposits. The amount of money in the economy has therefore increased by $1,000 since time deposits are not considered money. Total liquid wealth remains the same, however, and no member of the nonbank public has lost purchasing power. The results are the same if the depositor wants currency. The bank gives up an asset, vault cash, in return for a reduction in time deposit liabilities.[5] It should be noted that currency held by the commercial banking system as vault cash is neither money nor part of the liquid wealth system of the nonbank public. Vault cash is not owned by the nonbank public and hence cannot be used to purchase goods and services until distributed to the public by banks.

A switch from Postal Savings deposits to money will also lead to an increase in the nonbank public's money with no change in total liquid wealth. In this case there is a loss of either checking deposits or currency by the United States Treasury (which is not a part of the nonbank public either).

The Balance Sheet as a Tool of Analysis

The "T" account or "balance sheet" effectively illustrates what has been discussed in the preceding paragraphs. The balance sheet is simply a means of showing, at a moment of time, the balance between what one owns (*assets*) and what one owes (*liabilities* plus *capital accounts*). These are always equal. Here are a few simple rules that will help you analyze correctly the elementary balance sheets in this text:

---

[4] See Table 2–1 for a list of near monies.
[5] For reasons that will become clear in Chapter 7, it is assumed that banks have an adequate reserve base upon which to make these transactions.

1. Assets must always equal liabilities plus capital accounts.

2. If assets increase or decrease in their total size, then there must be a corresponding increase or decrease in the sum of liabilities plus capital accounts.

3. If there is an increase or decrease in the total of liabilities and capital accounts, there must be a corresponding increase or decrease in the total of assets.

4. An increase in one type of asset item will mean that some other asset will have decreased or that a liability and capital account item will have increased.

5. A decrease in an asset means an increase in the value of some other asset or a decrease in a liability and capital account.

6. An increase in a liability or capital account means a decrease in some other liability or capital account or an increase in an asset.

7. A decrease in a liability or capital account means an increase in some other liability or capital account or a decrease in an asset.

For example, take the case in which the depositor in a commercial bank wanted to switch his $1,000 savings deposit into demand deposits:

BALANCE SHEET CHANGES FOR COMMERCIAL BANK A

ASSETS	LIABILITIES + CAPITAL ACCOUNTS	
	Demand deposits	+$1,000
	Time deposits	−$1,000

BALANCE SHEET CHANGES FOR INDIVIDUAL 1

ASSETS		LIABILITIES + CAPITAL ACCOUNTS
Demand deposits	+$1,000	
Time deposits	−$1,000	

Here we see that the depositor has changed the nature of his assets while the bank has experienced a change in the type of its liabilities.

The analysis becomes somewhat more complicated when we take the case of the depositor in a savings and loan association who wants to convert his savings and loan shares into a demand deposit account.

BALANCE SHEET CHANGES FOR THE COMMERCIAL BANKING SYSTEM

ASSETS	LIABILITIES + CAPITAL ACCOUNTS	
	Demand deposits (of savings and loan association)	−$1,000
	Demand deposits (of Individual 1)	+$1,000

BALANCE SHEET CHANGES FOR INDIVIDUAL 1

ASSETS		LIABILITIES + CAPITAL ACCOUNTS
Savings capital	−$1,000	
Demand deposits	+$1,000	

BALANCE SHEET CHANGES FOR SAVINGS AND LOAN ASSOCIATION

ASSETS		LIABILITIES + CAPITAL ACCOUNTS	
Demand deposits	−$1,000	Savings capital	−$1,000

Here we see that there has been no change in the stock of money, but that total liquid wealth has decreased by $1,000 due to the reduced amount of savings capital. The commercial banking system, which formerly owed money to the savings and loan association, now owes it to the private individual depositor.

U.S. Government Securities as a Form of Wealth

Quantitatively, United States government securities are as important a form of liquid wealth as money itself. In March of 1964, U.S. government securities held by the nonbank public totaled $162.4 billion, whereas the supply of money was $150.9 billion.

Government securities are basically of two types: marketable and nonmarketable.

Nonmarketable securities are those bonds that cannot be transferred from one owner to another. To get back one's financial investment, the securities must be returned to the original issuer. Savings bonds are the principal type of nonmarketable securities held by individuals. These securities presently yield 3¾ percent interest at maturity. Thus, if a $25 savings bond were purchased for $18.75, in seven years and eleven months the bond could be redeemed for $25, or the purchase price plus the accumulated interest. There is no possibility of loss on these securities, except that which may occur in purchasing power if the price level in the economy increases sharply. These securities are redeemable upon demand only if they have been held by the purchaser for more than sixty days, however. Thus, during the initial period of ownership, nonmarketable securities are not as liquid as other forms of near money.

Marketable securities, on the other hand, may have their ownership transferred by sale and purchase. The market for them is composed of the nonbank public, commercial banks, and even various agencies of the federal government itself. For example, the Federal Reserve banks alone owned some $34 billion of these securities in May, 1964.[6]

---

[6] *Federal Reserve Bulletin*, June, 1964, p. 730.

Since there is a market for United States marketable securities, their prices are ultimately determined by supply and demand. If they are held to maturity, that is, if they are held until the time when the United States Treasury is obligated to redeem them, there is no possible price loss. If one chooses to redeem them prior to the redemption date, however, they must be sold on the open market for what they will bring. Thus there may be either a gain or a loss. Short-term securities that can be redeemed within one year are usually not subject to much appreciation or depreciation in value. Longer-term securities, however, may appreciate or depreciate in value significantly, depending upon market conditions. United States government securities yielding 2½ percent and due in 1967–72 were selling at 90

TABLE 2–2. PROBABLE EFFECTS ON THE STOCK OF MONEY AND TOTAL LIQUID WEALTH FOLLOWING CONVERSION OF NEAR MONIES INTO MONEY

FORM OF NEAR MONEY CONVERTED	DIRECTION OF CHANGE OF STOCK OF MONEY	DIRECTION OF CHANGE OF TOTAL LIQUID WEALTH
Time deposits in commercial banks	+	0
Time deposits in mutual savings banks	0	–
Time deposits in postal savings system	+	0
Savings and loan shares	0	–
Savings bonds	+	0
Marketable U.S. government securities	+*	0*
	0†	0†
Cash value of life insurance	0	–

* If redeemed by the U.S. government or purchased by the banking system.
† If purchased by other members of the nonbank public.

in July of 1964, for example.[7] This means that a $1,000 security of this type, if purchased when first issued for about $1,000, could be sold on the open market for only $900. This is a substantial loss. For this reason, marketable public securities are not usually considered to be good near monies: there is certainty of no loss only if held to maturity. On the other hand, they are immediately marketable and thus highly liquid. The funds obtained from sale of securities may quickly be used in payment of debt or purchase of goods and services.

When nonmarketable U.S. government securities are converted into money, the supply of money increases without changing the total of liquid wealth. The Treasury redeems these securities by drawing on its own deposit balances (which are not part of the money supply). This leads to an increase of the deposit balances of the nonbank public. If the Treasury redeems the marketable securities at maturity, the results are the same. Re-

---

[7] *Wall Street Journal*, July 24, 1964.

sults will vary, however, when marketable securities are bought and sold on the open market. For example, assume that one individual sells a security to another for $900:

BALANCE SHEET CHANGES FOR THE COMMERCIAL BANKING SYSTEM

ASSETS	LIABILITIES + CAPITAL ACCOUNTS
	Demand deposits (of Individual 1) −$900
	Demand deposits (of Individual 2) +$900

BALANCE SHEET CHANGES FOR INDIVIDUAL 1

ASSETS		LIABILITIES + CAPITAL ACCOUNTS
Demand deposits	−$900	
U.S. securities	+$900	

BALANCE SHEET CHANGES FOR INDIVIDUAL 2

ASSETS		LIABILITIES + CAPITAL ACCOUNTS
U.S. securities	−$900	
Demand deposits	+$900	

Individual 1, who purchases the security, does so by writing a $900 check on his checking account. Individual 2 receives the check, deposits it in his checking account, and turns the security over to the new owner, Individual 1. The whole transaction takes place within the nonbank public. Thus there is no change in total money holdings or in total liquid wealth of the nonbank public. This is merely a redistribution.

There is a different result when the banking system purchases the security. Assume that the security is sold by Individual 1 to the banking system for $900:

BALANCE SHEET CHANGES FOR THE COMMERCIAL BANKING SYSTEM

ASSETS		LIABILITIES + CAPITAL ACCOUNTS
U.S. securities	+$900	Demand deposits (of Individual 1) +$900

BALANCE SHEET CHANGES FOR INDIVIDUAL 1

ASSETS		LIABILITIES + CAPITAL ACCOUNTS
U.S. securities	−$900	
Demand deposits	+$900	

The banking system creates a demand deposit for the seller of the security, thus increasing the total money holdings of the nonbank public. Total liquid wealth remains unchanged, however, since the U.S. security component decreased by the same amount for the nonbank public.

We have included U.S. government securities among the principal forms of nonbank public liquid wealth holdings. Why not include privately issued stocks and bonds also? For several reasons. First, privately issued securities exhibit considerable variation in price depending upon (1) the financial condition of the firm issuing the securities and (2) the business prospects for the economy and the industry in general. If the firm has had stable earnings, the chances are good that its securities will sell well. But a brief setback in earnings, or a decline in the demand for the products of the firm and industry, could initiate a wave of security sales that will drive bond and stock prices down. These sales would cause security holders to suffer extensive capital losses. Thus, the liquidity of these securities, their ability to be converted into money quickly and without losses, is seriously hampered. Marketability is uncertain. Similarly, even with adequate earnings and good prospects, a firm may have difficulty marketing its securities if it is small in size or if its success depends on only a few key individuals. The securities of a larger, better-established firm will frequently command a higher price than those of smaller, younger corporations.

The prevailing rate of interest is another factor that influences the price of both public and private securities. If prevailing interest rates are higher than in the past, then previously issued securities must be sold by their holders at a lower price. There is an inverse relationship between interest rates and bond prices.[8] This factor also tends to reduce the liquidity of private and public securities.

Finally, private securities have less secure backing than federal securities. The U.S. government stands in back of its securities but only the issuing corporation guarantees its stocks and bonds. No one doubts the permanence of the U.S. government and its ability to redeem securities, but private enterprises have not exhibited such permanence. During each month of 1961, for example, business failures averaged about sixty per 10,000 concerns.[9]

Life Insurance as a Form of Liquid Wealth

The cash value of life insurance is another type of near money. As long as the insurance company remains in business, the policy holder can, within a matter of days, either acquire the cash surrender value of his policy or borrow on the basis of that value. Since life insurance companies are classified as part of the nonbank public, there is no change in the stock of money when policy holders choose to convert their life insurance into money. There is, however, a decrease in total liquid wealth. The policy

---

[8] This will be examined in more detail in Chapter 19.
[9] U.S. Department of Commerce, *Survey of Current Business* (1962).

holder also suffers a small loss by converting to cash. He loses insurance protection and the excess of premium payments over the cash value of the policy.

Summary

In this part of Chapter 2 we have (1) developed the "T" account as a tool of analysis and (2) classified the liquid wealth system of the United States by degrees of moneyness. Insured time deposits, savings and loan shares, and U.S. savings bonds are the safest and most liquid near monies available. There is no possibility of loss and they may quickly be converted into cash. Life insurance policies and marketable U.S. government securities, while usually safe and quickly convertible, are less safe as near monies because of possible losses. Table 2-2 summarizes the effects that the conversion of near monies has upon the stock of money and total liquid wealth. In a later chapter we will consider the importance of these liquid-wealth holdings to aggregate economic activity.

CURRENCY IN THE UNITED STATES

The American unit of account is the dollar. The dollar is divisible into 100 cents. Coins are made in convenient divisibles of 100: 1, 5, 10, 25, 50, and 100 cents. Similarly, paper currency comes in convenient 1, 2, 5, 10, 20, 50, 100, 500, 1,000, 5,000, and 10,000 dollar denominations. All of this currency must, by law, be accepted by creditors in payment of debt. It is, in other words, *legal tender*. The other component of our money supply, demand deposits, is *not* legal tender; it is only a generally accepted substitute for it. Issuing currency and defining the unit of account are the prerogatives of the federal government.

The Federal Reserve Note

Table 2-3 shows the present composition of currency in the United States. Clearly the most important type of currency is the Federal Reserve note, which is issued in denominations of $1 and up. These notes make up 85 percent of the total currency in circulation. They are liabilities of the Federal Reserve banks that issue them.

In 1945, Congress last fixed the backing of Federal Reserve notes at 25 percent in gold certificates and the remainder in United States government securities. This does not mean, however, that you can convert your Federal Reserve notes into gold certificates or government securities by merely presenting them at any Federal Reserve bank. As a matter of fact it is against the law for anyone in the private sector of the economy to hold gold certificates. If you want United States government securities, you will have to purchase them through your securities dealer. What is it, then, that makes Federal Reserve notes "good"? Two things: the fact that they are legal tender and the faith of the public.

TABLE 2–3. UNITED STATES CURRENCY IN CIRCULATION, APRIL 30, 1964
(IN MILLIONS OF DOLLARS)

KIND OF CURRENCY*		AMOUNT
Coins		
Silver dollars	482	
Dimes, quarters, and half dollars	1,933	
Nickels and pennies	724	
Total amount of coins		3,139
Paper currency—Treasury		
Silver certificates	1,699	
United States notes	322	
In process of retirement	163	
Total amount of treasury paper currency		2,184
Paper currency—Federal Reserve		
Federal Reserve notes		31,563
Total currency in circulation		36,886
Currency in commercial bank vaults		−4,886†
Currency in circulation outside of commercial bank vaults		32,000†

Source: *Federal Reserve Bulletin*, June, 1964, pp. 733, 735.
* Includes all currency outside of the Treasury and Federal Reserve Banks.
† Preliminary data.

Is there any limit on the number of Federal Reserve notes that may be issued? Federal Reserve banks owned $15.2 billion worth of gold certificates in April, 1964.[10] Some $4.1 billion of these certificates were needed to back bank deposit liabilities of the Federal Reserve. The remaining $11.1 billion was sufficient to support $44.4 billion in Federal Reserve notes. Thus, the Federal Reserve banks are able to issue substantially more notes than the $31.6 billion outstanding. The reason Federal Reserve banks have not issued more currency is that they issue and retire currency only in response to the demands of the public.

Assume, for example, that the public demand for currency in the form of Federal Reserve notes rises by $1 million. How may it get this additional amount? By writing checks out to "cash" at their bank. This causes the banks to lose both a liability, demand deposits, and an asset, vault cash.

[10] *Federal Reserve Bulletin*, June, 1964, p. 730.

BALANCE SHEET CHANGES FOR THE COMMERCIAL BANKING SYSTEM

ASSETS		LIABILITIES + CAPITAL ACCOUNTS	
Vault cash	−$1,000,000	Demand deposits	−$1,000,000

BALANCE SHEET CHANGES FOR THE NONBANK PUBLIC

ASSETS		LIABILITIES + CAPITAL ACCOUNTS
Demand deposits	−$1,000,000	
Currency	+$1,000,000	

Commercial banks now need to replenish their depleted currency holdings. Where do they get the currency? From the Federal Reserve banks. Commercial banks exchange their reserve accounts at the Federal Reserve banks for currency. The Federal Reserve banks then issue and turn over to the commercial banks the desired type of currency (in this case, Federal Reserve notes of various denominations). This transaction appears as follows:

BALANCE SHEET CHANGES FOR THE COMMERCIAL BANKING SYSTEM

ASSETS		LIABILITIES + CAPITAL ACCOUNTS
Reserves with Federal Reserve banks	−$1,000,000	
Vault cash	+$1,000,000	

BALANCE SHEET CHANGES FOR THE FEDERAL RESERVE BANKS

ASSETS		LIABILITIES + CAPITAL ACCOUNTS	
		Member bank reserves	−$1,000,000
		Federal Reserve notes	+$1,000,000

When the public wants less currency than it has, this process is reversed. People exchange currency for increased deposits at the commercial banks. The commercial banks, with excess holdings of vault cash, return them to the Federal Reserve banks, who increase the reserve accounts of the commercial banks. The Federal Reserve banks then retire the currency that has been returned.

Treasury Currency

The Treasury along with the Federal Reserve has a monopoly of currency issue. There are two types of Treasury currency: coin and paper. Coin amounts to approximately 8 percent of the total amount of currency in circulation. Treasury paper currency is less than 6 percent of all currency. Coins are issued by the Treasury Department in response to the needs of the public for "change." Silver certificates come in $1, $5, and $10 denominations and are issued on the basis of Treasury silver purchases.

United States notes are another type of Treasury money. They were first issued during the Civil War and are limited in quantity. Of the $347 million of these notes now in existence, only $322 million are presently in circulation. These notes usually come in $2 and $5 denominations. All other types of Treasury currency are being retired.

Treasury currency gets into circulation in much the same manner as Federal Reserve notes. When there is a need for this low-denomination Treasury currency, commercial banks may procure it from the Federal Reserve banks. There is this difference however: since the Federal Reserve banks do not issue this type of currency, they are giving up an asset, Treasury currency, which they previously purchased from the Treasury. The Treasury usually issues currency and sells it to the Federal Reserve banks after it has purchased silver from the public.

The Nature of Our Currency System

This discussion points up at least two important distinguishing characteristics of our currency system. First, in the United States, changes in the amount and composition of currency occur almost exclusively in response to the demands of the public. There are no accompanying changes in the money stock. When the amount of currency in the economy increases, there is a corresponding decrease in deposit money. When the supply of currency decreases, deposit money increases. This causes a constant redistribution of the components of the money supply, but not a change in the total supply itself. This is true whether the redistribution involves Treasury currency or Federal Reserve notes.

Secondly, the United States government does not issue currency to defray its expenses, to finance its own operations. In other words the United States has a managed paper currency system. It is a "paper" system because currency is the money of ultimate redemption. Paper currency holdings of United States citizens are redeemed with paper currency. It is a "managed" system because currency is self-regulatory, the money stock not changing when the currency total changes.

Supplementary Readings
Nussbaum, Arthur. *Money and the Law.* 2nd ed. New York, Foundation Press, 1950.

Data Sources
Board of Governors of the Federal Reserve System. *Federal Reserve Bulletin* (monthly).
————. *Annual Reports.*
————. *Banking and Monetary Statistics.* Washington, D.C., 1943.
————. *All Bank Statistics United States 1896–1955.* Washington, D.C., 1959.
U.S. Department of Commerce. *Survey of Current Business* (monthly).

Chapter 3

The Commercial Banking System
and the Economy

Economists frequently use income and employment statistics to measure the economic importance of a given industry. These statistics are thought to reveal the extent to which economic activities contribute to the national economy in terms of jobs created and income generated. In this chapter we will first use these statistics to assess the overall importance of the financial sector of the economy. Then we will discuss some of the special characteristics of the commercial banking system, our most important financial subsector.

FINANCE IN THE ECONOMY

Tables 3–1 and 3–2 show the contribution of various industries to the national income and employment for selected years since 1929. Ranking the various sectors of the U.S. economy in order of their contribution to national income for 1929 and 1962, we have:

1929	1962
Manufacturing	Manufacturing
Wholesale and retail trade	Wholesale and retail trade
Finance	Government
Services	Services
Agriculture	Finance
Transportation	Contract construction
Government	Agriculture
Contract construction	Transportation
Communications and public utilities	Communication and public utilities
Mining	Mining

The most impressive changes that occurred in the relative contribution of the various industrial sectors to national income were the decreased

TABLE 3–1. UNITED STATES NATIONAL INCOME BY INDUSTRY, 1929, 1940, 1950, 1960, AND 1962

INDUSTRY	INCOME CONTRIBUTED BY EACH SECTOR (IN MILLIONS OF DOLLARS)					PERCENT OF INCOME CONTRIBUTED BY EACH SECTOR				
	1929	1940	1950	1960	1962	1929	1940	1950	1960	1962
Agriculture, forestry, and fisheries	8,278	6,247	17,923	17,295	18,910	9.4	7.7	7.4	4.2	4.2
Mining	2,048	1,868	5,010	5,510	5,218	2.3	2.3	2.1	1.3	1.2
Contract construction	3,808	2,569	11,833	21,786	23,623	4.3	3.1	4.9	5.3	5.2
Manufacturing	21,888	22,336	74,371	121,025	130,546	24.9	27.4	30.7	29.2	28.8
Wholesale and retail trade	13,358	14,337	42,707	67,698	73,552	15.2	17.6	17.7	16.3	16.2
Finance, insurance, and real estate	12,693	8,208	21,789	42,586	46,063	14.5	10.1	9.0	10.3	10.2
Transportation	6,636	5,040	13,278	17,909	18,467	7.6	6.2	5.5	4.3	4.1
Communications and public utilities	2,864	3,056	7,198	16,808	18,326	3.3	3.7	3.0	4.1	4.0
Services	10,338	8,854	23,089	49,065	55,382	11.8	10.8	9.5	11.8	12.2
Government and government enterprises	5,093	8,762	23,490	52,528	60,393	5.8	10.7	9.7	12.7	13.3
Other	810	357	1,188	2,287	3,215	0.9	0.4	0.5	0.6	0.7
All industries (total)	87,814	81,634	241,876	414,497	453,695	100.0	100.0	100.0	100.1*	100.1*

Source: Office of Business Economics, U.S. Department of Commerce, *National Income, A Supplement to the Survey of Current Business,* Washington, 1954; *U.S. Income and Output, A Supplement to the Survey of Current Business,* Washington, 1958; *Survey of Current Business,* 1963 (July), p. 17.
* Does not equal 100.0 because of rounding.

TABLE 3–2. UNITED STATES NUMBER OF FULL-TIME EQUIVALENT EMPLOYEES BY INDUSTRY, 1929, 1940, 1950, 1960, AND 1962

INDUSTRY	FULL-TIME EQUIVALENT EMPLOYEES* (IN THOUSANDS)					PERCENT OF TOTAL CONTRIBUTED BY EACH SECTOR				
	1929	1940	1950	1960	1962	1929	1940	1950	1960	1962
Agriculture, forestry, and fisheries	3,530	2,781	2,219	2,060	2,017	9.8	7.3	4.6	3.6	3.4
Mining	993	927	916	674	624	2.8	2.4	1.9	1.2	1.1
Contract construction	1,484	1,285	2,381	2,846	2,870	4.1	3.4	4.9	4.9	4.8
Manufacturing	10,428	10,882	14,969	16,364	16,478	29.1	28.4	30.8	28.4	27.8
Wholesale and retail trade	5,846	6,526	9,005	11,041	11,330	16.3	17.0	18.5	19.2	19.1
Finance, insurance, and real estate	1,415	1,422	1,805	2,593	2,747	3.9	3.7	3.7	4.5	4.6
Transportation	2,873	2,072	2,652	2,459	2,369	8.0	5.4	5.4	4.3	4.0
Communications and public utilities	1,031	898	1,270	1,445	1,434	2.9	2.3	2.6	2.5	2.4
Services	5,112	5,274	6,073	7,830	8,298	14.2	13.8	12.5	13.6	14.0
Government and government enterprises	3,184	6,267	7,380	10,323	11,088	8.9	16.3	15.2	17.9	18.7
Other	0	2	5	4	4	—	—	—	—	—
All industries (total)	35,896	38,336	48,675	57,639	59,268	100.0	100.0	100.1†	100.1†	99.9†

Source: Office of Business Economics, U.S. Department of Commerce, *National Income, A Supplement to the Survey of Current Business*, Washington, 1954; *U.S. Income and Output, A Supplement to the Survey of Current Business*, Washington, 1958; *Survey of Current Business*, 1963, (July), p. 33.
 * Full-time equivalent employment measures man-years of full-time employment of wage and salary earners and its equivalent in work performed by part-time workers. Full-time employment is defined in terms of the number of hours which is customary at a particular time and place.
 † Does not equal 100.0 because of rounding.

importance of the agricultural sector and the increased importance of the government sector. The other major economic sectors maintained their respective positions for the most part. There was some percentage gain by manufacturing, but this has become stabilized. Mining has gradually declined. The finance sector, as one might expect, showed a sharp decline in the depression. Since then it has been unable to increase its contribution, possibly because it is subject to restrictive barriers to entry. Transportation is also less important because of the continually expanding private use of the automobile.

The employment figures tell much the same story as the income source figures. The greatest relative gain is found in government. The number of people employed by the government has risen from 8.9 percent of all employees in 1929 to 18.7 percent in 1962. Expansion of federal civilian payrolls during the depression was the immediate cause of this increase. In contrast, agriculture dropped from 9.8 percent in 1929 to 3.4 percent in 1962. Technological revolution in farm equipment and the higher income possibilities in other sectors of the economy are primarily responsible for this national movement away from agriculture. Transportation and mining were the only other industries to experience any substantial relative decline. Manufacturing, wholesale and retail trade, and services continued to be large employers.

Thus, as a direct source of income and employment, the financial sector of the economy has been one of the less important industries in the United States since the depression. In 1962 it was the source of only 10.2 percent of the income and 4.6 percent of the employment. In 1940 it contributed 10.1 percent of the income and 3.7 percent of the employment.

Why, then, is the financial sector of the economy thought to be so important? The answer is simple: *it is our most important creator of liquid assets.* Hence, it is in a unique position to affect the development of the American economy.

Although decisions regarding the direction of future expenditures and the timing of those expenditures are initially dictated by business and consumer desires, financial institutions, acting as sources of funds, also help shape those decisions. Whether they make direct consumer and business loans, or extend real-estate credit, these institutions help determine the use to which much of our money is put. By making one form of loan or security purchase and not another, they influence the nature of expenditures. As the money on loan is spent by borrowers, the demand for certain goods and services is increased. This in turn may stimulate investment in plant and equipment in those industries most affected by the increased demand. The economy's overall level of prosperity, its rate of growth, the level of employment, the rate of inflation, and the composition of the nation's output are all heavily influenced by the financial sector and the rate at which it finances various activities. Unlike other industrial sectors, therefore, the financial sector cannot accurately be evaluated in terms of its contribution to income and employment. Instead, it should be judged in terms of its functions.

The financial institutions that are most influential in shaping expenditure decisions are the commercial banks, savings institutions, insurance companies, and various governmental agencies. These institutions give rise to 34, 20, 17, and 29 percent respectively of the principal liquid wealth holdings of the nonbank public.[1] We shall first study the commercial banking system. Chapter 8 discusses the other financial subsectors.

THE COMMERCIAL BANKING SYSTEM

Distinguishing Characteristics

Like other financial institutions, banks are in the business of making loans and investments, taking deposits, acting as securities brokers, providing safety-deposit facilities, and administering estates. They may be distinguished from the other financial institutions, however, in that they are also able to *create money*, *destroy money*, and *allow their creditors to transfer claims through the use of checks*. No other private financial institution is able to do this.

When banks make loans they give the borrower either a deposit or cash. Most people and businesses prefer deposits to cash because they are more convenient. This deposit is money created by the bank. For example, say that someone borrows $500 to finance emergency medical payments. The "T" account entries would look like this:

BALANCE SHEET CHANGES FOR COMMERCIAL BANK A

ASSETS		LIABILITIES + CAPITAL ACCOUNTS	
Loans to individuals	+$500	Demand deposits	+$500

Thus, in the process of making a loan, the commercial bank has created money. Similarly, when the individual borrower repays the loan, he will do so with cash, or by check. The majority of loan repayments are also negotiated by check. Hence:

BALANCE SHEET CHANGES FOR COMMERCIAL BANK A

ASSETS		LIABILITIES + CAPITAL ACCOUNTS	
Loans to individuals	−$500	Demand deposits	−$500

---

[1] See Table 2–1.

Here money has been destroyed in the process of loan repayment.[2] Thus, as long as the total loan volume is not reduced, the granting of additional loans by commercial banks will increase the stock of money. Given stable prices, the ability of the public to purchase goods and services will thus be enhanced.

What is the difference when a borrower obtains a loan from a consumer finance company? Assume that the finance company gives the borrower a check. This check is not money created by the finance company; it is simply a check written on the finance company's checking account at a commercial bank.[3] The balance sheet changes that take place are as follows:

BALANCE SHEET CHANGES FOR CONSUMER FINANCE COMPANY

ASSETS		LIABILITIES + CAPITAL ACCOUNTS
Demand deposits	−$500	
Loans	+$500	

BALANCE SHEET CHANGES FOR THE COMMERCIAL BANKING SYSTEM

ASSETS	LIABILITIES + CAPITAL ACCOUNTS	
	Demand deposits (of consumer finance company)	−$500
	Demand deposits (of individual borrower)	+$500

The individual borrower deposits the check in his own account at the bank with which he does business. Subsequently, he writes checks out on his increased demand deposit account. Thus, there has only been a transfer of deposits from one part of the nonbank public to another. Likewise, when the loan is repaid, there is no corresponding reduction of the money supply.

Other financial institutions are in a position similar to that of the consumer finance company. When they make loans and investments they are merely transferring their money holdings. Only commercial banks can create and destroy money because only commercial banks are permitted to allow creditors to transfer claims through the use of checks.

Special Responsibility of the Commercial Banking System

The commercial banking system shares one very important characteristic with other members of the financial sector and the rest of the business com-

---

[2] We are assuming for the sake of simplicity that the bank collected interest on the loan in advance. Also note that the effects of these transactions on the stock of money would be the same if people took cash instead of deposits. Vault cash is not part of the money supply. Hence if it is given to a borrower by the bank, an increase in the money holdings of the nonbank public will result. Chapter 7 will examine the mechanics of money creation and destruction in more detail.

[3] It is assumed that the finance company has adequate funds to engage in lending, and therefore need not borrow from the banking system.

munity—the desire to maximize profits and expand its share of the market. Commercial banking is a profit-seeking enterprise. As such it shares with other businesses the same set of expectations concerning the "health" of the economy. When business opinion expects the future to be prosperous, businesses usually expand their operations. When the economy is expected to take a turn for the worse, businesses usually contract their plans for expansion, hire fewer new workers, or even contract their work force. Commercial banks follow suit. They tend to expand their loans during periods of economic upturn and contract their loans (or at least contract the rate of growth of loans) during economic downturn. In the absence of compensating actions taken by the government, this expansion and contraction of loans results in a parallel expansion and contraction of the deposit part of our money supply.

This in turn means that in periods of economic upturn, commercial banks add to the money supply and thereby help expand demand in the economy. However, once the economy arrives at full employment of men and resources, a continued expansion of loans and deposits simply adds to price-level increases. Once full employment has been reached, it is difficult to increase real production, except by increasing the utilization of men and equipment through a longer work week, adding a number of retired people, women, and students to the work force, or bringing obsolescent machinery back into production.

On the other hand, if banks contract loans in periods of mild economic decline, experience shows that we are not likely to have price-level drops. Prices in the United States seem to have some downward "stickiness." As a consequence, the reduced amount of deposits accompanying the reduction in loans usually tends to aggravate the downturn in demand and output.

In short, banks share the general business outlook on economic conditions. *Commercial banks, in the absence of regulation, tend to intensify whatever phase of the business cycle is current. They do this through their unique ability to create and destroy money when making loans and investments.*

An individual banker may counter the preceding analysis by arguing that all he really does is to respond to the loan demands of the public, that he supplies credit and money according to the needs of trade. His standards with respect to granting loans do not change. Rather, when people want more funds in periods of upturn, he supplies them. In periods of decline, when they want fewer loans, he responds to their wishes accordingly. Furthermore, he contends, this is a safe loan policy. On business loans, for example, the borrower uses the funds to purchase productive resources for the process of production. Shortly after the loan is made, the business borrower will have produced the goods that are to be sold. The proceeds from the sale of the goods can then be used to repay the loan.[4]

---

[4] This line of reasoning is sometimes called the "commercial loan theory of banking" or "real bills doctrine."

There are two loopholes in this line of reasoning. First, though it may be neither intentional nor conscious, such a procedure usually involves disproportionate stringency during periods of declining business. What may appear to be a sound loan on the upward side of the cycle may not appear to be safe on the downward side. In periods of economic decline, banks examine their loan applications more carefully in addition to reducing the amount of loans in response to the increased reluctance of businesses and individuals to borrow. This places additional downward pressure on loans during a period of decline when what is needed in the economy may well be added demand, further extension of loans, and more money creation.

Second, although many loans are granted on the basis of future production, no increase in production may occur if the economy is in a period of full employment. During upswings demand may outrun production. Future production which serves as the basis for bank loans may never materialize because resources are already in full use. All that a business can do is to use its borrowed funds to bid resources away from other enterprises. Thus, a shift in the type, but not the total amount of production, takes place. Prices of resources, and hence of final goods and services, are bid up in this process. If the business wants to renew its loan in the future to facilitate production, it will have to increase the amount of the loan because of the increased costs. A vicious circle of increased borrowing and rising prices may easily ensue.

This suggests that normal commercial bank loan operations can perversely affect the economy at both ends of the cycle, either worsening recession or feeding inflation. Yet commercial banks are given the right to create demand deposits, which constitute the major part of our money supply. Almost 80 percent of our money is in this form and about 90 percent of all transactions in the economy are check transactions. For this reason, commercial banks have a responsibility that transcends that of other business enterprises. Banks are responsible for the creation, destruction, and administration of our money. As a consequence, they are also responsible to a great extent for the welfare of the economy.

This dual responsibility—one to itself as a business enterprise and one to the nation—puts a tremendous burden on the individual commercial bank. If it acts in the national interest, it will often hurt its competitive position. If its lending policy is conservative during periods of prosperity and full employment, it reduces its potential profits. Borrowers will seek funds from competing banks and savings institutions. If its lending policy is liberal during periods of recession, unpaid loans may weaken its financial soundness. On the other hand, if it acts purely on the basis of self-interest, it may worsen the national economic picture.

Because of the contradictory nature of this dual responsibility, the federal government exercises considerable control over the commercial banking system. As we shall see later, various governmental bodies such as the Federal Reserve System, the Federal Deposit Insurance Corporation, the Comptroller of the Currency, and comparable state regulatory bodies are all engaged in the business of regulating commercial banks. Some agencies are just concerned with banks as businesses, seeing to it that the banks operate in the interest of their stockholders. Other agencies, such as the Federal Reserve System, are concerned with maintaining employment levels, stimulating economic growth, and holding the price line. These agencies regulate commercial banks and their money-creating activities with an eye to the national interest.[5] This permits banks to act in their own interest without too much concern for the national welfare. The government provides for the safety of our money supply and national interest.

SUMMARY

The financial sector of the economy is not particularly important as a direct source of income and employment. It is important, however, as a creator of liquid wealth. Commercial banks are our most significant financial subsector. They create and destroy demand deposits. Banks have a responsibility to their stockholders and to the nation as well. Because of the contradictory nature of this responsibility, banks are subject to extensive governmental regulation.

---

[5] As previously indicated, our other financial institutions also affect the national economy. Because of this, some economists argue that these institutions should also be subject to extensive regulation. Chapter 8 will further discuss this point.

Chapter 4

The Structure of the Commercial Banking System

The commercial banking system of the United States is composed of more than 13,500 banks. There are several ways to describe the structure of this system. Listed below are the types of bank and the types of banking with which we will be concerned in this chapter. Having defined our terms, we will then proceed to examine the structure of our banking system in some detail.

TYPES OF BANKS

Member bank. A bank that is a member of the Federal Reserve System. Banks of this type are classified by the system as reserve city or country banks.

Nonmember bank. A bank that is not a member of the Federal Reserve System.

National bank. A bank that holds a charter from the federal government. It must be a member of the Federal Reserve System.

State bank. A bank that has a state-granted charter. It may or may not be a member of the Federal Reserve System.

Insured bank. A bank whose deposits are insured by the Federal Deposit Insurance Corporation. All member banks must be so insured.

Noninsured bank. A bank whose deposits are not insured by the Federal Deposit Insurance Corporation.

TYPES OF BANKING

Unit banking. The operation of one banking office by a commercial bank.

Branch banking. The operation of two or more banking offices by a commercial bank.

Chain banking. The association of a number of commercial banks through an interlocking directorate.

Group banking. The control of two or more banks by a holding company that has controlling interest in the stock of the banks.

Correspondent banking. Commercial bank maintenance of checking deposit accounts with another bank in return for such services as bond and security purchases and check clearance.

MEMBER AND NONMEMBER BANKS

Table 4–1 summarizes data describing the commercial bank membership in the Federal Reserve System. As of December 20, 1963, there were 13,570 commercial banks in the United States and its possessions, yet only 6,112, or 45 percent, were members of the Federal Reserve System. These member banks accounted for 79 percent of commercial bank demand deposits, however, and 82 percent of time deposit liabilities. Average deposit liabilities of member banks at the end of 1963 amounted to $34 million, whereas for nonmember banks they came to only $6 million. Clearly, member banks figure more importantly in the economy than nonmember banks.

TABLE 4–1. COMMERCIAL BANKS IN THE UNITED STATES, DECEMBER 31, 1947, AND DECEMBER 20, 1963

TYPE OF BANK	NUMBER		DEMAND DEPOSITS (IN MILLIONS OF DOLLARS)*		TIME DEPOSITS (IN MILLIONS OF DOLLARS)*	
	1947	1963	1947	1963	1947	1963
Member banks						
National	5,005	4,615	53,541	76,836	19,278	61,288
State	1,918	1,497	27,068	40,725	9,062	29,642
Total member banks	6,923	6,112	80,609	117,562	28,340	90,930
Nonmember banks						
Insured state	6,478	7,173	12,366	23,140	6,558	19,793
Noninsured state	783	285	1,392	832	478	341
Total nonmember banks	7,261	7,458	13,758	23,972	7,036	20,134
Total commercial banks	14,184	13,570	94,367	141,534	35,376	111,064

Source: *Federal Reserve Bulletin*, June 1964, pp. 736–38.
* Exclude U.S. and interbank deposits.

The trend in Federal Reserve membership has been slightly downward in recent years. This decline in the number of Federal Reserve members is largely attributable to the fact that the consolidation and merger of existing members has outweighed the creation of new member banks. In addition, there has been some tendency for small member banks to withdraw from the system and become insured nonmember banks.

The total number of banks in the economy has also declined. The big drop, of course, came with the large-scale bank failures of the thirties. The number of banks almost halved during this period. Since then the total number has only declined slightly, through absorptions, consolidations, and mergers. Some increase in the number of banks is becoming apparent in the mid-sixties, however.

Banks wishing to become members of the Federal Reserve System must meet certain qualifications. Primary among these are that the banks (1) have sufficient capital relative to deposit liabilities and (2) redeem at par all checks drawn by their depositors and presented by out-of-town banks for collection. In addition there must be an examination of the bank's past operations, its solvency, and its managerial talent. Many banks do not meet these requirements and must therefore remain outside of the system. If a bank applies for and receives a national bank charter from the Comptroller of the Currency, however, membership in the Reserve System is automatic.

The Importance of the Capital Requirement

The requirement that banks have a relatively low ratio of deposits to capital accounts is important. The higher this ratio becomes, the smaller the margin of safety for depositors. With deposit insurance, of course, the average depositor need no longer worry about this. It is still the responsibility of the Federal Reserve System and other examining groups, however, to see that commercial banks do not engage in unsound practices that might lead to insolvency.

When a bank fails, creditors have first claim to the assets of the corporation; stockholders have only a residual claim to assets. They receive whatever funds are available after the claims of creditors have been met. Deposit claims constitute almost all of the liabilities of a commercial bank. Thus, if the capital accounts are low in relation to these deposit claims, nearly all the assets of the bank would be used to meet depositor claims. Furthermore, when corporate assets are sold in liquidation, they usually do not bring their full book value. As a consequence, if there is a high deposit/ capital ratio, all creditor claims may not be met. It is important, therefore, that commercial bank assets be of high quality. The examining authorities carefully study both the qualitative composition of assets and the deposit/ capital ratio. Cash, deposits at the Federal Reserve banks, and short-term U.S. government securities are considered very good assets since they are subject to almost no loss.

In recent years the deposit/capital ratio for all commercial banks has been about 10/1.[1] This may be a relatively safe ratio, since by "December 31, 1960, fewer than five thousand out of the approximately 1,452,000 depositors

---

[1] *Federal Reserve Bulletin,* June, 1964, p. 736.

in the insured banks which closed since the beginning of federal deposit insurance had not had their deposits in excess of the insurance maximum made available to them in full."[2] Also, almost 92 percent of the direct payments to depositors of liquidated banks have been recovered by the FDIC.[3]

The Par Collection Requirement

Any bank that is a member of the Federal Reserve System must remit checks drawn on it at par. Nonmember banks wishing to use Federal Reserve check-clearing facilities must also remit at par.[4]

Those banks that do not remit checks at par are called "nonpar" banks. They cannot be members of the Federal Reserve System, and the Federal Reserve banks will not accept their checks for collection. Only a small and declining number of banks are nonpar. In 1954 there were 1,787 nonpar banks; by the end of 1963 there were only 1,594 banks not on the par list.[5] These banks represent about 10 percent of the total number of banks in the United States, yet they generally control only about 2 percent of the total deposit liabilities of commercial banks.[6] Although nonpar banks are not particularly important in terms of the national economy, they are quite important regionally. Nonpar banks are concentrated in the South and in the west north-central states. States having more than fifty nonpar banks in 1961 were Alabama, Arkansas, Georgia, Louisiana, Minnesota, Mississippi, Missouri, North Carolina, North Dakota, South Carolina, South Dakota, and Tennessee.[7]

Nonpar banks usually impose a minimum "exchange charge" of 0.1 percent on checks presented for collection by out-of-town banks. Thus, on a $1,000 check, a nonpar bank will remit only $999. Any checks drawn on a nonpar bank and presented at the teller's window, however, will be paid at par.

Why do some commercial banks choose to operate in this manner? Nonpar bankers argue that an exchange charge is required to cover the costs of making payment to out-of-town banks. Expensive out-of-town checking deposit accounts must be maintained with the large out-of-town banks. Since most nonpar banks are small rural banks, this expense can be considerable. This is not a valid argument, however, since these banks must maintain deposit balances with out-of-town banks anyway in order to collect on the deposit of checks drawn on the out-of-town banks. The real

---

[2] Federal Deposit Insurance Corporation, *Annual Report* (1960), p. 6.
[3] *Ibid.,* p. 7.
[4] For a more complete account of the process of check clearing and collection see Chapter 10.
[5] *Federal Reserve Bulletin,* February, 1955, p. 209; February, 1964, p. 241.
[6] Board of Governors of the Federal Reserve System, *The Federal Reserve System— Purposes and Functions* (Washington: 1961), p. 219.
[7] *Federal Reserve Bulletin,* February, 1964, p. 241.

reason for staying nonpar is that the exchange charge is profitable. Since checks sent to large out-of-town banks for collection are paid at par, and checks drawn on nonpar banks are paid at less than par, a profit margin exists. Nonpar banks are typically small, rural banks that are not as efficient as the city banks, nor as skilled in making profitable investments; hence, some have come to rely on the exchange charge as a source of earnings. Furthermore, they are often located in one-bank towns where there is little competitive pressure to force them to abandon their nonpar status.

Other Member Bank Obligations and Privileges

Banks that are members of the Federal Reserve System must also meet certain other requirements. First, they must be insured by the FDIC. This comes automatically with system membership. Second, they are subject to periodic examination by the Reserve System. (Actually, the Federal Reserve System usually examines only state member banks, leaving the examination of national banks to the Comptroller of the Currency.) Third, they must subscribe to Federal Reserve bank stock. At present, a member bank must subscribe to an amount of stock equal to 3 percent of its own capital accounts. The Federal Reserve System also has the right to increase this requirement by as much as an additional 3 percent. Finally, member banks are required to maintain a certain level of reserves.

This *reserve requirement* is a *ratio of* vault cash plus deposits at the Federal Reserve banks *to* the bank's deposit liabilities. The amount of reserves required to back demand deposit liabilities is now 16½ percent for banks designated as reserve city banks by the Federal Reserve System and 12 percent for those designated as country banks. The requirement is 4 percent for time deposits in all banks.[8]

Reserve system membership carries with it certain privileges: (1) member banks may have their checks cleared and collected free of cost by the Federal Reserve banks; (2) currency may be obtained free of charge; (3) loans and advances may be obtained from the Reserve banks; (4) a 6 percent dividend is received by a member bank on its holding of Reserve bank stock; and (5) the bank gains a certain amount of prestige, stemming from the mere fact that it is a member bank.

Advantages of Nonmember Bank Status

Nonmember banks are typically small banks that either do not meet the necessary membership qualifications or do not care to become members. There are a number of reasons why a bank may choose not to be a member. For one thing, state banking authorities generally set lower reserve require-

---

[8] *Federal Reserve Bulletin*, June, 1964, p. 729.

ments for nonmember banks than the Federal Reserve sets for member banks. State bank *reserve requirements* are generally some ratio of vault cash plus deposits *at other commercial banks* (and, in some cases, plus certain types of U.S. government securities) to the bank's deposit liabilities. Member banks, by way of contrast, are not permitted to count their deposits at other commercial banks as part of their reserves. In short, a nonmember bank does not need to keep as large a percentage of its monetary resources idle as does a member bank.

Another advantage of nonmembership is that a nonmember bank is subject to audit by one less supervisory agency than a member bank: it is not audited by the Federal Reserve System.

Finally, many nonmember banks, particularly those that remit at par, are able to obtain most of the advantages of membership without any of its responsibilities. These banks usually maintain checking deposit balances with large "city correspondents" (and, in some instances, even with a Federal Reserve bank). Thus, the nonmember banks obtain the privileges of membership indirectly, since the correspondent banks are almost always member banks and can use the facilities of the Federal Reserve banks to clear checks, obtain currency, and arrange for loans on behalf of nonmember banks.

NATIONAL AND STATE BANKS

At the end of 1963 there were 4,615 national banks, 1,497 state member banks, and 7,458 state nonmember banks. The average deposit liability of national banks at that time was $30 million, as against $13 million for state banks. As previously indicated, average deposit liabilities were $34 million for member banks and $6 million for nonmember banks. Although one would expect that the deposit liabilities of state member banks would average less than those of the national banks, this is not the case. The average deposit liability of the national banks was $29 million at the end of 1963, whereas for state member banks the figure came to $47 million.[9]

There appear to be two principal reasons for the larger size of state member banks. One concerns the prestige factor. Many small banks apparently feel that they need "national status" in order to maintain their competitive position. Small "store front" national banks are not uncommon in small rural communities, for example. Many of these banks have held their charter since the early days of the National Banking System and are now reluctant to relinquish their "national" status. The officers of these banks believe that a change to a state charter would cause their customers to transfer deposits to a larger bank in the "big city." Thus, many national banks are quite small.

---

[9] See Table 4–1.

The other reason is really the opposite side of the same coin. A number of very large banks feel that the advantages of a state charter outweigh this "prestige" factor. Some of these banks are so large that a national charter probably could not add to their prestige anyway—principally the large downtown New York City banks, whose operations are international in scope.

National Bank Charter Requirements

The capital requirements for national banks vary with the size of the city in which the bank is located:

POPULATION	CAPITAL REQUIREMENT
Up to 6,000	$ 50,000
6,000–50,000	100,000
Over 50,000	200,000

The capital requirement for new state banks, on the other hand, is usually $25,000, although some states have somewhat larger requirements. Connecticut, for example, has a $100,000 requirement.

There are four basic criteria upon which the Comptroller of the Currency and the various state banking departments rely when judging an application for a charter: (1) the access of the community to other banking facilities, (2) the need of the community for additional banking facilities, (3) the talent of the managers of the proposed bank, and (4) the adequacy of the amount of capital proposed. These considerations, along with the proposed capital size of the bank, help the authorities determine whether or not to grant a charter.

INSURED AND NONINSURED BANKS

Almost all U.S. commercial banks are insured. At the end of 1963 only 295 banks, just under 2 percent of all banks, were not insured by the FDIC. Their deposits totaled only 0.5 percent of all deposit liabilities.

Banks that are members of the Federal Reserve System are automatically admitted to deposit insurance, whereas nonmember banks are admitted only after examination by the FDIC. Factors considered by the FDIC before admitting a bank to insurance are (1) the financial condition of the bank, (2) its prospective earnings, (3) its managerial talent, and (4) the needs of the community. Thus the FDIC examines bank qualifications on much the same basis as the Comptroller of the Currency and the Federal Reserve banks, thereby helping to maintain uniform qualification standards.

Insured banks are under certain obligations to the FDIC, too. They are subject to periodic FDIC examination,[12] they must secure FDIC permission before merging with another bank,[13] and they must pay an annual assessment fee.[14]

What privileges does the FDIC extend to insured banks? None. The main function of the FDIC is to insure deposit accounts, up to a maximum of $10,000 per account. This is a guarantee extended to the depositor, not to the insured bank. FDIC insurance does help a bank to maintain its competitive position, of course, since most depositors would hesitate to keep deposit accounts with noninsured banks.

THE AMERICAN BANKING SYSTEM: TYPES OF OPERATION

Unit and Branch Banking

Most American banks operate only one office and are not controlled by any other bank or corporation. This is known as unit banking. At the end of 1963 the United States had 13,582 commercial banks, of which 10,717 were unit banks and 2,865 were banks operating a total of 13,652 branches.[15] In contrast, foreign banking has developed extensive multiple banking office systems.

Our banking tradition has encouraged the growth of unit banking. Americans have always felt that those who were qualified should be free to set up banks where needed. This has tended to encourage the establishment of many small banks. By 1921, for example, there were 31,076 banks

---

[12] In practice, as previously indicated, the FDIC examines only state nonmember insured banks. The Comptroller of the Currency and the Federal Reserve banks examine all member banks and the FDIC simply reviews these reports.

[13] If the resulting bank is to be national, permission must be obtained from the Comptroller of the Currency. If the new bank is to be a state member bank, the Board of Governors of the Federal Reserve System must give its approval. If the bank is to be a nonmember insured bank, the FDIC must give its consent. This is a relatively recent regulation—see Public Law 86–463, signed by the President on May 13, 1960. Notice that the approving agency in the case of consolidation is the same as the examining agency for each class of bank.

[14] The assessment rate is $\frac{1}{12}$ of 1 percent. This rate is assessed against the average of deposits less 16⅔ percent of demand deposits and 1 percent of time deposits. Actually, the amount paid by the banks does not equal this rate. After deducting its expenses and losses from the total amount due according to the assessment rate, the FDIC credits two-thirds of what is left to the insured banks. This is also a relatively recent regulation —see Public Law 86–671, signed by the President on July 14, 1960. The total amount collected from deposit insurance assessments during all of FDIC history from 1933 through 1960 amounted to only $1.75 billion, while deposit insurance losses were even less, $29 million. (Federal Deposit Insurance Corporation, *Annual Report* [1960], p. 20.)

[15] See Table 4–2.

operating only 1,455 branches.[16] The large-scale bank failures of the twenties and thirties demonstrated, however, that there were too many small and inefficient banks. Because of this "overbanking," state and national authorities made it more difficult to set up a new bank. Today, banking is still "free" only to the extent that the authorities believe we need additional banks. A new bank must carefully demonstrate the need for its services and its ability to satisfy that need. For this reason there has been relative stability in the total number of bank members during the last twenty-five years. The small decline that has occurred is a result of the fact that recently there have been more mergers than newly chartered banks. Many of these mergers are the result of FDIC efforts to have small, inefficient bank operations taken over by larger banks.

With an expanding economy, a need arises for more banking facilities. This has been met, however, not through the establishment of larger numbers of new banks, but through the establishment of an increasing number of branches by existing banks. Branch banks are thought to be able to meet the needs of the community better than unit banks because of the greater financial resources at their disposal. Our statutes, however, continue to encourage unit banking and discourage other forms of banking operations. For example, the Supreme Court recently ruled that bank mergers are subject to the antitrust laws. This may discourage future bank growth via consolidations.

Table 4–2 summarizes the present status of unit and branch banking in the United States on a state-by-state basis. Here we see that in over one-third of the states, those having approximately 25 percent of all bank assets, unit banking is still the dominant form. In those states with extensive branch banking systems, we find that expansion is severely limited. Almost one-third of the states, for example, permit a bank to establish a branch only within its home-office county, or at best in a contiguous county.

These restrictions apply to national as well as to state banks. U.S. banks are national only in the sense that they may have a charter from the Comptroller of the Currency. They are still allowed to operate only within the confines of a state. None of our banks are permitted to establish branches outside of the state in which the home office is located.[17] Under present regulations, a national bank is allowed to establish branches only to the extent permitted by the statutes of the state in which it is located.

Even when a state does permit extensive branch banking, a national bank is not authorized to establish any desired number of branches. It must file an application with the Comptroller of the Currency for permission to establish each branch. When an application is presented, it is studied with a view not only to the need for the branch, but also to the potential effects

---

[16] Federal Deposit Insurance Corporation, *Annual Report* (1960), p. 29.

[17] This restriction, however, does not apply to the setting up of branches in U.S. territories and foreign countries.

TABLE 4-2. UNIT AND BRANCH BANKING IN THE UNITED STATES, DECEMBER 31, 1963

STATE AND TYPE OF BANKING OPERATION	NUMBER OF ALL OFFICES	NUMBER OF UNIT BANKS	NUMBER OF BANKS WITH BRANCHES	NUMBER OF BRANCHES	DEPOSITS (IN MILLIONS OF DOLLARS)
States permitting statewide branch banking					
Alaska	63	4	8	51	$ 253
Arizona	244	3	10	231	1,741
California	2,282	80	75	2,127	30,981
Connecticut	322	27	37	258	2,821
Delaware	80	12	8	60	799
District of Col.	90	3	11	76	1,933
Hawaii	124	4	8	112	808
Idaho	138	15	12	111	755
Maryland	455	66	52	337	3,017
Nevada	59	2	5	52	616
North Carolina	828	74	82	672	3,549
Oregon	285	26	25	234	2,475
Rhode Island	116	—	10	106	1,045
South Carolina	355	87	51	217	1,222
Utah	147	33	19	95	1,176
Vermont	92	34	15	43	477
Washington	437	60	33	344	3,228
States permitting branch banking within limited areas					
Countywide					
Indiana	836	286	151	399	5,362
Kentucky	546	257	91	198	2,834
Louisiana	419	120	79	220	3,459
Massachusetts	640	61	101	478	6,068
Michigan	1,095	214	153	728	11,189
New Jersey	807	85	150	572	8,559
New Mexico	140	26	35	79	893
Ohio	1,367	329	223	815	12,988
Tennessee	565	205	89	271	4,192
Other					
Alabama	371	207	35	129	2,557
Georgia	583	371	52	160	3,608
Maine	206	13	33	160	737
Mississippi	371	110	84	177	1,678
New York	2,062	191	169	1,702	52,186
Pennsylvania	1,669	399	222	1,048	16,859
Virginia	710	163	117	430	4,066
States where unit banking is prevalent					
With limited branch banking					
Arkansas	319	190	52	77	1,703
Iowa	886	509	165	212	3,660
Kansas	638	550	43	45	2,882
North Dakota	197	129	30	38	921
Oklahoma	435	369	32	34	3,135
South Dakota	244	140	33	71	926
Wisconsin	741	475	101	165	5,440

TABLE 4–2. (*Continued*)

STATE AND TYPE OF BANKING OPERATION	NUMBER OF ALL OFFICES	NUMBER OF UNIT BANKS	NUMBER OF BANKS WITH BRANCHES	NUMBER OF BRANCHES	DEPOSITS (IN MILLIONS OF DOLLARS)
Without branch banking*					
Colorado	234	221	6	7	$ 2,533
Florida	401	370	15	16	6,030
Illinois	1,013	1,005	4	4	21,164
Minnesota	715	703	4	8	5,050
Missouri	684	588	48	48	7,172
Montana	128	122	3	3	981
Nebraska	455	405	24	26	2,012
New Hampshire	80	72	4	4	499
Texas	1,444	1,053	46	45	14,860
West Virginia	182	182	—	—	1,491
Wyoming	64	62	1	1	505
United States	27,234	10,717	2,865	13,652	$276,230†

Source: Federal Deposit Insurance Corporation *Annual Report*, 1963, pp. 118–27.
* The few branches in these states were established prior to existing prohibitory legislation or under unusual circumstances.
† Does not equal the sum of the above due to rounding.

upon bank competition and concentration. Not every new branch application is approved. During 1963, for example, some 679 applications were filed with the Comptroller of the Currency. Of these, only 480 were approved; forty-one were rejected and thirty-two were withdrawn. The remaining 126 were still in process at the end of the year.[18]

Why do we impose these restrictions on branch banking? Why does state law apparently favor the unit banking system? Partly out of tradition. Our country was originally underpopulated, with great distances between population centers. Travel and communication was difficult. The economy was also primarily agrarian. These conditions tended to foster the development of unit banks—locally owned, operated, and controlled. This type of tradition is hard to put aside. In addition, many state legislatures are still dominated by the rural sectors of their states.[19] Legislatures of this type are concerned with "home rule" and fear a shift of political power to the urban centers. They are reluctant to permit an expansion of branch banking because they fear that the big banks in the urban areas would set up branches. Thus the competitive position of the country bank would be lessened and economic as well as political power would be transferred to the city.

[18] Comptroller of the Currency, *Annual Report* (1963), p. 9.
[19] The recent Supreme Court decision concerning legislative reapportionment may well cause this situation to change.

Arguments for and Against Branch Banking

A number of arguments may be advanced against branch banking. One of these has already been mentioned: branch banking leads to a concentration of economic power and lessens competition. Other arguments frequently cited follow: First, branch banks draw funds away from local areas and channel them to the big city. Second, the unit bank can make loan decisions more quickly, since the branch manager must first consult the home office before making a loan over a certain size. Third, the unit bank is best equipped to make correct loan and investment decisions because its managers are more aware of local conditions. Branch managers frequently come from out-of-town and do not have a "feel" for the community and its problems. Finally, the unit bank is able to meet almost any legitimate financial need of the local business community, because it maintains correspondent arrangements with large city banks.

Proponents of branch banking, on the other hand, counter these arguments as follows: First, the competitive position of large banks has, if anything, decreased in recent years. With the movement of the population to the suburbs, large city banks, even those with branches, have grown less rapidly than the banks in outlying areas. The city banks have often been prevented from expanding into these areas by the restrictive prohibitions against branch banking. As a result the suburban and rural banks are not faced with competition. This is particularly true in "one-bank" communities. This monopoly of banking power increases with the distance of the community from competing financial centers. Banks located in these areas frequently charge more for loans and pay less interest than banks located where alternative banking facilities are available. Further, if "increasing concentration is taken as evidence of declining competition, the data suggest that the banking system of the nation in the late 1950's, though less competitive than in 1920, was more competitive than in the middle 1930's or early 1940's."[20]

A second argument advanced in favor of branch banking is that the unit bank is frequently too small to handle the large borrower. It is also unable to provide skilled banking services such as investment counseling. The branch is able to do this through its contact with the home office.

Third, a large branch bank is usually financially sounder and more efficiently managed than a unit bank. Most of the bank mergers in recent years have been between large banks and small, weak banks. Most of the smaller banks were unit banks. For example, in 1960, ninety-nine banks having resources of $1.7 billion were absorbed by ninety-two banks having resources of $16.3 billion. Prior to the transaction, the number of offices operated by the absorbing banks was 964. The absorbed banks had operated

---

[20] Federal Deposit Insurance Corporation, *Annual Report* (1960), p. 59.

a total of 210 offices. After absorption, 1,143 offices were in operation, some thirty-one offices having been discontinued.[21]

Finally, when a branch needs funds, it is able to acquire them through the home office from branches that have a surplus. Hence a branch may immediately draw upon the resources of the whole bank. Unit banks, on the other hand, may be embarrassed by a shortage of loan funds.

Certainly there are valid points on each side of this controversy. The unit bank probably does know the needs of the community best, and through its correspondents it is able to provide almost as many services as a large branch bank. On the other hand, it tends to be monopolistic where there is a lack of competing bank facilities. The large bank and its branches, in competition with other large banks and their branches, do provide a greater variety of services. In addition, they charge relatively low interest rates on loans and pay close to the maximum interest allowed on deposits. Both types of bank operations, therefore, have their advantages. It is probable, however, that our system will soon no longer be dominated by unit banking. Recently the tendency has been to restrict the growth of the number of banks, while the number of branches has substantially increased even in the face of the existing restrictive state statutes.

Chain Banking

Chain banking is a term used to describe the association of a number of commercial banks through an interlocking directorate. It is not an important feature of American banking. Each bank in a chain is counted as a separate bank; some may operate branches. Control over the chain is exercised by an individual or group of individuals who own stock in or are directors of the separate banks in the chain.

This type of banking originated in the 1880's in the South and central Northwest. It reached the peak of its popularity about 1920. Since then it has declined markedly, primarily because individual control has tended to give way to corporate control.

Group Banking[22]

Group banking exists in either of two forms. In one, a nonbanking corporation, sometimes called a bancorporation, owns the stock of the constituent banks and acts as the controlling agency. In the other form, one bank controls the stock of the other banks in the group. Both of these are

---

[21] *Ibid.*, p. 10.

[22] Mr. James F. Gallagher of Fordham University made some material available for the preparation of this section. James F. Gallagher, *The Bank Holding Company in New York State*, Ph.D. dissertation in process, Fordham University.

holding company arrangements. Each of the banks in a group is counted as a separate bank; some of these banks even operate branches.[23]

As a whole, bank holding company groups are not a very important factor in American banking. As of December 31, 1963, there were 52 bank holding companies operating 454 banks and 1,278 branches. These groups accounted for 6.5 percent of all bank offices and held 8 percent of all deposits in the United States.[24] There has been no relative growth of bank holding companies since the 1920's, either. If anything, there has been a decline since 1936, when these group banks operated 7 percent of the offices and controlled 14 percent of all deposits. This decline is surprising, since the holding company has certain advantages over branch banking as a form of expansion. The holding company device can be used to establish systems that cross city, county, and even state lines. This is the only way that banks are able to cross state lines. Despite this advantage, holding companies have not increased in number for the following reasons: First, the liberalization of branch banking laws in some states has led some banking groups to convert into branch bank systems. Second, in 1938 President Roosevelt publicly advocated the abolition of bank holding companies. This proposal placed group banking in a position of uncertainty which did not really end until the passage of the Bank Holding Company Act of 1956. During the intervening eighteen years, unit banking interests waged an extensive campaign against group banking.

The arguments for and against group banking are similar to those for and against branch banking. It has been contended on one side that group banking concentrates banking power, decreases competition, and is not concerned or able to cope with the problems of the small financial centers. On the other side, it is argued that the bank holding company can increase competition and is a sounder financial institution than the unit bank.

Group banking, like branch banking, has also encountered some restrictive legislation. According to the provisions of the Bank Holding Company Act of 1956, all bank holding companies (1) must register with the Board of Governors of the Federal Reserve System, (2) must obtain permission of the Board prior to the purchase of additional bank voting stock, and (3) can hold no stock in subsidiaries that are not engaged in banking.

State legislation is silent, for the most part, concerning group banking. As of October 1, 1960, thirty-four states placed no legal restraints on the growth of bank holding companies. Three states required state approval for the incorporation of bank holding companies. The remaining thirteen states either restricted or prohibited the setting up or expansion of banking groups.[25]

---

[23] This means that single banks in a unit will be counted as unit banks, while those operating branches will be counted as branch banks. Our methods of counting banks, therefore, fail to distinguish clearly between unit, branch, and group banking.

[24] *Federal Reserve Bulletin*, June, 1964, p. 783.

[25] Donald L. Rogers, *Compilation of State Laws Affecting Bank Holding Companies* (Washington, D.C.: Association of Registered Holding Companies, 1960).

Correspondent Banking

A correspondent bank is one that maintains checking deposit accounts for other, usually smaller, customer banks. These deposits are called interbank deposits. As of May 27, 1964, there were $14.3 billion in interbank deposits, $13.7 and $0.6 billion of this amount respectively in demand and time.[26]

Maintaining these accounts benefits both the correspondent and customer banks. To the correspondent bank the deposit is a source of funds like any other new deposit; thus, when a small bank with excess funds makes a new interbank deposit of $1,000, the "T" account entries would look as follows:

BALANCE SHEET FOR A LARGE MEMBER BANK

ASSETS		LIABILITIES + CAPITAL ACCOUNTS	
Cash assets	+$1,000	Interbank deposits	+$1,000

The large bank, on the basis of the increased cash assets, is in a position to extend its loans and deposits.[27] The total cash assets of the small bank, however, remain unchanged. To the small bank the deposit at the big bank is as good as cash, since it is subject to call on demand.

Small banks maintain these deposit balances because of the variety of services provided by the larger banks. Among these are (1) the clearing and collection of checks for both members and nonmembers, (2) security analysis, (3) the handling of bond and security purchases, (4) currency shipments, (5) participation in loans that the small banks cannot handle alone, (6) the making of loans to customer banks, and (7) the providing of foreign monies (exchange) so that the customers of small banks may buy and sell abroad.

SUMMARY

In this chapter we have outlined the structure of the U.S. banking system. More than half of our banks are not members of the Federal Reserve System, but they account for only 21 percent of demand deposit liabilities. Almost all banks, however, do participate in deposit insurance.

Unit banking is by far the principal form of U.S. banking. In recent decades, however, the growth of the number of unit banks has fallen off, whereas the number of new branch offices has expanded markedly.

On several occasions we mentioned the question of competition and concentration in banking. It does not appear that either bank consolidations or the development of branch banking and holding companies constitute a

---

[26] *Federal Reserve Bulletin*, June, 1964, p. 736.
[27] See Chapter 7 for a more complete account of deposit creation.

serious monopolistic threat to competition under existing law. If anything, the law still tends to favor small unit banking and, for many one-bank communities, this means a lack of competition. The 100 largest commercial banks had 42, 54, 57, 45, and 46 percent of commercial bank deposits in 1929, 1934, 1940, 1949, and 1958 respectively.[28] This type of concentration would be taken as indicative of a high degree of competition in most other industries.

Supplementary Readings

Alhadeff, David A. *Monopoly and Competition in Banking*. Berkeley, University of California Press, 1954.

Board of Governors of the Federal Reserve System. *The Federal Reserve System: Purposes and Functions*. Washington, D.C., 1961, Chapter 4.

Cartinhour, G. T. *Branch, Group and Chain Banking*. New York, Macmillan, 1931.

Commission on Money and Credit. *Money and Credit: Their Influence on Jobs, Prices, and Growth*, Englewood Cliffs, N.J., Prentice-Hall, 1961, Chapter 6.

Nadler, Marcus, and J. I. Bogen. *The Bank Holding Company*. New York, Graduate School of Business Administration, New York University, 1959.

Data Sources

Comptroller of the Currency. *Annual Reports*. Washington, D.C.
Federal Deposit Insurance Corporation. *Annual Reports*. Washington, D.C.
See also the end of Chapter 2.

---

[28] Federal Deposit Insurance Corporation, *Annual Report* (1960), p. 51.

Chapter 5

Commercial Bank Sources of Funds

Preceding chapters examined the structure of commercial banking and the relative importance of the financial community to the U.S. economy. We have seen that commercial banks differ from other members of the financial community in their unique ability to create and destroy money. In Chapter 7 we will examine this peculiar money-creating ability of the commercial banking system in some detail. In this chapter and the next we shall concern ourselves with commercial bank operations as they are summarized on a bank balance sheet. The focus is upon the sources and uses of commercial bank funds. What are the sources of funds? To what uses do banks put these funds? Are they invested in securities, loans, or real estate, or are they merely held idle in the form of cash? What do the differing sources and uses of funds mean for the national economy? for bank earnings and operations? These are some of the questions that will concern us in Chapters 5 and 6.

THE BALANCE SHEET
FOR A REPRESENTATIVE COMMERCIAL BANK

The balance sheet of a commercial bank shows the financial position of that bank at a moment of time. Table 5–1 gives a simplified hypothetical balance sheet for a typical commercial bank. The *asset side* of the balance sheet shows what the bank owns, that is, the uses to which the bank has put its funds. In this balance sheet we see that the bank has $1 million in *cash assets*. These assets consist of cash in the bank's vaults and demand deposits maintained with other banks. They are idle assets, for they do not enhance the bank's earning powers and are kept on hand primarily for the purpose of enabling the bank to meet reserve requirements and the cash demands of depositors.

Almost one-third of our bank's assets are in the form of *security holdings*. These consist primarily of U.S. government securities. In addition, the bank holds substantial quantities of state and local government securities. Relatively small quantities of privately issued stocks and bonds are held. Government securities are viewed as secondary reserves by banks. They have ready marketability and can be converted to cash quickly to meet depositor demands for cash.

The largest category in the list of assets for our bank is *loans and discounts.* It is composed primarily of real estate loans, business loans, and loans to individuals. This is the most profitable and the most important use to which commercial banks can put their funds and is the principal source of their earnings.

Miscellaneous assets is a catchall category representing all non-income-yielding assets such as the "book value" of the bank's premises, furniture, and fixtures.

The claims of creditors to the assets of the bank are termed *liabilities.* *Capital accounts* are the residual claims of stockholders to the assets of the

TABLE 5–1. HYPOTHETICAL BALANCE SHEET
FOR A TYPICAL COMMERCIAL BANK

ASSETS		LIABILITIES + CAPITAL ACCOUNTS	
Cash assets	$1,000,000	Demand deposits	$3,500,000
Securities	2,000,000	Time deposits	1,900,000
Loans and discounts	3,000,000	Miscellaneous liabilities	200,000
Miscellaneous assets	100,000	Capital accounts	500,000
Total	$6,100,000	Total	$6,100,000

bank. Both liabilities and capital accounts are sources of funds for the commercial bank. As a bank's liabilities and capital accounts increase, it is provided with the funds that enable it to acquire earning assets. More will be said of this later in the chapter.

We have said that *demand deposits* are claims upon the commercial bank that may be transferred on demand by the use of checks. The owners of these checking deposit accounts are the depositors of the bank. Deposit liabilities, as our balance sheet shows, are almost always the largest category of liabilities. Because any amount of these liabilities may be demanded by depositors at any given time, the commercial bank must maintain assets that it can liquidate quickly in the event of demands for cash by depositors. Cash assets and U.S. government securities usually perform this function.

The second form of deposits on our hypothetical balance sheet is *time deposits.* This amounts to $1.9 million, or almost one-third of all liabilities and capital accounts. Time deposits, unlike demand deposits, are not legally subject to call upon demand. Banks may demand up to thirty days' notice on time deposit withdrawal, however. In addition they yield interest to the depositors. These deposits are an important source of funds to the commercial bank because commercial banks are not asked to redeem time deposits as often as demand deposits. Consequently, to cover time deposits banks need not maintain idle cash reserves as large as those covering demand deposits.

The principal forms of *miscellaneous liabilities* consist of rediscounts and borrowings. A *rediscount* refers to money that a bank has raised by selling assets, such as loans to other banks. It is treated as a liability because the bank is liable for the note in the event of default in payment by the borrower. *Borrowings* arise when banks borrow funds, principally from the Federal Reserve banks. Both rediscounts and borrowing will be discussed in more detail in Chapter 12.

Capital accounts are the last items on the bank's balance sheet. They consist of cash surplus and the par value of the bank's common and preferred stock. Most of the surplus is created when the bank has profits.

LIABILITIES AND CAPITAL ACCOUNTS

To this point we have briefly described the components of a bank's balance sheet. We began our discussion with the balance sheet because it serves as a convenient outline of the more detailed discussion that follows. Chapter 6 will deal with uses of funds. This section examines the right hand side of the balance sheet–liabilities and capital accounts–in some detail. First, we shall see how these accounts provide funds for the commercial bank. Second, we shall examine the composition and size of our banking system's sources of funds. And third, we shall consider how certain changes in sources of funds might affect the national economy.

How Liabilities and Capital Accounts Provide Funds for a Bank

When a commercial bank accepts deposits, sells stock, or borrows funds from other banking institutions, it is provided with funds that it can use to expand earning asset holdings. For example, when an individual deposits $1,000 in cash into either his checking or savings deposit account, the bank acquires an asset, $1,000 in cash, and creates a liability for the individual depositor of $1,000 in deposits. The "T" account entries for this transaction are as follows:

BALANCE SHEET CHANGES FOR COMMERCIAL BANK A

ASSETS		LIABILITIES + CAPITAL ACCOUNTS	
Reserves (vault cash)	+$1,000	Deposits	+$1,000

The asset entry is recorded as an increase in reserves rather than as a vault cash increase because vault cash is usually part of a bank's reserves. If the depositor deposits a check drawn on some other bank, the "T" account entries remain the same, because once the checks written on other banks are collected, the reserves of Bank A will increase, while the banks on which the checks were drawn will experience a decrease in reserves.✓

Very much the same thing occurs when a bank sells stock. If a bank sells stock for cash, reserves are increased and common stock, under capital account entries for such a transaction are

BALANCE SHEET CHANGES FOR COMMERCIAL BANK A

ASSETS		LIABILITIES + CAPITAL ACCOUNTS	
Reserves	+$1,000	Common stock	+$1,000

Likewise, if the stock is paid for with checks drawn on other commercial banks, both reserves and common stock increase by $1,000.[1] Other banks, of course, are faced with a decrease in their reserves. *The reserves that the acquiring bank receives provide it with the basis for an expansion of its earning assets.*

A bank, however, will sometimes not receive cash or deposits drawn on other banks when it sells stock. This occurs when a bank's own depositors purchase stock. A bank frequently attempts to induce its depositors to become stockholders. Although this does not provide the bank with additional funds, its lending ability is enhanced nevertheless! Assume that a depositor of Bank A purchases $1,000 in Bank A stock by drawing $1,000 from his checking deposit account. The "T" account entries are:

BALANCE SHEET CHANGES FOR COMMERCIAL BANK A

ASSETS		LIABILITIES + CAPITAL ACCOUNTS	
		Demand deposits	−$1,000
		Common stock	+$1,000

Note that no change has occurred in assets. The bank has not acquired funds through the sale of stock. Nevertheless, its lending ability has increased because its deposit liabilities have decreased. A bank must maintain reserves, as we have seen, to cover its demand deposit liabilities. If the demand deposits decrease, the commercial bank will have more reserves relative to its demand deposit liabilities than formerly, and may, accordingly, grant new loans and create new deposits.

Commercial banks also obtain funds by borrowing from other banks. A common source of borrowings is the Federal Reserve System. Thus if a bank wants to increase its lending operations or feels that it is short of

---

[1] If it so happens that the stock is sold for more than the par value of the stock, common stock is increased by $1,000, and another item under capital accounts, surplus, is increased by the difference between the amount received by the bank for the stock and the par value of the stock. Reserves will increase by the amount of the proceeds received from the sale of the stock. On the other hand, if the stock sells for less than its par value, surplus will be reduced by the amount that the par value exceeds the receipts from the sale of the stock, and common stock increased by the par value of the stock. Reserves will again increase by the amount received from the stock sale.

funds, it may borrow funds from its district Federal Reserve bank. The "T" account entries for such a transaction are

BALANCE SHEET CHANGES FOR COMMERCIAL BANK A

ASSETS		LIABILITIES + CAPITAL ACCOUNTS	
Reserves	+$1,000	Borrowings	+$1,000

Commercial banks and other business institutions differ in their use of funds. When a nonbanking business enterprise receives additional funds from operations, from sales of stock, or from outside lenders, it is likely to spend these funds sooner or later to acquire income-producing assets. If these funds are used to purchase a $50,000 machine, this increase in the company's income-producing assets is accompanied by an equal decrease in its cash holdings. The balance sheet changes are recorded as items a:

BALANCE SHEET CHANGES FOR COMPANY A

ASSETS		LIABILITIES + CAPITAL ACCOUNTS
Cash	−$50,000 (a)	
Plant and equipment	+$50,000 (a)	
Cash	−$50,000 (b)	
Loans	+$50,000 (b)	

If Company A were to extend a loan to some other business, there would normally be an equal and offsetting increase and decrease in the corresponding asset items, also. This is illustrated by the b entries in the above balance sheet.

When a commercial bank receives additional funds from new deposits, borrowings, or sales of stock, however, it does not use its cash increase directly to make loans and investments. As mentioned previously, when a commercial bank grants a loan, it acquires both an asset and a liability. The bank acquires an interest-earning loan and it creates a demand deposit liability for its customer. In Bank A, the entries would be as follows:

BALANCE SHEET CHANGES FOR COMMERCIAL BANK A

ASSETS		LIABILITIES + CAPITAL ACCOUNTS	
Loans	+$50,000	Demand deposits	+$50,000

An increase in demand deposit liabilities necessitates an increase in bank reserves to back these additional liabilities. Consequently, banks add additional incoming funds to reserves, instead of lending them or investing them directly. When the bank has more reserves than it needs to meet its legal reserve requirement (see Chapters 4 and 7), it may then expand its loans by the amount permitted by its excess reserves.

Most borrowers would rather have a demand deposit than cash when receiving a loan, since demand deposits are easier to handle for all but very small amounts. When cash loans are made, however, the bank uses its vault cash reserves directly. Thus, on a cash loan, reserves will decline by an amount equal to the loan.

Generally a bank should not expand its loans and create new deposits beyond an amount equal to excess reserves. A fuller discussion of excess reserves is found in Chapter 7, but for the present we may define *excess reserves* as the amount by which the reserves of a bank exceed what it legally must have to back its outstanding deposit liabilities.

This general rule is important. When a commercial bank lends and creates deposits, it cannot expect its borrowers to do business only with those firms and individuals that maintain accounts with the same bank. If Individual 1 borrows $1,000 from Bank A, he will probably use the money to purchase goods or services from Individual 2, who maintains deposit balances with some other bank, Bank B. Hence, when Individual 1 writes checks on his increased checking account, those checks will find their way into the deposit accounts of Individual 2, increasing the reserves of Bank B, while Bank A loses reserves. The appropriate "T" account entries are

BALANCE SHEET CHANGES FOR COMMERCIAL BANK A

ASSETS		LIABILITIES + CAPITAL ACCOUNTS	
Loans	+$1,000 (a)	Demand deposits of individual 1	+$1,000 (a)
Reserves	−$1,000 (b)	Demand deposits of individual 1	−$1,000 (b)

BALANCE SHEET CHANGES FOR COMMERCIAL BANK B

ASSETS		LIABILITIES + CAPITAL ACCOUNTS	
Reserves	+$1,000 (b)	Demand deposits of individual 2	+$1,000 (b)

Entries a show the results of Bank A lending to Individual 1. Entries b show the effects of Individual 1 purchasing $1,000 worth of goods and services from Individual 2, who then deposits the check in his account with Bank B. Bank B in turn collects from Bank A, and the checking account of Individual 1 is decreased.

If Bank A had had only $500 in excess reserves, it would now be $500 short of its legal reserve requirement. It would probably be forced to reduce its loans or borrow additional reserves from the Federal Reserve System. Either alternative is costly, however, since the Federal Reserve banks charge for borrowed reserves, and since fewer loans mean less income.

We can see, therefore, that a commercial bank should expect to lose reserves to other banks when it makes a loan. Hence, when it acquires additional funds, it should only expand loans and investments by an amount equal to its excess reserves. Thus an increase in funds indirectly permits the bank to expand its loans and investments. A stable volume of funds means that the bank should maintain about the same total volume of loans and investments, since continuous repayment of outstanding loans enables it to make new loans even though it is not receiving additional excess reserves.

There appears to be a paradox in this line of reasoning, however. Demand deposit liabilities of commercial banks have been described as a source of funds. Deposits of checks drawn on other banks or deposits of cash provide funds; in return for the use of these funds, commercial banks create demand deposit liabilities for the depositors. The funds provided in this manner enable banks to make loans and create additional demand deposits. These additional deposits are *not* sources of funds, however. Only the first kind of deposit provides a bank with additional funds. Such a deposit is called a *primary deposit*, a deposit that increases the bank's holding of reserves. Those deposits created when a bank makes loans are called *derivative deposits*. Only primary deposits are sources of funds for the bank. Derivative deposits can only become sources of funds when they are used and thus increase the reserves and deposits of some other bank. Such a case was described in the last "T" account illustration under entry b.

Composition and Size of Bank Sources of Funds

Table 5–2 shows that demand deposits are the chief source of bank funds. They comprise 52.3 percent of all liabilities and capital accounts. Time deposits are the second largest source of funds, accounting for 35.7 percent of liabilities and capital accounts. Only 8.2 percent of the total are in the form of capital accounts.

Individuals, partnerships, and corporations, the U.S. government, state and local governments, U.S. banks, and foreign banks all own demand deposits in U.S. banks. More than 75 percent of these deposits are held by individuals, partnerships, and corporations. This group also owns over 90 percent of all time deposits. The U.S. government and domestic commercial banks keep almost all of their funds in the form of demand deposits. State and local governments and foreign banks, on the other hand, maintain substantial amounts in time deposits, principally for the purpose of earning interest.

Demand deposits. The demand deposits owned by individuals, businesses, and state and local governments are usually held for transaction purposes, that is, in order to have money readily available for purchase of goods and services. Deposits held at commercial banks by the U.S. government, on the other hand, are not used to purchase goods and services. The Treasury uses its balances with the Federal Reserve banks for this purpose.

The Treasury's deposit balances at commercial banks are called *Tax and Loan Accounts.* These balances normally increase as commercial banks sell U.S. government savings bonds, as they purchase new issues of government

TABLE 5–2. ALL COMMERCIAL BANK LIABILITIES AND CAPITAL ACCOUNTS,
DECEMBER 20, 1963
(IN MILLIONS OF DOLLARS AND PERCENT OF TOTAL)

TYPE OF LIABILITY OR CAPITAL ACCOUNT	MILLIONS OF DOLLARS	PERCENT OF TOTAL
Demand deposits		
Interbank		
Domestic	14,048	
Foreign	1,218	
U.S. government	6,729	
State and local government	12,256	
Certified and officers' checks, etc.	4,494	
Individuals, partnerships, and corporations	124,784	
Total	163,529	52.3
Time deposits		
Interbank	526	
U.S. government and Postal Savings	269	
State and local government	7,908	
Individuals, partnerships and corporations	102,886	
Total	111,589	35.7
Borrowings	3,664	1.1
Other liabilities	8,314	2.7
Capital accounts	25,677	8.2
Total liabilities and capital accounts	312,773	100.0

Source: *Federal Reserve Bulletin*, June, 1964, pp. 736, 740.

securities, and as employers make social security and income-withholding payments. The purpose of these accounts is to help banks avoid the reserve losses that would otherwise occur when the private sector of the economy makes payments to the government.

Tax and Loan Accounts decrease when the Treasury orders the commercial banks to transfer a portion of the accumulated deposits to the U.S. government balances with the Federal Reserve banks. This is reflected on the balance sheets as follows:

BALANCE SHEET CHANGES FOR THE COMMERCIAL BANKING SYSTEM

ASSETS	LIABILITIES + CAPITAL ACCOUNTS
Reserves −$1,000,000	U.S. government demand deposits −$1,000,000

BALANCE SHEET CHANGES FOR THE FEDERAL RESERVE BANKS

ASSETS	LIABILITIES + CAPITAL ACCOUNTS

	Deposits
	   Member bank reserves −$1,000,000
	   U.S. government general account
	       +$1,000,000

The Treasury orders the above type of decrease in its balances at commercial banks when the government needs money to meet its obligations. This is generally done at regular intervals. As the "T" account entries show, commercial banks lose reserves when the Treasury balances are transferred to the Federal Reserve banks. As the Treasury spends funds, however, bank reserves are built back up. In the meantime, to offset possible adverse economic repercussions of this decrease in reserves, the Federal Open Market Committee will usually see to it that banks are provided with additional reserves from other sources. More will be said of this in Chapter 13.

Interbank demand deposits, as indicated in Chapter 4, are maintained at large banks by small banks in return for the variety of services which the larger banks provide. The interbank deposits are important as a source of funds for the large banks—as these deposits increase, so do their reserves.[2]

Time deposits. Time deposits constitute the second most important source of funds for commercial banks. In recent years these deposits have increased in significance. Demand deposits (adjusted) increased from $92.3 billion at the end of 1950 to $124.6 billion at the end of 1963, an increase of almost one-third. In the same period, however, all commercial bank time deposits increased from $36.3 to $110.8 billion—a 205 percent increase.[3] The increased interest yield now allowed by the Federal Reserve System is one possible reason for this growth of time deposits. The maximum interest rate payable on time and savings deposits from 1936 to 1957 was 2½ percent. This was raised to 3 percent in 1957 and to 4 percent in 1962. A $15 billion increase in time deposits occurred after the rise in early 1962.[4] Another reason for the increase in time deposits may be that commercial banks are making a more active attempt to acquire these sources of funds. Reserve requirements on time deposits are lower than on demand deposits. Consequently, for every new deposit going into a savings rather than a checking account, the bank is able to create a substantially greater amount of loans and demand deposits.

What forms do time deposits take? Principally three: savings deposits, certificates of deposit, and open-account time deposits. Of these, *savings deposits* are the most familiar and the most important. These accounts are held principally by individuals. They are payable upon presentation of a passbook (and are usually paid on demand—few banks enforce the legal thirty-day waiting period).

Businesses, however, may not hold savings deposits. Instead they may invest idle funds in time certificates of deposit or in open-account time

---

[2] It should be noted that interbank demand deposits are excluded from the data on the money supply in Table 2–1.

[3] *Federal Reserve Bulletin,* June, 1964, p. 735. Adjusted demand deposits include all demand deposits other than interbank and U.S. government less cash items in process of collection. Commercial bank time deposits include all commercial bank time deposits other than interbank, Treasurer's open account, and those of the Postal Savings System in banks.

[4] *Ibid.,* pp. 729, 735.

deposits. *Certificates of deposit* are offered by banks to both their corporate and noncorporate customers. The certificates may or may not be negotiable. They have become of increasing importance since 1961 when

several large money market banks in New York City began to offer CD's [time certificates of deposit] in readily marketable form to their corporate depositors. . . . A special survey by the Federal Reserve of 410 member banks indicates that such certificates outstanding at these banks had reached $6.2 billion by December 5, 1962. This compares with just over $1 billion at the end of 1960 and $3.2 billion at the end of 1961.[5]

Open-account time deposits are similar to the time certificates of deposit in that payment will not be made by the bank until some specific date. On the other hand, the open-account deposit is not for a fixed amount; it may be increased.

Borrowings. Borrowings, as previously indicated, are liabilities that a bank incurs when it borrows funds from the Federal Reserve district banks or other commercial banks. Borrowings usually take place when banks are temporarily deficient of reserves or wish to expand earning assets. Only 1.1 percent of bank liabilities and capital accounts are in this form.

Capital accounts. Capital accounts consist of the sum of a bank's surplus and the par value of its stock. Surplus is a general category which usually includes capital surplus, undistributed profits, and reserves. Capital stock increases when a bank issues new stock. Surplus changes when a bank receives more or less than par value from the proceeds of the sale of newly issued stock. Undistributed profits increase when a bank has profits on its operations and does not distribute all of them to its stockholders. Undistributed profits decrease when the bank has losses. Banks frequently reduce the size of undistributed profits by setting up reserves. Actually, this involves no transfer of cash or setting aside of funds. The reserve account is merely a segregation of undistributed profits which is designed to reduce stockholder claims to these profits.

As mentioned in an earlier chapter, the total of capital accounts is simply a measure of the claims of stockholders to the assets of the bank. Thus, accounts such as surplus and undistributed profits are claims to bank assets. The bank does not segregate any of its cash assets for the purpose of distributing them to stockholders. If the bank has earnings, it is highly probable that it will reinvest the funds in income-producing assets like loans or securities. (Consequently there is no cash surplus that can be used to pay stockholders dividends.) Profitable banks generally pay dividends, however, but not by as much as the total of profits. Undistributed profits, then, are profits remaining after dividend payments have been made.

As a source of funds, capital accounts have recently increased in importance. The ratio of capital accounts to assets increased from 5.5 percent

---

[5] *Federal Reserve Bulletin*, April, 1963, p. 458.

in 1945 to 12.2 percent in 1963.[6] Most of the increase is accounted for by a rise in retained profits. In the period 1947 to 1959 "retained profits provided 82 percent of new capital and new stock sales 18 percent."[7]

There are numerous reasons for this limited volume of new bank common stock sales. First, there is the memory of the depression, when the number of banks was cut almost in half between 1929 and 1933. Earnings were poor throughout the thirties. Second, many small banks are either family dominated or controlled by a small group of individuals who do not want to expand bank ownership for fear of losing control. Third, *bank earnings are low in comparison with many other industries.* This third factor has probably been the source of most of the difficulty in expanding stock ownership.

Thus, the banking industry is faced with a dilemma: To acquire additional funds through the sale of stock, banks must increase earnings. To raise earnings, banks must grant more loans and make more investments. In order to make more loans and investments, however, they need more funds (reserves). Additional usable reserves for the commercial banking system are provided when the monetary authorities lower reserve requirements or purchase U.S. government securities on the open market. Thus the ability of the commercial banking system to get additional reserves does not depend upon its own decisions, but on those of our regulatory agencies. True, individual banks can compete more aggressively with one another for deposits and thus acquire additional reserves, but this would only benefit some banks at the expense of others.

How can banks increase earnings when additional reserves are not available to them? One obvious solution is to reduce expenses. In a competitive industry like banking, however, most firms are already striving for reduction in costs. The other solution is to make relatively more high-income-producing loans and investments. Higher yielding loans and investments, however, are likely to be risky. An increased proportion of risk assets would impair the quality of bank assets in the view of government supervisory agencies. The ratio of capital accounts to risk assets had already

declined to 14.2 percent by 1959, the lowest level for the quarter of a century since 1935, despite the growth of capital funds that occurred in the interim. This ratio was 19.7 percent in 1930, at the start of the depression. This trend is significant, for should risk assets and capital funds of insured commercial banks grow at the same rate in the 1960's, the risk asset ratio would sink to 9.5 percent by the end of 1969. Such a decline would be unacceptable to supervisory authorities and to bankers.[8]

Supervisory authorities may hamper bank efforts to expand funds through increasing yields on loans and investments. Nevertheless, in recent decades

---

[6] *Federal Reserve Bulletin,* May, 1963, p. 664. See also Table 5–2.

[7] The American Bankers Association, *The Commercial Banking Industry,* (Englewood Cliffs, N.J.: Prentice-Hall, 1962), p. 325.

[8] *Ibid.,* p. 325.

supervision has resulted in a very low rate of bank failure and deposit loss. Thus, some limitation on growth in risk assets has enabled capital accounts to perform adequately what many regard as their principal function—the provision of a margin of safety for bank depositors.

Ultimately it appears that the solution to what many bankers view as a serious problem—the inadequacy of bank capital—lies in the creation of more usable reserves by the Federal Reserve System. With increased reserves, banks would be able to make more loans and investments, increase earnings, and thereby induce greater stock sales. With increased stock sales, the ratio of capital accounts to assets would rise. This would then provide a greater margin of protection for bank depositors.

THE NATIONAL ECONOMY
AND SOURCES OF FUNDS

The contribution of the commercial banking system to economic growth and stability depends in large part upon the uses to which the banks put their funds. To help promote growth, the banks need expanding sources of funds. Bank sources of funds have not grown proportionately with the rest of the economy, however. From 1945 to 1963, commercial bank liabilities and capital accounts increased 83 percent while gross national product rose almost 175 percent. Other financial institutions have increased their lending activity relative to the commercial banking system. Life insurance company assets increased by more than three times from 1945 to 1963 while savings and loan association assets increased by eleven times.[9]

The relative decline of commercial banks as direct contributors to the pecuniary assets of the economy is partly a consequence of the characteristic that sets them off from other financial institutions: their creation and administration of the principal part of our money supply, demand deposits.

The stock of money is closely related to the level of economic activity. When the money supply is allowed to increase rapidly, inflation generally follows. Depressions, on the other hand, are usually accompanied by a fall in the stock of money. In our economy, the monetary authorities attempt to prevent inflation and recession by manipulating interest rates and the money supply. In an attempt to manipulate the money supply, the Federal Reserve regulates the reserve position of the commercial banking system. In periods of high employment levels, the Federal Reserve System thus limits the ability of the commercial banking system to create demand deposits.

When these limitations are imposed upon the banking system, borrowers turn to other lending institutions. This worsens the competitive position of

---

[9] Computed from *Federal Reserve Bulletin*, June, 1964, pp. 736, 749, and 778; and Board of Governors of the Federal Reserve System, *Supplement to Banking and Monetary Statistics*, Section I (1962), p. 25.

the commercial banking system. When one borrows from a lender other than a commercial bank, money is not created. The other financial institutions lend funds directly, and these funds usually consist of demand deposits at commercial banks. The balance sheet changes that occur when other financial institutions lend are as follows:

BALANCE SHEET CHANGES FOR NONBANK LENDING INSTITUTIONS

ASSETS	LIABILITIES + CAPITAL ACCOUNTS
Demand deposits at commercial banks −$10,000	
Loans and investments +$10,000	

BALANCE SHEET CHANGES FOR THE COMMERCIAL BANKING SYSTEM

ASSETS	LIABILITIES + CAPITAL ACCOUNTS
	Demand deposits of the nonbank lending institutions −$10,000
	Demand deposits of the borrowers +$10,000

As a result, the dollar volume of loans and investments made by commercial banks decreases in relation to those of other institutions. For the economy as a whole there is an increase in economic activity. The total of the money stock is unchanged but there has been an increase in its turnover. The velocity with which the money stock changes hands in the economy has increased, in other words.

These lending institutions obtained the funds that they lent by successfully competing with commercial banks for the idle cash and deposits of individuals in the economy. For example, here is what happens to the balance sheet when a depositor in a commercial bank is induced to switch from deposits (either time or demand) in a commercial bank to a savings and loan share account:

BALANCE SHEET CHANGES FOR THE COMMERCIAL BANKING SYSTEM

ASSETS	LIABILITIES + CAPITAL ACCOUNTS
	Deposits of individual depositor −$1,000
	Deposits of savings and loan association +$1,000

BALANCE SHEET CHANGES FOR THE SAVINGS AND LOAN ASSOCIATION

ASSETS	LIABILITIES + CAPITAL ACCOUNTS
Deposits at the commercial banking system +$1,000	Savings and loan share accounts +$1,000

The savings and loan association is now in a position to make a loan, probably a mortgage loan.

When this situation prevails throughout the economy in a period of full employment and rising prices, there is an added incentive for the monetary authorities to impose tighter controls. The Federal Reserve System can be expected to restrict commercial bank lending activity in hopes of causing interest rate increases that will discourage borrowers. The effects of such restraint will fall directly upon the commercial banking system. The effects on other financial institutions will only be indirect—that is, to the extent that rising interest rates will also discourage borrowers from seeking funds at those institutions.

The fact that monetary policy works directly only upon commercial banks limits their ability to compete for funds. Ironically, the tighter the restraint applied by the Federal Reserve System on commercial banks, the less direct control the Federal Reserve has over the economy. Increased lending activity by nonbank financial institutions increases the demand for goods and services just as loans by the commercial banks would have done, but the Federal Reserve has no direct control over these institutions.

The 1950's and 1960's have been years of relatively high employment levels and rising prices. While there has been some concern about excess productive capacity and a slow rate of economic growth since the 1957–58 recession, these problems have not been so severe as to call for aggressive monetary expansion and government spending programs. As a result, the Federal Reserve System has often tended to restrain the growth of bank sources of funds and usable reserves. The only periods in which the Federal Reserve has actively sought to provide commercial banks with additional reserves (exclusive of seasonal needs) has usually been during recessions, although general monetary ease existed from 1961 to 1964. Such action is designed to stimulate the economy. Recessions, however, are periods in which the demand for loans falls off, when commercial banks purchase government securities because they cannot actively expand loans. The increased availability of loans cannot force anyone to borrow if he sees no profitable uses for such funds. The increase in reserves that occurs in these periods probably does not help the economy reach an upturn, but only provides the basis for the commercial banking system to help the economy expand, once expansion is already under way.

From this discussion, we see that the monetary policy of the Federal Reserve System may hamper the ability of banks to compete for loans and sources of funds. Probably it cannot be otherwise in light of our government's continued emphasis on monetary policy as the principal means of regulating the economy. To enhance the competitive position of the commercial banking system, monetary controls may well have to be extended to nonbank financial institutions, a measure which does not seem politically feasible at this time. More will be said of this in Chapter 21.

SUMMARY

In this chapter we have examined bank sources of funds. Commercial bank funds, in order of importance, are demand deposits, time deposits, and capital accounts. The increase in bank sources of funds has not kept pace with the growth of other financial institutions. Part of this is attributable to the exercise of controls over the economy by our monetary authorities in an era of relatively high output and employment.

Supplementary Readings

American Bankers Association. *The Commercial Banking Industry*. Englewood Cliffs, N.J., Prentice-Hall, 1962, Chapters 2 and 12.
Robinson, Roland I. *The Management of Bank Funds*. New York, McGraw-Hill, 1962, Chapter 23.

Chapter 6

Commercial Bank Uses of Funds

COMPOSITION AND NATURE
OF COMMERCIAL BANK USES OF FUNDS

The asset composition of a commercial bank's balance sheet indicates the many ways in which that bank is able to make use of available funds. It may hold funds idle, it may extend credit to business firms, consumers, farmers, financial institutions, and buyers of real estate, and it may invest in corporate and government securities. As recently expressed by one study, a "characteristic of commercial banks is the multifunctional nature of bank lending and investing. In contrast, savings banks and nonbank financial institutions are essentially specialized institutions, although a few lend to more than one category of borrower. Commercial banks, on the other hand, deal in a wide variety of debts and accommodate all types of borrowers."[1]

Table 6–1 shows the asset side of the combined balance sheets of all commercial banks in the United States. The banks described by this table are the same as those described by Table 5–2, which gave the liability and capital account data. Note that the total of assets in Table 6–1 equals the total of liabilities and capital accounts in Table 5–2.

CASH ASSETS

Cash assets consist of reserves with the Federal Reserve banks, vault cash (currency and coin), balances with domestic banks, and other cash assets. This last category refers to a very small amount of deposit balances held with foreign banks, and a large volume of cash items in process of collection.

Cash assets, as indicated in Chapter 5, have several functions. First, they are used to meet the legal reserve requirements imposed by the Federal Reserve System and by the various states. For member banks the require- ments of the Federal Reserve are satisfied by deposits at the Federal Re- serve banks and by vault cash. For nonmember banks the state requirements

---

[1] The American Bankers Association, *The Commercial Banking Industry*, (Englewood Cliffs, N.J.: Prentice-Hall, 1962), p. 1.

are usually satisfied by vault cash and by deposits with other domestic banks.

Second, cash assets provide banks with funds to meet the demands of depositors for cash. When used for this purpose, cash assets are in the form of vault cash. And third, cash assets, in the form of deposit balances with

TABLE 6–1. ALL COMMERCIAL BANK ASSETS, DECEMBER 20, 1963

ASSETS	MILLIONS OF DOLLARS	PERCENT OF TOTAL
Cash Assets		
Reserves with Federal Reserve banks	17,150	
Currency and coin	4,048	
Balances with domestic banks	12,312	
Other	17,201	
Total cash assets	50,711	16.2
Loans		
Commercial and industrial	52,947	
Agricultural	7,470	
For purchasing or carrying securities		
To brokers and dealers	5,353	
To others	2,509	
To financial institutions		
To banks	3,605	
To others	9,479	
Real estate	39,056	
Other to individuals	34,550	
Other	4,034	
Total loans	159,003	50.8
Investments		
U.S. government securities		
Bills	11,059	
Certificates	1,658	
Notes	22,415	
Bonds	28,065	
State and local government securities	29,786	
Other securities	5,173	
Total investments	98,156	31.4
Other assets	4,903	1.6
Total assets	312,773	100.0

Source: *Federal Reserve Bulletin*, June, 1964, pp. 736, 740, 741.

the Federal Reserve and other banks, are used to redeem checks drawn by bank customers and presented for collection by other banks.

Cash items in process of collection are simply the value of checks drawn on other banks and not as yet collected. These cash assets are not considered usable as a source of funds. Bankers realize that the items which they have for collection on other banks will probably be matched by the checks that other banks will present.

Finally, some banks use their cash assets to secure valuable services from larger city banks and from foreign banks. Smaller banks, for example, often leave substantial sums of money on deposit with large city banks in return for such services as security analysis, the handling of bond and security purchases, the clearing and collection of checks, and participation in loans that the small banks cannot handle alone. These deposits are termed inter-bank deposits and represent another function of cash assets.

BANK LOANS

Bank loans are the largest category of bank assets; more than 50 percent of all assets are in the form of loans. Table 6–1 shows the diversity of these loans.

Commercial and Industrial Loans

The greater part of commercial bank lending has traditionally taken the form of commercial and industrial loans. These loans are extended to manufacturing, mining, wholesale trade, retail trade, transportation, public utility, construction, and service concerns. In short, commercial and industrial loans are made to all types of business enterprises except competing financial institutions and farms, which are covered by other types of loans.

Commercial loans may be secured or unsecured and of any duration. The most important type of *unsecured loan* made by a commercial bank is the loan that is created when a firm draws on its *line of credit*. Since a loan made on the basis of a line of credit is unsecured, only firms with excellent credit ratings are granted a line. Under the terms of a line of credit, a business enterprise may borrow up to a predetermined limit (provided that it maintains a compensating balance—usually around 10 percent of the line of credit) and repays the loan annually. Assume, for example, that a firm has a $100,000 line of credit and a 10 percent compensating balance requirement. This means that to utilize the line of credit, the business must maintain an average deposit account of $10,000 with the lending bank. Having a line of credit, however, does not necessarily mean that the firm has borrowed from the bank. Only when the line of credit is used is a debt created and interest collected by the bank. Many firms scarcely ever use their line, since they maintain it simply for purposes of prestige or to have funds available in cases of extreme emergency.

Like many secured loans, *unsecured* commercial loans are primarily designed to provide businesses with funds to take care of possible discrepancies between receipts and expenditures. For example, a business may borrow to meet a monthly payroll, and repay the loan through the month as receipts come in. A retailer may borrow substantial amounts in the fall of the year to build up inventories prior to heavy Christmas sales. When businesses borrow for *seasonal* reasons, such as these, the maturity of the loan is usually short. Unsecured loans generally have a shorter life than secured loans, too. On the other hand, when the borrowing is designed to expand plant and equipment, the loan life is of greater duration.

Most commercial and industrial loans are secured loans. The collateral used to secure them may be plant and equipment, accounts receivable, or even the stock and bond holdings of the borrowing firm.[2]

As previously indicated, the maturity of both secured and unsecured loans varies considerably. Approximately two-thirds of all commercial and industrial loans mature within a year, however, and very few have a maturity of over five years.

Agricultural Credit

A second form of credit extended by commercial banks to borrowers is agricultural credit. Although agricultural loans comprise only 5 percent of all bank loans, they are, nevertheless, an important source of funds for the agricultural sector of the economy, and a major source of earnings for a large number of U.S. commercial banks. In 1958, there were 21,736 banking offices in the United States. Of these, 9,643 were located in primarily rural population centers of less than 5,000 people.[3]

Agricultural loans are made principally to provide the farmer with seasonal funds to take care of current expenses. Banks also provide farmers with funds to make investments in livestock and machinery, however, and these loans usually have a longer maturity than those designed to meet current expenses. Still other loans are made to repay debts and to finance real-estate purchases.

Real-Estate Credit

Real-estate credit is the second most important type of credit extended by commercial banks. Nearly 25 percent of all bank loans are mortgage loans, and almost all of these are for residential construction. Since the real-estate assets purchased by the borrowers have a long life, the maturity of mortgage loans will usually run from ten to twenty-five years.

Many commercial banks compete aggressively for mortgage loans. Because of their long maturities, mortgage loans provide a steady source of income. For this reason, banks like to have a large volume of mortgages in their portfolios. These loans have acquired great importance for banks in the postwar period. In 1963, for example, commercial banks had $39.0 bil-

---

[2] An account receivable is created when a firm delivers merchandise to the purchaser and does not receive payment until some future date.

[3] Federal Deposit Insurance Corporation, *Annual Report* (1960), p. 48.

lion in mortgages, as compared with $9.4 billion in mortgages in 1947.[4]
Part of the explanation for this increased interest in mortgages is attributable
to the federal government's insurance programs in residential housing. The
Federal Housing Administration and Veteran's Administration underwrite
many different types of mortgages for residential construction and for re-
modeling and rehabilitation loans. FHA and VA insurance remove almost
all of the risk on mortgage loans for lenders. Some $9.9 billion of commer-
cial bank residential mortgage loan holdings in 1963 were insured and guaranteed; $16.5 billion were uninsured conventional mortgage loans.[5]

Consumer Credit

Loans to consumers are another important use to which commercial
banks put their funds. Most of the $34.6 billion listed under "Other to in-
dividuals" on Table 6–1 consists of consumer loans. These loans are quite
varied. They may be made on an installment or a noninstallment basis. Some

TABLE 6–2. CONSUMER CREDIT, DECEMBER 30, 1963
(IN MILLIONS OF DOLLARS)

TYPE OF CREDIT	TOTAL CREDIT	CREDIT HELD BY COMMERCIAL BANKS
Installment		
Automobile paper	22,199	11,249
Other consumer goods paper	13,766	3,123
Repair and modernization loans	3,389	2,361
Personal loans	14,391	4,877
Total	53,745	21,610
Noninstallment		
Single-payment loans	5,959	5,047
Charge accounts	5,871	—
Service credit	4,315	—
Total	16,145	5,047
Total consumer credit	69,890	26,657

Source: *Federal Reserve Bulletin*, June, 1964, pp. 764–65.

are used to finance the purchase of automobiles. Others are used for personal loans, for repairs and modernization, or for the purchase of various
consumer durables. Banks make some consumer loans directly, but they also
purchase the installment paper created by the sellers of consumer goods.

Table 6–2 shows the amount of consumer credit outstanding in the
economy in 1963 and the relative importance of the commercial bank in

---

[4] *Federal Reserve Bulletin*, June, 1964, p. 740.
[5] *Ibid.*, p. 761.

furnishing this credit. Out of a total $69.9 billion in consumer credit in 1963, $26.7 billion was furnished by commercial banks. Collectively, they are the largest supplier of consumer credit in the economy. Sales finance companies, retail outlets, credit unions, and consumer finance companies follow in that order as additional suppliers of consumer credit.[6]

This strong position of commercial banks in consumer credit is a relatively recent phenomenon. For the most part it has developed since the 1930's. With the weak credit demands of traditional business borrowers during the depression, commercial banks increased the variety of their lending activities, particularly in the area of consumer credit. By 1939, commercial banks accounted for 24 percent of all consumer credit. This figure has continued to grow. Banks presently extend almost 40 percent of total consumer credit.[7]

Other Lending Activity

Banks lend to one another and to various financial intermediaries, too. For example, finance companies, which make personal loans to individuals, may borrow from commercial banks. There are many other ways in which commercial banks lend to competing financial institutions. The amount of loans to financial intermediaries in 1963 was $13.1 billion.

Banks also lend to brokers, dealers, and individual purchasers of securities. The total volume of such loans in 1963 came to $7.9 billion. When individuals wish to purchase stock but have insufficient funds to cover the full purchase price, they may borrow up to a certain percentage of the purchase price from the bank. The Federal Reserve determines how low this minimum percentage, or margin, may be.[8] Banks also lend directly to securities brokers who put up their customers' securities as collateral.

INVESTMENTS

Commercial bank holdings of investments consist primarily of U.S. government securities. In 1963, all commercial banks held $63.2 billion in U.S. government securities. These holdings represented approximately 20 percent of all bank assets. In addition, banks held $29.8 billion in state and local government securities and $5.2 billion in other securities.

U.S. Government Securities

Commercial banks purchase U.S. government securities for a variety of reasons. First, they are very safe; there is no risk that the U.S. government,

---

[6] *Ibid.*, pp. 764–65.
[7] *Ibid.*
[8] See Chapter 13 for a discussion of margin requirements.

like a private borrower, will default on its obligations. Second, they are highly liquid. There is a wide market for these securities; when banks need cash, they can quickly find purchasers for their security holdings. Third, banks are permitted to use U.S. government securities as collateral when borrowing reserves from the Federal Reserve banks. Finally, banks earn interest on their security holdings. *In short, commercial banks purchase and hold U.S. government securities because they are safe, highly liquid, interest-yielding assets.*

This is not to say, of course, that banks never lose money on U.S. government securities. For example, while there is no risk of default on the part of the U.S. government, the danger does exist that a commercial bank may lose on its U.S. government security holdings if they are sold prior to maturity. For the same reasons, a security sold prior to maturity may occasionally lead to a capital gain, and a bond purchased at less than par may yield a profit when redeemed. When a bank purchases a $1,000, 3 percent U.S. government security at time of issue for $1,000, for example, and interest rates on comparable U.S. government securities subsequently increase to 3.5 percent, the market price of the 3 percent security will decline. For a 3 percent, $1,000 security to be sold in the face of such competition, its price must be sufficiently low to give the purchaser the same return on his investment that he could get on the 3.5 percent securities which are now available to him. What will this be? The $1,000, 3 percent security yields $30, and $30 is 3.5 percent of $857. Hence, figuring backward, the old security probably cannot be sold for more than $857. Therefore, if a bank originally purchased the old security for $1,000 and decides to sell at this point, it will lose $143 on the transaction. On the other hand, if the security had been purchased when it was selling at less than par, the purchasing bank would have acquired a gain either by holding on to the security until maturity or by selling it when interest rates on comparable securities had eased and their prices had consequently risen.

Therefore, when government bonds held by commercial banks have a lower nominal interest yield than is currently available on comparable new government security issues, the older bonds can no longer be described as highly liquid. They can no longer be quickly converted into cash assets without substantial loss. They must now be held to maturity or until such time as their prices again increase. This situation leads to what economists call the *"lock-in effect."*[9] The hypothesis is that, rather than experience losses, commercial banks will hold on to their U.S. government securities and thus be "locked in" to their investments in these securities.[10] Furthermore, with commercial bank funds tied up in U.S. government securities,

---

[9] "The Influence of Monetary Policy on Lenders and Borrowers," *Federal Reserve Bulletin*, May, 1953; and "The Lock-in Effect: Bank Reactions to Security Losses," *Monthly Review* (Federal Reserve Bank of Kansas City, June, 1960).

[10] Actually, commercial banks are only occasionally locked in. See Table 6–4.

banks will be unable to expand bank loans. In a period of full employment and rising prices, this restraint on bank lending activities is thought to act as a deterrent to inflation.

If it is true that holding U.S. government securities tends to restrain commercial bank lending operations in periods of rising interest rates and strong demand for loans, why do banks bother to hold any U.S. government securities? For several of the reasons already given: they are safe investments and they may be used as collateral when borrowing reserves. Furthermore, almost a quarter of the U.S. government securities held by banks have a short maturity. Most government bills mature in 90 to 92 days, most certificates in less than a year, most notes in one to five years, and most bonds at the end of five years. With this high proportion of short-term U.S. government securities in their investment portfolios, many banks are able to overcome the lock-in effect in periods of inflation by gradually replacing some of their U.S. government securities as they come due with higher-yielding private investments and loans. Caution must be observed, however, since private securities and loans involve more risk and can be illiquid on the downward side of the business cycle. Banks must be careful not to sacrifice too much safety for higher yields.

State and Local Government Securities

Investment in state and local government securities represents the final major use to which commercial banks put their funds. Approximately 9 percent of all bank assets are in this form.

State and local government securities are tax exempt. This makes them a highly attractive investment for commercial banks and for individuals who are in a high-income tax bracket. The after-tax yield of these securities is generally higher than that of comparable non-tax-exempt securities. Thus, if a tax-exempt security yields 4 percent, the actual return to the security holder is substantially higher than that on a comparable but taxable investment. For example, if the bondholder is a bank and in the 52 percent corporation income tax bracket, the 4 percent tax-exempt security is equivalent to an $8\frac{1}{3}$ percent taxable security.[11] For this reason, tax-exempt securities tend to carry a lower nominal yield than private securities with a comparable face value. This difference in nominal yields tends to diminish the actual yields of tax-exempt securities.

Nevertheless, the actual yields of most tax-exempt securities are higher than the after-tax yields of taxable securities of a comparable face value,

---

[11] A $1,000, 4 percent tax-exempt security yields $40 per year. What rate of interest would a $1,000 security subject to tax have to yield for the bondholder to be left with $40 after taxes? Let X be the rate of interest. Then $(\$1,000)(X) - (.52)(\$1,000)(X) = \$40$; solving for X, we get $8\frac{1}{3}$ percent.

largely for competitive reasons. A large volume of municipal securities has been issued since World War II. Our expanding population calls for more local sewage, water, electric, and gas facilities. The rapidly growing school population needs additional classrooms. All of these needs are provided by local governments and financed, in part, by an increase in the supply of local issues. Local governments, in order to increase their ability to get needed funds, must offer higher yields. Thus, a favorable spread is maintained by state and local governments between the after-tax yields on taxable securities and the yields on tax-exempt securities.

Investment in state and local government securities by commercial banks does pose several problems, however. First, banks are subject to community pressures to purchase securities that may be somewhat risky. Second, the market for tax-exempt securities is limited. Banks and individuals in high-income tax brackets are the principal purchasers of tax-exempt securities. This limited market, in turn, means that the relative liquidity of these securities is reduced. Consequently, when banks purchase tax-exempt securities, they tend to hold them to maturity.

Other Securities

Finally, commercial banks also purchase privately issued securities in limited numbers. These consist primarily of corporate bonds. Government agencies closely regulate bank purchases of privately issued securities; banks are not permitted to buy stocks as investments.

BANK EARNINGS

Bank revenue comes almost exclusively from its earning assets, its loans and investments. Table 6–3 shows bank sources of income in 1963 and how this income was accounted for. Here we see that over 60 percent of all bank revenue in 1963 came from loans. Bank ownership of securities provided another 22 percent. In comparison, all other sources of income were relatively insignificant.

It may seem peculiar that bank loans earned almost three times as much as investments despite the fact that their dollar volume was only about 50 percent greater than that of investments. The differing characteristics of these assets are responsible for this striking difference in return. Loans are held primarily for return, whereas investments are held primarily for safety and liquidity. Since investments are less risky and more liquid than loans, their yield is lower. To put it another way, the higher interest returns on loans are a way of compensating commercial banks for the risks they assume.

How did commercial banks dispose of this income? A quarter went into wages, salaries, and fees. Dividend distributions and interest paid on time and savings deposits were 7 and 25 percent, respectively, of income. Taxes took another 9 percent of income.

When compared with other industries, banks have a relatively low (but steady) level of earnings. Higher rates of return can, of course, be obtained

TABLE 6–3. SOURCES AND DISPOSITION OF TOTAL INCOME, INSURED COMMERCIAL BANKS IN THE UNITED STATES, 1963

INCOME	AMOUNTS (IN THOUSANDS OF DOLLARS)	PERCENT OF TOTAL*
Total income	$13,978,163	
Sources		
Interest on U.S. government obligations	2,176,454	15.6
Interest and dividends on other securities	921,060	6.6
Interest and discount on loans	8,516,837	60.9
Service charges and fees on bank loans	155,478	1.1
Service charges on deposit accounts	728,857	5.2
Other service charges, commissions, fees and collection and exchange charges	248,362	1.8
Trust department	573,252	4.1
Other current operating earnings	189,413	1.4
Recoveries, transfers from reserve accounts, and profits	468,450	3.4
		100.1
Disposition		
Salaries—officers	1,183,264	8.5
Salaries and wages—employees	2,101,111	15.0
Officer and employee benefits	457,033	3.3
Fees paid to directors and members of executive, discount and other committees	67,469	0.5
Interest on time and savings deposits	3,464,308	24.8
Interest and discount on borrowed money	106,517	0.8
Occupancy expense of bank premises—net	608,462	4.4
Furniture and equipment	311,518	2.2
Other current operating expenses	1,415,298	10.1
Losses, charge-offs, and transfers to reserve accounts	883,637	6.3
Federal taxes on net income	1,130,629	8.1
State taxes on net income	96,154	0.7
Dividends and interest on capital	993,374	7.1
Net additions to capital from income	1,159,389	8.3
		100.1

Source: Federal Deposit Insurance Corporation, *Annual Report* (1963), pp. 152–53.
* Figures do not add up to 100.0 because of rounding.

by increased lending activity. Over half of bank revenue comes from loans already, however. A substantial increase in lending activity at the expense of investments would thus reduce the liquidity of the banking system and lower the ratio of capital accounts to risk assets. The solution, as we suggested in Chapter 5, would seem to be for the monetary authorities to provide banks with reserves sufficient to enable them to expand both loans and investments, and thereby increase earnings. The soundness of such an approach, of course, depends on the national economic situation.

BANK USES OF FUNDS
AND THE NATIONAL ECONOMY

In Chapter 5 we suggested that the monetary policy of the Federal Reserve System may hamper the ability of banks to compete for loans and sources of funds. During inflationary periods, for example, the actions of other financial institutions may cause the Federal Reserve to impose monetary restraints that only work directly on commercial banks.

This should not be taken to suggest that commercial banks always exert a stabilizing influence on economic fluctuations. On the contrary, as stated in Chapter 3, commercial banks, in the absence of regulation, tend to intensify whatever phase of the business cycle is current, through their unique ability to create and destroy money when making loans and investments. Put another way, the uses to which banks put their funds when lending and making investments may intensify the upward and downward swings of business fluctuations, necessitating action by the monetary authorities.

The Behavior of Bank Loans and Investments and Gross National Product

Table 6–4 compares the growth of the loans, investments, and "other demand deposits" of all commercial banks with the growth of gross national product from 1951 to 1964. Here we can see that there is a close relationship between bank loan and investment activity and the condition of the economy. The growth of bank loans slackened in the recession years, 1954, 1958, and 1961. Gross national product remained steady in 1954 and 1958, and increased by 3 percent in the very mild recession of 1961. Bank investments, on the other hand, rose substantially in each of these years. Conversely, during economic recovery and prosperity, bank loans increased rapidly, while investments declined or remained steady (1962, as we shall discuss in a moment, was an exception; in that year both loans and investments increased sharply).

For the most part our policy during this period was one of ease in the recession years and gradually increasing restraint through recovery and prosperity, on the theory that in recession we need an expansion of loans, and in prosperity some restraint.

Yet this did not come about. Bankers argue that loan volume does not grow during recessions because demand is slack. As a result, banks place their funds into safe investments, primarily U.S. government securities.

With prosperity, however, demand for loans increases sharply. Banks are eager to expand their loan volume to increase their earnings, but restriction of bank reserve positions by the Federal Reserve may prevent this. Consequently, banks cut back on their investments in low-interest-yielding government securities so as to make more profitable use of their funds in loans. Thus, we find that in all years of relative prosperity, bank investments remained comparatively steady or declined—except in 1962, the exception that proves the rule. Although the economy was in some respects prosperous

TABLE 6–4. LOANS, INVESTMENTS, NONINTERBANK AND U.S. GOVERNMENT DEMAND DEPOSITS FOR ALL COMMERCIAL BANKS AT MIDYEAR, 1951–1964; GROSS NATIONAL PRODUCT, 1951–1964

(IN BILLIONS OF DOLLARS)

YEAR	LOANS	TOTAL INVESTMENTS	U.S. GOVERNMENT SECURITIES	OTHER DEMAND DEPOSITS*	GROSS NATIONAL PRODUCT
1951	54.8	71.2	58.5	96.3	329.0
1952	59.2	75.2	61.2	103.4	347.0
1953	65.0	73.0	58.6	105.7	365.4
1954	67.3	79.1	63.5	107.0	363.1
1955	75.2	80.1	63.3	113.0	397.5
1956	86.9	73.1	56.6	115.8	419.2
1957	93.3	72.3	55.5	115.7	442.8
1958	93.6	84.0	64.2	117.1	444.5
1959	104.5	81.4	60.9	121.6	482.7
1960	114.8	74.1	54.2	119.5	502.6
1961	118.0	83.8	61.8	125.2	518.2
1962	129.2	91.5	64.4	128.8	554.9
1963	145.0	97.0	63.5	133.6	585.1
1964	160.9†	94.9†	59.1†	133.0†	624.0‡

Source: *Federal Reserve Bulletin*, June, 1964, p. 736; June, 1963, p. 808; December, 1962, p. 1650; Board of Governors of the Federal Reserve System, *Supplement to Banking and Monetary Statistics*, Section 1 (1962), pp. 26–28. See Table 21–1 for gross national product sources.

* Other demand deposits exclude interbank and U.S. government demand deposits.

† Preliminary data for May 27, 1964.

‡ Estimated by the author.

that year the Federal Reserve System retained an expansive monetary policy because of continued high unemployment levels. This permitted banks to expand both loans and investments. In addition, almost all of the growth in investments in that year came in state and local government securities, which have high interest yields. Banks showed a strong demand for tax-exempts because they needed high-interest long-term investments to provide funds for the rising interest rates on increasing volumes of time deposits.

For the period 1951–64 as a whole, bank uses of funds were expansive. Loans increased from $54.8 to $160.9 billion, a 194 percent increase. Investments, however, rose only from $71.2 to $94.9 billion, a 33 percent rise.

Thus, bank loans, which tend to stimulate demand in the economy more than bank investments, increased almost 6 times as such as bank investments. During this period demand deposits increased only 38 percent, yet gross national product rose 90 percent. This means that bank loan and investment activity, coupled with federal monetary restraint, has resulted more in increased use than in an increased volume of demand deposits. The monetary restraints used by the federal authorities have forced banks to economize on their creation of demand deposits. This is what the Federal Reserve wants to accomplish. But such Federal Reserve action could be self-defeating, since the velocity of money increases. The section below discusses this more fully.

The Commercial Banking System's Role in Economic Fluctuations

The manner in which commercial banks build up loans and decrease investments in prosperity, and hold down loan growth and increase investments in recessions, suggests the following conclusions concerning the role of the commercial banking system during economic fluctuations.

First, it shows that banking activities as a whole were not always effectively circumscribed by the "lock-in effect." Banks may readily decrease investments in prosperity by failing to reinvest as bonds mature or by selling off some of their holdings—and they were apparently not afraid to do so, even when some capital losses were incurred by these sales.

Second, commercial-bank loan creation in periods of recovery helps to increase demand deposits and stimulates demand, output, and employment in the economy. The data show that demand deposits have grown slowly in the last decade and a half and that most of the growth came in the year or two following each recession. These were periods of monetary ease when commercial banks had adequate reserves.

Third, when banks put their funds in investments rather than in loans during recessions, it slows down the pace of potential recovery. This is also partially responsible for the fact that demand deposits remain virtually unchanged in recessions. The money balances held by borrowers are active and stimulate the economy, but the money balances used in the purchase and sale of securities are relatively inactive.

Finally, commercial bank activity may also have an adverse effect on the economy during periods of high employment, rapidly growing gross national product, and rising prices. In these periods, banks are able to avoid monetary restrictions by reducing their investments and increasing loans. This transfers money balances from security purchasers (relatively inactive) to borrowers (active spenders). Thus, even with no change in the money supply, bank loan and investment policy may increase the velocity of money, adding to the demand for goods and increasing inflationary pressures.

A balance sheet transaction may be used to illustrate this last situation:

BALANCE SHEET CHANGES FOR THE COMMERCIAL BANKING SYSTEM

ASSETS		LIABILITIES + CAPITAL ACCOUNTS	
Investments	−$1,000,000 (a)	Demand deposits of security purchasers	−$1,000,000 (a)
Loans	+$1,000,000 (b)	Demand deposits of borrowers	+$1,000,000 (b)
		Demand deposits of sellers of goods to borrowers	+$1,000,000 (c)
		Demand deposits of borrowers	−$1,000,000 (c)

Transaction a records a sale of securities by the commercial banks. Those who purchase the securities from the banks do so by drawing down their checking accounts. This reduces the demand deposit liabilities of the commercial banking system and frees reserves that the banks can use to back loans in the amount of $1 million. The new deposits created by these loans are recorded in transaction b, where bank loans and the demand deposit accounts of borrowers are increased by $1 million. Subsequently, the borrowers purchase goods and services, and the $1 million in demand deposits are transferred to the sellers of goods and services. This is recorded in transaction c.

Thus, despite Federal Reserve monetary controls, commercial banks tend to lend less during deflations and more during inflations, thus intensifying the cyclical swings of the economy rather than dampening them.

SUMMARY

This chapter has described the uses to which banks put their funds. Cash assets are held for reserve purposes, investments for safety and return, and loans for their return. Commercial banks, through their lending activities, can serve as a stabilizing force in the economy, but more often they intensify recessions or inflations.

The following chapter demonstrates how commercial banks create and destroy money. The potential economic impact of their money-creating power, of great significance for the role of banks in the business cycle, will also be considered.

Supplementary Readings

American Bankers Association. *The Commercial Banking Industry*. Englewood Cliffs, N.J., Prentice-Hall, 1962, Chapters 4–8, 10.

Beckhardt, Benjamin, ed. *Business Loans of American Commercial Banks*. New York, Ronald Press, 1959.

Chapter 7

Commercial Banks
and the Creation of Money

Preceding chapters have repeatedly emphasized the importance of the commercial banking system in the creation and destruction of the principal component of our nation's money supply, demand deposits. It has been explained that individual commercial banks create deposits when they accept new deposits, grant loans, or make investments. This chapter will demonstrate how this is done. Deposit creation will then be studied from the larger perspective of the entire banking system.

THE CREATION AND DESTRUCTION
OF DEPOSITS BY INDIVIDUAL BANKS

Commercial Bank Creation of Deposits

Primary deposits. A commercial bank creates deposits when it accepts *deposits of cash.* Assume that Individual 1 deposits $1,000 in currency with Bank A. This results in a $1,000 increase in Bank A's reserves (since vault cash is part of a bank's reserves) and a $1,000 increase in its deposit liabilities:

BALANCE SHEET CHANGES FOR COMMERCIAL BANK A

ASSETS		LIABILITIES + CAPITAL ACCOUNTS	
Reserves	+$1,000	Deposits of Individual 1	+$1,000

The deposits thus created are called *primary deposits* because they result from the deposit of cash.

Primary deposits may also result from the *deposit of checks drawn on other banks.* These checks will also increase the reserves of the receiving bank. Suppose that Individual 1 wishes to deposit a $1,000 bonus check from his employer. If the individual makes the deposit with Bank A, and if the employer writes the check out on the company account at Bank B, the appropriate balance sheet changes, after the check has cleared,[1] are as follows:

BALANCE SHEET CHANGES FOR COMMERCIAL BANK A

ASSETS		LIABILITIES + CAPITAL ACCOUNTS	
Reserves	+$1,000	Deposits of Individual 1	+$1,000

BALANCE SHEET CHANGES FOR COMMERCIAL BANK B

ASSETS		LIABILITIES + CAPITAL ACCOUNTS	
Reserves	−$1,000	Demand deposits of employer	−$1,000

Notice that no distinction is made between the time and demand deposits of Individual 1 since he may choose to increase either account.

What are the overall effects of the creation of these primary deposits upon the total money supply? If Individual 1 chooses to keep his funds in the form of demand deposits, the money supply is not affected. A cash deposit decreases the currency holdings of the nonbank public but it increases the funds in demand deposit. Thus there is no change in the total money supply. Similarly, when deposits are transferred from one part of the nonbank public (i.e., the employer) to another part (Individual 1), there is no effect on the total money supply. On the other hand, if Individual 1 puts his cash in a time deposit there is a *decrease* in total money supply. Before time deposits become active money, before they may be used in the purchase of goods and services, they must be converted into either currency or demand deposits. Thus they are not considered part of the total money supply. The *total liquid wealth* holdings of the nonbank public undergo no change, however, because both time and demand deposits are part of liquid wealth.

Derivative deposits. When commercial banks make *loans and investments*, deposits are also created. Assume that Individual 1 borrows $1,000 from Bank A. He will probably receive the proceeds of the loan in the form of a demand deposit increase.[2] Thus, bank loans and bank demand deposits increase by $1,000:

BALANCE SHEET CHANGES FOR COMMERCIAL BANK A

ASSETS		LIABILITIES + CAPITAL ACCOUNTS	
Loans	+$1,000	Demand deposits of Individual 1	+$1,000

[1] Check clearing is discussed in Chapter 10.
[2] Of course, the borrower always has the option of increasing his time deposits. If he does, bank total deposit liabilities increase but there is no increase in the money stock. Total liquid wealth increases because of the increase in time deposits. This sequence of events, however, is unlikely to occur, because most borrowing is done for purposes of spending or repayment of debt.

These newly created deposits are called *derivative deposits*. They increase the money stock and liquid wealth holdings of the economy and they contribute to economic expansion by increasing spending power. They do *not* increase the reserves of the lending bank, however.

Investment expansion also causes an increase in the money supply. Suppose that Bank A decides to increase its holdings of securities by $10,000 and pays for them by writing a cashier's check on itself. The seller of the securities will deposit the check in his checking account at Bank B. This will increase Bank B's reserves and decrease Bank A's reserves as follows:

BALANCE SHEET CHANGES FOR COMMERCIAL BANK A

ASSETS		LIABILITIES + CAPITAL ACCOUNTS
Reserves	−$10,000	
Securities	+$10,000	

BALANCE SHEET CHANGES FOR COMMERCIAL BANK B

ASSETS		LIABILITIES + CAPITAL ACCOUNTS
Reserves	+$10,000	Demand deposits of securities seller +$10,000

For the banking system as a whole, demand deposit liabilities have increased, security holdings have increased, but reserves remain unchanged. Thus, although the money holdings of the nonbank public have increased, there has been no change in total liquid wealth as a result of the sale of securities to Bank A.

Are the deposits created in the second transaction primary or derivative deposits? From the point of view of Bank B, the new deposits are primary because they increased reserves in an amount equal to the deposit liability increase. From the view of the whole banking system, however, they are derivative deposits because there has been no increase of the total volume of bank reserves.

Commercial Bank Destruction of Deposits

When cash is withdrawn, when loans are repaid, when bank investments are sold, and when reserves decline, commercial bank deposits are destroyed.

Assume that Individual 1 needs additional cash for vacation expenses and draws $1,000 from his checking account:

BALANCE SHEET CHANGES FOR COMMERCIAL BANK A

ASSETS		LIABILITIES + CAPITAL ACCOUNTS
Reserves	−$1,000	Demand deposits of Individual 1 −$1,000

As the balance sheet changes show, the bank loses reserves and deposit liabilities. The nonbank public experiences no change in either money supply or liquid wealth because it has merely exchanged one form of money, demand deposits, for another, currency. This bank and the banking system as a whole have lost reserves, however. Hence, as we shall discuss in a moment, commercial bank lending activity will be restricted.

A bank also loses reserves and deposits when its depositors make checks payable to those maintaining accounts with other banks. This was the situation confronting Bank B in the illustration on page 77 when the employer paid Individual 1. A primary deposit was made at Bank A and, as a consequence, Bank B's deposit liability and the reserves behind that deposit were destroyed.

Loan repayments also cause deposit destruction. Assume that Individual 1 repays a $1,000 loan with Bank A. He repays by drawing down his checking account. The "T" account entries are as follows:

BALANCE SHEET CHANGES FOR COMMERCIAL BANK A

ASSETS		LIABILITIES + CAPITAL ACCOUNTS	
Loans	−$1,000	Demand deposits of Individual 1	−$1,000

If the loan repayment is made with checks drawn on other banks, $1,000 in demand deposits are destroyed for the entire banking system. Bank A does not experience this loss directly, however.

BALANCE SHEET CHANGES FOR COMMERCIAL BANK A

ASSETS		LIABILITIES + CAPITAL ACCOUNTS
Reserves	+$1,000	
Loans	−$1,000	

BALANCE SHEET CHANGES FOR THE REST OF THE COMMERCIAL BANKING SYSTEM

ASSETS		LIABILITIES + CAPITAL ACCOUNTS	
Reserves	−$1,000	Demand deposits	−$1,000

Finally, deposits are destroyed when banks reduce their investments. Suppose, for example, that Bank A sells $10,000 in U.S. government securities. If the purchasers are members of the nonbank public, payment is usually made with checks drawn on commercial banks. Assume that Bank A sells the securities and depositors of Bank B are the ultimate purchasers. The balance sheet changes that record this transaction are as follows:

BALANCE SHEET CHANGES FOR COMMERCIAL BANK A

ASSETS		LIABILITIES + CAPITAL ACCOUNTS
Reserves	+$10,000	
U.S. government securities	−$10,000	

BALANCE SHEET CHANGES FOR COMMERCIAL BANK B

ASSETS		LIABILITIES + CAPITAL ACCOUNTS	
Reserves	−$10,000	Demand deposits	−$10,000

Here the money supply of the nonbank public has decreased, while total liquid wealth and the reserves of the banking system remain unchanged.

LIMITATIONS TO INDIVIDUAL BANK DEPOSIT CREATING AND DESTROYING ABILITIES

Deposit Creation and the Reserve Requirement

The ability of an individual commercial bank to create deposits is not unlimited. The reserve requirement and the volume of each bank's reserves restrict its power to create deposits.

The reserve requirement is the legally required ratio of those cash assets defined by law as reserves to deposit liabilities. Reserves are divided into two categories: required and excess. *Required reserves* are those which a bank must have to meet its reserve requirement. *Excess reserves* are the amount of reserves that a bank has in excess of its required amount. When required reserves exceed actual reserves, the bank has a *deficiency (or shortage) of reserves.*

Assume, for example, that a bank has $1 million in reserves, a 20 percent reserve requirement, and $4 million in deposit liabilities. The bank's required reserves are $800,000. Since its actual reserves are $1 million, the bank has $200,000 in excess reserves. On the basis of this volume of excess reserves, it may expand loans and investments by $200,000 and create up to $200,000 in demand deposits. Of course, the bank could expand beyond this amount, but it would consider this a very risky policy. On the basis of past experience, the bank expects to lose reserves in an amount equal to its loan and investment expansion, unless it has a favorable clearing balance—as we shall discuss in a moment.

What would happen if some of the givens in this illustration changed? If the volume of reserves increases by $50,000 because of loan repayments, the lending and money-creating ability of our bank increases by $50,000. Similarly, if the legal reserve requirement drops to 15 percent, then the excess reserves of our bank increase from $200,000 to $400,000. In general terms, the lower the reserve requirement, the greater the amount of excess reserves, and hence the greater the lending and money-creating ability of the bank. Also, the greater the volume of reserves available to meet a fixed reserve requirement, the greater the volume of excess reserves, and hence the greater the lending and money-creating abilities of the bank.

Deposit Destruction and the Reserve Requirement

If the bank becomes deficient in reserves, it will stop expanding its loans and investments. It may even cut back on its loans and investments. For example, if the bank discussed in the preceding section had had $600,000 instead of $1 million in reserves, it would have had a $200,000 shortage of reserves. In such a situation the bank might refuse to renew $100,000 in loans and it might sell $100,000 in investments. If those who repay the loans and purchase the investments do so with checks drawn on other commercial banks, then our bank will no longer be deficient in reserves. Other banks will have lost reserves:

BALANCE SHEET CHANGES FOR COMMERCIAL BANK A

ASSETS		LIABILITIES + CAPITAL ACCOUNTS
Reserves	+$200,000	
Loans	−$100,000	
Investments	−$100,000	

These methods of meeting reserve requirements have several shortcomings. First, it is not good business practice to refuse to renew loans for customers. The refusal to renew may hurt future lending opportunities. In a subsequent period, when the bank has adequate excess reserves, borrowers may decide to go elsewhere for a loan. Second, too great a reduction of investments may jeopardize the safety and liquidity of the bank. Third, a reduction of loans lowers bank earnings. Finally, if those who repay loans do so with checks drawn on the deficient bank itself, a contraction in an amount greater than the deficiency of reserves will be necessary:

BALANCE SHEET CHANGES FOR COMMERCIAL BANK A

ASSETS		LIABILITIES + CAPITAL ACCOUNTS	
Loans	−$200,000	Demand deposits	−$200,000
Addenda: Original deficiency of reserves		$200,000	
New deficiency of reserves		$160,000	

When depositors repay $200,000 in loans, a corresponding amount of demand deposits are destroyed. With $200,000 less in deposit liabilities, the required reserves of the bank are reduced by 20 percent of $200,000, or $40,000. Thus, there is still a shortage of reserves amounting to $160,000. To make up a $200,000 deficiency in required reserves in this fashion, the bank would have to reduce its loans by $1 million:

BALANCE SHEET CHANGES FOR COMMERCIAL BANK A

ASSETS		LIABILITIES + CAPITAL ACCOUNTS	
Loans	−$1,000,000	Demand deposits	−$1,000,000
Addenda: Original deficiency of reserves		$200,000	
Reduction in required reserves		$200,000	
New deficiency of reserves		0	

Thus, to improve Bank A's reserve position by not making new loans once the old loans have been repaid, the total dollar volume of loans must be reduced by an amount five times as large as the initial deficiency in reserves. Required reserves are only reduced by $1 for every $5 dollar decrease in deposit liabilities when the reserve requirement is 20 percent. The reason for this effect is quite simple: Since *$200,000 in reserves* represents 20 percent, or one-fifth, of a given amount of demand deposits, it will take *$200,000 in demand deposits*, multiplied by the reverse or reciprocal of one-fifth (five), to restore an equivalent amount in lost reserves.

How Banks with a Shortage of Reserves Get Additional Reserves

For these reasons banks try not to rely solely on a contraction of loans and investments as a means of eliminating a deficiency in reserves. Instead, they use a variety of techniques. They may reduce investments slightly to bring in some reserves from other banks. They may also reduce loans through granting fewer new loans than are currently running off. This will bring in some reserves and lower deposit liabilities, since some loans will be repaid with checks drawn on other banks.

There are other ways to make up a deficiency in reserves. The bank may *borrow* reserves from other banks, if it appears that the shortage of reserves is to be temporary. Banks with a surplus of excess reserves are willing to lend them to other banks in what is termed the *federal funds market*. "The federal funds market refers to the borrowing and lending of a special kind of money—deposit balances in the Federal Reserve banks—at a specified rate of interest."[3] These reserves, maintained at Federal Reserve banks in the form of deposit balances, are usually loaned to deficient banks on an overnight basis. Banks may also borrow reserves from their district Federal Reserve banks, which almost always meet legitimate requests for borrowings.

When banks borrow reserves from other banks or from their district Federal Reserve bank, the balance sheet entries are as follows:

BALANCE SHEET CHANGES FOR COMMERCIAL BANK A

ASSETS		LIABILITIES + CAPITAL ACCOUNTS	
Reserves	+$200,000	Borrowings	+$200,000

[3] Board of Governors of the Federal Reserve System, *The Federal Funds Market—A Study by a Federal Reserve System Committee* (Washington: 1959), p. 1.

Thus Bank A's $200,000 deficiency in reserves is removed without reducing its earning assets. The borrowed funds will have to be repaid with interest, of course, but it is hoped by the bank that future operations will provide the means of repayment. Borrowing reserves permits banks with temporary reserve deficiencies to provide credit continuity to customers.

Other Factors Affecting Commercial Bank Money-creating Abilities

There are many other factors that affect the ability of a commercial bank to create and destroy demand deposit money. Some of the more important of these are (1) the demands of the nonbank public for currency, (2) the relative preferences of the nonbank public for time and demand deposits, (3) the clearing balances of the commercial bank, (4) the unpredictability of business conditions, (5) the willingness of the bank to lend and the borrower to borrow, and (6) government economic policy.

The demand for currency. The reserve position of a commercial bank, and, for that matter, of the whole banking system, depends in part upon the willingness of the nonbank public to maintain its present distribution of currency and demand deposits. When people decide that they need more currency, they draw down their deposit balances. This reduces commercial bank reserves and deposits by an equal amount. The effect of a $1,000 cash withdrawal upon a bank that has extended as many loans as its reserves will permit and is faced with a 20 percent reserve requirement is shown by the following "T" account entry:

BALANCE SHEET CHANGES FOR COMMERCIAL BANK A

ASSETS		LIABILITIES + CAPITAL ACCOUNTS	
Reserves	−$1,000	Demand deposits	−$1,000
Addenda: Changes in reserves		−$1,000	
Change in required reserves		−$ 200	
Change in excess		−$ 800	

Since only 20 percent of $1,000, or $200, was required to back the $1,000 in demand deposit liabilities, required reserves decreased by only $200. The remaining $800 was used as excess reserves. To make up the resulting deficiency in reserves, the bank must either contract loans, investments, and deposits, or borrow additional reserves. This type of currency drain usually occurs seasonally. More currency is needed during vacation periods, for example, when people travel, and during the Christmas season, when people make more cash purchases than usual. Fortunately, the Federal Reserve System generally provides banks with the needed reserves in such periods.

During other periods, such as those following the holiday seasons, there are sizable influxes of currency into the banking system, and reserves, excess reserves, and deposits all increase. This would seem to be an ideal time for the commercial bank to expand its loans. Unfortunately, the demand for loans typically falls off during the same periods. In addition, the Federal Reserve System usually takes measures to mop up the excess reserves.

The demand for time deposits. Up to this point we have assumed similar reserve requirements for both time and demand deposits, in order to keep the numerical illustrations comparatively simple. Actually, reserve requirements vary a great deal, depending on the location of the bank and the type of deposit. In 1964, for example, the reserve requirements for member banks were 4 percent for time deposits, 12 percent for demand deposits at country banks, and 16½ percent for demand deposits at reserve city banks.

This difference in reserve requirements means that commercial bank reserve positions are weakened by a switch from time to demand deposits. Suppose that reserve requirements are 4 percent for time deposits and 15 percent for demand deposits and that Bank A is initially loaned up. Then a change occurs. Depositors decide to increase their demand deposits by $100,000 and decrease their time deposits by an equal amount:

BALANCE SHEET CHANGES FOR COMMERCIAL BANK A

ASSETS	LIABILITIES + CAPITAL ACCOUNTS	
	Demand deposits	+$100,000
	Time deposits	−$100,000
Addenda: Changes in existing amount of reserves	0	
Change in required reserves	+$11,000	

Bank A is now deficient in reserves by $11,000. The reduction in time deposits releases $4,000 in required reserves, but the demand deposit increase calls for an increase of $15,000 in reserves. The net effect is that Bank A needs $11,000 more in reserves.

On the other hand, when a bank's customers decide to shift funds from demand deposits to time deposits, the reserve position of the bank is improved. The amount of reserves released by the reduction in demand deposits is greater than the amount of reserves required to back the new time deposits. Thus, the bank receives additional excess reserves.

Favorable and adverse clearing balances. A bank continually receives checks drawn on other banks. Conversely, it is also continually redeeming checks drawn on it by its depositors and presented for collection by other banks. If the total value of the checks to be collected from a bank is less than the value of the checks that it presents to other banks for collection, then that bank is said to have a *favorable clearing balance.* If the reverse is true, then the bank has an *adverse clearing balance.*

A bank that continues to experience a favorable clearing balance over a period of time is in a position to expand loans and deposits beyond its excess reserves. On the other hand, if it regularly has an adverse clearing balance, it must limit its expansion of loans and deposits to an amount less than the volume of excess reserves.

Assume, for example, that Bank A has $10,000 in excess reserves, a 20 percent reserve requirement, and a consistently favorable clearing balance equal in value to 2 percent of its newly created demand deposits. What additional volume of loans and deposits can the bank create? Without a favorable or adverse clearing balance it could create $10,000 in loans and deposits, the amount of its excess reserves. With the favorable balance, a $10,000 deposit creation would lead to a $200 deposit return to the bank. Thus the bank can create more than $10,000 in deposits. It can create 1/.984 times the volume of excess reserves.[4]

The following "T" account entries show the effects of Bank A's expanding by 1/.984 times its excess reserves.

When the new loan is made,

BALANCE SHEET CHANGES FOR COMMERCIAL BANK A

ASSETS		LIABILITIES + CAPITAL ACCOUNTS	
Loans	+$10,163	Demand deposits	+$10,163

When all of its checks have been cleared,

BALANCE SHEET CHANGES FOR COMMERCIAL BANK A

ASSETS		LIABILITIES + CAPITAL ACCOUNTS	
Reserves	−$9,960	Demand deposits	−$9,960

Addenda: Net increase in demand deposits after all transactions	$ 203
Net increase in required reserves	$ 40
Net decrease in total reserves	$ 9,960
Former volume of excess reserves	$10,000
New volume of excess reserves	0

The checks presented by other banks for collection are 2 percent less than the volume of newly created deposits. Hence, total deposit liabilities

---

[4] The figure 1/.984 is based upon the following formula:

$$p = \frac{1}{1 - q + (r)(q)}$$

where r is the reserve requirement, q is the percentage of new deposits which return to the bank, and p is that multiple of its excess reserves by which the bank may expand its loans and deposits. As study of the formula shows, q acts as an expansive force on deposit creation, while r acts as a contractive force. As deposits return to the bank, the reserve requirement calls for an increase in excess reserves.

This same formula is used when a bank has an adverse clearing balance. In this case p and r have the same meaning, but q now refers to the percentage by which checks drawn on the bank exceed the volume of newly created deposits. Under these circumstances, q takes a negative value and tends to hold down deposit creation, while r, the reserve requirement, helps maintain it.

are $203 greater than they were at the start of these transactions and required reserves have increased by $40. The bank lost $9,960 in reserves. Without the favorable clearing balance the bank would have lost $10,000 in reserves.[5] Thus, a favorable clearing balance of 2 percent enabled the bank to expand loans and deposits beyond its excess reserves.

Other banks are not so fortunate, however. If one bank has a favorable balance, some other bank must be in an adverse position. Thus, for the entire banking system there can be neither a favorable nor an adverse clearing position. To the individual bank, however, an adverse clearing balance means that it cannot create loans and deposits to the full extent of its excess reserves.

Assume that Bank B has excess reserves of $10,000, a reserve requirement of 20 percent, and a consistently adverse clearing balance equal to 2 percent of its newly created deposits. This bank would experience difficulty if it expanded to the extent of its excess reserves. If it expanded loans and deposits by $10,000, for example, it would lose $10,200 in reserves. Therefore Bank B should expand demand deposits by only 1/1.016 times its excess reserves (see footnote 4):

When the new loan is made,

BALANCE SHEET CHANGES FOR COMMERCIAL BANK B

ASSETS		LIABILITIES + CAPITAL ACCOUNTS	
Loans	+$9,843	Demand deposits	+$9,843

When all of its checks have been cleared,

BALANCE SHEET CHANGES FOR COMMERCIAL BANK B

ASSETS		LIABILITIES + CAPITAL ACCOUNTS	
Reserves	−$10,040	Demand deposits	−$10,040

Addenda: Net decrease in demand deposits after all transactions $ 197
           Net decrease in required reserves $ 39
           Net decrease in total reserves $10,040
           Former volume of excess reserves $10,000
           New volume of excess reserves   0

Various factors affect the clearing position of a bank. For instance, a bank located in an area of economic growth may expect to gain reserves at the expense of banks in areas of declining economic activity. This shifting of reserves to a growing area is considered necessary by the gaining bank, of course. Growing areas generally experience a shortage of funds, since the demand for loans is strong relative to the supply.

A bank with increasing loans and reserves is not necessarily one with a

---

[5] All figures have been rounded to even dollars.

favorable clearing balance, however. The very extensiveness of the bank's lending activity may produce an adverse clearing balance: if a bank is rapidly expanding credit, it may usually expect sharp drains on its reserves. On the other hand, banks that make few loans may find their reserves rising. Thus the movement of reserves to a district with a growing economy may simply offset expected losses attributable to the increased volume of bank lending activity.

The willingness to borrow and lend. Changes in the reserve requirement, in the demand for currency, in the demand for time deposits, and in clearing balances, all tend to affect a commercial bank's reserve position, and thus its money-creating ability. In addition, the extent to which a bank creates new deposits through loans also depends upon its own willingness to lend and upon the demand of borrowers.

For example, banks are more willing to lend when there is prosperity in the community and the economy. In recession, they generally follow a more cautious lending policy, expanding investments instead.

Although most banks tend to vary the size of their loan and investment portfolios according to changes in the business cycle, there are, of course, many individual differences between banks. Some have a fundamentally conservative lending policy and keep a relatively large proportion of their assets in safe investments. Other banks follow a more liberal lending policy.

The attitude of borrowers is also important. When businesses expect a decline in sales volume, for example, they borrow less and repay loans. If economic conditions are expected to improve, however, businesses want to be prepared for the anticipated increase in demand and therefore increase their borrowings from banks, in order to build up their inventories.

Bank creation of money, therefore, depends upon more than the reserve position. It depends also upon the willingness of the bank to lend and the borrower to borrow at any given time.

The unpredictability of business conditions. While a bank may expect transfers from time to demand deposits, cash drains, and adverse clearing balances to confront it regularly, it cannot always predict the size and timing of these occurrences. Random disturbances, such as unanticipated cash drains, occur frequently. Since these disturbances cannot always be precisely anticipated, a bank must set aside a certain proportion of its excess reserves against these contingencies.

Small banks lack the skilled personnel and the specialized knowledge of the money markets that large banks have. As a result, small banks are not as well able to economize on reserves; they must often maintain substantial amounts of excess reserves as precautionary balances. The large banks must maintain precautionary balances, too, but in smaller volumes relative to their deposit liabilities. Although regularly maintained precautionary balances of excess reserves help to cover the unexpected demands for cash and reserve losses, they also cut down the lending ability of the bank because they do not permit it to expand to the full extent of its excess reserves.

Government economic policy. In many ways, government economic policy is the single most important determinant of commercial bank money-creating powers. When the federal government feels that the economy needs expansion, it attempts to stimulate the economy through various agencies. The Federal Reserve System, for example, may lower the reserve requirement for member banks. This action will directly increase the lending ability of each member bank. The improved reserve position, of course, does not guarantee that the banks will actually increase their lending activity, but it is a step in the right direction.

The Federal Reserve System may also aggressively expand its holdings of U.S. government securities. When this happens, commercial bank reserves increase because the sellers of the securities receive checks drawn on the Federal Reserve banks and deposit them in checking accounts at commercial banks.[6] Although this action is expansive, it is not directly felt by every bank. Only those banks whose depositors are the sellers of the securities are initially affected. Other banks participate indirectly, depending upon the lending actions of the banks that receive the additional reserves.

Other government agencies also help stimulate the economy. Their actions only affect commercial banks indirectly, however. The federal government may increase its rate of spending, for example. If the federal government's demand for goods and services is increased in this fashion, businesses may be stimulated to borrow at commercial banks so as to meet this added demand. Thus there may be increased willingness to borrow and more lending activity.

Also, bank reserves may increase as businesses deposit checks received from the federal government in payment for its increased orders of goods and services. The federal government usually draws these checks on its accounts at the Federal Reserve banks. The deposit of these checks with commercial banks increases both the deposit liabilities and reserves of commercial banks. Suppose, for example, that the federal government increases its spendings by $50 million in an effort to stimulate the economy:

BALANCE SHEET CHANGES FOR THE FEDERAL RESERVE BANKS

ASSETS	LIABILITIES + CAPITAL ACCOUNTS
	Deposits
	Member bank reserves
	+$50,000,000
	U.S. Treasurer—general account
	−$50,000,000

---

[6] This type of transaction by the Federal Reserve System is called an open market operation. See Chapter 13 for a full discussion.

BALANCE SHEET CHANGES FOR THE COMMERCIAL BANKING SYSTEM

ASSETS		LIABILITIES + CAPITAL ACCOUNTS	
Reserves	+$50,000,000	Demand deposits	+$50,000,000

The checks deposited by businesses were drawn on the government accounts at the Federal Reserve banks. When commercial banks present these checks for collection, the Federal Reserve banks pay them by increasing commercial bank reserve accounts and decreasing the Treasury deposit accounts. Not all commercial banks participate in this increase in reserves initially. As the banks that receive these additional reserves expand loans and investments, however, other banks will receive increased amounts of reserves and deposits.

During prosperity and inflation, government economic policy may be the reverse of that just described. The Federal Reserve System may attempt to restrain inflationary pressures in the economy by restricting commercial bank lending activity. To accomplish this, the Federal Reserve System may sell U.S. government securities to the nonbank public. The purchasers of the securities will pay for them with checks drawn on their demand deposit accounts at commercial banks. The Federal Reserve banks, when they receive these checks, will collect by lowering the reserve balances of member banks. The Federal Reserve System could also raise reserve requirements to reduce inflationary pressure, but this is not the normal procedure.

Federal government spending may also be restricted in a period of inflation. A decrease in the federal government's demand for goods and services is thought to bring about reduced spending and borrowing by the nonbank public. Also, as the rate of federal spending decreases, government receipts relative to expenditures tend to increase. Thus, Treasury balances with the Federal Reserve banks increase, while commercial bank reserves and deposit liabilities diminish.

Summary. This part of Chapter 7 has dealt with some of the more important factors influencing the ability of a commercial bank to create money. The analysis has concentrated on the *potential* influences on bank money creation. The focus, for the most part, has been upon the individual commercial bank. The ability of the commercial bank to create demand deposit money depends principally on its reserve position. In general, the commercial bank may create demand deposits in an amount equal to its excess reserves. Whether the bank actually expands to this extent depends upon its willingness to lend, the demand for loans, its clearing balances, and its precautionary margin of excess reserves. If the bank has a shortage of reserves, it must either contract its loans and investments or obtain additional reserves. Government economic policy and changes in the demand for time deposits and currency affect banks principally by altering reserve positions.

THE CREATION AND DESTRUCTION OF DEPOSITS BY THE COMMERCIAL BANKING SYSTEM

The ability of the entire banking system to create and destroy money differs from that of the individual bank. It is true that the ability of the banking system to create and destroy money, like that of individual banks, depends upon reserve positions. The individual bank may create new deposits only to the extent of its excess reserves, however, whereas the banking system may create new deposits by a multiple of banking system excess reserves.

Banking System Creation of Deposits

To illustrate the multiple money-creating ability of the commercial banking system, let us begin by making the following assumptions: (1) the reserve requirement is 20 percent; (2) the deposit liabilities of the banking system are $140 billion; (3) the reserves of the banking system are $28 billion; (4) there is normally no cash drain or influx; (5) unless specified otherwise, all transactions are by check; (6) there are no time deposits; (7) banks require no minimum amount of precautionary reserve balances; and (8) monetary-fiscal policy is neutral in its effects on commercial bank lending and investing activities. Under conditions such as these, banks would be loaned up; required reserves are $28 billion and are equal to actual reserves.

Now, imagine that there is a $100 million influx of cash into the banking system. These deposits of cash increase both commercial bank reserves and demand deposit liabilities by $100 million. Required reserves increase by $20 million. Excess reserves are no longer zero; they now amount to $80 million. What has happened to the lending and money-creating ability of the commercial banking system? It has increased not by the amount of the excess reserves, but by a multiple of that amount.

Initially the banks will only increase deposits by the amount of their excess reserves, $80 million. They expect to lose their excess reserves to other banks as borrowers pay off debts to depositors of other banks. This will not cause a loss in reserves for the entire banking system, however. Deposit creation will continue to occur because the reserves stay in the banking system. As the newly created funds are spent, other banks receive these reserves and create new primary deposits to the extent of $80 million. These banks now have excess reserves. With $80 million more in deposits and reserves, they have $64 million in excess reserves and may create additional deposits to this amount.

Summarizing the discussion to this point in "T" account form, we have

1. A hypothetical initial balance sheet for the commercial banking system when loaned up:

BALANCE SHEET FOR THE COMMERCIAL BANKING SYSTEM
(IN BILLIONS OF DOLLARS)

ASSETS		LIABILITIES + CAPITAL ACCOUNTS	
Reserves	$ 28	Demand deposits	$140
Other assets	122	Other liabilities and capital accounts	
			10

2. Balance sheet changes that occur when people make cash deposits of $100 million (banks receiving these deposits are called Group 1 banks):

BALANCE SHEET CHANGES FOR GROUP 1 BANKS
(IN MILLIONS OF DOLLARS)

ASSETS		LIABILITIES + CAPITAL ACCOUNTS	
Reserves	+$100	Demand deposits	+$100

BALANCE SHEET CHANGES FOR THE COMMERCIAL BANKING SYSTEM
(IN MILLIONS OF DOLLARS)

ASSETS		LIABILITIES + CAPITAL ACCOUNTS	
Reserves	+$100	Demand deposits	+$100

3. Balance sheet changes that occur when the banks acquiring the $100 million in cash deposits create loans and derivative deposits:

BALANCE SHEET CHANGES FOR GROUP 1 BANKS
(IN MILLIONS OF DOLLARS)

ASSETS		LIABILITIES + CAPITAL ACCOUNTS	
Loans	+$80	Demand deposits	+$80

BALANCE SHEET CHANGES FOR THE COMMERCIAL BANKING SYSTEM
(IN MILLIONS OF DOLLARS)

ASSETS		LIABILITIES + CAPITAL ACCOUNTS	
Loans	+$80	Demand deposits	+$80

4. Balance sheet changes that occur when the newly created deposits are spent and passed to other (Group 2) banks:

BALANCE SHEET CHANGES FOR GROUP 1 BANKS
(IN MILLIONS OF DOLLARS)

ASSETS		LIABILITIES + CAPITAL ACCOUNTS	
Reserves	−$80	Demand deposits	−$80

BALANCE SHEET CHANGES FOR GROUP 2 BANKS
(IN MILLIONS OF DOLLARS)

ASSETS		LIABILITIES + CAPITAL ACCOUNTS	
Reserves	+$80	Demand deposits	+$80

BALANCE SHEET CHANGES FOR THE COMMERCIAL BANKING SYSTEM

ASSETS	LIABILITIES + CAPITAL ACCOUNTS
0	0

5. Balance sheet changes that occur when Group 2 banks create loans and deposits:

BALANCE SHEET CHANGES FOR GROUP 2 BANKS
(IN MILLIONS OF DOLLARS)

ASSETS		LIABILITIES + CAPITAL ACCOUNTS	
Loans	+$64	Demand deposits	+$64

BALANCE SHEET CHANGES FOR THE COMMERCIAL BANKING SYSTEM
(IN MILLIONS OF DOLLARS)

ASSETS		LIABILITIES + CAPITAL ACCOUNTS	
Loans	+$64	Demand deposits	+$64

The above entries show that $100, $80, and $64 million in new demand deposits have successively been created. Theoretically, in the banking system as a whole, banks will continue to create deposits in this fashion until all of the excess reserves in the banking system become required reserves. Under our assumptions, this point will be reached when the total of the newly created deposits is five times the initial increase in reserves of the commercial banking system. This means that the banking system as a whole, with an initial increase in reserves of $100 million, can theoretically expand deposits by $500 million. Since, in our illustration, the first $100 million created were primary deposits, the remaining $400 million were, in a general sense, *derivative deposits* created when banks made loans and investments in that amount. Thus, the total nonbank public holdings of money have increased by $400 million.

The essential difference between individual bank and banking system deposit creation is this. When the individual bank makes investments, it expects to lose reserves in equal amount; when it makes loans and creates deposit liabilities, it expects to lose those deposit liabilities and reserves in an equal amount. When the banking system makes loans and investments and creates demand deposit money, however, there is no change in reserves. They are merely redistributed among the individual banks in the system.

Banking System Destruction of Deposits

The banking system, like individual banks, must contract when it is short of reserves. Unlike an individual bank, however, the banking system as a whole must contract its deposits by a multiple of the deficiency of reserves. An individual bank may make up its shortage of reserves by getting reserves from other banks. It does this by reducing loans and investments and by borrowing reserves in the Federal Funds Market. Such an act by an individual bank, however, does not relieve other banks in a system that is short of reserves. Instead, this only makes the problems of other banks more severe. This is particularly true when the Federal Reserve System, for purposes of restraining inflation, does not undertake to provide commercial banks with additional reserves.

To explain the multiple deposit destruction which occurs in the commercial banking system, let us start with the same initial set of assumptions we used in our illustration of the multiple expansion of deposits. The banking system is initially loaned up. Now, let us imagine that there is an increase in the reserve requirement from 20 to 21 percent. Let us assume further that additional reserves are not available. What happens in the banking system?

The required amount of reserves increases from $28 to $29.4 billion. With only $28 billion in reserves, banks now have a $1.4 billion deficiency of reserves. The banking system must contract its loans and investments. Assume that banks try to get additional reserves by lowering their investment holdings. Since each bank will try to acquire enough additional reserves to remove its deficiency, each bank will contract its investments by that amount. Thus, all banks sell off investments worth $1.4 billion. The purchasers of the investments will probably be members of the nonbank public, since it is unlikely that banks, being short of reserves, will purchase the securities. The nonbank public pays for the securities with checks written on its demand deposit accounts. As a result, the commercial banking system's deposit liabilities contract by $1.4 billion. The banks have been unsuccessful in their attempt to get additional reserves:

BALANCE SHEET CHANGES FOR THE COMMERCIAL BANKING SYSTEM
(IN BILLIONS OF DOLLARS)

ASSETS		LIABILITIES + CAPITAL ACCOUNTS	
Investments	−$1.4	Demand deposits	−$1.4

Addenda: Initial shortage of reserves $1.4
Decrease in required reserves after decrease in demand deposits 0.294
New deficiency of reserves 1.106

The sale of securities results in no change in reserves for the banking system. The parallel decrease in demand deposit liabilities, however, reduces required reserves by 21 percent of $1.4 billion, or $294 million. Thus, the banking system is still $1.106 billion short in its reserves.

Given our assumptions, the banking system will continue to contract. Another means of contraction open to banks is loan reduction. As loans come due, depositors usually repay with demand deposits. If, prior to loan repayment, depositors build up their accounts with creditor banks by depositing checks received from others who have accounts with other banks, the creditor banks acquire reserves. These banks also lose reserves, however, since other banks are in approximately the same position. With a $1.106 billion shortage of reserves, all banks together may reduce loans and deposits by $1.106 billion. Are banks still short of reserves? Yes, because a $1.106 billion deposit reduction only reduces required reserves by 21 percent of $1.106 billion, or $232.26 million. The deposit, investment, and loan contraction must continue.

At this point deposits have already dropped by $1.4 and $1.106 billion, a multiple of the initial $1.4 billion shortage in reserves. They must continue to fall, however, until the overall decrease in demand deposits equals 1/.21 times the $1.4 billion shortage in reserves. These overall changes must occur in the banking system's balance sheet before the system has no shortage of reserves:

BALANCE SHEET CHANGES FOR THE COMMERCIAL BANKING SYSTEM
(IN BILLIONS OF DOLLARS)

ASSETS		LIABILITIES + CAPITAL ACCOUNTS	
Loans and investments	−$6.67	Demand deposits	−$6.67

Addenda: Decrease in required reserves (.21)($6.67) = $1.4
Initial deficiency of reserves $1.4
Present level of excess reserves 0

Thus, the system must contract until demand deposit liabilities are reduced by a total of $6.67 billion in order to make up a $1.4 billion shortage in reserves.

A Shorthand Formula
to Predict Deposit Creating and Destroying Potentialities
of the Commercial Banking System

The results of the preceding analysis may be more readily obtained by mean of the formula

$$D = \frac{R}{r} \qquad\qquad [7\text{--}1]$$

where r is the reserve requirement, R the volume of reserves in the commercial banking system, and D the amount of demand deposits that a given volume of reserves (R) can support. For example, if R is $28 billion and r is 20 percent, then D is $140 billion, the initial demand deposit figure in the balance sheet given on page 91.

So long as R and r are unchanged, the formula shows the volume of deposits the banking system may maintain as a maximum. But if r were to increase to 21 percent, for example, then D would equal $133.33 billion. A 1 percent increase in the reserve requirement would thus lead to a $6.67 billion drop in deposits. On the other hand, a 1 percent decrease in the reserve requirement would lead to a $7.368 billion increase in deposit liabilities:

$$D = \frac{\$28 \text{ billion}}{.19} = \$147.368 \text{ billion}$$

Given the reduction in the reserve requirement, the formula will indicate to what level of deposits the commercial banking system may expand. There is no requirement that the banking system must expand to this extent, of course, but the profit motive may encourage it to do so.

The formula may also be used to demonstrate the effects of a change in the volume of reserves. For example, if the level of reserves is increased by $100 million, the lending ability of the banking system is increased by $500 million:

$$D = \frac{\$28.1 \text{ billion}}{.20} = \$140.5 \text{ billion}$$

Similarly, a $100 million decrease in reserves would lead to a $500 million decrease in the money-creating ability of the banking system.

Banking System Deposit Creation and Destruction
Under Relaxed Assumptions

The assumptions we have made to illustrate bank deposit creation and destruction capabilities are quite unrealistic, of course. They were made simply to show the theoretical extent to which a given level of reserves and a given reserve requirement can be used to support deposits. In the following section we will consider what happens when certain of these limiting assumptions are relaxed.

First, let us allow for cash drain and cash influx. The nonbank public tends to maintain a relatively stable ratio of currency to deposits. The stability of this ratio is important in terms of commercial bank reserve position changes. An increase in nonbank public demand deposit holdings is typically accompanied by an increased demand for currency. This tends to modify the potential increase in deposits and loans that seemed possible given the initial increase in the volume of excess reserves. When deposits contract, nonbank public holdings of currency also tend to decrease and currency flows into the banking system, building up commercial bank reserves.

Ironically, the very lending activities of banks that lead to deposit creation tend to restrain the money-creating abilities of the banking system. For example, when banks make loans, some people prefer to take cash, and others take both cash and deposits. These withdrawals of cash reduce the system's reserves, and hence its lending and money-creating abilities. If businesses that get loans for payroll purposes take deposits, cash withdrawals also take place. Employees generally have a higher ratio of cash to deposits than do employers. Paychecks are usually converted into both cash and deposits by employees.

On the other hand, when loans are repaid, they are not repaid solely with demand deposits. Instead, some portion of the repayments are in the form of cash. This means that loan repayment usually leads to reserve increases for the banking system. If banks reduce investments, some security purchasers will use cash. This also leads to reserve increases. Thus, if banks contract because of a reserve deficiency, the extent to which they must contract will be reduced by the resultant cash inflow.

The ability of the banking system to create and destroy money, with this change in assumptions, is now determined by R, the level of reserves; r, the reserve requirement; and c, the ratio of currency to deposits desired by the nonbank public. The formula for the deposits which can be maintained by the banking system remains equation 7–1. Changes in the volume of demand deposits that can be maintained by the banking system, given changes in reserves, however, are governed by the equation

$$\Delta D = \frac{\Delta A}{r + c} \qquad [7\text{--}2]$$

where ΔD is the change in demand deposit liabilities and ΔA is some beginning change in the volume of reserves.

Assume that R originally equals $28 billion, r is .20, c is .10, and that R then increases by $1 billion (that is, $\Delta A = \$1$ billion). If R were to remain at the new higher level of $29 billion, equation 7–1 would give us $140 and $145 billion for R of $28 billion and $29 billion respectively. The cash drain created when banks grant loans, however, holds down the money-creating ability of the banking system. From equation 7–2 we see that banks will create only an additional $3.33 billion in deposits. For every billion increase in demand deposit liabilities, the banking system must allow for a $100 million cash drain, which means, of course, a withdrawal of $100 million from commercial bank reserves. If banks were to attempt to expand deposits by $5 billion on the basis of the $1 billion in additional reserves, they would experience a $500 million loss in cash reserves. This would leave them, on balance, with $4.5 billion in additional demand deposit liabilities and only $500 million in additional reserves, whereas legally $900 million in additional reserves would be required. Thus banks will instead expand demand deposits by $3.33 billion, lose $333 million of the initial $1 billion increment in reserves, and be left with $667 million of that $1 billion in reserves to cover the .20 reserve requirement against the newly created demand deposits. Bank loan and investment expansion during this time will total $3.66 billion: $3.33 billion extended to those customers who took deposits and $.33 billion extended to those who took currency. Equation 7–1 now gives

$$D = \frac{\$28.66 \text{ billion}}{.20} = \$143.333 \text{ billion}$$

On the other hand, if R were initially reduced by $1 billion, the cash inflow that occurs would hold down the potential deposit destruction to $3.333 billion.

Second, many banks tend to maintain precautionary and working balances of excess reserves. This is an additional factor that further reduces the extent to which the banking system can create and destroy demand deposits. Assume that $R = \$28$ billion, $r = .20$, $c = .10$, and that banks wish to have excess reserves equal to 5 percent of their demand deposit liabilities. Let the symbol i' represent this percentage. The formula for the volume of demand deposits that the banking system can support now becomes

$$D = \frac{R}{r + i'} \qquad [7-3]$$

Thus, in terms of our hypothetical situation,

$$D = \frac{\$28 \text{ billion}}{.20 + .05} = \$112 \text{ billion}$$

Now, suppose that R increases by an initial $1 billion ($\Delta A = \$1$ billion). Banks must now have reserves sufficient to cover the reserve requirement, precautionary demands for excess reserves, and cash drain. As a consequence, the formula for changes in the volume of demand deposits that can be maintained by the banking system, given changes in reserves, is now

$$D = \frac{\Delta A}{r + c + i'} \qquad [7-4]$$

Now, for every $1 billion increase in demand deposit liabilities, the banking system must allow for a $100 million cash drain and build up excess reserves by $50 million. Consequently, banks will only create a maximum of $2.857 billion.

On the other hand, a $1 billion decrease in reserves results in a $2.857 billion drop in deposits, instead of $5 billion drop. Thus, the tendency of banks to maintain working balances of excess reserves dampens both the money-creating and the money-destroying capacities of the banking system.

Finally, banks create both time and demand deposits. Equations 7–1 and 7–3, however, are only applicable for a banking system with no time deposits and no reserve requirement for time deposits. Although we are primarily concerned with the ability of the banking system to create demand deposit money, we need to know the volume of reserves required to cover time deposits in order to ascertain this.

Let r be the reserve requirement for demand deposits, r' the reserve requirement for time deposits, and TD the volume of time deposits. If $r' = .04$ and $TD = \$60$ billion, then $2.4 billion in reserves is needed to meet the reserve requirement for time deposits. If total reserves, R, are $28 billion, then $25.6 billion in reserve is available to support demand deposits. Thus, the formula for the demand-deposit-supporting ability of the commercial banking system is

$$D = \frac{R - r'(TD)}{r + i'} \qquad [7-5]$$

If $R = \$28$ billion, then $D = \$102.4$ billion.

$$D = \frac{\$28 \text{ billion} - (.04)(\$60 \text{ billion})}{.20 + .05} = \frac{\$25.6 \text{ billion}}{.25} = \$102.4 \text{ billion}$$

The greater the volume of time deposits and the larger the reserve requirement for time deposits, the less is the ability of the banking system to create demand deposits. This statement also holds true in reverse.

Although these statements are basically true, they should not be taken too literally. For, as previously indicated, if people can be persuaded to switch from demand to time deposits, the ability of the banking system to make loans and create deposits (both demand and time) is increased. A switch from demand to time deposits allows some of R to become excess reserves, since the reserve requirement for time deposits is lower than that for demand deposits. Equation 7–5 simply tells us how much in demand deposits the banking system can maintain. Clearly, if there are more time deposits, fewer demand deposits can be maintained, but the total dollar volume of time and demand deposits is greater. This means, moreover, that all bank loans and investments can be increased.

SUMMARY AND PREVIEW

It has been demonstrated that the ability of the banking system to create and destroy demand deposit money depends upon (1) r, the reserve requirement for demand deposits, (2) r', the reserve requirement for time deposits, (3) R, the volume of reserves, (4) TD, the volume of time deposits, (5) c, the ratio of currency to demand deposits which the public desires to maintain, and (6) i', the ratio of excess reserves to demand deposits that commercial banks wish to maintain. These six variables are all direct determinants of D, the volume of demand deposits that the banking system may maintain. Changes in any of the variables will change D. Equations 7–4 and 7–5 incorporate all these determinants.

Three determinants, r, r', and R, are controlled by the monetary authorities. The current values of these variables are easy to ascertain.[7] Two determinants, TD and c, are determined by the nonbank public. One determinant, i', is controlled by the commercial banking system. To explain and predict movements in the money supply successfully, we must understand how the banking system and the nonbank public reacts to changes in excess reserves and our monetary base, R.

Chapter 15 is devoted to a study of contemporary money supply theory. That chapter will first show quantitatively how our actual volume of reserves and our money supply is determined. Second, it will develop behavior relations showing how the banking system reacts to changes in economic conditions and the monetary base, to help determine the level of money in the economy. We do not turn to this study now because it is essential that we first understand the influence of other financial institutions and our monetary authorities upon our monetary resources. This is discussed in Chapters 8 through 14.

Supplementary Readings

Board of Governors of the Federal Reserve System. *The Federal Reserve System: Purposes and Functions.* Washington, D.C., 1963, Chapter 4.

Crick, W. F. "The Genesis of Bank Deposits," reprinted in American Economic Association, *Readings in Monetary Theory.* Homewood, Ill., Irwin, 1951, pp. 41–53.

Orr, Daniel, and W. J. Mellon. "Stochastic Reserve Losses and Bank Credit," *American Economic Review* (1961), pp. 614–23.

Pritchard, Leland J. *Money and Banking.* Boston, Houghton Mifflin, 1964, Chapter 6.

---

[7]There is, it is true, a spectrum of reserve requirements for demand deposits. They differ for member banks that are country and reserve city banks. They also differ for member and nonmember banks. Yet, by calculating the percentage of deposits subject to each of the differing requirements, it is possible to calculate an average reserve requirement for the commercial banking system. For example, if 75 percent of deposits are subject to a 10 percent requirement and the remaining 25 percent of deposits come under a 20 percent requirement, then the average reserve requirement, r, would be 12.5 percent.

Chapter 8

Nonbank Financial Institutions: Sources and Uses of Funds

Commercial banks, in the process of increasing or decreasing their loans and investments, create and destroy money, our most important financial asset. Commercial banks are not the only private financial institutions that help to shape the growth and progress of the economy, however. Other financial institutions create and destroy financial assets that compete with currency and the deposits of banks for primacy in the nonbank public's distribution of liquid-wealth holdings. The greater the success of these nonbank financial institutions in attracting funds from the nonbank public, the greater the total liquid wealth of the nonbank public, the greater the loan and investment activity of these financial institutions, and the weaker the direct control of our monetary authorities over the economy.

Previous chapters have examined some of the problems that are created for banks and the economy in general as a result of the fact that the principal regulatory devices used by the monetary authorities have their initial impact upon commercial banks. This chapter discusses briefly those financial institutions that compete with commercial banks, and, as is sometimes claimed, escape the brunt of federal monetary regulation. We shall first study those institutions that create forms of liquid assets with a high degree of moneyness—mutual savings banks, savings and loan associations, and life insurance companies. Other financial institutions will then be considered. Finally, the relationship between these nonbank financial institutions and the national economy will be examined. (Government financial institutions will be treated in later chapters.)

PRINCIPAL NONBANK FINANCIAL INSTITUTIONS

Mutual Savings Banks

Mutual savings banks are the only financial institutions, other than commercial banks, that create deposits in large volume. Here the similarity ends, however. Commercial banks create both time and demand deposits; mutual savings banks today create only time deposits. This occurs when individuals cash or deposit checks drawn on commercial banks. These deposits are subject to withdrawal only after notice, but, in practice, depositors at mutual savings banks, like those at commercial banks, need give no advance notice.

As Table 8–1 indicates, deposits are the principal source of funds for mutual savings banks. They constituted almost 90 percent of total mutual savings bank liabilities and surplus accounts in 1964. The remaining funds were provided by other liabilities and surplus accounts.[1]

TABLE 8–1. MUTUAL SAVINGS BANKS, SOURCES
AND USES OF FUNDS, MARCH 31, 1964
(IN BILLIONS OF DOLLARS)

Assets (uses of funds)	
Financial assets	
Mortgage loans	$36.9
Other loans	0.7
U.S. government securities	6.1
State and local government securities	0.4
Corporate and other securities	5.2
Total	$49.3
Cash assets	0.9
Other assets	0.8
Total	51.0
Liabilities and surplus accounts (sources of funds)	
Deposits	45.8
Other liabilities	1.0
Surplus accounts	4.2
Total	51.0

Source: *Federal Reserve Bulletin*, June, 1964, p. 748.

Mortgages and other investments represent the principal uses to which mutual savings banks put their funds. In 1964, more than 70 percent of all their assets were in the form of mortgages, and an additional 27 percent were in federal, state, local, and corporate securities. Not quite 2 percent of assets were in cash form. This would appear to be a dangerously low ratio of cash assets to deposits (.018) when contrasted with the types of reserve requirements that commercial banks are required to maintain. For institutions like mutual savings banks, however, this is not a dangerous ratio.

Mutual savings banks were initially set up to provide a place of safe-keeping for the funds of small savers. These funds were found to have a slow rate of turnover and, as a consequence, the savings banks did not feel that they had to maintain a large volume of cash. Furthermore, the investment policy of mutual savings banks has traditionally been very conserva-

----

[1] We use the term "surplus accounts" rather than "capital accounts" since mutual savings banks, like other *mutual* organizations, have no stockholders. Surplus arises when operations are profitable.

tive; they almost never make risky loans on which they could sustain a loss. Thus, although the assets of mutual savings banks are quite illiquid, the slow rate of deposit turnover and the fact that many of them have deposit insurance with the Federal Deposit Insurance Corporation preclude the probability of substantial losses on those assets during periods of relative prosperity.

Mutual savings banks have had an excellent record of performance. Even during the depression of the 1930's there were few failures. Yet despite this favorable record, mutual savings banks have not increased in numbers. Their assets have increased substantially, but they have not risen as quickly as those of other nonbank financial institutions. Table 8–2 shows the recent growth in the financial assets of various types of financial institutions. Only

TABLE 8–2. FINANCIAL SECTOR STATEMENT OF FINANCIAL ASSETS, 1945–1962

AMOUNTS OUTSTANDING AT END OF YEAR

(IN BILLIONS OF DOLLARS)

YEAR	COMMER- CIAL BANKS	MUTUAL SAVINGS BANKS	SAVINGS AND LOAN ASSOCIA- TIONS	CREDIT UNIONS	LIFE INSUR- ANCE COM- PANIES	NON- INSURED PENSION PLANS	OTHER INSUR- ANCE COM- PANIES	OTHER FINAN- CIAL INSTI- TUTIONS
1945	141.2	16.9	8.3	.3	43.4	2.3	9.0	11.0
1946	133.6	18.5	9.8	.3	46.4	2.8	9.6	10.5
1947	137.2	19.5	11.3	.4	49.8	3.3	10.8	10.8
1948	138.2	20.5	12.7	.5	53.2	3.9	12.0	12.9
1949	140.3	21.5	14.2	.7	57.1	4.5	13.7	15.0
1950	148.4	22.4	16.4	.9	61.0	5.9	15.1	17.9
1951	157.5	23.3	18.7	1.0	64.9	7.3	16.4	19.0
1952	166.5	25.1	22.2	1.3	69.6	8.8	18.1	22.3
1953	170.7	27.0	26.2	1.7	74.4	10.6	19.6	24.8
1954	180.0	29.1	31.0	2.1	79.9	13.6	22.2	28.6
1955	185.3	31.1	37.0	2.5	85.4	16.7	24.2	35.6
1956	190.8	33.1	42.1	3.0	90.4	19.0	25.0	37.7
1957	196.4	34.9	47.1	3.5	95.2	21.2	25.3	39.2
1958	211.2	37.5	54.0	4.1	101.0	26.5	28.3	44.5
1959	216.4	38.6	62.2	4.8	106.4	30.8	30.4	50.0
1960	225.7	40.2	70.0	5.3	111.9	34.3	32.3	55.7
1961	243.0	42.4	80.2	6.0	118.6	41.6	36.0	64.8
1962	262.8	45.7	91.4	6.8	125.0	42.2	37.0	66.9

Source: Board of Governors of the Federal Reserve System, *Flow of Funds Accounts, 1946–1962; 1963 Supplement*, pp. 15–22; 26.

commercial bank financial asset growth has been slower than that of mutual savings banks. What accounts for this relatively slow rate of growth? The principle reason is probably the provincial character of the mutual savings banks.

Mutual savings banks are almost exclusively a phenomenon of the Middle Atlantic and New England states. They were first started in these states in the early 1800's. As the economy expanded through the nineteenth and twentieth centuries, the mutual savings form of financial institution did not move geographically.

Another limiting factor in the growth of mutual savings banks has been the competition of savings and loan associations. As previously indicated, mutual savings banks were initially formed to provide a place of safekeeping for the funds of small savers. Little thought was given to the investment of funds for earnings; safety was the primary consideration. As a consequence, mutual savings banks preferred to make short-term mortgage loans and required relatively large down payments. In recent years, many mutual savings banks have departed from these traditions. In New York State, many will make thirty-year mortgage loans on as little as 10 percent down payment. This is clearly competitive. Savings and loan associations had come to dominate this field of lending long before mutual banks became competitive. Savings and loan associations have also offered strong competition to mutual savings banks for the savings of depositors. The dividend return on savings and loan share accounts is usually about ½ percent higher than the interest return from the competing mutual savings bank deposit accounts.

Savings and Loan Associations

In contrast to mutual savings banks, savings and loan associations are specifically organized for the purpose of making mortgage loans. Savings and loan share accounts are their principal source of funds, and mortgages represent their primary use of funds. Table 8–3 states that out of a total of $109.6 billion in assets in 1964, $93.1 billion was in the form of mortgages. Cash assets amounted to 3.3 percent of all assets.

The funds that savings and loan associations use to expand their holdings of mortgages are acquired when individuals purchase savings and loan share accounts. Purchasers of these accounts often believe that the accounts are the same as savings accounts with commercial and mutual savings banks. This is not usually true, however. In a savings and loan association a depositor usually owns a share of the assets of the association. Fortunately, this ownership is not the same as ownership in a business corporation, for the market price of the stock of a corporation varies. To get cash for one's stock in a corporation the owner must sell the stock. He may sustain either a loss or a gain. This is not usually possible with the shares of a savings and loan association. The shares of most associations carry some type of insurance. Those associations regulated by the Federal Home Loan Bank Board, for example, have their share accounts insured by the Federal Savings and Loan Insurance Corporation.

It should be observed that a few savings and loan associations do have the same type of ownership as most business corporations. These savings and loan associations issue stock which is regularly traded in the securities market. The savings accounts that are sources of funds for these corporations are liabilities, and thus are comparable to the "savings deposits" created by commercial banks and mutual savings banks.

Like mutual savings banks, savings and loan associations receive their funds in the form of either cash or checks drawn on commercial banks. When the associations accept these deposits, they create savings and loan share accounts, thus increasing the volume of near money in the economy.

TABLE 8–3. SAVINGS AND LOAN ASSOCIATIONS,
SOURCES AND USES OF FUNDS, MARCH 31, 1964
(IN BILLIONS OF DOLLARS)

Assets (uses of funds)	
Mortgages	93.1
U.S. government securities	6.7
Cash	3.6
Other	6.2
Total	109.6
Liabilities (sources of funds)	
Savings capital	93.5
Reserves and undivided profits	7.2
Borrowed money	4.3
Loans in process	2.4
Other	2.1
Total	109.6*

Source: *Federal Reserve Bulletin,* June, 1964, p. 749.
* Totals may differ because of rounding.

The funds received by the associations are then deposited in their checking accounts at commercial banks and are subsequently used to make mortgage loans or to purchase some other type of asset, such as United States government securities.

When the mortgage loans made by savings and loan associations are received by borrowers, the funds become active money in the economy and stimulate demand and spending. Thus savings and loan associations act as financial intermediaries; they help to transfer funds from those who save, the holders of savings and loan share accounts, to those who borrow, the mortgagors. In this fashion funds pass from less active to more active spenders. In the process, the volume of liquid wealth and the claims to money in the economy increase.

As shown in Table 8–2, savings and loan associations have grown faster in recent decades than almost any other type of financial institution. This is probably attributable to their active lending habits and the fact that their dividend rates are usually higher than the interest rates paid by competing mutual savings banks and commercial banks.

Another reason that is often suggested for the rapid growth of savings and loan associations in recent years is the fact that they are not subject to the same type of reserve requirements as commercial banks. There is quite a bit of truth in this argument. Cash holdings are used directly by savings and loan associations when redeeming share accounts. When additional funds are needed to redeem share accounts, U.S. government security holdings are sold, or loans are secured from a Federal Home Loan bank (if the association is a member of the Federal Home Loan Bank System). As collateral for these loans the associations put up their mortgages. Furthermore, savings and loan associations seem to have little reluctance toward borrowing. Borrowings were $4.3 billion, 4 percent of assets, in March, 1964. These borrowings exceeded cash assets in volume. Commercial bank borrowings, on the other hand, were $3.3 billion, or only 1 percent of total assets; and bank borrowings were far exceeded by cash assets, which totaled $47.9 billion.[2]

At the present time, savings and loan associations that are members of the Federal Home Loan Bank System are operating under a reserve requirement of 7 percent. The Federal Home Loan Bank Board is authorized to vary these requirements from 4 to 8 percent of each association's savings and loan share accounts. Cash deposits with a Federal Home Loan bank and U.S. government securities are the principal assets used to meet this requirement. Were savings and loan associations subject to the same reserve requirements as Federal Reserve member banks, however, only cash assets could be used to satisfy the requirement. This means that in 1964 savings and loan associations would have needed $10.2 billion in cash assets instead of their actual $3.6 billion.[3] This would seem to put savings and loan associations at a distinct competitive advantage over commercial banks.

Life Insurance Companies

Life insurance companies, with $143.1 billion in assets as of March 31, 1964, are the second most important financial subsector of the economy.[4] They are second only to commercial banks, which had total assets of $309.3 billion at the end of the same month.[5]

Like other savings institutions, life insurance companies are financial intermediaries. They collect savings and then put these funds to use by making investments. Thus the process of getting funds from the ultimate lenders (savers) to borrowers is considerably eased.

The principal sources of life insurance company funds are the premiums that they collect from the sale of life insurance, annuities, and accident and

---

[2] *Federal Reserve Bulletin,* June, 1964, p. 736.
[3] Calculated on the assumption that the average reserve requirement on commercial bank time and demand deposits for member banks in 1964 was 11 percent.
[4] See Tables 8–2 and 8–4.
[5] *Federal Reserve Bulletin,* June, 1964, p. 736.

health insurance. The sale of term life insurance and accident and health insurance provides the insured with protection. Annuities and nonterm life insurance, however, not only provide protection but also add to the volume of near monies in the economy, as the policies acquire a cash surrender value. Thus, the total claims to the money supply are increased.

The uses to which life insurance companies put their funds are primarily long-term, consisting mostly of mortgage loans and bonds of business enterprise. Table 8–4 shows that life insurance company holdings of mortgages in March, 1964, totaled $51.4 billion, some 36 percent of total life insurance company assets. Holdings of corporate bonds amounted to $54.3 billion, or 38 percent of all life insurance company assets. Life insurance companies put a large percentage of their funds into these long-term

TABLE 8–4. LIFE INSURANCE
COMPANY ASSETS, MARCH 31, 1964
(IN BILLIONS OF DOLLARS)

Government securities		
United States	5.7	
State and local	3.8	
Foreign	2.8	
Total		12.4*
Business securities		
Bonds	54.3	
Stocks	5.9	
Total		60.2
Mortgages		51.4
Real estate		4.4
Policy loans		6.8
Other assets		7.8
Total assets		143.1*

Source: *Federal Reserve Bulletin*, June, 1964, p. 749.
* Totals differ because of rounding.

assets because they provide a steady source of revenue that can be used to meet insurance benefit payments. Mortality tables enable insurance companies to predict approximately how much in benefits they will have to pay each year and reduce the need for a large volume of short-term assets that can quickly be converted into cash to meet unanticipated expenses.

The purchase of corporate securities by life insurance companies may well have a significant impact on the direction of growth in the U.S. economy. This is because life insurance companies are an important source of long-term funds for business enterprise. Long-term funds are used primarily for expansion of plant and equipment, a major source of economic growth. There are four main sources of such funds: retained earnings, depreciation, proceeds from the sale of bonds, and proceeds from the sale of stock. What proportion of these long-term funds are supplied by life insurance companies? In 1962 there was a net increase of $6.0 billion in outstanding corporate and foreign bonds. In that same year life insurance companies added $2.4 billion to their portfolio holdings of corporate bonds.[6] Thus the increase in life insurance company holdings of corporate securities accounted for 40 percent of the 1962 increase in outstanding corporate and foreign bonds. The importance of life insurance companies as a source of long-term funds for business enterprise is further illustrated by the fact that of a total of $101.2 billion in outstanding corporate and foreign bonds, $53.1 billion worth of these securities were held by life insurance companies in 1962.[7]

Life insurance company holdings of corporate stock are comparatively small. Most states have legal prohibitions on the amount of stock a life insurance company may hold. In New York, for example, a life insurance company can have no more than 5 percent of its assets in common stock holdings. Net stock issues totaled $2.6 billion in 1962, but only $0.4 billion was purchased by life insurance companies.[8]

In what type of businesses do life insurance companies tend to invest their funds? There were life insurance company holdings of $3.5 billion in railroad bonds, $17.3 billion in public utility bonds, and $30.7 billion in industrial and miscellaneous bonds.[9] Life insurance companies also held $101 million in railroad stocks, $2.5 billion in public utility stocks, and $4.8 billion in industrial and miscellaneous stocks.[10] Clearly life insurance companies direct their funds toward industrials and utilities. In industrials the tendency is to invest in the bonds of chemical-, machinery-, and petroleum-related manufacturing industries. The concentration in these areas depends largely on yield and the demand for funds by business. The issues purchased today by life insurance companies tend to be direct placements. Life insurance companies are purchasing fewer and fewer public issues.

OTHER NONBANK FINANCIAL INSTITUTIONS

There are a host of other financial institutions that provide funds for the American public and business enterprise. Some are principally savings institutions like credit unions and pension plans. Others, such as finance companies, do not collect savings but act as intermediaries between bor-

---

[6] *Flow of Funds Accounts, 1946–1962: 1963 Supplement*, p. 82. Foreign bonds were an insignificant part of the total of corporate and foreign bonds.
[7] *Ibid.*, pp. 3, 19.
[8] *Ibid.*, p. 83.
[9] Institute of Life Insurance, *Life Insurance Fact Book, 1963* (New York: 1963), p. 64. The total of these figures differs from the $53.1 billion mentioned above. This difference is attributable to different data sources and the fact that the $53.1 billion includes a small amount of foreign bonds.
[10] *Ibid.*, p. 84. Data include both common and preferred stock.

rowers and savers nonetheless. In fact, finance companies themselves often borrow from other financial institutions, using the proceeds of the borrowings to lend to consumers.

Credit Unions

A credit union is a savings institution that collects funds by selling shares to its members. This method of collecting funds is comparable to that employed by savings and loan associations. The uses to which credit unions put their funds, however, differ sharply from those of savings and loan associations. The latter will lend to many different qualified borrowers, principally for long-term mortgage loans. Credit unions lend to a very restricted group of borrowers, and usually on a short-term basis.

Membership in a credit union is limited to a specific group of people. The group may consist of the members of a religious organization located in a particular community, or members of the same occupational group. In the United States, almost a third of all credit union members are industrial employees. An additional 14 percent are government employees.[11]

Group members are the principal source of funds for the credit union. Lendings to these members also represent the primary use to which the institutions put their funds; the lending activity of the credit union is almost always limited to its members.

In recent years credit unions have experienced phenomenal growth. As is shown in Table 8–3, their financial assets grew from $300 million in 1945 to $6.8 billion in 1962. No other type of savings institution, not even the rapidly growing savings and loan association, has had a faster rate of growth. The relative importance of credit unions as a financial institution is still minor, however.

Credit union assets consist primarily of short-term loans to credit members. Unlike other savings institutions, credit unions concentrate on consumer installment debt. Out of a total $53.8 billion in installment credit held by financial institutions in March, 1964, some $5.7 billion was held by credit unions. Only commercial banks ($21.9 billion) and sales finance companies ($13.8 billion) had extended more installment credit.[12] The principal types of installment loan made by credit unions are for the purchase of automobiles, home improvements, and the consolidation of debt.

The major problem facing credit union members is the lack of savings protection comparable to that provided depositors in commercial and mutual savings banks by the Federal Deposit Insurance Corporation and for shareholders in federal savings and loan associations by the Federal Savings and Loan Insurance Association. As a result, the risk attached to holding credit union shares is greater than for other forms of liquid wealth.

---

[11] *International Credit Union Yearbook, 1963*, p. 8.
[12] *Federal Reserve Bulletin*, June, 1964, p. 764.

Pension Funds

Pension funds are designed to provide income for people after retirement. There are two types of pension plan: insured and noninsured. Insured plans are administered by insurance companies; uninsured plans are administered by corporations, unions, or trustees appointed by them. The uninsured pension plans have become increasingly popular in recent decades. This is largely due to the fact that there are legal limitations on insurance company investments in common stock. This has made the uninsured plans, which do not usually have such legal limitation, more attractive.

Pension plans may be funded or nonfunded. Companies with nonfunded plans meet pension payment requirements out of current income; in funded plans, funds are collected and invested to help meet future benefit payments. Employer and employee contributions to such plans supply the funds, of course. If the plan is insured, the uses to which these funds are put are no different from the uses for any other funds available to life insurance companies.

Uses of funds in uninsured pension plans differ markedly, however. Table 8–5 lists the total financial assets of noninsured pension plans as of December, 1962. Out of a total $42.2 billion of financial assets, some $36.9 billion, or 87 percent, were in the form of corporate stocks and bonds. In the same year, by way of comparison, life insurance company holdings of corporate stocks and bonds amounted to only 44 percent of their total financial assets. The contrast is even more striking when we compare the holdings of corporate stock. Life insurance company holdings of stocks were only 5 percent of financial assets; uninsured pension plans, however, held $19.9 billion, or 47 percent, of their financial assets in this form.[13] The reasons for this difference, as previously indicated, are the legal restrictions that are imposed on life insurance company investment in stocks. In a period of relative prosperity, like that of the post-World War II economic world, stocks will usually appreciate in value and hence be viewed as a better investment than bonds. Thus, there is a strong inducement to invest the funds of pension plans in stocks.

Other Insurance Companies

Other insurance companies consist primarily of fire and casualty insurance firms. These companies differ from life insurance companies in their use of funds. Like life insurance companies, their sources of funds are principally in premium payments. Unlike them, however, capital accounts also provide a substantial source of funds for the fire and casualty insurance companies.

The uses of funds by fire and casualty insurance companies differ sharply

---

[13] *Flow of Funds Accounts, 1946–1962: 1963 Supplement*, p. 19.

from those of life insurance companies, too. Fire and casualty insurance company assets are, for the most part, highly liquid. As is shown in Table 8–5, a total of $8.4 billion, or 23 percent, of fire and casualty financial assets were in the form of demand deposits and U.S. government securities in 1962. In contrast, life insurance companies had only 6 percent of their financial assets in this form.[14]

TABLE 8–5. INSURANCE SECTOR: FINANCIAL ASSETS AND LIABILITIES FOR NONINSURED PENSION PLANS AND OTHER INSURANCE COMPANIES, DECEMBER 31, 1962

(IN BILLIONS OF DOLLARS)

TYPE OF ASSET AND LIABILITY	NONINSURED PENSION PLANS	OTHER INSURANCE COMPANIES*
Financial assets		
Demand deposits and currency	0.7	1.6
Credit and equity market instruments		
Federal obligations	3.0	6.8
State and local obligations	—	10.6
Corporate bonds	17.0	3.4
Corporate stock	19.9	11.3
1-to-4 family mortgages	1.5	—
Mortgages	—	1.0
Other loans (policy loans)	—	0.1
Total	41.5†	33.1†
Trade credit		2.4
Total financial assets	42.2	37.0†
Total liabilities	42.2	19.6

Source: *Flow of Funds Accounts, 1946–1962: 1963 Supplement*, p. 19.
* Fire and casualty companies, fraternal orders, and nonprofit medical plans.
† Totals may differ because of rounding.

This difference is largely attributable to the nature of the financial obligations that the respective institutions are likely to incur. Life insurance companies can predict their total future financial responsibilities with a high degree of accuracy on the basis of mortality tables. Hence, they need not keep large quantities of their funds in a highly liquid form. Fire and casualty companies, on the other hand, cannot know in advance the claims that will be made in a given year as a result, for example, of fire or the vagaries of the weather. While one may expect increases in aggregate liability payments from year to year, this is of little assistance to the individual insurance company. Its powers to predict claims are relatively weak.

---

[14] *Ibid.*, p. 19.

As a consequence, fire and casualty companies tend to concentrate their fund placement in assets that can be quickly converted into cash, such as demand deposits and government securities. They also invest heavily in corporate stock; this is permitted because of their relatively low debt/equity ratio.

Finance Companies

Finance companies differ from the other financial institutions we have discussed principally in terms of their sources of funds. Commercial banks, savings banks, savings and loan associations, and credit unions all receive their funds from depositors and shareholders, and, in the process, create near monies. Life insurance companies receive their funds principally from premium payments; other insurance companies receive their funds from premium payments and capital accounts. Finance companies, however, get their funds principally from borrowings and capital accounts.

The two most important types of finance company are consumer finance and sales finance companies. Consumer finance companies deal directly with the public; they usually make installment loans to help in the purchase of automobiles and consumer durables. Although the proceeds of the loans are generally used for these specific purposes, the actual loan is generally unsecured.

Sales finance companies, on the other hand, do not normally deal directly with the public. Instead, they purchase the installment contracts that consumers sign with the sellers of goods and services. This provides the retailer with funds that he can immediately use in his business operations. His liquidity position is increased and he is often freed from the expense and bother of collecting the installment payments. Most installment contract purchases are in the field of auto financing. Sales finance companies frequently lend directly to automobile dealers at relatively low rates of interest, thus permitting the dealer to build up his stock of automobiles. Once the cars are sold, the dealer may extinguish the debt by paying cash or selling the installment contracts of his customers.

Table 8–6 shows the overwhelming importance of consumer credit as a use of funds for finance companies. At the end of 1962, the financial assets of finance companies amounted to $31.9 billion, with 54 percent in consumer credit. Total assets, however, were actually somewhat higher because of land and building ownership. Liabilities at the end of 1962 were $23.4 billion. Thus, capital accounts were a source of at least $8.5 billion dollars of finance company funds.

As is shown in Table 8–7, sales finance companies and consumer finance companies, in 1963, together accounted for over $18 billion in installment debt out of a total of $54 billion. Commercial banks, of course, held the largest amount, almost $22 billion. This is to be expected; commercial banks hold the largest volume of financial assets of any financial institution in the economy. Consumer credit is less important, however, for commercial banks than for finance companies. Commercial banks provide a wide variety of financial services for the public, whereas finance companies specialize in consumer credit.

TABLE 8–6. FINANCIAL ASSETS AND LIABILITIES FOR FINANCE COMPANIES, SECURITY BROKERS AND DEALERS, AND OPEN-END INVESTMENT COMPANIES, DECEMBER 31, 1962

(IN BILLIONS OF DOLLARS)

TYPE OF ASSET AND LIABILITY	FINANCE COMPANIES	SECURITY BROKERS AND DEALERS	OPEN-END INVESTMENT COMPANIES
Financial assets			
Demand deposits and currency	2.3	0.6	0.6
Federal obligations		1.8	0.7
Corporate bonds			1.8
Corporate stock			18.1
Mortgages	2.6		
Other securities		2.1	
Consumer credit	17.2		
Other loans	9.8		
Security credit		4.6	
Other			
Total	31.9	9.2*	21.3*
Liabilities			
Corporate bonds	11.2		
Bank loans	7.5		
Other loans (open market paper)	4.7		
Customer credit balances		1.3	
Security loans from agencies of foreign banks		0.7	
Security loans from banks		5.1	
Total	23.4	7.2*	

Source: *Flow of Funds Accounts, 1946–1962: 1963 Supplement*, p. 22.
* Totals differ from sum of individual items because of rounding.

Open-End Investment Companies

Open-end investment companies are still another important financial institution. These investment companies are commonly called *mutual funds*. They obtain funds by selling their stock directly to the public. The proceeds are then used to purchase the stocks and bonds of other corporations.

New stock is issued to meet the demands of the public. This stock may be purchased only from the investment company itself. When a stockholder of an open-end investment company wishes to redeem his shares, he does so by selling his stock back to the company. Thus, annual variations in the amount of open-end investment company stock outstanding depend upon the difference between new stock sales and stock redemptions. In 1963, open-end investment companies sold $2.46 billion of their own shares. They also retired $1.504 billion of their own shares, however. This left a net increase of $952 million.[15]

TABLE 8–7. CONSUMER CREDIT, MARCH 31, 1964

(IN MILLIONS OF DOLLARS)

TYPE OF CREDIT AND INSTITUTION		AMOUNT
Installment credit		
Commercial banks		
Automobile paper	11,466	
Other consumer goods paper	3,195	
Repair and modernization loans	2,303	
Personal loans	4,955	
Total		21,919
Sales finance companies		
Automobile paper	8,265	
Other consumer goods paper	3,603	
Repair and modernization loans	152	
Personal loans	1,782	
Total		13,802
Credit unions		5,668
Consumer finance companies		4,597
Other financial institutions		1,667
Retail outlets		
Department stores	3,044	
Furniture stores	1,022	
Appliance stores	273	
Automobile dealers	334	
Other	1,469	
Total		6,142
Total installment credit		53,795
Noninstallment credit		
Single payment loans		6,002
Charge accounts		4,634
Service credit		4,482
Total noninstallment credit		15,118
Total consumer credit		68,913

Source: *Federal Reserve Bulletin*, June, 1964, pp. 764–65.

Such an excess of sales over redemptions constitutes an increase in shares outstanding. It does *not* mean that the liquid wealth of mutual fund stockholders has increased, however. The value of a mutual fund's shares only increase when the company wisely invests the funds it receives from its stock sales, for, as Table 8–6 shows, mutual fund income is used principally to purchase the stock of other companies.

---

[15] *Federal Reserve Bulletin*, June, 1964, p. 758.

Because of the large volume of funds received, the open-end investment company is able to purchase the stocks of a diverse number of companies. Presumably this cuts down the possibility of loss attendant upon holdings that are concentrated in particular stocks. It is entirely possible that a falling market will undermine the greater part of an open-end company's portfolio of stock investments, too, however. Mutual funds took substantial losses in the stock market decline of 1962. On the other hand, if the market is rising, as has been usual during recent decades, the value of an open-end investment company's stock investments will increase, and its own stock will rise, too. Mutual fund investment company assets have risen in market value from $3.9 billion at the end of 1952 to $25.2 billion at the end of 1963. Part of this $21.3 billion increase is attributable to an increase in net sales of mutual fund stocks amounting to $11.8 billion during the period. The remaining $9.5 billion increase in market value of assets, however, is almost wholly due to the increased value of the stock investments made by these open-end investment companies.[16]

How good a form of liquid wealth is stock ownership in a mutual fund? Clearly the possibility of loss and the lack of any federal insurance on this type of asset indicate that shares of ownership in mutual funds possess only a small degree of moneyness. They may be fairly good investments during an extended period of economic prosperity, however.

Open-end investment companies are not the only form of investment company; there are also *closed-end investment companies*. The two types of companies differ primarily in their techniques for the purchase and issue of their own stock. Closed-end companies issue only a fixed amount of stock that is not sold directly to the public; it is usually sold through an investment bank. Nor, once the stock has been purchased by the public, can it be sold back to the company, like the stock of an open-end investment company. Closed-end investment company stock can only be resold through some form of stock exchange to other individuals who are willing to purchase it. (The data on these companies is relatively incomplete, so none is presented here.) Closed-end and open-end investment companies *are* comparable, however, in that their fundamental purpose is to make earnings by wise investments in the stocks of other corporations.

SUMMARY

We have now briefly examined the sources and uses of the funds of our major financial institutions. The results of this survey are summarized in Table 8–8. In general, those financial institutions which receive a large proportion of their funds from savers tend to put their funds into uses that

---

[16] *Ibid.,* p. 758. Market value is measured as market value at end of period less current liabilities.

yield a return over a long period of time. This is characteristic of mutual savings banks, savings and loan associations, and life insurance companies. Credit unions are a clear-cut exception. They appear to fill a gap left by other financial institutions; no other credit institution concentrates in extending short-term credit to small savers in the relatively low-income groups.

Those financial institutions which receive a large fraction of their funds from capital accounts and borrowings tend to put their funds to uses that produce a high yield, but are also highly liquid. Financial institutions that

TABLE 8–8. PRINCIPAL SOURCES AND USES OF FUNDS, BY TYPE OF
FINANCIAL INSTITUTION

TYPE OF FINANCIAL INSTITUTION	PRINCIPAL SOURCES OF FUNDS	PRINCIPAL USES OF FUNDS
Commercial banks	Demand deposits Time deposits	Commercial and industrial loans Real estate loans Consumer credit U.S. government bonds U.S. government short-term securities State and local government securities Cash assets
Mutual savings banks Savings and loan associations Life insurance companies	Deposits Savings capital Premium payments Earnings	Mortgages Mortgages Corporate bonds Mortgages Government securities
Credit unions Pension funds (noninsured)	Savings capital Premium payments	Consumer credit Corporate stock Corporate bonds
Other insurance companies	Premium payments Capital accounts	Corporate stock State and local government securities U.S. government securities
Finance companies	Borrowings Capital accounts	Consumer credit
Investment companies	Capital accounts	Corporate stock

need funds on short notice to pay casualty claims (fire and casualty insurance companies), to repay borrowings (finance companies), or to redeem shares of stock (open-end finance companies) tend to invest their funds in highly liquid assets that can quickly be converted into cash. Of course, these assets are also somewhat risky, which accounts for their relatively high yield. Principal among these uses of funds are corporate stock and consumer credit. Uninsured pension funds are, to a certain extent, an exception. They receive their funds from premium payments and are able to predict with considerable accuracy their annual need for funds. Nevertheless, they tend to invest in both stocks and bonds. One important reason for this is probably the high yield obtained from stocks in our relatively prosperous postwar era.

The sources and uses of commercial bank funds differ sharply from those of other financial institutions. The main reason for this is the wide range of services that banks in the United States provide for their customers. Demand deposit accounts are maintained; these accounts can be converted into cash on demand. Hence, large volumes of commercial bank uses of funds must be of a highly liquid nature. Short-term government securities, commercial and industrial loans, and consumer credit fill this need. Banks also maintain time deposit accounts, such as savings deposits, which have a relatively slow turnover rate. Funds from time deposits permit commercial banks to invest in relatively safe, long-term, interest-yielding assets such as real-estate loans and U.S. government bonds.

NONBANK FINANCIAL INSTITUTIONS AND THE ECONOMY

Most nonbank financial institutions are financial intermediaries that help channel funds from savers to borrowers. This is certainly a useful, and apparently innocent, function. Financial intermediaries create many problems for the economy, however.

Nonbank financial institutions create forms of liquid wealth that compete with money. There are many forms of wealth; real wealth and the liquid-wealth claims are the two inclusive categories. People are confronted with a choice between the alternative forms of both liquid and non-liquid wealth. As was shown in Chapter 5, the greater the extent to which nonbank financial institutions successfully induce people to maintain their liquid-wealth holdings in the form of savings bank deposits, savings and loan association share accounts, or life insurance policies instead of money, the weaker the control of our monetary authorities over the economy becomes. Monetary policy operates directly only on commercial banks. This is the first problem created for our economy by the operations of nonbank financial institutions; they are responsible for an apparent weakening of our economic control mechanism. Should there be increased regulation of nonbank financial institutions? This is but one of the numerous policy questions that are considered in Part IV of the text.

A second problem arising out of increased nonbank financial institution operations is that of increased spending during periods of economic boom. Such periods call for spending restraint. Our monetary authorities, by limiting commercial bank lending activity, attempt to dampen spending and hence reduce the demand for goods. If, at this same time, savers are induced to switch from holding demand or time deposit accounts at commercial banks to the liquid-wealth forms created by nonbank savings institutions, however, funds may become activated. Savings institutions do not hold their increased money balances idle. They lend them to consumers in the form of installment loans, to home buyers for home construction and improvement purposes, or to businesses for capital expenditure. When the borrowed funds are spent, spending increases. The demand for goods and services rises. In a relatively high employment economy, spending and the demand for goods may rise faster than the ability of the economy to furnish the desired goods and services. Thus, the result is a rise in prices rather than an increased output of goods and services.

There does not have to be a change in the stock of money for this to occur, merely an increase in its use. A rise in the velocity of circulation of money acts in the same manner on total spending as the spending of an increased stock of money—it raises it. Nonbank financial institutions contribute to these inflationary pressures by helping to transfer money balances from savers, who are not active spenders, to actively spending borrowers.

There is some evidence that this is the process by which a substantial part of the price rises and output increases of the 1950's occurred. Consider the following two periods of rapid growth: 1951 and 1955–57. Wholesale prices increased 11 percent in 1951. The stock of money in that year increased from $115.5 billion at the end of 1950 to $122.1 billion at the end of 1951. Gross national product rose from $284.6 to $329.0 billion. The income velocity of money, or the number of times that the supply of money is spent on gross national product during a year, is computed by dividing gross national product by a representative stock of money figure for the year in question. Applying this measure to the case at hand, we find that income velocity rose from 2.52 in 1950 to 2.77 in 1951.[17] Thus, while gross national product increased 16 percent, the stock of money rose only 5 percent. This money therefore had to circulate more rapidly, and, indeed, velocity increased approximately 11 percent. This increase in velocity was twice as important for the growth in gross national product in 1951 as the increase in the stock of money.

In the second period, the recession year of 1954 through prosperous 1957, the stock of money increased from an average money supply of $130.0 billion in 1954 to a supply of $136.0 billion in 1957, an increase of only 5 percent. Prices in that period increased from 110.3 percent of 1947–49 wholesale prices to 117.6 percent in 1957. Gross national product, however, rose from $363.1 billion to $442.8 billion, an increase of 22 percent. Income velocity rose from 2.79 in 1954 to 3.26 in 1957, an increase of 17 percent. Here again, increased velocity was more important than increased money balances as a means of financing the growth of gross national product— more than three times as important! This clearly illustrates that if increased money balances are not available to finance increased output, then the

---

[17] The data in this section are taken from various issues of the *Federal Reserve Bulletin.* The stock of money figures used in the computation of income velocity is the average of successive end-of-year figures.

increase in output will stop or the existing money supply will be utilized more intensively.

Much of this increase in velocity is attributable to the lending activity of nonbank financial institutions. The relatively rapid growth of nonbank financial intermediaries, as shown in Table 8–2, supports this view. Of course, it would be unfair to ascribe all of the increase to these financial institutions. Increased loan activity of commercial banks in a period of prosperity can be another source of increased spendings. Householders also tend to increase their rate of spending during such periods. All of this increased spending of a slowly rising money supply leads to an increase of both the output of goods and services and the prices of that output. As full employment is approached, the effects will tend to be concentrated on price-level increases.

The third problem created by the growth of nonbank financial institutions is that of the multiplication of claims to real wealth in the economy. It has already been pointed out that the claims created by these institutions make monetary control of the economy more difficult. Actually, the enormous magnitude of these claims relative to the stock of money is itself a potential source of economic difficulty. Liquid wealth is a claim to real wealth. While an increase in the volume of liquid wealth may induce increased spending, and hence increased output, the mere multiplication of claims does not itself increase the physical volume of real wealth in the economy.

Furthermore, real wealth can only be purchased with money. The more other forms of liquid wealth increase relative to money, the more difficult it may become to convert them into money. In the event of economic stress people may want to convert the liquid wealth created by these institutions into money, since that is the most liquid of all assets. In periods of rapidly rising prices, people may come to expect a continuation of rising prices. As a consequence most forms of liquid wealth, including money itself, will be losing purchasing power. There may then be an attempt to "get out of" other liquid wealth and into money, for the ultimate purpose of getting into goods. The total amount of liquid wealth, however, is several times the volume of money in the economy. Hence, not all the claims to money can actually be redeemed. A concerted attempt of the American public to transform a major portion of their liquid-wealth holdings into money could conceivably result in financial chaos comparable to that of the early 1930's.

Fortunately, several forms of non-money liquid wealth, such as time deposits in commercial banks and mutual savings banks, and savings and loan association share accounts, carry some form of federal insurance. Although the present assets of the federal insuring corporations are inadequate to meet all possible demands for converting insured liquid wealth into money, it is generally believed by economists that the mere existence of the insurance may prevent the public from starting a financial panic. This "psychological" restraint on panics, however, applies only to recession situations. What about "runs" on financial institutions that might occur with the expectation of sharply rising prices? Deposit insurance here would do little good because people would be demanding money in order to spend it. Thus, insurance would not restrain people from converting "near money" into money. Hopefully we shall not be confronted with this situation if the relatively conservative monetary-fiscal policies of the last decade are continued. It is usually only when a nation's spending and money-creating activities are unrestrained that great inflations take place and there is a general abandonment of both money and other liquid-wealth holdings.

These three problems—a weakening of the effectiveness of our monetary controls, increased velocity in periods of prosperity, and the multiplication of claims to real wealth—are not problems created by nonbank financial institutions alone. Commercial banks, individuals, and government all contribute to them. We have concentrated on nonbank financial institutions, however, because their lending activities and liquid-wealth creation have expanded more rapidly than those of commercial banks and thus contributed significantly to the policy problems discussed. A further development of these problems is reserved for the theory and policy discussions of Parts III and IV.

Supplementary Readings

Gurley, John G., and Edward S. Shaw. *Money in a Theory of Finance.* Washington, D.C., Brookings Institution, 1960.

Simons, Henry C. "Rules Versus Authorities in Monetary Policy," reprinted in American Economic Association, *Readings in Monetary Theory*, Homewood, Ill., Irwin, 1951, pp. 337–68.

Tobin, James, and William C. Brainard. "Financial Intermediaries and the Effectiveness of Monetary Controls." *American Economic Association Papers and Proceedings*, (1963), pp. 383–400.

PART II

*Money
and Government*

Chapter 9

The Historical Development
of Banking in the United States

Money consists of currency created by the federal government and demand deposits created by the commercial banking system. From the earliest days of our nation's history the American government has attempted to regulate money. At various times in our history Congress has placed the United States on bimetallic, gold coin, paper, and modified gold monetary standards. Congress has also created the First Bank of the United States, the Second Bank of the United States, a National Banking System, and, finally, our present Federal Reserve System. This chapter briefly examines the historical development of monetary standards and banking in the United States, with emphasis on the shaping influence of the government.

MONETARY STANDARDS
IN THE UNITED STATES

It will be recalled that the dollar is the unit of account in the United States. All debts, prices, and types of money are counted in terms of the dollar. Once a price for a good is established, we know how much money must be given up to acquire the good. Today this unit of account, the dollar, is an abstract measure of value; it is no longer domestically tied to a specific commodity. Officially the dollar is tied to gold: an ounce of gold is defined by law as being worth $35. However, no form of money, currency or deposits, can be redeemed in gold by citizens of the United States. Currency is our money of ultimate redemption. For this reason we say that the United States presently has an *internal paper standard;* that is, money can be redeemed only by currency, most of which is in the form of paper currency. Externally, of course, the United States is on the *gold standard,* since foreign claims on the United States must be met in gold at the discretion of foreign governments.

This distinction between our internal and external monetary standards has prevailed since the passage of the Gold Reserve Act of 1934. It has taken a long time for this characteristic of the contemporary American economy to be recognized by the general public, however. The Federal Reserve System continues to print currency bearing the designation, "will pay to the bearer on demand _____ dollars." The recent issues of $1 and $5 Federal Reserve notes, however, simply state, "_____ dollars." The designation "will pay to the bearer on demand _____ dollars" has been dropped, in recognition of the fact that currency, not gold, is the actual money of ultimate redemption. Nonetheless, this change in the labeling of our currency caused considerable consternation among Congressmen.

U.S. currency and the unit of account have not always been divorced internally from specific commodities such as gold or silver. This is a comparatively recent development, which began on a permanent basis in 1934. For most of its history, the United States has been on some type of metallic standard.

The Period of Bimetallism

1792–1834. Under a bimetallic standard the unit of account is tied to two money metals, usually gold and silver. The first monetary standard in the United States was bimetallic. The *Coinage Act of 1792* defined the dollar as being equal either to 371.25 grains of silver or to 24.75 grains of gold. This meant that anyone bringing gold or silver to the mint could have it coined without charge. The legally defined mint ratio of silver to gold was 15 to 1 (371.25/24.75 = 15). A given amount of gold was, therefore, legally worth 15 times as much as an equal amount of silver. At that time, however, the actual market exchange ratio of silver to gold was about 15.5 to 1. Thus Congress undervalued gold and overvalued silver. As a consequence only one money metal, silver, circulated in the United States. The intent of Congress had clearly been that both gold and silver coin should circulate, however, since the amount of either metal in the United States was insufficient by itself to meet domestic currency needs. If the bimetallic standard had legally priced gold and silver closer to the market ratio, both metals would probably have circulated. The disparity between the mint and world ratios for gold and silver drove gold from circulation. Since gold in the United States was worth less silver at the mint than in the world market, little gold was brought to the mint for coinage. Silver, however, had a high price at the mint and a large amount of silver coinage took place.

Other circumstances combined to prevent even the freshly minted silver coin from having a wide circulation within the United States. American silver dollars found their way into the West Indies where Spanish and American silver dollars circulated side by side, each equally acceptable. Unworn Spanish dollars were actually heavier than American silver dollars, however, so a trade in Spanish and American silver dollars developed. American dollars were exchanged for the Spanish dollars with the heavier silver content and then were melted and minted in the United States into new American silver dollars. Thus there developed a flow of American silver dollars to the West Indies, and a return flow of a roughly equivalent number of Spanish dollars to the United States. Once these were melted, a greater number of American silver dollars were minted; these then flowed back to the West Indies. As a result, American silver dollars failed to circulate in the United States. Lower denomination American coin and light weight, worn foreign coin circulated in the United States.[1] To put a halt to the outflow of silver caused by the failure of American silver dollars to remain in circulation in the United States, the treasury stopped coining silver in 1805. This suspension continued until 1834.

During the period *1792 to 1834*, therefore, the *United States was legally on a bimetallic standard*, but *in fact, it was on a silver standard*. The currency in circulation consisted of worn foreign coin, small denomination American coin, and banknotes. More will be said about banknotes in a subsequent section of this chapter.

Gresham's Law. The reasons for the outflow of gold and high denomination silver coin during this period may also be explained by reference to a principle called *Gresham's Law*, which states that "bad money drives out good." This simply means that a money form will be used where its value is the greatest. Under the bimetallic standard, when the mint ratio departs from the market ratio, there will tend to be an outflow of one money metal to where its value is greatest. Gold was undervalued in the United States from 1792 to 1834, so it flowed abroad. Silver was overvalued in the United States during the same period, so it flowed into the United States. The heavier weight of Spanish silver dollars offset this inflow, however, and led to an outflow of the lighter weight American dollars to the West Indies.

1834–1861. The United States continued on the bimetallic standard from 1834 to 1861, but during this period the standard became a *de facto gold standard*. This began in 1834 when Congress changed the legal ratio of silver to gold. Silver was kept at 371.25 grains to the dollar, but gold was changed to 23.22 grains to the dollar. This boosted the mint ratio to approximately 16 to 1. Congress hoped that the new mint ratio would return the United States to a de facto bimetallic standard, but again Congress miscalculated. The United States was too small a nation at the time to dominate the world price of gold and silver; changes in the American mint ratio had little influence on world gold and silver market prices. Since the market ratio of gold to silver was still approximately 15.5 to 1, gold became overvalued and silver undervalued in the United States.

---

[1] At that time it was legally permissible for foreign coin to circulate freely in the United States. This privilege was gradually restricted and finally terminated in 1857.

Gold was now brought to the U.S. mint for coining instead of silver. The outflow of large denomination silver coins increased. Small denomination silver coins remained in circulation, but there was little new minting of silver coin. This contributed to a shortage of low denomination coin. It was impractical to mint low denomination gold coins. Since the mint price of gold was 16 times that of silver, a low denomination gold coin would have had to be either very small in size or a mixture of a small amount of gold and a large amount of some other metal. Hence, to increase the amount of coins in circulation, Congress reduced the silver content of subsidiary silver coins in 1853. From that date to the present, our subsidiary silver coin has not contained an amount of silver equal in value to the face value of the coin.

1861–1873. The United States officially continued on a bimetallic standard until 1873. From 1861 to 1879, however, we were actually on a *paper standard*. Faced with the necessity of financing the Northern war effort, Congress authorized the Treasury to issue $450 million in "greenbacks," an irredeemable paper currency designed to serve as legal tender. It was not until 1879 that redemption of these greenbacks in gold specie was permitted. Greenbacks are now known as "United States notes" and are still being issued today. The total issuance of United States notes is limited by law to $347 million, however.

The Gold Standard

The silver question. The United States continued on a de facto paper standard from 1873 to 1879, but the period of the legal gold standard started prior to the resumption of specie payments in 1879. The Coinage Act of 1873 made no provision for coining silver dollars. In effect, this failure to provide for silver coinage put the United States on a legal gold standard, although low denomination subsidiary silver coin could still be minted.

At the time this action meant little, since greenbacks were not being redeemed in either gold or silver. It came to have meaning, however, when, due to a sharp increase in world silver production, there was a fall in the market price of silver. This produced a clamor for "free silver" and a silver standard in the United States. The agitation was so strong that silver purchase acts were passed in 1878 and 1890. These acts provided that the Treasury should purchase silver at a given price and issue silver coin and silver certificates.

The silver purchase acts of 1878 and 1890 were the first of a long series of acts designed to protect silver-producing interests in the United States. Additional silver purchase acts were passed in 1893, 1918, 1934, 1939, and 1946. These acts provided a firm market price for silver producers. Whenever the market price tended to fall beneath the Treasury buying price, producers could sell their output to the Treasury. This policy of protection continued until 1963, when Congress repealed the silver purchase acts and permitted the Federal Reserve System to replace silver certificates with Federal Reserve notes. Silver is now used only in coins and as backing for silver certificates still outstanding.

Actually, the concessions made to the silver interests by the various silver purchase acts were comparatively minor. Silver-backed paper currency and silver coin have remained a small part of our total currency supply.

1873–1933. Although the United States was legally on the gold standard in 1873, the de facto paper standard continued until 1879. The *Resumption Act of 1875* required that the U.S. Treasury begin the redemption of greenbacks in 1879. Actual resumption, the conversion of currency into gold on demand, started in *1879.* It was this action that placed the United States on both a *legal and a de facto gold standard.* Gold coins were minted and gold certificates were issued that were fully backed by gold held in the Treasury.

Some doubt existed, however, concerning the legality of the gold standard. The widespread demands for "free silver" are indicative of this. The controversy was finally settled by the *Gold Standard Act of 1900,* which explicitly stated that the United States, like the leading European powers, was on a gold standard. The United States continued on this standard until 1933. With the exception of the World War I period, 1917 to 1919, U.S. currency could be redeemed in gold until 1933.

1933; 1934–1964. Until 1933 gold coins, gold certificates, Federal Reserve notes, and the various forms of Treasury currency circulated in the United States. All were considered legal tender. The volume of gold coins and gold certificates in circulation, however, tended to diminish after the establishment of the Federal Reserve System. After 1917, member banks were required to keep all of their reserves in the form of deposits with the Federal Reserve banks. This caused a large transfer of gold from the vaults of member banks to those of the Federal Reserve banks. In addition, the Federal Reserve replaced gold certificates in circulation with its own Federal Reserve notes. These actions led to a reduction of the amount of gold and gold certificates in circulation.

In the 1930's it became increasingly difficult for the large industrialized nations to remain on the gold standard. The depression caused the principal trading nations of the world to abandon the gold standard in favor of monetary policies more conducive to internal economic stability (see Chapter 26 for a discussion of this point). By 1933 the United States was one of the few nations continuing on the gold standard. The widespread bank failures that accompanied the depression in 1933 then caused the United States to *abandon gold.* The nonbank public and the commercial banks were required to turn in all holdings of gold coin, bullion, and certificates to the Federal Reserve banks. This action took the United States off the gold standard internally. In addition, the United States stopped exporting gold; this took the United States off the gold standard externally as well. Thus, in 1933, the United States went on a *legal and de facto paper standard both domestically and externally*. Obligations could only be redeemed in paper currency.

In *1934* the United States returned to a gold standard, but one which may be more accurately described as a *modified gold standard*. Prior to 1934, an ounce of gold was legally worth $20.67. The new legal price of gold as set forth in the *Gold Reserve Act of 1934* was $35 an ounce. It remains at this level today.

In addition, the Gold Reserve Act of 1934 prohibited any further gold coinage and declared all gold certificates to be the property of the Federal Reserve, and all gold coin and bullion the property of the U.S. Treasury. As a result, gold coin and certificates can no longer be used for transactions within the United States. The private sector of the economy is prohibited from owning gold except as jewelry or for industrial purposes. Paper currency is now the money of ultimate redemption. Thus the United States has been on a *de facto paper standard internally since 1934*, even though the dollar is legally defined as having a gold content.

The Gold Reserve Act of 1934 also authorized the Treasury to regulate the export of gold. Since that time the Treasury has used gold to settle international claims on American dollars. This means that the United States is on both a *legal and a de facto gold standard in international transactions*.

BANKING IN THE UNITED STATES FROM *1791* TO THE PRESENT

The First Bank of the United States, 1791–1811

Congress has often readjusted our monetary standard, the principal changes having come in 1834, 1861, 1873, 1879, 1933, and 1934. Similarly, the development of banking in the United States has been shaped largely by governmental action.

In 1791, Congress chartered the First Bank of the United States. The establishment of this bank was due largely to the efforts of Alexander Hamilton, our first Secretary of the Treasury, and other advocates of a central banking institution.

At the time, there were only three commercial banks in the United States. Their ability to issue currency was limited, and state governments were forbidden to print currency. The bimetallic standard was still in the process of being moved through Congress under Hamilton's guidance; coinage of gold and silver by the U.S. mint would not start until after the Mint Act of 1792. As a consequence, there was generally a shortage of money. The First

Bank of the United States was designed to be a source of currency convertible into specie and to operate both as a commercial bank and as fiscal agent for the U.S. government.

The First Bank of the United States received its charter from Congress in 1791 and began operations with its head office in Philadelphia. In time it operated eight branches in important domestic trading centers. In brief, the principal provisions of the charter authorized the First Bank to (1) have a capitalization of $10 million (25,000 shares were to be issued with a value of $400 each, of which $2 million in stock was to be purchased by the government and the remaining $8 million was to be sold to the public; foreigners could own stock, but only U.S. citizens could vote their shares by proxy), (2) issue up to $10 million in paper currency in denominations of $5 and up (these notes were the equivalent of legal tender because they could be used to pay debts to the U.S. government), (3) receive deposits, (4) make loans, (5) act as fiscal agent for the federal government, and (6) act as a clearing mechanism for other banks. Among the restrictions placed on the Bank was the provision that forbade loans on real estate and commodities. This prevented the Bank from engaging in speculative ventures that had frequently been the downfall of less well-managed state banks.

Opposition to the establishment of the Bank was strong. Thomas Jefferson was a leading opponent, for example, arguing that the Bank was unconstitutional. Others contended that the First Bank would inhibit the development of private banking in the United States, that it would be a monopoly and abrogate the powers of state governments. Even after its chartering, the First Bank of the United States encountered strong opposition. Rural interests that needed easy credit to meet the demands for funds in the expanding frontier areas, farm debtors, and commercial banks were particularly vocal in their opposition.

Commercial banks, for example, objected to the Bank's unwillingness to accept the notes of banks that refused to redeem their notes in specie (gold and silver). This policy made it difficult for many commercial banks to expand loans. Banks at that time created bank notes in much the same way as they create demand deposits today.[2] Each commercial bank could create paper currency (bank notes) when extending loans. Borrowers usually took the proceeds of their loans in the form of bank notes rather than in specie. As these bank notes were spent, they passed into circulation in the economy. The notes were liabilities of the issuing bank and were presumedly redeemable in gold and silver coin. If the issuing bank had a good reputation and adequate specie reserves to cover demands for specie, its notes achieved a wide circulation. On the other hand, a bank that was illiquid, made risky loans, overextended note issues relative to specie holdings, or made it difficult for noteholders to redeem its currency soon found that its notes had become generally unacceptable. By refusing to accept and redeem notes of

---

[2] Today, only the Federal Reserve and the U.S. Treasury can create paper money.

overextended banks, the First Bank of the United States hoped to restrain excessive issues of state bank notes. This encountered strong state bank opposition.

In addition, the First Bank's combination of public and private functions aroused strong state bank resentment. They felt that this represented unfair competition. The First Bank was the only private commercial bank operating with a national charter. It also acted as a central bank by regulating state bank note issues and, as fiscal agent for the Treasury, it held federal funds.

There were also many who objected to the large volume of Bank stock held by foreigners, even though this stock did not carry voting privileges except by proxy. In sum, the opposition to the Bank was so strong that Congress failed to renew its charter in 1811. The First Bank of the United States, by assuming the responsibilities of a central bank in regulating the nation's currency, had run counter to rural interests, proponents of state rights, and commercial banks.

State Banking, 1811–1816

When the First Bank of the United States closed its doors for the last time in 1811, the restraint on unsound bank note issues was eliminated. The United States then entered into a period of rapid state bank growth. The number of commercial banks' rose from 88 in 1811 to 246 in 1816. Bank mismanagement also increased, however.

Speculative excesses occurred and inflation ensued. By 1814 state banks were no longer able to redeem notes in specie. Paper currency had been issued to excess. It has been estimated that the volume of state bank notes in circulation tripled from 1811 to 1816.[3]

Not all of this financial difficulty was caused by the closing of the First Bank. This was also the period of the Napoleonic Wars, in which the United States became involved through the War of 1812. Europe, like the United States, was experiencing currency problems. For example, from 1797 to 1821 the Bank of England refused to redeem its notes in specie; as a consequence, overissue occurred and inflation followed. The American experience was not unique.

The absence of a central bank hampered the financing of the War of 1812. The Treasury could have refused to accept depreciated state bank notes in payment of debt, but it did not choose to do so. Instead, it tried to persuade state banks to resume specie payments. This effort proved unsuccessful. It appears, therefore, that part of our difficulties arose from the failure of the Treasury to act as a monetary authority in the absence of a central bank.

[3] Leon M. Schur, "The Second Bank of the United States and the Inflation after the War of 1812," *The Journal of Political Economy* (1960), pp. 118–34.

The Second Bank of the United States, 1816–1836

The drive for specie resumption led to the establishment of the Second Bank of the United States in 1816. The charter provisions passed by Congress were not unlike those of the First Bank. The major difference was that the Second Bank was larger. Its capitalization was greater, and it eventually operated a total of twenty-five branches.

The principal charter provisions authorized the bank to (1) have a capitalization of $35 million, 20 percent going to the government and 80 percent to the public; (2) issue up to $35 million in paper currency in denominations of $5 and up (these notes were to be legal tender for payments of debts to the United States government); (3) receive deposits; (4) make loans; (5) act as fiscal agent for the federal government; and (6) act as a clearing mechanism for other banks. The Bank's charter was to run for twenty years.

The Second Bank had an even stormier history than the First Bank. In its early years, the Second Bank was badly managed. Loans were made to stockholders who used stock as collateral. Investments were expanded too swiftly; the Second Bank's own note issue was increased too quickly. The Bank's first president, William Jones, a political appointee who was not a banker, actually speculated in the Bank's stock. Jones finally resigned in 1818 and Langdon Cheeves, another nonbanker, became the Bank's second president. He succeeded in bringing some stability to operations, however.

Although the Second Bank of the United States was mismanaged in its early years, the principal charge against it was that it failed to prevent inflation in 1817 and 1818. It will be recalled that one of the primary reasons for establishing the Second Bank had been to put a stop to the inflation that had been caused by the excessive issue of state bank notes. This inflation was not halted by the founding of the Second Bank. Part of the blame, however, has to be placed upon the Secretary of the Treasury, William Crawford, who pressured the Second Bank into accepting the notes of banks with questionable reserves. Crawford was primarily interested in minimizing losses to the Treasury that could result from the closing of over-extended state banks.[4]

The Second Bank finally began to follow a restrictive policy in the latter part of 1818. It refused to accept the notes of state banks that did not redeem in specie and it also restricted its own lending activity. It did this chiefly because its own specie reserve position was in danger. Unfortunately, the timing of this restrictive action was bad; it aggravated a sharp economic contraction that subsequently occurred in 1818 and 1820. This depression of 1818–20 was probably initiated by a drop in the foreign demand for agricultural goods, but the decrease in the stock of money result-

---

[4] *Ibid.*, p. 120.

ing from the Bank's restrictive policy certainly accelerated the depression. At the time, however, the Second Bank received almost all of the blame for the depression. The Bank's opposition even went so far as to instigate an unsuccessful attempt to have its charter revoked.

From 1820 on, the Second Bank operated on a relatively sound basis, particularly after Nicholas Biddle became the Bank's president in 1823. Biddle operated the Bank both as a private profit-making commercial bank and as a central bank for the nation. He tried to restrain excessive state bank note issues, particularly those of southern and western banks and, with increased Bank pressure, resumption of specie payments became fairly widespread.

With the election of Andrew Jackson to the U.S. Presidency in 1828, political difficulties again beset the Second Bank. Jackson was sympathetic to southern and western interests, which were mistrustful of eastern bankers, among other things.

In 1832, four years prior to charter expiration, Congress rechartered the Second Bank. Jackson vetoed the bill, however. In 1833, Jackson transferred federal deposits from the Second Bank to various private "pet banks." Biddle countered this action by contracting the Second Bank's assets and demand liabilities.[5] The result was a nationwide economic contraction. Needless to say, there was no renewal of the Bank's charter when it expired in 1836.[6] This "bank war" between Biddle and Jackson spelled the end of central banking in the United States until the establishment of the Federal Reserve System in 1913.

State Banking, 1836–1863

The period 1836 to 1863 was an era of state banking. Most legitimate banks operated on charters obtained from state legislatures or state banking authorities. There was no one central banking authority charged with supervising the stability of state bank notes or with regulating speculative lending operations by commercial banks.

As a result, there was financial chaos throughout most of this period. The number of banks increased rapidly in good times and decreased rapidly in recession; successive price inflations and deflations occurred. Many unsound loans were made, including illegal loans to stockholders. It was not uncommon for banks to have inadequate specie reserves, so that they were unable to redeem their bank note liabilities in specie. In fact, payment of specie was almost completely suspended from 1837 to 1842. The variety of bank

---

[5] For a discussion of this period see Jacob P. Meerman, "The Climax of the Bank War: Biddle's Contraction, 1833–34," *The Journal of Political Economy* (1963), pp. 378–88.

[6] For some years, the Bank tried to operate with a Pennsylvania charter, but it finally failed in 1841.

notes in circulation ran into the thousands, many, as might be expected, being counterfeit. Books were published describing which notes were good and which were bad, but the books were out-of-date even before they were printed.

Attempts were made to reform and regulate the banking system, but these were primarily regional efforts that did little to improve the nation-wide banking problem. The three main programs of reform were (1) the Suffolk System, (2) the Safety Fund System, and (3) free banking.

The Suffolk System was established in New England as early as 1824. Prior to 1824, the notes of banks outside of Boston had moved toward that city because of its financial importance in the New England area. Frequently, the notes of these outside banks did not circulate at par, whereas the notes of most Boston banks did. In fact, the more difficult it was for Boston banks to redeem the notes of outside banks, the greater the discount from par that these notes bore.

Thus, in conformity with Gresham's law, the good notes of the Boston banks were driven from circulation. People hoarded the notes of the Boston banks and used the depreciated currency of distant banks in their daily transactions. To remedy this situation, the Suffolk System was set up. Under this system, banks outside of Boston that wished to have their notes redeemed at par within the Boston area were required to maintain at least a $2,000 redemption fund account with the Suffolk bank. All notes of non-Boston banks received by the Boston banks were to be cleared by the Suffolk bank. If the "outside" banks refused to join the Suffolk System, the Suffolk bank would collect a large volume of their notes and then request redemption in specie. Naturally any bank with inadequate specie reserves was unable to meet such a sudden large demand for specie. In this fashion the Suffolk System rather effectively eliminated most speculative and excessive note issues from the New England area. Eventually almost all New England commercial banks became members of the system. It was only with the establishment of the National Banking System in 1863 that the need for the Suffolk System was eliminated.

The Safety Fund System was set up in 1829 by the New York state legislature. The principal function of this system was to protect depositors in the event of bank failure. Each bank in New York that was to receive a new charter or that requested renewal of its old one by the legislature was required to contribute an amount of money to the fund (to be held by the State Treasury) equal to 3 percent of its capital stock. Payments from the fund were to be made to creditors of banks that failed.

For a time the Safety Fund System worked successfully. This was during periods when bank failures were not widespread, however. With the demise of the Second Bank of the United States in 1836, bank failures became more extensive, particularly during the 1837–42 recession. The Safety Fund soon found that it did not have adequate funds to meet the claims of the creditors of all the banks that failed in this period. Legislation was then passed limiting insurance to the claims of noteholders only, not all creditors. The Fund continued to operate under the new arrangements for several decades, but it rapidly diminished in importance after 1846.

There are several reasons why the Safety Fund System gradually became less important. First, the bank failures from 1837 to 1842 demonstrated that a fund limited in scope to a small area of the country is unlikely to be able to stave off nationwide financial panic. Second, New York adopted "free banking" in 1846. Under free banking new banks were no longer required to get their charters from the state legislature, as banks that were members of the Fund had had to do. Finally, the establishment of the National Banking System in 1863 provided nationwide note stability.

Although the Safety Fund became relatively unimportant, it was the first major attempt in our banking system to insure bank creditors. Today, of course, Federal Reserve notes are legal tender, and for funds on deposit we have a nationwide system of deposit insurance under the auspices of the Federal Deposit Insurance Corporation.

Free banking was another answer to the excesses of state banking. Free banking started first in the State of New York with the passage of the Free Banking Act of 1838. A similar program was adopted at about the same time in Michigan. Under the New York plan any group of people could set up a bank, provided they deposited various state and United States bonds with the state comptroller in an amount equal to the volume of notes to be issued. In the event of bank failure, the comptroller was to pay the note-holders out of the proceeds of the sale of these assets deposited with him. The purpose of the act was to standardize procedures for the establishment of banks and to free banks from dependency upon the whims and political pressures of state legislatures. No longer, for example, could legislators demand bank stock in exchange for their vote in favor of granting a bank a charter.

Some fifteen states adopted free banking laws prior to 1860. One difficulty with the free banking system of this period was that frequently it was too easy for individuals to set up banks that complied with state requirements. Reserve requirements often did not exist, or were far too lenient. As a result, too many banks were established within a relatively short period of time, many with inadequate specie reserves, and too many risky loans were made.

Thus, *in the period of state banking from 1836 to 1863, the absence of a uniform currency and a central bank led to financial chaos.* There were a tremendous number of different bank notes in circulation, many of which were counterfeit. Charters came to be granted too freely. As a consequence, too many banks were weak and badly managed, and too many risky loans were made. Efforts at reform were regional in scope and thus unable to offer a solution to the national banking problem.

Much of this difficulty was caused by the closing of the Second Bank of the United States. At the time it was thought that the Treasury could regulate the banking system effectively by keeping federal funds in various "pet banks." These banks were supposed to maintain separate specie reserves to cover Treasury deposits. Frequently, however, these banks used Treasury deposits as a basis for expanding their own loans and note issues. Consequently, when these banks experienced financial difficulty, the Treasury often discovered that its funds could not be withdrawn.

Finally, the Treasury itself lost confidence in the "pet banks," and, after various abortive attempts at solutions, Congress set up the *Independent Treasury System* in 1846. Under this system, a series of subtreasuries were set up in various cities across the nation, where the Treasury could amass its funds. In this fashion, the Treasury gave up what few powers of monetary regulation it had had. Instead of using its deposits to keep state bank notes safe throughout the nation, it now confined itself to safeguarding its own funds. The Independent Treasury System did, in fact, safeguard federal funds, but in the process it left the banking system totally unregulated and it created some new difficulties.

For example, Treasury tax collections and Treasury expenditures did not coincide. When collections temporarily exceeded payments, a surplus would arise. Funds were withdrawn from the economy and held by the Treasury. This reduced the amount of specie reserves held by commercial banks and thereby lessened their ability to redeem notes. On the other hand, when Treasury payments exceeded tax collections, an increased amount of funds would flow to the banking system and provide the basis for bank note and loan expansion, some of which was speculative.

The Independent Treasury System continued to operate until 1920. As early as 1863, however, the Treasury was again permitted to keep funds in commercial banks in addition to its own Independent Treasury System. Gradually the Treasury came to realize that it should use its deposits at commercial banks in a way that would not affect bank specie reserves adversely.

The National Banking System, 1863–1913

The shortcomings of state banking were obvious. The problem was how to rectify the situation. There was considerable pressure for bank reform, but it was not until the Civil War that this agitation brought positive results with the passage of the National Banking Acts of 1863 and 1864. These acts did not reinstate centralized regulation of banking, but they did correct some of the deficiencies of state banking.

The National Banking Acts were designed to meet two broad goals—(1) to establish a safe currency system, and (2) to assist the Treasury in financing the Civil War. It is probable that it was the financial pressure of the war that caused this banking legislation to be passed. According to the terms of these acts, national banks were to be established that would issue paper currency and provide a market for U.S. government securities. As it developed, the national banks did not purchase a large volume of U.S. government securities during the Civil War, and thus they never became a principal source of funds for the Treasury.

The national banks, which, taken together, constituted the National Banking System, did provide a safe currency system for the United States, however. This was accomplished by limiting the amount of notes that national banks could issue to a maximum of 90 percent of their holdings in U.S. government securities. Since the federal government had budget surpluses throughout much of the time in which the National Banking System existed, there were several reductions in national debt which limited the supply of notes and contributed to their safety.

Principal Provisions of the National Banking Acts

In addition to a provision for the issuance of bank notes based upon U.S. government security holdings, the National Banking Acts of 1863 and 1864 had provisions concerning the chartering of banks, capital requirements, reserve requirements, government security holdings, and bank lending operations.

The granting of charters. Under the National Banking Acts, any group of five or more persons could apply for a charter from the Comptroller of the Currency in Washington, D.C. In essence, this amounted to a new system of free banking, although the Comptroller was often strict in his granting of charters. Banks receiving their charters from the Comptroller were called "national banks," to distinguish them from "state banks," which received their charters from state banking authorities. This distinction between state and national banks remains with us today, as will be recalled from Chapter 4.

Capital requirements. The minimum capital requirements for the establishment of national banks were (1) $50,000 for banks in cities of under 6,000 inhabitants, (2) $100,000 for banks in cities from 6,000 to 50,000 inhabitants, and (3) $200,000 for banks in cities with still larger populations. These requirements still apply today to national banks. Some 50 percent of the capital had to be paid in to the bank's managers before the bank could begin operations. Each share had a par value of $100. Stockholders were subject to double liability; that is, if the bank failed, the stockholder could be required to pay an amount of money equal to his original stock purchase. The funds would be used to meet the claims of the bank's creditors. This provision is no longer in effect.

Government security deposits and bank notes. Prior to beginning operations, a bank was required to deliver a given volume of U.S. government securities to the U.S. Treasury. These securities had to have a value of $30,000 or one-third the value of the bank's capital stock, depending on which figure was larger. Once the bonds were delivered to the Treasury, the banks could start issuing national bank notes in an amount equal to 90 percent of the value of the securities. In 1900 banks were permitted to issue an amount of notes equal to a full 100 percent of the value of the securities. In addition, each national bank was obligated to redeem the notes of any other national bank at par.

Although each national bank was authorized to issue notes if it met the preceding requirements, the actual printing of the currency was done by the U.S. Treasury so as to minimize the risk of counterfeiting.

These notes were not legal tender, but since they could be used to pay federal taxes at par, they were the equivalent of legal tender, just like the earlier notes of the First and Second Banks of the United States. It was not until 1933 that Congress declared national bank notes to be legal tender. Today there are still a few national bank notes in circulation, but they are all in process of retirement; no national bank notes have been issued since 1935. Private commercial banks are no longer permitted to issue paper currency. Only the Federal Reserve and the U.S. Treasury are authorized to issue paper currency and coin money.

As further insurance for the safety of national bank notes, Congress provided in the National Banking Acts of 1863 and 1864 that no bank could issue notes in excess of the volume of its own stock and that the total volume of national bank notes could not exceed $300 million. A particular bank's share in the $300 million depended on its size and location. These limitations were removed in 1875.

In the event of the failure of a national bank, the Comptroller of the Currency was authorized to sell the securities that had been deposited by the bank and to use the proceeds to redeem its notes. In addition, the national banks were required to maintain a "redemption fund" with the Comptroller equal to 5 percent of their outstanding notes.

Reserve requirements. National banks initially had one set of reserve requirements for both currency and deposit liabilities. The reserve requirements stipulated that banks designated as *central reserve city* and *reserve city* banks maintain reserves equal in value to 25 percent of their bank note and deposit liabilities. Banks in other cities were called *country banks*. They were to maintain reserves of 15 percent against notes and deposits. At first only New York was a central reserve city. In 1887, however, Chicago and St. Louis were also included in this category.

The reserves of central reserve city banks were to be vault cash in the form of "lawful money," by which was meant legal tender–specie and Treasury currency. National bank notes, of course, could not be used as reserves. Reserve city banks, on the other hand, needed to keep only one-half of their reserve requirement in the form of vault cash. The remaining portion could be in the form of deposits with central reserve city banks. The terms were even more lenient for country banks; only 40 percent of their reserves had to be in the form of vault cash. The remaining 60 percent could be in the form of deposits with either reserve city or central reserve city banks.

In 1874 the reserve requirement for notes was dropped altogether; reserves were now only required for deposits. As we shall discuss in a moment, the composition of the assets used to satisfy the reserve requirement turned out to be one of the principal shortcomings of the National Banking System.

Other charter provisions. The major limitation on the lending activity of national banks was the banning of real-estate loans. This rule is no longer in effect. In addition, loans to any one borrower could not exceed 10 percent of the value of the capital stock of the bank. This regulation still applies to national banks. Finally, national banks were permitted to serve as fiscal agents of the U.S. government.

The Tax on State Bank Note Issues; Renewed Growth of State Banking

The National Banking Acts were successful in providing a safe uniform currency. Although the number of state banks declined markedly in the face of competition from national banks, those remaining in operation continued to issue paper currency and many of these state banks issued excessive amounts of notes. Thus the National Banking Acts did not substantially improve the quality of *all* bank note issues. To correct this deficiency, Congress passed an act in 1865 that placed a 10 percent annual tax on all state bank note issues. This tax was so prohibitive that within a few years all state bank note issues were withdrawn from circulation. This, also caused the number of state banks to decline sharply.

The National Banking System did not spell the end of state banking, however. Banks had always considered the right of note issue a fundamental prerequisite for banking, but revolution was occurring in the banking habits of businesses and individuals, which soon invalidated that assumption. Following the Civil War, increasing use was made of deposit money; people found it more convenient to use demand deposits as a medium of exchange. State banks soon discovered that they could continue operations by creating deposits rather than currency. Bank customers seeking loans were willing to accept demand deposits in lieu of bank notes and, except for periods of financial panic, the turnover of deposits proved quite predictable. Thus, banks could operate much as they always had, now with reserves a fraction of deposits instead of a fraction of notes and deposits. Once banks became accustomed to operating under the new conditions, the number of state banks increased markedly. The number of national banks continued to mount also, but at a substantially slower rate than state banks.

Although many new banks felt that it would be to their advantage to give up the right of note issue for the prestige they would attain by becoming national banks, there were, nonetheless, several distinct advantages to a state charter. The rules and regulations of state authorities were more lax than those of the Comptroller of the Currency, even as they are today. Reserve requirements and required capitalization was usually lower for state than for national banks. State banks could make real estate loans, whereas national banks could not.

Principal Defects of the National Banking System

Inelasticity of bank note issue. The National Banking System did not provide for the needed seasonal, cyclical, or secular variation in currency. At seasonal peaks of business activity, for example, more currency and deposit money are needed. The volume of national bank notes was tied to the national debt, however, and the national debt is determined by federal surpluses and deficits, not by seasonal business activity. Thus, there was no room for a seasonal expansion of the currency supply.

More important than the seasonal inelasticity of national bank note issues was the cyclical and secular inelasticity of national bank notes. As the economy expands on the upward swing of the cycle, more currency is needed to carry on business activity. To the extent that expansion of business is in real output, an increase in money helps to finance the rise in economic activity. A growing economy needs additional currency and deposits to carry on a growing volume of transactions. Under the National Banking System, however, there was no mechanism for automatic note expansion. In point of fact, during the upward phase of the cycle, the federal government often found itself with a surplus which it used to retire part of the national debt. As national debt was retired, of course, the support for national bank notes decreased and their volume had to be reduced. Treasury surpluses were common throughout the 1880's and, as a consequence, the volume of national bank notes fell from $339 million in 1880 to a low of $165 million in 1891.[7] In later years surpluses were not as frequent, and by 1913 the volume of national bank notes had climbed to $745 million.[8] Thus national bank note variations were geared to national debt changes rather than to the economy's need for currency.

Other forms of currency did not have the desired elasticity in this period either. The volume of gold and silver coins in circulation depended upon foreign and domestic production of the money metals. This was also the

---

[7] Milton Friedman and Anna Schwartz, *A Monetary History of The United States, 1867–1960* (Princeton, N.J.: National Bureau of Economic Research, 1963), p. 131.
[8] *Ibid.*, p. 180.

case with paper gold and silver certificates, since they had to be backed fully by money metals. The greenbacks issued during the Civil War, which today we call United States notes, were limited in amount by Act of Congress. These limitations, together with the limits placed upon national bank note expansion, effectively prevented the needed flexibility in our paper currency and coinage.

Pyramiding of reserves. Another major shortcoming of the National Banking System was that it made possible a pyramiding of reserves. It will be recalled that, legally, the reserves of national banks consisted of vault cash and deposits at other national banks. The *ultimate reserves* of all national banks, however, consisted of vault cash, not deposits at other banks, since only vault cash could be used to redeem deposit liabilities.

Nonetheless, as country and reserve city banks made cash deposits with either reserve city or central reserve city banks, the total volume of reserves held by national banks would increase, and, accordingly, the loan and demand-deposit-creating ability of the banking system would rise also.

Assume, for example, that country banks had $1 million in vault cash and no deposits at other banks. Since country banks could maintain as much as three-fifths of their reserves as deposits at non-country national banks, under these conditions country banks could transfer $600,000 in cash to reserve city banks. Assume that country banks deposit $600,000 in cash with reserve city banks. This is shown by entries a:

BALANCE SHEET CHANGES FOR COUNTRY BANKS

ASSETS	LIABILITIES + CAPITAL ACCOUNTS
Reserves 　Vault cash　　　　−$600,000 (a) 　Deposits at reserve city banks 　　　　　　　+$600,000 (a)	

BALANCE SHEET CHANGES FOR RESERVE CITY BANKS

ASSETS	LIABILITIES + CAPITAL ACCOUNTS
Reserves 　Vault cash　　　+ $600,000 (a) 　Vault cash　　　− $300,000 (b) 　Deposits at central reserve city 　　banks　　　　+$300,000 (b)	Demand deposits due country banks 　　　　　+$600,000 (a)

BALANCE SHEET CHANGES FOR CENTRAL RESERVE CITY BANKS

ASSETS	LIABILITIES + CAPITAL ACCOUNTS
Reserves 　Vault cash　　　+$300,000 (b)	Demand deposits due reserve city 　　banks　　　　+$300,000 (b)

Country bank total reserves have not changed, but those of reserve city banks have risen by $600,000.

The process need not stop here. Reserve city banks were required to keep at least one-half of their reserves in the form of vault cash. Thus, reserve city banks could now transfer $300,000 in cash to deposit accounts at central reserve city banks. This transaction, as shown in the entries b above, results in another increase in reserves; central reserve city bank reserves have increased by $300,000. Thus, the initial $1 million in vault cash reserves has been pyramided to $1 million in vault cash reserves and $900,000 in reserves in the form of deposits at other banks.

So far this caused no economic difficulties. However, if reserve city and central reserve city banks expand loans and deposits on the basis of these increased reserves, then in the event of a call for cash from other banks, there could well be a shortage of cash reserves. A shortage of cash reserves could force banks to suspend specie payments and this might precipitate financial panic. As knowledge of a lack of liquidity became general, people would fear for the safety of their deposits and demand more cash. This would place added strain on the resources of the banking system. The financial panics of 1873, 1884, 1893, and 1907 were in large part an outgrowth of such reserve pyramiding and excessive deposit creation by reserve city and central reserve city banks. These panics were triggered by the currency drains that took place in periods of relative prosperity when banks were loaned up.

These difficulties could have been avoided if reserve city and central reserve city banks had kept enough vault cash on hand to back the deposit liabilities they owed other banks. Instead, as reserve city and central reserve city banks received cash deposits from other banks, they tended to consider this cash as part of their own reserves, and expanded loans and deposits as if they were receiving cash deposits from individuals. This is not to say that reserve city banks did not recognize their responsibility for maintaining funds to cover the deposits to other banks. The city banks were fully aware of this responsibility, particularly the large New York banks. They were private profit-seeking corporations in a highly competitive industry, however. As a result they felt obliged to keep their excess reserve positions low. Possible demands for cash by other banks were covered by the New York banks through call loans to stockbrokers. When pressed for funds from other banks, the New York banks could "call" back their funds from the brokers. These call loans were considered highly liquid.

The problem was, however, that if there were a widespread demand for cash throughout the economy, these call loans would prove to be non-liquid. Stockbrokers would not be able to get funds without selling stocks and causing a collapse of stock prices. Financial panic would follow in either case. Frequently these calls for cash would come when lending activity was high. Country banks would call for funds when farmers needed cash to help harvest and distribute crops in the fall. At the same time, however, central reserve city and reserve city banks were faced with loan demands from their own seasonal borrowers. There was no central bank to provide additional funds at such times, either.

If this was the case, why didn't the banks keep all reserves in cash form? Primarily for two reasons. First, demand deposits, until 1934, earned interest. Therefore, these funds were a source of earnings for banks with temporarily idle funds. Second, country banks maintained deposits with reserve city banks to secure the advantages of correspondent banking.

Another problem related to the pyramiding of reserves was the lack of any means of accumulating cash for the purpose of helping a bank in emergency. Each bank was prohibited from drawing down its vault cash beneath the required level. In effect, cash reserves were frozen at each national bank. As a result, although one bank might have a large volume of vault cash, it could not send any substantial amount to a bank in difficulty if this would entail a reduction in its own vault cash beneath the legal minimum. Once a bank's vault cash had sunk to its legal minimum, it had to close its vaults even if it had more than enough cash to cover a bank run.

Thus, under the National Banking System, cash flowed toward central reserve city and reserve city banks and, as this occurred, the loans and deposits of these banks increased. When, however, the depositing country banks converted their deposits into cash, reserve city and central reserve city banks were forced to contract these loans and investments so as to re-establish a favorable reserve position. If they were unable to do so, they suspended cash payment and precipitated a financial panic.

Rigid reserve requirements. A third shortcoming of the National Banking System was that for the time that a bank was short of reserves, it was required to suspend the granting of new loans. This type of regulation made for uncertainty for both borrowers and bank managers. Just when the demand for borrowing was strong, banks frequently had to halt the granting of new loans.

Inadequate check-clearing facilities. Finally, the clearing and collection mechanism for checks used by the National Banking System was archaic. There was no central check-clearing agency comparable to the system presently maintained by the Federal Reserve System (see Chapter 10). With a unit banking system consisting of thousands of banks, checks had to be cleared through an elaborate network of correspondent banking relationships. Had the United States had only a few banks with many branch offices like many European countries, the need for adequate check-clearing facilities would not have been so important. As it was, however, the correspondent clearing facilities were cumbersome. The cost of transferring funds between distant points was expensive, long delays frequently occurred in check clearing, and many banks did not redeem out-of-town checks at par.

Establishment of the Federal Reserve System

The shortcomings of the National Banking System became increasingly apparent with each successive financial panic. After the panic of 1907, a National Monetary Commission was set up to make a study of the situation. It made its report in 1910. On the basis of the findings in this report, a plan for bank reform called the *Aldrich Plan* was submitted to Congress. It called for the creation of a National Reserve Association that was to act as a central bank for the United States.

The Aldrich Plan, largely backed by the Republican party, encountered widespread opposition and was not brought out of committee by a Democratic House of Representatives. Reform legislation was needed, however, and Congress then passed the Federal Reserve Act in 1913 (largely a House bill) establishing the Federal Reserve System.

As originally conceived, the Federal Reserve System was designed not as a single strong central bank, but as a federation of largely autonomous regional central banks. Each regional bank was to be responsive to the unique needs of its area. It was hoped that this federated system could avoid the charge of "monopoly." People at that time feared centralization, as many do even today, equating it with authoritarianism and lack of individual freedom. In spite of the adverse experiences with state banking and the National Banking System, the public was not yet ready to accept central bank regulation. Many feared that under a centralized system our unit banks would be dominated by eastern banking interests; anything akin to either the First or Second Banks of the United States would have met fierce opposition.

This reluctance to accept a system of central banking the purpose of which was to help provide the economy with safe banks and a sound currency was a peculiarly American attitude. Other advanced nations of the Western world had long possessed central banks, some of which were even engaged in commercial banking, as the First and Second Banks of the United States had been. The Bank of England was established in 1694 and had a virtual monopoly of note issue very early in its history. The Bank of France, founded in 1800, has an extensive commercial banking operation, organized along branch banking lines. The German Reichsbank was set up in 1875, but it was actually an outgrowth of the Bank of Prussia, which was founded in 1765. Other European nations had long operated similar institutions.

The commercial banking systems of most of these nations differed from that of the U.S., however, in that they were generally dominated by a few large banks with extensive branch networks. Europeans were accustomed to big, powerful banks, and this may have made it easier for them to accept regulation from a strong central bank. The American tradition of small unit banking, of laissez faire, of private enterprise, made us naturally suspicious of any agency that appeared to foster bigness and regulation.

Federal Reserve Correction of National Bank Deficiencies

The Federal Reserve System was initially set up to correct the deficiencies of the National Banking System; it was not specifically designed to regulate the economy for purposes of economic stabilization, which is today the Federal Reserve System's most important function.

How did the Federal Reserve correct the shortcomings of the National Banking System? *First*, it introduced a mechanism for correcting inelasticity in the currency supply. Federal Reserve banks were authorized to issue a new type of bank note, Federal Reserve notes. Member banks could use their deposit accounts at Federal Reserve banks to acquire additional Federal Reserve notes as needed. If a bank's deposits at Federal Reserve banks were insufficient for this purpose, it could borrow from the Federal Reserve banks. Thus, commercial banks could always get additional currency from the Federal Reserve System. It was thought that this would help avoid the panics that had started when the customers of commercial banks feared that currency would not be available on demand. The new currency could also expand and contract to suit the demands of the public. The Federal Reserve Act did not eliminate other currency forms, however, it simply added a currency, Federal Reserve notes, which had the feature of elasticity. Today Federal Reserve notes have become our principal currency form.

Second, pyramiding of reserves became impossible for member banks. All national banks were required to become members of the new Federal Reserve System. Member banks maintained reserve deposit accounts with the Federal Reserve banks; deposits at other commercial banks no longer counted as member bank reserves. The Federal Reserve banks, in sharp contrast to central reserve city national banks, did not also operate as private commercial banks. Thus, when the district Federal Reserve banks received cash deposits from member banks, no expansion of loans and deposits could take place in the private sector of the economy.

Third, the Federal Reserve banks were to operate as banks for commercial banks. If commercial banks were short of reserves, they could borrow reserves from the Federal Reserve banks. This meant that member banks always had a source of additional reserves; they did not have to stop extending loans because they were temporarily deficient of reserves.

Fourth, the Federal Reserve banks provided an efficient mechanism for clearing and collecting checks throughout the country. This mechanism is briefly described in Chapter 10.

Early Shortcomings of the Federal Reserve System

Although the Federal Reserve System was able to solve many of the problems of the National Banking System, it also had some defects of its own. *First*, the Federal Reserve System did not make provisions for the safety of demand deposit money. It took the depression of the 1930's to bring this needed reform with the establishment of the Federal Deposit Insurance Corporation in 1934.

Second, according to the terms of the act it was not recognized that a central bank also has the important responsibility of stabilizing the economy. The Federal Reserve was originally viewed simply as a banker's bank. Federal Reserve banks were to be sources of currency and funds to meet the credit needs of the commercial banking system. This was a recurrent theme throughout the aforementioned corrections to the National Banking System. The Federal Reserve Act provided that the Federal Reserve banks "discount notes, drafts and bills of exchange issued or drawn for agricultural, industrial or commercial purposes, or the proceeds of which have been used for such purposes. . ."[9] This feature was included not only to protect banks and businesses in crisis, but also to take care of the ordinary needs of business for funds.

This amounted to an acceptance of the "real bills doctrine" or the "commercial loan theory of banking," which was briefly described in Chapter 3. In essence it was thought that the debts, or "paper," of its customers that a bank put up for borrowed funds should arise out of current production, since the production of real goods was believed to be the real source of funds for loan repayment. As was discussed previously, however, loans can prove illiquid in times of economic stress. Furthermore, expanding and contracting loans in accord with the "needs of trade" is a procyclical action. If full employment is reached, then the needed funds go to finance the operations of firms that successfully bid productive resources away from their competitors. Total output, however, remains unchanged. Thus, applying the real bills doctrine in periods of full employment only adds to inflationary pressures.

Fortunately, the Federal Reserve recognized the potential dangers of following the real bills doctrine as early as the 1920's. It was also during this period, as we shall discuss in some detail in Chapters 12 and 13, that the Federal Reserve began developing a sense of responsibility for the stabilization of economic activity.

Third, many economists believe that the depression of the thirties demonstrated that there was a shortage of contracyclical monetary tools at the disposal of the Federal Reserve. Accordingly, these powers were expanded to include reserve requirement manipulation and open-market policy

---

[9] Federal Reserve Board, *Annual Report* (1914), p. 17.

manipulation in the 1930's. As early as the 1920's it was made easier for member banks to borrow reserves. All of these techniques will be considered in Chapters 12 and 13.

Finally, the federated structure of the system created policy coordination problems. At first, the Federal Reserve Bank of New York tended to dominate the system, but the other district Federal Reserve banks sought to exercise more authority of their own. These organizational difficulties were resolved in the 1930's with the creation of our present Board of Governors.

As subsequent chapters will demonstrate, the Federal Reserve System has proved to be a valuable institution, which has been able to adapt successfully to changing economic circumstances. However much economists may disagree concerning the system's effectiveness, it can at least be said that the Federal Reserve has become aware of its responsibility for promoting economic stability.

Supplementary Readings

Friedman, Milton, and Anna Schwartz. *A Monetary History of the United States, 1867–1960*. Princeton, N.J., National Bureau of Economic Research, 1963.

Hammond, Bray. *Banks and Politics in America from the Revolution to the Civil War*. Princeton, N.J., Princeton University Press, 1957.

Sprague, O. M. W. *History of Crises under the National Banking System*. Washington, D.C., Publications of the National Monetary Commission, 1910.

Chapter 10

The Structure and Nonregulatory Functions of the Federal Reserve System

As presently constituted, the Federal Reserve System acts as a central bank for the United States. It has as its primary function the regulation of the domestic economy through the manipulation of money and credit. Its goals are stable prices, high employment levels, and economic growth. As subsequent chapters show, however, these may be mutually contradictory goals. A fourth major objective of contemporary central banking policy is to influence the flows of goods and money between domestic and foreign markets. The overriding concern of the Federal Reserve, however, is to help achieve a prosperous and growing domestic economy. No longer is the Federal Reserve concerned merely with maintaining an elastic currency or being a banker's bank.

Later chapters discuss in detail how the Federal Reserve System attempts to achieve these goals through the administration of monetary policy. They also summarize the contemporary controversy on economic policy. The scope of this chapter, however, is limited to an examination of the structure of the Federal Reserve System and its nonregulatory functions.

THE STRUCTURE OF THE FEDERAL RESERVE SYSTEM

There are five principal elements in the organizational structure of the Federal Reserve System: (1) the Board of Governors, (2) Federal Open Market Committee, (3) Federal Advisory Council, (4) the twelve Federal Reserve banks and their branches, and (5) the member banks.

Board of Governors

The Board of Governors is the single most important part of the Federal Reserve System. The Board consists of seven men appointed to fourteen-year terms by the President of the United States with the approval of the U.S. Senate. The members of the Board are ultimately responsible for the operations of the entire Federal Reserve System. Monetary policy is formulated by the Board. Decisions on whether policy will be restrictive or whether easy money conditions are to prevail are made by the Board. The Board of Governors is also engaged in more routine activities. It supervises the Federal Reserve banks and regulates the member banks of the system. It also interprets the Federal Reserve Act and issues various regulations under that Act.

The varied nature of the activities of the Board of Governors is well illustrated by the following résumé of some of its activities during 1963.[1]

Economic policy actions.

1. In July, the Board approved actions taken by the directors of the Federal Reserve banks to raise discount rates. It also revised Regulation Q so as to permit member banks to increase to 4 percent the maximum rate of interest payable on time deposits and certificates with maturities from ninety days to one year. These actions were primarily designed to help reduce the adverse U.S. balance of payments, not to limit the extension of credit in the economy.

2. In August and September, the Board revised Regulations M, H, and K affecting banks and corporations engaged in foreign banking and financing, and operating bank branches abroad under the Federal Reserve Act. The purpose of the revisions was to permit U.S. banking operations abroad to compete more effectively in foreign countries.

3. The Board raised margin requirements for the purchase of stock. This took place in November.

Actions to enhance domestic competition in banking. The Board issued numerous orders under the Bank Merger Act approving and disapproving proposed mergers. It also issued orders under Section 3 of the Bank Holding Company Act approving and disapproving applications for the establishment of bank holding companies.

Routine administrative actions.

1. The Board admitted various state banks to membership in the Federal Reserve System.

---

[1] Compiled from *Federal Reserve Bulletin*, 1963.

2. It appointed Federal Reserve bank directors and branch directors. There were also Board staff changes.

Bank examination and supervision.

1. The Board examined all state member banks. Such examinations take place at least once a year. The Board does not normally examine national banks. The Comptroller of the Currency examines national banks and makes copies of the examinations available to the Board of Governors.

2. The Board's Department of Examinations also examined the Federal Reserve banks and their branches.

Revisions of regulations; interpretations of the Federal Reserve Act.

1. In January, the Board suspended its 1959 interpretation that a bank holding company can lawfully invest in the stock of small business investment companies up to 1 percent of the holding company's capital accounts.

2. Also in January, the Board revised Regulation I pertaining to the issue and cancellation of capital stock of Federal Reserve banks.

3. In February, the Board amended Regulation G to define "noncash items" as consisting of checks, drafts, and other items with special instructions or requiring special handling.

4. In February, the Board issued an opinion concerning "grace periods" in computing twelve months' interest on savings deposits.

The Board and legislation. The chairman and members of the Board of Governors frequently appeared before Congress to give their opinions on proposed banking and economic policy legislation. For example, in April, the Board argued against raising maximum coverage of deposit and share insurance to $25,000. The Board also argued in favor of a bill authorizing the Federal Reserve System to issue Federal Reserve notes in $1 and $2 denominations. This bill subsequently passed Congress as Public Law 88–36 in June of 1963.

These were just some of the actions taken by the Board of Governors in 1963. In addition, the members of the Board of Governors serve on the Federal Open Market Committee. As members of this committee, they exert a dominant influence over the purchase and sale of U.S. government securities by the Federal Reserve System, our most important instrument of monetary policy. The Board also has the authority to alter reserve requirements for member bank deposit liabilities; this is another important instrument of monetary policy. The Board did not exercise this power in 1963, however.

Federal Open Market Committee

The Federal Open Market Committee, or FOMC, consists of twelve members, seven of whom constitute the Board of Governors. Thus, as previously indicated, the Board (if it has unanimity) has the controlling voice in FOMC deliberations. The remaining five members are the presidents of five of our twelve Federal Reserve banks. The president of the Federal Reserve Bank of New York is vice-chairman of the committee and serves as a permanent member because of the crucial role the New York bank plays in the purchase and sale of securities. The other four positions on the committee are rotated among the remaining presidents of Federal Reserve banks. The chairman of the committee is also the chairman of the Board of Governors. Although only five members of the Federal Open Market Committee are presidents of Federal Reserve banks, in practice all twelve presidents attend committee meetings.

The FOMC meets approximately every three weeks for the purpose of determining Federal Reserve policy with respect to the purchase and sale of securities, principally U.S. government securities on the open market. Open market policy decisions have crucial importance for the U.S. economy because, as the next chapter will demonstrate, open market transactions in government securities by the Federal Reserve System strongly influence the reserve position of the commercial banking system, and thus constitute an important instrument of control over the money supply. In addition, the FOMC also directs the system's purchase and sale of foreign currencies.

The FOMC is a policy-setting organization. It does not itself execute the policies that it selects as most appropriate for the current economic situation. The actual purchase and sale of securities and currencies is performed by the Federal Reserve Bank of New York because New York is the center of the government securities and foreign exchange markets in the United States. All private government securities dealers have their main offices in New York. When securities and currencies are purchased by the Federal Reserve Bank of New York, they are apportioned among all Federal Reserve banks according to each bank's share of total Federal Reserve bank assets.

The policies determined by the FOMC are issued as directives to the manager of the System Open Market Account and the special manager in foreign currency. Working in the Federal Reserve Bank of New York, these men direct the purchase of securities and foreign exchange within the context of the directives given by the FOMC.

These directives are formulated at each meeting of the FOMC. They are usually very broad in scope. For example, the current economic policy directive issued to the Federal Reserve Bank of New York on December 18, 1962, stated:

It is the current policy of the Federal Open Market Committee to accommodate moderate further increases in bank credit and the money supply, while aiming at money market conditions that would minimize capital outflows internationally. This policy takes into account the lack of any significant improvement in the U.S. balance of payments and the recent substantial increase in bank credit, but at the same time recognizes the unsatisfactory level of domestic activity, the continuing underutilization of resources, and the absence of inflationary pressures.

To implement this policy, operations for the System Open Market Account during the next three weeks shall be conducted with a view to offsetting the anticipated seasonal easing of Treasury bill rates, if necessary through maintaining a firmer tone in money markets, while continuing to provide moderate reserve expansion in the banking system.[2]

With such a broad directive, the account manager and special manager have a great deal of latitude with respect to how FOMC policies are executed. These managers have day-to-day contact with the currency and government securities markets; they are continually receiving information on the various forces directly affecting commercial bank reserve positions and the U.S. balance of payments situation. Consequently, within the context of the current directives, they may make rapid adjustments to offset undesired changes in our reserve and currency positions. For example, the previously quoted directive implies that in terms of domestic policy the Federal Reserve banks' holdings of U.S. government securities should be expanded. Yet, at a given time, the account manager may actually be contracting Federal Reserve bank holdings of U.S. government securities. Why? Because other forces may be operating to expand commercial bank reserves. What is needed, under such a directive, is not an actual expansion of Federal Reserve holdings of securities, but a *net expansion of commercial bank excess reserves*. This is just one aspect of Federal Reserve open market operations; Chapters 11 and 13 discuss these operations in detail.

Federal Advisory Council

The Federal Advisory Council consists of twelve members, one from each of the twelve Federal Reserve districts. Each member is selected by his district Federal Reserve bank. He is usually a representative banker of his district. This council is strictly an advisory group. It meets at least four times a year, surveying the general business conditions of the economy and formulating appropriate policy recommendations to be presented at its meetings with the Board of Governors. There is no obligation on the part of the Board, however, to execute the recommendations of the council.

Today it can be argued that there is little reason for the continuation of the Federal Advisory Council, since it has no powers. Originally, however, there was some justification for its establishment. When the Federal Reserve Act was passed, there was commercial bank opposition to the formation of a Federal Reserve Board; bankers felt that the Board would not be responsive to banking interests and needs. Consequently, the Federal Advisory Council was set up to provide the banking industry with a means of directly informing the Federal Reserve Board of its needs and wishes.

---

[2] Board of Governors of the Federal Reserve System, *Annual Report* (1962), p. 109.

The Federal Reserve Banks

The Federal Reserve System is composed of Federal Reserve banks and twenty-four branch offices. Geographically, the United States is divided into twelve Federal Reserve districts, each with a Federal Reserve bank and branches.

FIGURE 10–1. Boundaries of the Federal Reserve districts and their branch territories.

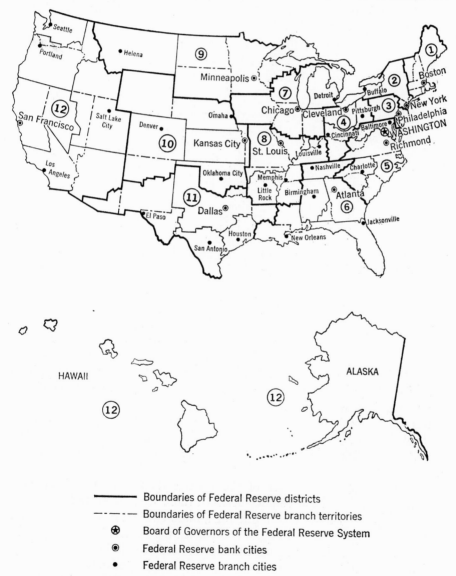

Boundaries of Federal Reserve districts
Boundaries of Federal Reserve branch territories
Board of Governors of the Federal Reserve System
Federal Reserve bank cities
Federal Reserve branch cities

Source: Board of Governors of the Federal Reserve System, Washington, D.C.

The location of these banks and their branches is shown in Figure 10-1. Federal Reserve banks are located in Boston, New York, Philadelphia, Cleveland, Richmond, Atlanta, Chicago, St. Louis, Minneapolis, Kansas City, Dallas, and San Francisco. The banks vary greatly in size. Table 10–1 shows the relative capitalization of the various Federal Reserve banks. The Federal Reserve Bank of New York is the largest, with total assets of $14.0 billion in 1964. This is to be expected, since New York is the money market center of the nation. The Federal Reserve banks of Chicago and San Francisco follow in size with $9.6 and $7.1 billion in assets respectively. The smallest

TABLE 10–1. ASSETS OF EACH FEDERAL
RESERVE BANK, MAY 31, 1964
(IN MILLIONS OF DOLLARS)

DISTRICT NUMBER	FEDERAL RESERVE BANK	ASSETS
1.	Boston	2,998
2.	New York	14,018
3.	Philadelphia	3,117
4.	Cleveland	4,677
5.	Richmond	3,922
6.	Atlanta	3,350
7.	Chicago	9,603
8.	St. Louis	2,275
9.	Minneapolis	1,241
10.	Kansas City	2,451
11.	Dallas	2,362
12.	San Francisco	7,144
	Total	57,158

Source: *Federal Reserve Bulletin*, June, 1964, p. 731.

is the Federal Reserve Bank of Minneapolis, with $1.2 billion in assets. This difference in capitalization among district Reserve banks roughly conforms to the percentage of total commercial bank assets held by the commercial banks within each district. Initially it was hoped that the size of each Federal Reserve bank would be approximately equal. It has not been possible to attain equality because of the concentration of financial business in a limited number of cities.

The decentralized character of the Federal Reserve System is an outgrowth of the traditional conflict between those who advocate local banking autonomy and those who argue for a more efficient centralized system. Local banking interests were quite vocal when the Federal Reserve Act was passed in 1913, and it was thought that local needs would best be served by regional Federal Reserve banks that were loosely federated under the Federal Reserve Board. Thus, at one time, each Federal Reserve bank had a substantial amount of authority in its district. This gradually changed over time as the need for more centralized operations became apparent. The Banking Act of 1935 recognized the need for centralization by giving the new Board of Governors of the Federal Reserve System strong powers.

Today, the principal function of each Federal Reserve bank is to supervise the operations of the member banks within its own district. The district Federal Reserve banks maintain member bank reserve deposits, clear and collect checks for the member banks of the district, lend them reserves, and supply them with currency. In addition, each district bank sets the discount rate for its district. This power, however, is subject to review by the Board of Governors.

Each Federal Reserve bank has the same type of administrative structure. Each is supervised by Class A, Class B, and Class C directors. There are a total of nine directors, three of each class. Class A and B directors are selected by the member banks of the district. Two directors, one Class A and one Class B, are chosen by the small banks of the district, two by the medium-size banks, and two by the large banks. Class A directors may be bankers. Class B directors must not be bankers, but should be actively engaged in commerce, agriculture, or industry in the district. The remaining three directors (Class C) are chosen by the Board of Governors. One of them is appointed chairman and another, deputy chairman of the board of directors by the Board of Governors. Class C directors cannot be actively engaged in the banking business. The directors of each district bank formulate policy for the bank and appoint its president and vice-president, as well as certain other employees of the bank. The appointment of these bank officials, however, may be disapproved by the Board of Governors.

Each Federal Reserve bank is a corporation which has a charter from the federal government. Its stockholders are the member banks. Ownership of the stock of its district Federal Reserve bank is a requirement for commercial banks that wish to be members of the Federal Reserve System. The amount of stock held by a member bank must, at present, equal 3 percent of its own capital accounts. Thus, the amount of Federal Reserve bank stock subscribed to by member banks varies as member bank capital accounts change and as the number of member banks in the Federal Reserve System changes.

Although a Federal Reserve bank is in fact a corporation, it is unlike a private corporation in many ways. A Federal Reserve bank's fundamental purpose is to regulate the operations of the member banks in its district within the confines of the monetary policies articulated by the Board of Governors. Hence, Federal Reserve banks are not profit-seeking corporations. True, a Federal Reserve bank in the course of its operations does make profits. Stockholders (member banks), however, by law, receive dividends equal to only 6 percent of the value of their subscription to Federal Reserve bank stock; member banks have no claim to additional dividends. Nor do they have a residual claim to the assets of a Federal Reserve bank. In addition, ownership of Federal Reserve bank stock, unlike the common stock of most corporations, is not transferable; there is no market for the stocks of the Federal Reserve banks. In the event of liquidation, the total value of the surplus and the par value of the common stock (assuming the Federal Reserve bank assets would yield their book value) would go to the U.S. government. Such a liquidation, however, is highly unlikely, given our tradition of at least some decentralization in central banking activities.

Member Banks

The last element of the Federal Reserve System is the member banks themselves. Member banks, of course, are private profit-seeking corporations, which, like all commercial banks, possess the unique ability to create and destroy money in the process of making loans and investments. To possess member bank status, a bank must meet the membership qualifications set forth by the Federal Reserve Act. Member banks constitute only 45 percent of all commercial banks in the United States, but they account for 83 percent of bank demand deposit liabilities.

NONREGULATORY FUNCTIONS OF THE FEDERAL RESERVE BANKS

Many of the functions performed by the Federal Reserve banks are not directly connected with the implementation of Federal Reserve monetary policy. Several of these services have already been mentioned briefly: (1) lending reserves to member banks, (2) supplying member banks with currency, and (3) clearing and collecting checks. All three of these functions are part of the main job of a Federal Reserve bank, the maintenance of member bank reserve deposits. A fourth nonregulatory function of the Federal Reserve banks is to act as fiscal agents of the U.S. government.

Maintenance of Member Bank Reserve Accounts

Each member bank is required to maintain reserves at its district Federal Reserve bank in the form of vault cash and deposits. Commercial bank deposits at district Federal Reserve banks do more than meet legal reserve requirements. The funds in these accounts do not lie idle; on the contrary, they are very active. Reserve deposits at Federal Reserve banks are constantly increasing and decreasing. The activity of these accounts demands careful supervision by both the member banks and the Federal Reserve banks so that minimum member bank reserve requirements are met.

How are the funds in these accounts employed? First, there is the *lending of reserves* to member banks by the Federal Reserve banks. Member banks are usually able to borrow reserves from their district Federal Reserve bank to meet temporary shortages of reserves, provided they have the proper collateral. Frequent trips by a member bank to the "discount window," however, may cause the Federal Reserve bank to restrict the amount it will loan to the member bank.[3] When a member bank borrows reserves, the Federal Reserve bank simply marks up the member bank's deposit balance. When the member bank repays the loan, it simply uses its reserve account. Member bank borrowing of reserves is discussed at greater length in the next chapter.

Member bank reserve deposits are also the *mechanism through which the economy is supplied with currency.* As described in Chapter 2, when the nonbank public's demand for currency increases, commercial bank demand deposit liabilities and vault cash holdings are reduced. Where do the commercial banks get currency to meet the increased demand? Nonmember banks buy it from member banks, who in turn purchase it from the Federal Reserve banks. Member banks "purchase" currency by accepting a decrease in their reserve accounts at Federal Reserve banks. When, subsequently, there is an influx of currency into the banking system, the excess currency is returned to the Federal Reserve banks, and member bank reserve deposits are increased.

Third, when banks have excess funds in their reserve accounts they may lend this excess to banks with a shortage of reserves. Negotiations of this sort take place in the *federal funds market.* The reserve accounts of lending banks are reduced, and those of borrowing banks increased.

Fourth, when the *Treasury transfers funds* from its accounts at member banks to its general accounts at Federal Reserve banks, member bank reserve deposits are decreased.

Finally, it is through member bank reserve accounts that many *checks are cleared and collected.* This is one of the most valuable functions that a Federal Reserve bank can perform for a member bank. A member bank's reserve deposits are increased when it sends checks drawn on other banks to the Federal Reserve bank for collection. Conversely, a member bank's reserve account is decreased when checks written by its depositors are presented for collection to the Federal Reserve banks by the member banks.

Check-clearing and Collection Operations by the Federal Reserve System

The volume of Federal Reserve bank check-clearing operations is almost staggering. In 1963, Federal Reserve banks handled 4,069,111,000 packages of non-U.S. government checks. The total value of these packages of checks

---

[3] "Federal Reserve banks do not discount eligible paper or make advances to member banks automatically; the discount facilities are made available to member banks as a privilege of membership in the system and not as a right." Board of Governors of the Federal Reserve System, *The Federal Reserve System—Purposes and Functions* (Washington, D.C.: 1961), p. 43.

handled was $1,363,949,957,000.[4] The bulk of these checks are now processed electronically, although several Federal Reserve banks and their branches still do some manual processing.

The nationwide clearing and processing of checks was one of the principal functions that the Federal Reserve System was designed to perform under the Federal Reserve Act. The Federal Reserve System has been quite successful in fulfilling this task. Here is how the process looks. Assume that an individual in New York has sold goods valued at $1,000 to someone in Chicago. These goods are paid for with a check drawn on a Chicago member bank. The New York businessman deposits the check with his bank in New York City. Assuming that the New York bank is also a member bank, there are several changes that may occur on its balance sheet.

For example, the Chicago bank may be a customer bank. If so, then the New York bank may increase the deposit account of the seller who presented the $1,000 check and, at the same time, reduce the deposit account of the Chicago bank. The check is then returned to the Chicago bank, which in turn reduces the account of the person who wrote the check. The net result of this transaction in terms of the commercial banking system is that the Chicago bank will have lost an asset—deposits with the New York bank.

If the Chicago bank is not a customer bank, however, the check-clearing and collection procedure is considerably more complicated. First there are the balance sheet changes that occur upon deposit of the check by the businessman. These are the following entries a:

BALANCE SHEET CHANGES FOR NEW YORK CITY MEMBER BANK

ASSETS		LIABILITIES + CAPITAL ACCOUNTS	
Due from banks	+$1,000 (a)	Demand deposits	+$1,000 (a)
Due from banks	−$1,000 (b)		
Reserves	+$1,000 (b)		

The New York bank must now collect on this check. It does this by sending the check to the Federal Reserve Bank of New York. This results in a change in the balance sheet of the Federal Reserve Bank of New York. Entries a show that the Federal Reserve Bank of New York has received

BALANCE SHEET CHANGES FOR THE FEDERAL RESERVE BANK
OF NEW YORK

ASSETS	LIABILITIES + CAPITAL ACCOUNTS
Cash items in process of collection +$1,000 (a)	Deferred availability cash items +$1,000 (a)
	Deferred availability cash items −$1,000 (b)
	Member bank reserve deposits +$1,000 (b)

[4] Board of Governors of the Federal Reserve System, *Annual Report* (1963), p. 226.

a check (cash items in process of collection), the value of which has not yet been credited to the account of the New York member bank (deferred availability cash items). Shortly after the check is received by the Federal Reserve Bank of New York, the reserve account of the New York member bank is increased.[5] The balance sheet of the New York bank is now adjusted to show that its reserve position has increased. This is recorded as entries b on the New York member bank balance sheet. The balance sheet of the Federal Reserve Bank of New York has also changed. These are recorded as entries b on the balance sheet of the Federal Reserve Bank of New York.

The Federal Reserve Bank of New York must still collect on the $1,000 check. If the member bank on which the check is drawn were a member bank in District Number 2 (the district of the Federal Reserve Bank of New York), it would have a reserve deposit account with the Federal Reserve Bank of New York. The reserve account of the member bank would be reduced, as would cash items in process of collection. But, in our example, the member bank on which the check is drawn is in District Number 7. Under these circumstances, the Federal Reserve Bank of New York must send the check to the Federal Reserve Bank of Chicago for collection. The Federal Reserve Bank of Chicago in turn lowers the reserve deposit account of the Chicago member bank and forwards the check to it. The Chicago member bank lowers the deposit account of the businessman who first wrote the check. The balance sheet changes for this member bank are as follows:

BALANCE SHEET CHANGES FOR THE CHICAGO MEMBER BANK

ASSETS		LIABILITIES + CAPITAL ACCOUNTS	
Reserves	−$1,000	Demand deposits	−$1,000

Thus the check has traveled from the Chicago businessman to the New York businessman, to the New York member bank, to the Federal Reserve Bank of New York, to the Federal Reserve Bank of Chicago, to the Chicago member bank, and back again to the Chicago businessman. The demand deposits of the New York businessman have increased; those of the Chicago businessman have decreased. The New York member bank has gained reserves; the Chicago member bank has lost reserves.

There is still one debt created during this process that remains unresolved. The Federal Reserve Bank of New York sent the check to the Federal Reserve Bank of Chicago for collection. Since the check was written on a bank in District 2, the Federal Reserve Bank of Chicago now owes $1,000 to the Federal Reserve Bank of New York. Debts of this type among Federal

---

[5] Usually a Federal Reserve bank increases the reserve deposit account of member banks before it collects on the checks. As a result, cash items in process of collection are normally greater than deferred availability cash items. The difference between these two items is known as "Federal Reserve float" and has an influence on commercial bank reserve positions. The influence of "float" on the economy is discussed more fully in the next chapter.

Reserve banks are cleared through the Federal Reserve System's *Interdistrict Settlement Fund.* Each Federal Reserve bank owns gold certificates on deposit with the Interdistrict Settlement Fund in Washington, D.C. When one Federal Reserve bank is in debt to another, its gold certificate fund is reduced by the amount of the debt. In turn, the creditor Federal Reserve bank has its gold certificate holdings increased.[6] This transaction through the Interdistrict Settlement Fund is recorded on the balance sheets of the Federal Reserve banks and the Interdistrict Settlement Fund as follows:

BALANCE SHEET CHANGES FOR THE FEDERAL RESERVE BANK
OF CHICAGO

ASSETS	LIABILITIES + CAPITAL ACCOUNTS
Gold certificate reserves −$1,000	Member bank reserve deposits −$1,000

BALANCE SHEET CHANGES FOR THE FEDERAL RESERVE BANK
OF NEW YORK

ASSETS	LIABILITIES + CAPITAL ACCOUNTS
Gold certificate reserves +$1,000	Member bank reserve deposits +$1,000

BALANCE SHEET CHANGES FOR THE INTERDISTRICT SETTLEMENT FUND

ASSETS	LIABILITIES + CAPITAL ACCOUNTS
	Gold certificate reserves Federal Reserve Bank of Chicago −$1,000 Federal Reserve Bank of New York +$1,000

Gold certificate assets and member bank reserves have decreased at the Federal Reserve Bank of Chicago, and they have increased at the Federal Reserve Bank of New York.

The preceding illustration of our check-clearing procedures, as complicated as it may seem, is really simple compared to the overall check-clearing process. Remember that trillions of dollars worth of checks are cleared by the Federal Reserve banks each year. Checks are continually flowing back and forth in the economy. Our illustration merely showed the movement of one check through the clearing system. In practice, each member bank daily presents checks to its Federal Reserve bank for collection, and also has checks presented to it. Thus, member bank reserve changes reflect net flows of checks. If the value of the checks that a member bank presents for collection is greater than the value of the checks forwarded to it for collection, its reserves increase. If not, it loses reserves.

---

[6] These gold certificate funds are the reserve assets of the Federal Reserve banks.

Similarly, there are continual daily shifts of gold certificate funds from one Federal Reserve bank to another. Each Federal Reserve bank daily forwards checks to the other eleven Federal Reserve banks, and in turn has checks presented to it. When the total value of checks forwarded by one Federal Reserve bank to other Federal Reserve banks exceeds the value of those presented, it gains gold certificates for that day.

The clearing and collection of checks by the Federal Reserve System is not the only check-clearing mechanism in the economy. There is often a clearinghouse for banks having head offices within a particular city. Representatives of these banks meet daily in this clearinghouse and present checks to one another for collection. Debts which exist between the banks are then extinguished by a transfer of reserve balances from debtor to creditor banks. If the clearing is not done with Federal Reserve funds, the payment may be made to a city correspondent, which increases the accounts of creditor banks and lowers those of the debtor banks.

The Federal Reserve System not only clears and collects checks for member banks, but also for nonmember banks. Typically, when a Federal Reserve bank receives checks written on accounts in nonmember banks, it increases the reserve account of the depositing member bank. The checks are then forwarded to those member banks that serve as correspondents for the nonmember banks. The reserve deposits of these member banks are decreased. In turn, the demand deposit balances of nonmember banks at the correspondent member banks are reduced. As indicated in Chapter 4, a Federal Reserve bank will only perform this function of clearing for a nonmember bank when the nonmember bank is on the par list.

Fiscal and Foreign Agent Functions of the Federal Reserve Banks

The Federal Reserve banks also serve as fiscal agents and depositories for the U.S. government. In this capacity, the Federal Reserve banks maintain checking deposit accounts for the Treasury department, which makes almost all of its payments by drawing down its deposit accounts at the various Federal Reserve banks. As Treasury payments are made, the deposit accounts of the nonbank public are increased and member banks forward the U.S. government checks to the Federal Reserve banks for collection. Member bank reserves are increased.

On the other hand, when the Treasury receives tax revenues and funds from the sale of government securities, the funds are placed in the Treasury tax and loan accounts at commercial banks. Subsequently, as funds are needed to cover government payments, the funds are periodically transferred to the Treasury deposit accounts with the Federal Reserve banks. At that time, member bank reserve deposit accounts are decreased and treasury deposits increased at the Federal Reserve banks.

Treasury payments and receipts do not coincide; this is the principal reason for the maintenance of tax and loan accounts by the Treasury. For example, if all tax receipts were placed immediately in the Treasury's general accounts with the Federal Reserve banks, a serious drain in commercial bank reserves would occur as depositors made tax payments. This would necessitate commercial bank contraction in the absence of open market purchases by the Federal Reserve banks.

Not only do the Federal Reserve banks clear and collect checks for the Treasury, but they also assist in public debt transactions. Federal Reserve banks act as agents in the sale of new U.S. government securities; they process the applications of the purchasers of new security issues, deliver the securities to the purchasers, and receive payment for the securities.

The Federal Reserve Act designated the Federal Reserve banks as the fiscal agent and depository for the U.S. government. The performance of these functions extends beyond handling some of the financial transactions of the U.S. Treasury. The Federal Reserve banks also act as depositories and fiscal agents for such varied agencies as the FDIC, Federal Home Loan Banks, Federal Savings and Loan Insurance Corporation, Public Housing Administration, Small Business Administration, Federal National Mortgage Association, and the Commodity Credit Corporation. In addition, the Federal Reserve banks act as fiscal agent for those government agencies that guarantee loans extended to contractors and subcontractors engaged in the production and delivery of goods vital to national defense.

The activity of the U.S. government deposit accounts maintained with the Federal Reserve banks is intense. In 1963, the Federal Reserve banks handled 454,576,000 packages of Treasury checks having a total value of $131,795,729,000.[7] The general accounts of the U.S. government averaged $793 million in 1963.[8] Dividing the value of U.S. government check handlings by the average size of the U.S. general accounts gives us a measure of the turnover of U.S. government balances—166. This is a very active turnover, many times in excess of individual deposit account turnover at commercial banks. The annual rate of demand deposit turnover in New York, the most active financial center, was 85 in 1963.[9]

Finally, the Federal Reserve banks perform valuable services in the area of international economic relations. They are authorized to act as depositories for the International Monetary Fund, International Development Association, Inter-American Development Bank, and International Finance Corporation. The Federal Reserve banks are also authorized to accept the deposits of foreign monetary authorities. In practice, most foreign operations are carried on by the Federal Reserve Bank of New York for all the Federal Reserve banks; foreign deposits are recorded on the balance sheet

---

[7] Board of Governors of the Federal Reserve System, *Annual Report* (1963), p. 226.

[8] Computed by adding the end-of-month U.S. Treasurer general account deposits for the period December 31, 1962, through December 31, 1963, and dividing the total by 13. Source of data are the *Federal Reserve Bulletin* tables on the consolidated statement of condition of all Federal Reserve banks.

[9] *Federal Reserve Bulletin*, June, 1964, p. 732.

of each Federal Reserve bank in proportion to its share of total Federal Reserve bank assets.

The Federal Reserve Bank of New York also buys and sells foreign currencies for the U.S. government. Until recently this type of intervention in the exchange market was not done to influence exchange rates. Formerly the purpose was simply to provide the government with exchange needed in its foreign operations. Now, however, there is an economic regulatory purpose as well: to alleviate the pressure on the U.S. balance of payments. The manager of the special account handles all purchases and sales of foreign currency for the FOMC. More is said of this in later chapters on economic policy.

SUMMARY

This chapter has described the structure and nonregulatory functions of the Federal Reserve System. We have seen that the Board of Governors is the most important regulatory body of the Federal Reserve System, it is ultimately responsible for the determination of the monetary policy of the nation. The various Federal Reserve banks carry out these economic and regulatory policies according to the instructions of the Board of Governors. These Federal Reserve banks, in turn, regulate the operations of the member banks. Actually, it is the member banks that are the most important component of the Federal Reserve System, for they deal directly with the American public. In their daily operations of extending credit and creating money, the member banks become the instrument whereby Federal Reserve policy is executed.

Of the various Federal Reserve banks, it is the Federal Reserve Bank of New York that is most important. Because of its location in the nation's principle financial center, the Federal Reserve Bank of New York acts for the other Reserve banks and the FOMC in the purchase and sale of U.S. government securities and foreign exchange.

All Federal Reserve banks provide member banks with important services, too. These are (1) the maintenance of member bank reserve deposit accounts, (2) the clearing and collection of checks, (3) the supplying of currency, and (4) the lending of reserves.

The Federal Reserve banks are the fiscal agents of the U.S. government. Member banks also provide services for the government. They maintain tax and loan accounts for the Treasury and assist in the sale and payment of interest on government securities.

Supplementary Readings
Board of Governors of the Federal Reserve System. *The Federal Reserve System: Purposes and Functions.* Washington, D.C., 1963, Chapters 2 and 17.

Chapter 11

Assets and Liabilities
of the Federal Reserve System

Chapter 7 stressed the importance of the reserve position of commercial banks as the basis for credit extension and money creation. This chapter discusses how variations in the assets and liabilities of the Federal Reserve banks may alter commercial bank reserves and hence the lending ability of the commercial banking system. The emphasis is not upon how the Board of Governors, through a manipulation of the Federal Reserve bank assets and liabilities, may affect commercial bank reserves and hence economic activity, however. Instead, we are concerned with the alterations in commercial bank reserves that are caused by changes in Federal Reserve bank assets and liabilities. Chapters 12 and 13 then examine the instruments of Federal Reserve policy and explain how they may be manipulated so as to effect alternative policy goals.

FEDERAL RESERVE BANK ASSETS

Gold Certificate Reserves

Table 11–1 is a detailed balance sheet for all Federal Reserve banks as of December 31, 1963. The first asset of major importance on the balance sheet is that of gold certificate reserves.

Gold certificates are the legal reserves of the Federal Reserve banks. The Federal Reserve Act states: "Every Federal Reserve bank shall maintain reserves in gold certificates of not less than 25 per centum against its deposits and reserves in gold certificates of not less than 25 per centum against its Federal Reserve notes in actual circulation. . . ."[1]

The Federal Reserve banks do not use their reserves in the same manner as commercial banks. Federal Reserve banks almost always maintain large

---

[1] Board of Governors of the Federal Reserve System, *The Federal Reserve Act as Amended through October 1, 1961*, p. 57.

TABLE 11–1. DETAILED STATEMENT OF CONDITION OF ALL FEDERAL RESERVE
BANKS COMBINED, DECEMBER 31, 1963
(IN THOUSANDS OF DOLLARS)

ASSETS

Gold certificate reserves			
Gold certificates on hand			
Held by Federal Reserve banks	316,055		
Held by Federal Reserve agents	2,500,000		
Gold certificates due from U.S. Treasury			
Interdistrict Settlement Fund	6,613,088		
Federal Reserve Agents' Fund	4,390,000		
		13,819,143	
Redemption fund for Federal Reserve notes		1,417,709	
Total gold certificate reserves			15,236,852
Federal Reserve notes of other Federal Reserve banks			497,156
Other cash			
United States notes		24,676	
Silver certificates		136,263	
Standard silver dollars		4,526	
National bank notes and Federal Reserve bank notes		389	
Subsidiary silver, nickels, and cents		16,838	
Total other cash			182,692
Loans and securities			
Discounts and advances			
Secured by U.S. government securities			
Discounted for member banks	30,310		
Discounted for others	—		
Other discounts and advances			
Discounted for member banks	—		
Foreign loans on gold	32,000		
Total discounts and advances		62,310	
Acceptances			
Bought outright		69,978	
Held under repurchase agreement		91,742	
U.S. government securities			
Bought outright			
Bills	4,141,422		
Certificates	7,066,231		
Notes	17,729,041		
Bonds	4,645,407		
Total bought outright		33,582,101	
Held under repurchase agreement		10,800	
Total U.S. government securities		33,592,901	
Total loans and securities			33,816,931
Cash items in process of collection			
Transit items		6,836,729	
Exchanges for clearing house		252,368	
Other cash items		701,778	
Total cash items in process of collection			7,790,875
Bank premises			
Buildings (including vaults)	103,839		
Fixed machinery and equipment	58,780		
Total buildings	162,619		
Less depreciation allowances	−85,377		

TABLE 11–1. (*Continued*)

ASSETS (*Continued*)

	77,242	
Land	26,296	
Total bank premises		103,538
Other assets		
Denominated in foreign currencies	152,620	
Reimbursable expenses and other items receivable	2,948	
Interest accrued	222,771	
Premium on securities	15,316	
Deferred charges	1,956	
Real estate acquired for banking house purposes	1,476	
Suspense account	523	
All other	3,361	
Total other assets		400,971
Total assets		58,029,015

LIABILITIES AND CAPITAL ACCOUNTS

Liabilities			
Federal Reserve notes			
Outstanding (issued to Federal Reserve banks)		34,318,269	
Less: Notes held by issuing Federal Reserve banks	1,308,224		
Notes forwarded for redemption	131,854		
		−1,440,078	
Federal reserve notes, net (includes notes held by U.S. Treasury and by Federal Reserve banks other than issuing bank)			32,878,191
Deposits			
Member bank reserves		17,047,234	
U.S. Treasurer—general account		880,465	
Foreign		171,014	
Other deposits			
Nonmember bank clearing accounts	46,606		
Officers' and certified checks	9,394		
Reserves of corporations doing foreign banking or financing	26,688		
International organizations*	96,972		
All other	113,202		
Total other deposits		292,862	
Total deposits			18,391,575
Deferred availability cash items			5,192,859
Other liabilities			
Accrued dividends unpaid		—	
Unearned discount		357	
Discount on securities		74,475	
Sundry items payable		5,964	
Suspense account		957	
All other		63	
Total other liabilities			81,816
Total liabilities			56,544,441
Capital accounts			
Capital paid in			494,858
Surplus			989,716
Other capital accounts†			—
Total liabilities and capital accounts			58,029,015
Contingent liability on acceptances purchased for foreign correspondents			91,852

TABLE 11–1. (*Continued*)

Source: Board of Governors of the Federal Reserve System, *Annual Report* (1963), pp. 212–13, Table I.
* Includes Inter-American Development Bank, International Bank for Reconstruction and Development, International Finance Corporation, International Monetary Fund, etc.
† During the year this item includes the net of earnings, expenses, profits, etc., which are closed out on December 31.

volumes of excess reserves, whereas commercial banks tend to hold down their excess reserves. This difference is caused by the difference in the fundamental goals of a profit-seeking commercial banking system and those of a central bank concerned with administering economic policy.

The Federal Reserve banks, for example, had $15.2 billion in total gold certificate reserves on December 31, 1963. These reserves more than met the 25 percent reserve requirements for their $18.4 billion in deposit liabilities and $32.9 billion in Federal Reserve notes. Federal Reserve banks had $2.4 billion in excess reserves. Member banks, by way of contrast, had only $21.073 billion in reserves, of which $20.517 billion were required during the four-week period ending January 8, 1964. Thus, member bank excess reserves were only $556 million, some $432 million of which was concentrated in country banks.[2] Theoretically, on the basis of $2.4 billion in excess reserves, Federal Reserve banks could have expanded their Federal Reserve notes and deposit liabilities (which consist primarily of member bank reserve deposits) by $9.6 billion. Member banks with only $556 million in excess reserves, at best, could have expanded their total deposit liabilities by $5.3 billion. If the Federal Reserve banks had actually expanded their member bank reserve deposits by $9.6 billion, however, the member banks in turn could, theoretically, have expanded their total deposit liabilities by $91.4 billion.[3] Such is the potential power of these excess Federal Reserve gold certificate holdings! Of course the Federal Reserve System did not allow such a potential expansion to take place.

How do the Federal Reserve banks get gold certificates? By purchasing them as they are issued by the U.S. Treasury. How do Federal Reserve banks lower their holdings of gold certificates? In effect, by selling them back to the Treasury. The Federal Reserve banks may not legally own gold; they may only have gold certificates, which are claims to the gold held by the U.S. Treasury. As a rule, Federal Reserve bank holdings of gold certificates increase and decrease in volume according to the amount of gold

[2] *Federal Reserve Bulletin*, February, 1964, p. 183.
[3] With a 25 percent reserve requirement, the Federal Reserve banks can support deposits and Federal Reserve notes in a volume four times the volume of gold certificate reserves. The $5.3 billion and $91.4 billion figures for commercial banks assume an average reserve requirement against time and demand deposits of 10.5 percent, no cash drain, and no desire for minimum working balances of excess reserves.
A diminishing U.S. gold supply has cut the excess reserve position of the Federal Reserve in recent years. This led to President Johnson's early 1965 proposal to remove the gold certificate requirement for Federal Reserve deposits.

owned by the U.S. Treasury. Commercial bank reserves also usually increase and decrease in proportion to Treasury gold holdings.

Increases in Treasury gold holdings occur when the U.S. government buys gold from foreign governments or domestic producers. When a foreign government sells gold to the U.S. Treasury, Federal Reserve banks decrease the checking deposit account of the U.S. Treasury and raise that of the foreign government.[4] Assume, for example, that gold is purchased by the Treasury at a cost of $1 million. The effects on the balance sheet of the Federal Reserve banks are the following entries a:

BALANCE SHEET CHANGES FOR THE FEDERAL RESERVE BANKS

ASSETS	LIABILITIES + CAPITAL ACCOUNTS	
Gold certificate reserves +$1,000,000 (b)	Deposits	
	U.S. Treasurer	−$1,000,000 (a)
	Foreign	+$1,000,000 (a)
	U.S. Treasurer	+$1,000,000 (b)
	Foreign	−$1,000,000 (c)
	Member bank reserves	+$1,000,000 (c)

The Treasury then issues gold certificates in an amount equal to the value of the gold purchase. These certificates are added to the gold certificates that the Treasury already holds for the Federal Reserve banks, which in turn increase the deposit accounts of the Treasury. These transactions are recorded as the above entries b.

So far there has been no change in commercial bank reserves. The change only occurs as the foreign government spends the funds in the United States or transfers them to deposit accounts held with commercial banks. Then, on the balance sheet of the Federal Reserve banks, there is a decrease in foreign deposits and a corresponding increase in member bank reserve deposits (entries c above). Member bank deposit liabilities also increase. These deposits will be held by either foreigners or those U.S. citizens that have sold goods and services to foreigners.

The balance sheet entries are roughly the same when the Treasury acquires gold from domestic gold producers. There is one difference, however. Member bank reserves increase directly when the Treasury buys gold. This occurs because the gold producers deposit the checks they receive from the Treasury in deposit accounts at commercial banks. They in turn collect on these checks by forwarding them to the Federal Reserve banks, which increase the member bank reserve deposits. When the Treasury issues the gold certificates, gold certificate reserves and Treasury deposits again increase as in the preceding illustration.

The Treasury also experiences drains on its gold supply. A foreign gov-

---

[4] Actually transactions of this type will take place through the Federal Reserve Bank of New York.

ernment, for example, may choose to convert its holdings in U.S. currency on deposit with commercial banks into gold, for the purpose of switching this money into another currency. Using checks written on deposit accounts with commercial banks, the foreign government will probably first build up its deposit accounts at the Federal Reserve Bank of New York. This will decrease both commercial bank deposit liabilities and reserves by an equal amount, thereby reducing both commercial bank required and excess reserves. Subsequently the foreign government will use its increased deposit accounts at the Federal Reserve Bank of New York to purchase the desired gold from the Treasury. Thus, foreign deposits are reduced and Treasury deposits increased. Lower Treasury gold holdings mean reduced gold certificate claims to gold, however. Consequently, the Treasury withdraws gold certificates in an amount equal to the gold drain and Treasury deposits decrease. The results of a $1 million purchase of gold by foreigners can be shown as balance sheet changes by reversing the plus and minus entries on the preceding balance sheet.

The gold certificate holdings of the Federal Reserve banks increase and decrease according to the amount of gold held by the U.S. Treasury. This, in turn, means that commercial bank reserves generally increase as Treasury gold holdings increase, and decrease as those Treasury gold holdings decrease. Hence, if the effects of a change in the gold supply upon commercial bank reserves are viewed as undesirable in light of the general economic situation, the Federal Reserve System will take offsetting action, usually through the purchase and sale of U.S. government securities. As a matter of fact, the Federal Reserve System usually takes such action whenever commercial bank reserves fluctuate beyond a certain point because of forces over which the Federal Reserve banks have no direct control. A change in our gold stock is merely one of these forces.

Our gold stock is directly affected by our balance of payments.[5] In recent years, foreign dollar claims against the United States have exceeded the claims of the United States against foreign currencies. As a result, some foreign nations have chosen to take part of their additional claims in the form of gold rather than increased holdings of dollars in U.S. commercial banks. Thus, we have experienced gold losses and gold certificate reductions. These forces would have reduced commercial bank reserves and lending ability if the Federal Reserve System had not taken the type of offsetting action previously mentioned.

Other Cash

Other cash consists of Federal Reserve bank holdings of Treasury currency. Two circumstances may lead to an increase in this balance sheet item: (1) an issuance of new currency by the Treasury, which is purchased

---

[5] See Chapter 25 for a discussion of the balance of payments.

by the Federal Reserve banks; or (2) a return of Treasury currency to the Federal Reserve banks by member banks. On the other hand, a retirement of currency by the Treasury or a demand for Treasury currency by commercial banks would lead to a decrease in "other cash" holdings of the Federal Reserve banks.

When the Federal Reserve banks purchase currency from the Treasury, they make payment by increasing Treasury deposit accounts. Similarly, when the Treasury retires currency, it does so by drawing down its deposit accounts at the Federal Reserve banks. At present, a substantial volume of Treasury currency is in the process of being retired. Much of our present Treasury paper currency, silver certificates, is being replaced by Federal Reserve notes. This action will free silver that the Treasury has been holding as backing for silver certificates for the minting of additional subsidiary silver coin and for the sale of additional silver to domestic users.

These actions, the issuance and retirement of Treasury currency, have no direct effect on member bank reserves. Indirectly, however, there is some effect. When the Treasury spends the deposits it receives from a sale of currency to the Federal Reserve banks, the deposit liabilities and reserve deposits of member banks increase. The checks written by the Treasury are received by the nonbank public and deposited in commercial bank demand deposit accounts. Commercial banks then send the checks to the Federal Reserve banks for collection. Federal Reserve banks in turn increase member bank reserve deposits and lower Treasury deposits.

On the other hand, when member banks ask for additional Treasury currency, or send unneeded Treasury currency to the Federal Reserve banks, the total value of member bank reserves is in no way affected. Only a change in the composition of member bank reserves takes place. Member bank reserves consist of both vault cash and reserve deposits at the Federal Reserve banks. A shipment of Treasury currency to the Federal Reserve banks by member banks decreases the amount of reserves held in the form of vault cash, but the Federal Reserve banks make payment by increasing member bank reserve deposits.

Fluctuations in the amount of Treasury currency holdings at the Federal Reserve banks, like gold certificates, are another variable over which the Federal Reserve has no direct control.

Discounts and Advances

Federal Reserve bank holdings of discounts and advances are a factor over which the Reserve banks do have some control. Discounts and advances usually arise when member banks borrow reserves. There are three principal types of discounts and advances: (1) discounts and advances secured by eligible paper; (2) advances secured by U.S. government securities; and (3) advances secured to the satisfaction of the lending Federal Reserve bank.

Discounts are made when member banks sell "eligible paper" to a Federal Reserve bank. Eligible paper consists of notes, drafts, and bills of exchange arising out of agricultural, industrial, and commercial loans made by the borrowing bank. Such paper, at the time of discount, must have a maturity of less than ninety days, except for agricultural paper, which may have a maturity of nine months. For instance, if the paper has a value of $1 million and the current discount rate is 3 percent, then the Federal Reserve bank pays for the paper by increasing the member bank's reserve deposits by $970,000. If the member bank wants an *advance*, rather than a discount, secured by eligible paper, then the member bank's reserve deposits are still increased by $970,000. The member bank must subsequently repay the loan, however, since it still owns the paper.

The total volume of discounts and advances based on eligible paper is actually very small. Almost all member bank borrowing of reserves is based upon the second form of borrowing, advances secured by U.S. government securities. Here the security is a promissory note signed by the bank that deposits U.S. government securities as collateral with the lending Federal Reserve bank. The reserve deposit account of the member bank is then increased by the amount of the loan less the interest charged. Thus, discounts for eligible paper and advances secured by government securities are mechanically identical.

The third way in which a member bank may borrow reserves is through advances secured to the satisfaction of the lending bank. This means that member banks may borrow reserves even if they do not wish to secure the advances with eligible paper or U.S. government securities. The lending Federal Reserve bank will determine what other assets are acceptable as collateral. The maximum maturity of such a loan is four months. Advances of this sort carry a penalty rate of interest, however, which is usually ½ percent higher than the discount rate of advances secured by U.S. government securities. When the Federal Reserve banks received authority in 1935 to make this type of loan to member banks, it was expected that such borrowing would only be done under exceptional circumstances. Instead, it has now become a routine operation.

Generally banks apply for one of these three types of loan for the purpose of meeting a deficiency of reserves or to increase the level of reserves prior to expanding loans and investments. Many banks make frequent trips to the "discount window" for these reasons. As mentioned in Chapter 10, the Federal Reserve banks are usually ready to grant such loans to member banks, but they are not extended automatically. In practice, the Federal Reserve banks do not control the volume of member bank borrowings so much by loan limitation as they do by manipulation of the discount rate. Thus, if the Board of Governors believe that the lending activity of the commercial banking system should be restricted, they increase the discount rate. On the other hand, if the economy is in need of an increase in spending, they reduce the discount rate. The next chapter discusses in more detail how discount rate manipulation is used as an instrument of monetary policy.

In addition to lending reserves to member banks, the Federal Reserve banks are also permitted to make advances to individuals, partnerships, or corporations. These loans are made when alternative lending sources are unable to do so. These advances have a maximum maturity of ninety days and must be secured by U.S. government securities. The rate charged for these loans usually varies from ½ to 1½ percent higher than the discount rate on advances to member banks secured by U.S. government securities. The variation in these rates depends upon economic conditions in the various Federal Reserve districts. Direct loans of this type are very rare in today's prosperity economy. As a matter of fact, Table 11–1 shows that as of December 31, 1963, there were no loans of this type outstanding. When they are made, however, they tend to increase commercial bank reserves. As the borrowers use the proceeds of the loans, member banks acquire checks drawn on the Federal Reserve banks. When member banks present these checks for payment, the Federal Reserve bank increases member bank reserve deposit accounts. Conversely, loan repayments reduce member bank reserve deposits.

Acceptances

One of the functions that the Federal Reserve Bank of New York performs for all the Reserve banks and for the FOMC is the purchase and sale of bankers' acceptances in the open market.

A bank or a business may draw up an order for a commercial bank to pay. The credit of the firm serves as collateral here. If the commercial bank accepts the order to pay, the document becomes a bankers' acceptance. Since the bank has accepted the order, it is obligated to pay, and the acceptance becomes fully negotiable. These bankers' acceptances are often created when importers want to facilitate their purchase of goods and services abroad. In foreign trade, the seller may know little about the credit of the buyer, but is willing to accept the credit of a commercial bank. The importer, of course, will supply the bank with the necessary funds before maturity of the acceptance. An importer under these circumstances will have the foreign exporter draw a bill on the importer's bank. Once the bank accepts the bill, the bankers' acceptance that has been created can be sold by the exporter. This is how he receives payment for the goods and services sold.

How does the purchase and sale of bankers' acceptances affect commercial bank reserves? When the Federal Reserve Bank of New York purchases bankers' acceptances, it pays for them with checks drawn on itself. The checks are deposited by the recipients in their deposit accounts at commercial banks, and these banks present the checks for payment to the Federal Reserve Bank of New York. Payment is made on the checks by increasing the reserve accounts of the member banks. On the other hand, when the Federal Reserve Bank of New York sells bankers' acceptances, purchasers pay for them with checks written on their commercial banks. The Federal Reserve Bank of New York collects on these checks, decreasing member bank reserve deposits.

When the Federal Reserve buys and sells bankers' acceptances, this operation is called an "open market operation." It is not the only type of open market operation conducted by the FOMC. In fact, most of its dealings involve U.S. government securities instead of bankers' acceptances. More is said of open market operations in U.S. government securities in both the next section of this chapter and in Chapter 13.

Quantitatively, Federal Reserve bank holdings of bankers' acceptances amounted to only $162 million at the end of 1963. This represents, however, a substantial increase in such holdings over other years in the recent past.

U.S. Government Securities

Quantitatively, U.S. government securities are the most important asset held by the Federal Reserve banks. Out of a total $58.0 billion in assets held by the Federal Reserve banks at the end of 1963, some $33.6 billion was in the form of U.S. government securities. These securities are purchased by the account manager at the Federal Reserve Bank of New York for all of the Federal Reserve banks. Purchases are made either directly or on a repurchase agreement basis from government securities dealers. When made under a repurchase agreement, the securities dealer agrees to repurchase the securities within a specified period of time, normally fifteen days or less. Purchases of this sort by the Federal Reserve System are generally designed to provide banks with additional reserves in periods of temporary reserve shortages.

The securities issues bought and sold by the Federal Reserve are almost always old U.S. government securities. Rarely do the Federal Reserve banks acquire new security issues directly from the U.S. Treasury. The Federal Reserve Act provides that the Federal Reserve banks at any one time cannot hold more than $5 billion in securities purchased directly from the Treasury. This limitation presumably limits the ability of the Federal Reserve to assist the Treasury in inflationary financing of Treasury deficits. Actually, when such purchases are made, they are usually for the purpose of helping the Treasury adjust to a lack of synchronization between its tax receipts and payments. As shall be discussed in Chapter 13, purchase of old securities can also lead to inflationary pressures.

The securities purchased today by the Federal Reserve System are of varying maturities, both long and short term. This is a relatively recent development. For the period 1951 to 1961, Federal Reserve System purchases concentrated on short-term securities. Since February, 1961, however, the Federal Reserve banks have acquired both short- and long-term government securities. These purchases of longer-termed securities are designed to help bring about two policy ends: a stable domestic economy and a favorable balance of payments. In a less than full employment economy, Federal Reserve open market operations, if concentrated in securities with short maturities, can only tend to satisfy the requirements of policies designed to achieve economic stability. Purchases of short-term securities at this time tend to increase reserves (as we shall demonstrate in succeeding paragraphs), lower short-term interest rates, and induce an outflow of dollars from the U.S. economy (see Chapters 25 and 26). To compensate for this maladjustment in policy the Board of Governors decided that the Federal Reserve banks should buy and sell throughout the maturity range of U.S. government securities. At the end of 1961, the Federal Reserve banks held $17.7 billion in securities that were to mature within a year and $11.2 billion in securities that were to mature in more than a year. At the end of 1962, they held $17.7 billion in short-term securities and $13.1 billion in long-term securities, a $1.9 billion increase in long-term holdings.[6] By expanding long-term instead of short-term holdings, bank lending ability was expanded and short-term interest rates maintained, thus presumably reducing a possible flow of funds abroad. It should be pointed out, however, that it is difficult to judge the success of these policies from the evidence at hand. For example, in 1961, the year of the policy change, short-term holdings of the Federal Reserve banks actually increased and long-term holdings decreased. Still, short-term interest rates did not drop as sharply as in other recessions.

How do Federal Reserve operations in U.S. government securities affect member bank reserve positions? In precisely the same manner as the purchase and sale of bankers' acceptances by the Federal Reserve. The Federal Reserve buys U.S. government securities from government securities dealers who specialize in the trading of these securities and pays for them with checks written on itself. When a government securities dealer deposits this Federal Reserve check in his deposit account at a commercial bank, his deposits are increased. When his bank presents the check to the Federal Reserve for collection, it receives an increase in its reserve deposits. The following balance sheets show the effects of a purchase of $1 million in securities:

BALANCE SHEET CHANGES FOR THE FEDERAL RESERVE BANKS

ASSETS	LIABILITIES + CAPITAL ACCOUNTS
U.S. government securities +$1,000,000	Deposits Member bank reserves +$1,000,000

[6] *Federal Reserve Bulletin,* November, 1963, p. 1565.

BALANCE SHEET CHANGES FOR THE COMMERCIAL BANKING SYSTEM

ASSETS		LIABILITIES + CAPITAL ACCOUNTS	
Reserves	+$1,000,000	Demand deposits	+$1,000,000

The increase in the demand deposits of the securities dealer are only temporary, however, since he must pay whoever sold him the securities that the Federal Reserve System purchased.

When the Federal Reserve System sells government securities, just the reverse of this procedure takes place. The account manager tells the dealer in securities that he wishes to sell. The buyers of the securities pay the brokers with checks written on their demand deposit accounts at commercial banks. The securities dealer delivers the U.S. government securities to the buyers and pays the Federal Reserve System with a check drawn on his account at a commercial bank. The Federal Reserve then collects on the check by lowering the reserve deposits of the commercial bank.

Thus, a sale of securities by the Federal Reserve System means a decrease in commercial bank reserves, and a purchase means an increase in reserves. As we shall see later, the Federal Reserve System is continually buying and selling securities. What is important for commercial banks and economic policy is the net effect of these transactions on commercial bank reserves and lending practices.

Float

Federal Reserve "float" is not an asset. It is simply the difference between an asset, cash items in process of collection, and a liability, deferred availability cash items. Cash items in process of collection are simply checks that the Federal Reserve banks have received but not as yet collected on by decreasing member bank reserves. Deferred availability cash items are checks that the Federal Reserve banks have received and not as yet paid by increasing member bank reserves. Theoretically, these two items should equal one another. In point of fact, however, they do not, since the Federal Reserve banks generally increase the accounts of depositing banks prior to collecting from the banks on which the checks were drawn. As a result, there is a time gap and cash items in process of collection will be larger than deferred availability cash items. This difference is termed the "float." Variations in the float can significantly affect member bank reserve positions.

Deferred availability cash items are usually paid within two days of the receipt of checks by the Federal Reserve banks. This is done almost automatically. It usually takes longer than this to collect on checks, however. The checks received may have been written on banks in another Federal Reserve district. If so, they must be mailed to that district's Federal Reserve bank and thence to the bank on which the check was drawn. This takes time. If for some reason the mails are delayed, the accounts of the depositing banks will still be increased within two days even though the collection of the cash items is delayed. The result is an increase in member bank reserves. An increase in the volume of checks being written, and hence being cleared, will also increase float and reserves. A larger volume of checks being cleared strains the check-clearing mechanism of the Federal Reserve banks and slows up the collection process. Such increases in check payments regularly occur at mid-month and year end.

Increased collection of checks, on the other hand, will reduce float and, accordingly, member bank reserves.

Other Assets

Other Federal Reserve bank assets consist primarily of the physical property composing bank premises and accrued interest. The value of bank premises changes slowly. Any increase in these assets would involve an increase in member bank reserves, since the assets would be paid for by checks drawn on the Federal Reserve banks. When these checks are deposited in commercial bank deposit accounts, the commercial banks forward them to the Federal Reserve banks for payment in the form of increased reserve deposits.

Accrued interest is a somewhat different matter. This item consists principally of interest that has accrued on Federal Reserve holdings of U.S. government securities. Changes in this asset will not normally affect commercial bank reserve positions. As accrued interest increases, Federal Reserve surplus accounts increase. When the interest is paid, Treasury deposit accounts and accrued interest decrease. Commercial bank reserves are unaffected by these transactions. To the extent, however, that the Treasury has to transfer funds from its tax and loan accounts at commercial banks in order to meet the interest payments, commercial bank reserves decrease.

FEDERAL RESERVE BANK LIABILITIES

Federal Reserve Notes

Federal Reserve notes were described in Chapter 2. They are liabilities of the Federal Reserve banks that issue them. What are the effects of Federal Reserve note increases upon the member bank reserves? There is no direct effect until member banks distribute them to the nonbank public. Member banks purchase currency (both Treasury and Federal Reserve currency) by drawing down their reserve deposit accounts. At this point, the reserves of the bank have merely been switched from one form, reserve deposits, to another, vault cash. However, as soon as the nonbank public demands the currency, commercial bank vault cash reserves will be reduced. Conversely, return of currency to the banks will lead to an increase in reserves. Chapter 7 explained the effects of cash drains and inflows upon bank lending capacity; this topic will be raised again in Chapter 15 in a summary of all the various factors that determine bank reserves and the money supply.

Deposits

Member bank reserves. After Federal Reserve notes, member bank reserve deposits are the main liability of the Federal Reserve banks. At the end of 1963 there were $17.0 billion in member bank reserves, which in turn supported $229.5 billion in member bank deposit liabilities.

Movements in member bank reserve deposits do not occur independently of other items on the balance sheet of the Federal Reserve banks. On the contrary, member bank reserves change in response to changes in other balance sheet assets, liabilities, and capital accounts. The central concern of this chapter has been to demonstrate how member bank reserve deposits behave in response to other Federal Reserve bank balance sheet entries.

Thus, member bank reserve deposits are the residual item that the Federal Reserve System attempts to regulate in order to promote domestic economic stability. Later in this chapter there will be a summary showing how changes in all of the various assets and liabilities of the Federal Reserve banks affect member bank reserves.

U.S. Treasurer—general account. Earlier chapters have discussed the meaning of the general account of the U.S. Treasurer. It is principally through these deposit accounts that the U.S. government makes expenditures. Variation in the size of these Treasury accounts at Federal Reserve banks will usually affect member bank reserve positions.

Whenever the Treasury uses its balances at the Federal Reserve banks to make payments to the nonbank public or to the commercial banking system, there is an increase in member bank reserves. Assume, for example, that the Treasury uses $1 million of its deposits at Federal Reserve banks to retire U.S. government securities held by members of the nonbank public. The Treasury retires the securities with checks drawn on its accounts at the Federal Reserve banks. When the nonbank public deposits these checks in its checking accounts, the demand deposit liabilities of the commercial banking system increase by $1 million. Assuming a 15 percent reserve requirement, required reserves increase by $150,000. Excess reserves also increase, however. When the Treasury checks deposited by the nonbank public are presented to the Federal Reserve banks for collection, member bank reserves are increased by $1 million. Since required reserves only amount to

$150,000, excess reserves have increased by $850,000. This permits a substantial increase in the lending activity of commercial banks. The balance sheet changes of such a debt retirement operation are summarized in the following balance sheets:

BALANCE SHEET CHANGES FOR THE FEDERAL RESERVE BANKS

ASSETS	LIABILITIES + CAPITAL ACCOUNTS
	Deposits
	Member bank reserves +$1,000,000
	U.S. Treasurer −$1,000,000

BALANCE SHEET CHANGES FOR THE COMMERCIAL BANKING SYSTEM

ASSETS		LIABILITIES + CAPITAL ACCOUNTS	
Reserves	+$1,000,000	Demand deposits of the nonbank public	+$1,000,000

Precisely the same balance sheet changes occur when goods and services are purchased by the U.S. government from the nonbank public. There would be some difference, however, if the Treasury used its balances with the Federal Reserve banks to retire government securities held by commercial banks or to make other types of payments to the commercial banks. Then there would be no direct effect upon demand deposit liabilities of the commercial banking system. Commercial bank reserves would increase, however, because when Treasury checks are presented to the Federal Reserve for collection, payment is made by increasing member bank reserves.

On the other hand, not all decreases in Treasury deposits with the Federal Reserve banks will affect commercial bank reserves. There are transactions that take place between the Federal Reserve banks and the Treasury that may not initially involve either the commercial banks or the nonbank public. For example, if the Treasury uses its deposit balances to retire public debt held by the Federal Reserve banks, then Federal Reserve bank assets in the form of U.S. government securities are reduced, as are liabilities in the form of U.S. government deposits. The commercial banking system is in no way involved.

How do increases in Treasury deposits at the Federal Reserve banks affect member bank reserves? If the transaction is one that involves only the Federal Reserve banks and the Treasury, then there is no direct effect. As previously mentioned, a purchase of gold certificates by the Treasury will increase gold certificate holdings and demand deposits at the Federal Reserve banks. It must be remembered, however, that the overall operation of gold certificate issue may have involved the purchase of gold from gold producers who are members of the nonbank public. If this is the case, the gold purchase entails a payment to the nonbank public and hence an increase in member bank reserve deposits.

If the increase in Treasury deposits with the Federal Reserve banks involves the commercial banking system, a decrease in member bank reserves takes place. If, for example, the Treasury decides to transfer $1 million from its tax and loan accounts at commercial banks to its general accounts with the Federal Reserve banks, the reserves of the banks decrease by $1 million, and so do their deposit liabilities. The reduction in deposit liabilities means a decrease in required reserves, but since actual reserves have decreased in an equal amount, the net effect is a reduction of some magnitude in member bank excess reserve positions. Assuming a 15 percent reserve requirement, a $1 million decline in member bank demand deposits and reserves means an $850,000 decrease in excess reserves.

Foreign deposits. Foreign governments and foreign central banks maintain deposit accounts with our Federal Reserve banks and with commercial banks. Some mention of this was made in Chapter 10. When foreigners need funds to purchase goods and services in the United States, there is a transfer of funds from foreign dollar holdings at the Federal Reserve banks to commercial banks. This results in an increase in member bank deposit liabilities and a simultaneous increase in reserves. A reverse flow, from checking deposit accounts at member banks to foreign Federal Reserve accounts, means a reduction in commercial bank deposit liabilities and reserve deposits.

Other deposits. "Other deposits" consist primarily of nonmember bank clearing accounts, deposits of businesses engaged in foreign banking, deposits of various international organizations, and deposits of some government agencies. An increase in the total of "other deposits" usually decreases member bank reserves.

Nonmember banks that remit at par may maintain checking deposit accounts with the Federal Reserve banks. These deposit accounts are maintained primarily to facilitate the clearing of checks for nonmember banks. It is not necessary, however, that a nonmember bank have deposit accounts with the Federal Reserve banks in order to have access to the Federal Reserve clearing process. Large city correspondent banks will handle the clearing of nonmember bank checks.

An increase in nonmember bank deposits with the Federal Reserve banks will tend to decrease member bank reserves, but not necessarily all commercial bank reserves. In Connecticut, for example, nonmember banks may keep part of their reserves with Federal Reserve banks and part with commercial banks. If a Connecticut nonmember bank transfers some of its reserve deposits from member banks to Federal Reserve banks, a decrease in the reserves of the member banks would occur, but there would be no change in nonmember bank reserves. If the Connecticut nonmember bank transfers to Federal Reserve banks its deposits in a member bank that is not authorized by the state's commissioner to hold nonmember bank reserves, however, there is an increase in nonmember bank reserves and a decrease in member bank reserves. The precise effects on all bank reserves of changes in the location of nonmember bank reserves and deposits with other banks depends upon the various state statutes governing nonmember bank reserves.

It is also difficult to know precisely how the remaining components of "other deposits" will affect bank reserve positions. Fortunately, however, the relative importance and activity of these accounts is not great. The changes that take place in these deposits are not subject to the direct control of the Federal Reserve banks. Therefore, if changes in these accounts affect commercial bank reserves in an undesired manner, the Federal Reserve System usually takes offsetting action through the use of open market operations.

CAPITAL ACCOUNTS

Capital Paid In

Capital paid in refers to the par value of the stock of the Federal Reserve banks that has been purchased by the member banks. It will be recalled that when banks become members of the Federal Reserve System or as they become larger, they must purchase stock in their district Federal Reserve bank. To the extent that member bank reserve deposits are used in the purchase of Federal Reserve bank stock, member bank reserves decrease. A retirement of stock, on the other hand, means an increase in member bank reserves.

Surplus

Surplus changes with earnings by the Federal Reserve banks. These earnings are substantial because the receipts of the Federal Reserve banks on the interest on U.S. government security holdings and discounts and advances are far in excess of their operating expenses. Table 11–2 shows the earnings and expenses of the Federal Reserve banks in 1963. The current net earnings were $964 million. Most of this, however, instead of being transferred to surplus, was paid to the Treasury. The Federal Reserve banks, at present, pay a 6 percent statutory dividend to member banks and increase the surplus by enough to keep the surplus account approximately twice the size of the capital stock paid in. All remaining earnings are paid to the Treasury. Thus, most of the interest earned on U.S. government securities is turned back to the Treasury. In 1963, the Treasury paid more than $1 billion in interest to the Federal Reserve banks, and received almost $880 million back, technically in the form of interest on Federal Reserve notes.

TABLE 11-2. EARNINGS AND EXPENSES OF THE FEDERAL RESERVE BANKS
DURING 1963
(IN DOLLARS)

CURRENT EARNINGS		
Discounts and advances		8,865,844
Acceptances		1,728,755
U.S. government securities		1,138,167,465
Foreign currencies		2,039,600
All other		318,396
Total		1,151,120,060
CURRENT EXPENSES		
Salaries		
Officers		7,530,851
Employees		99,257,976
Retirement and other benefits		17,517,934
Fees—directors and others		571,122
Traveling expenses		2,144,063
Postage and expressage		21,333,562
Telephone and telegraph		1,735,398
Printing and supplies		8,376,360
Insurance		389,900
Taxes on real estate		5,000,399
Depreciation (building)		6,368,389
Light, heat, power, and water		1,930,003
Repairs and alterations		1,852,828
Rent		154,229
Furniture and equipment		
Purchases		3,097,943
Rentals		9,125,749
All other		3,303,310
Interbank expenses		—
Subtotal		189,690,014
Federal Reserve currency		10,062,901
Assessment for expenses of Board of Governors		7,572,800
Total		207,325,716
Less reimbursement for certain fiscal agency and other expenses		−20,052,359
Net expenses		187,273,357
PROFIT AND LOSS		
Current net earnings		963,846,704
Additions to current net earnings		
Profits on sales of U.S. government securities (net)	312,355	
All other	490,787	
Total additions	803,140	
Deductions from current net earnings	−188,309	
Net deductions from (−) or additions to current net earnings		614,834
Net earnings before payments to Treasury		964,461,538
Dividends paid		−28,912,019
Paid Treasury (interest on Federal Reserve notes)		−879,685,219
Transferred to surplus		55,864,300
Surplus, January 1		933,851,400
Surplus, December 31		989,715,700

Source: Board of Governors of the Federal Reserve System, *Annual Report* (1963), pp. 222–23.
Details may not add to totals because of rounding.

The net effect of this Federal Reserve policy is that there are only small yearly changes in surplus. Nevertheless, an increase in surplus means a decrease in member bank reserves. Payments by the Federal Reserve banks to employees, the U.S. Treasury, and member banks increase reserves, but the receipts remaining after these payments have been made tend to decrease reserves. Thus, an increase in surplus reflects an excess of receipts over payments, and this involves some decrease in member bank reserves.

SUMMARY

This chapter has studied the components of the balance sheet of the Federal Reserve banks. The focus has been upon the effect of various changes in this balance sheet on the reserves of commercial banks. Although our discussion has been almost exclusively in terms of member banks, it should be remembered that the reserves of nonmember banks will be affected in a manner similar to those of member banks.

In general, when Federal Reserve assets increase and there is no offsetting increase in other liabilities (defined as total liabilities less member bank reserve deposits) or capital accounts, member bank reserves will increase. If Federal Reserve assets decrease, and there is no corresponding decrease in other liabilities or capital accounts, member bank reserves decrease. If, on the other hand, Federal Reserve bank assets remain constant, and the total of other liabilities and capital accounts increases, there is a decrease in member bank reserves. Conversely, a decrease in other liabilities and capital accounts means an increase in member bank reserves.

This summary, however, merely reflects the truisms inherent in the construction of the balance sheet. What is of more relevance is the impact on reserves of a change in a specific balance sheet item. As the preceding analysis has shown, it cannot be predicted precisely that a change in a specific asset, other liability, or capital account will necessarily affect member bank reserves; possibly some other balance sheet asset, liability, or capital account will change instead. In spite of these difficulties, however, some specific conclusions can be derived.

First, an increase in discounts and advances to member banks will increase member bank reserves and a repayment of discounts and advances by member banks will decrease member bank reserves.

Second, a purchase of bankers' acceptances in the open market by the Federal Reserve banks will increase member bank reserves and a sale of bankers' acceptances in the open market will decrease member bank reserves.

Third, a purchase of U.S. government securities in the open market by the Federal Reserve banks will increase member bank reserves and a sale of these securities will reduce member bank reserves.

Finally, an increase in float will increase member bank reserves and a decrease in float will decrease member bank reserves.

Concerning changes other than those just mentioned, the most we can say is that changes in assets, other liabilities, and capital accounts will be associated with certain types of changes in member bank reserves. The most important of these changes are summarized as follows: (1) increases and decreases in gold certificate holdings tend to be associated with increases and decreases in member bank reserves; (2) increases and decreases in Federal Reserve notes result in equivalent decreases and increases respectively in member bank reserve deposits, without changing the total of member bank reserves; and (3) increases and decreases in U.S. Treasury general account deposits tend to cause decreases and increases respectively in member bank reserve deposits.

Supplementary Readings

Board of Governors of the Federal Reserve System. *The Federal Reserve System: Purposes and Functions.* Washington, D.C., 1963, Chapter 11.

"Collateral for Federal Reserve Credit," *Federal Reserve Bulletin* (September, 1963), pp. 1235–36.

Federal Reserve Bank of Chicago. *Modern Money Mechanics: A Workbook on Deposits, Currency, and Bank Reserves.* Chicago, May, 1961.

Chapter 12

The Development
of Federal Reserve Instruments
# of Monetary Control, Part I

At present the Federal Reserve System has three tools at its disposal that it may use to manipulate commercial bank reserve positions and thereby implement monetary, fiscal, and international economic policy. These instruments of control are (1) the reserve requirement, (2) the discount rate, and (3) open market operations. They are called *general monetary controls*. They are "general" because they do not directly affect commercial bank lending operations in specific types of credit extension. Commercial banks still have a free hand in determining which types of loans and investments they will make. In addition, the Federal Reserve System has one type of *selective credit control*. This is the power to manipulate margin requirements for the purchase and carrying of securities.

Chapters 12 and 13 examine these Federal Reserve instruments of monetary control in some detail. First, we shall consider how the Board of Governors may be expected to use these instruments of policy in alternative economic situations. Second, we shall examine the history of each policy instrument to see how it has actually been employed; some attempt will be made to assess whether or not these uses have been appropriate. Finally, we shall discuss the difficulties inherent in the use of these instruments.

APPROPRIATE USE
OF FEDERAL RESERVE MONETARY CONTROLS

Recession

A period of recession, a time in which human and nonhuman resources are less than fully employed, calls for increased spending. When either the public or private sectors of the economy actually increase their spending, an increase in the demand for goods and services takes place, incomes rise, and employment of resources increases. Before additional spending can take place, however, funds are needed. A desire to spend will affect the economy only to the extent that it is financed. This can be done in either of two ways: (1) by increasing the supply of money, (2) by utilizing more intensely the present supply of money; that is, an increase in the velocity of circulation. In the absence of these two conditions, an increase in the desire to spend cannot be implemented, and hence will not lead to increased employment levels.

Encouraging an increase in total spendings can be difficult; it depends in part on how the increase is financed. For example, an increase in federal government expenditures will be financed through increased taxes or through borrowing. If financed through taxation, the effects of increased government spending may in part be cancelled out by reductions in spending by taxpayers who face higher taxes. If increased expenditures are financed by the sale of government securities, the effects of increased spending will depend on who purchases the securities. If the nonbank public buys the securities with idle funds, spendings will actually rise in the economy. However, if the nonbank public makes the purchase with funds that would have been spent on goods and services, then the increased government spending may not have the full desired impact. If Federal Reserve banks buy the securities, public spending will be strongly stimulated, for the use of funds provided by the Federal Reserve banks will lead to an increase in the total money supply and in commercial bank reserves.[1]

An increase in private spending can only be induced by manipulating the determinants of private spending. These determinants are examined in detail in Chapter 19. In general, however, a drop in interest rates charged consumers and businesses for borrowings tends to lead to increased borrowing and spending. Second, a general increase in income brought about by increased government spending tends to induce an increase in private spending. Third, increased profit expectations by businesses often lead to greater investment spendings. Finally (a tricky thing to establish empirically, but important analytically), increased liquid wealth holdings tend to induce people to spend more liberally. These are some of the more important factors that encourage increased private spending.

The Federal Reserve System plays a significant role in this process of economic stimulation. Appropriate use of Federal Reserve instruments of monetary control can directly increase commercial bank lending ability and the supply of money. With increased borrowings from commercial banks by business firms and consumers, more funds are made available to the economy and spending should increase.

---

[1] The potential effects of federal government spending operations on the stock of money and commercial bank reserve positions are discussed in Chapter 14. The theory behind the analysis of how effective demand increases by the federal government affect the economy is outlined in the model of economic activity developed in Part III of this text.

Some economists argue that Federal Reserve action in periods of recession is inadequate for the purpose of actually reversing an economic decline. This may be true in many instances, but appropriate policy action will at least ease the path taken in recovery. Although monetary policy action may not be able to reverse a decline in the economy, it can intensify the speed of recovery once it is under way. On the other hand, inadequate creation of reserves by the Federal Reserve banks during recession and recovery can limit the increases in commercial bank lending operations, and hence slow down the recovery of the economy.

What, then, are the appropriate uses of the instruments of central bank policy during recession?

First, reserve requirements should be lowered. A reduction of reserve requirements will increase excess reserves and hence the lending ability of the commercial banking system.

Second, discount rates should be reduced. A drop in discount rates will make it easier for commercial banks to borrow reserves for the purpose of expanding lending operations.

Third, the Federal Reserve Bank of New York should purchase U.S. government securities and bankers' acceptances in the open market.

Purchases of securities will directly increase the volume of commercial bank reserves. More important than this, they will also increase the excess reserves of the commercial banking system. In addition, to the extent that the securities purchased were originally held by the nonbank public, the money stock is increased.

All of these policy actions will make it easier for banks and other financial institutions to lend. Interest rates, because of abundant reserves and a plentiful money supply, will ease, and this will further stimulate borrowing and spending. True, the interest rate structure of the economy during a recession will probably be low already; monetary policy can keep them low during recovery, however, and this will speed up the recovery process.

During a recession the Federal Reserve can also ease up in its selective credit controls; it can lower margin requirements for the purchase and carrying of securities. Today, however, most economists do not consider margin requirement changes an effective means of inducing increased spending in the economy. Instead, the consensus is that this instrument should be used primarily to minimize the use of borrowed money to finance speculation in the stock markets.

The capabilities of our three fundamental policy recommendations, however, should not be accepted without reservation. As we shall see later, they are subject to a number of limitations. Some instruments are more difficult to employ than others. In fact, open market operation is the only instrument whose power can be regulated with some degree of precision. Caution must be exercised in the use of the other instruments; otherwise, open market operations may have to be utilized to compensate for the errors of judgment made in applying the other tools of monetary policy.

Different types of recession call for different types of monetary action. A deep depression clearly calls for an aggressive use of all policy tools. A very mild recession, however, may necessitate only a very small increase in Federal Reserve bank holdings of U.S. government securities and bankers' acceptances. It is even possible that no acquisition of securities and acceptances would be needed at all, since by the time the effects of the purchase are felt in the economy, a recovery may be underway. Thus, a purchase in a mild recession may only serve to intensify inflationary tendencies in the next boom in the economy.

Qualifications such as these raise serious questions concerning the effectiveness of our policy instruments. Some economists even go so far as to argue that the Federal Reserve System should engage in no discretionary use of the monetary instruments of policy at all. Instead, these men believe that some type of automatic policy may be needed, one that would eliminate perverse variations in the stock of money as a source of economic instability. Such policies might consist of the automatic use of the instruments of monetary action for some purpose such as maintenance of price stability. Others suggest using open market operations only to maintain a steady increase in the money suppply fixed at some low predetermined rate. Several of these alternative policy proposals are evaluated in the discussion of the relationship between money and financial policy in Part IV.

The instruments recommended by monetary policy for recession—the lowering of reserve requirements, the reduction of discount rates, and the purchase of U.S. government securities and bankers' acceptances—should not, therefore, be advocated without qualification. Instead, they are only mentioned briefly to indicate the nature of the policies which might serve to mitigate a recession.

Economic Boom

As long as there are unemployed resources available in the economy, money stock increases and excess demand should not normally lead to substantial price level increases. Once, however, productive resources are fully utilized, then, in the absence of countermeasures, money stock increases and excess demand leads to rising prices. The rise in output that occurs during the early part of a boom, before resources are fully employed, is usually desirable. However, the increased price level and consequent deterioration of the purchasing power of most liquid wealth which are apt to result from a further extension of the boom are in themselves undesirable. If the inflationary problem becomes sufficiently serious, countermeasures should be taken. These measures may take several forms. Economic controls or price controls may be imposed, for example. Such measures deal only with the symptoms, not the causes of inflation, however. Prices have risen because of excess spending and increased costs. The full employment output of goods and services has produced a low supply relative to the effective demand. In a serious inflation the source of the excessive spending has to be eliminated, or the price controls will have to be supplemented by a second pricing mechanism, a rationing system.

If the inflationary period occurs during wartime, the increased spending which produces the inflationary pressures is made up of government military outlays which cannot be reduced. Therefore, taxes may have to be increased—an unpopular measure at any time—in order to decrease demand in the private sector of the economy. In the absence of increased taxation, the only alternatives are control measures which prevent the increased wartime incomes from being spent.

In peacetime, many economic controls are politically unacceptable in a democracy like the United States and hence different ways must be found to reduce spending. Public pressure can force the government itself to reduce its expenditure rate. Pressure may also be brought against business and consumer expenditures. Labor unions may be persuaded to postpone demands for wage increases.

Generally, however, in the absence of increased taxation, the most frequently employed restrictive policy is of the monetary variety. To succeed in reducing the effective demand for goods and services, either the money supply or its velocity must be decreased.[2] As previously indicated, there are three basic ways in which monetary policy attempts to fulfill these goals: (1) reserve requirements may be raised, thereby reducing commercial bank excess reserves and lending ability; (2) discount rates may be increased, making it more difficult for commercial banks to borrow additional reserves, and reducing the spread between the rates that commercial banks make on loans and the rates they pay for borrowed reserves; and (3) the Federal Reserve Bank of New York may sell bankers' acceptances and U.S. government securities, thereby reducing the money supply and bank reserves directly. A fourth policy action would be to raise margin requirements, halting thereby any speculation in stocks that is taking place on the basis of borrowed funds. These policy actions raise interest rates, making it more difficult for businesses and individuals to borrow. This should reduce spending in the economy.

Previously it was argued that a policy of monetary ease might not actually be able, by itself, to bring about an economic recovery. The converse of this statement is not true, however. A policy of monetary restriction *can* generally bring an unwanted inflation to an end. The three tools of monetary policy *are* strong enough to reverse almost any type of boom

---

[2] It would be well to keep in mind the boom had to be financed in some manner. Thus, increased spendings may well have resulted because of an over-easy application of money-increasing policy instruments during the preceding period of economic recovery.

other than one caused by excessive federal budget deficits accompanied by sharp money stock increases. In fact, the danger of applying our monetary instruments to curb inflation is not that they will not be able to halt an inflation, but rather that the instruments are so strong that they may throw the economy into a sharp recession if used improperly. Thus, while an increase in excess reserves *may* cause banks to expand credit, a deficiency of reserves *must* cause commercial banks to curtail credit, and even contract loans, investments, and demand deposit liabilities. Too sharp a reduction in reserves, therefore, may curtail spending drastically. For this reason, just as caution must be used in employing credit-easing monetary techniques, even more care must be taken in using credit-restricting devices. One example of an apparently inappropriate application of restrictive monetary policy was the doubling of reserve requirements from 1936 to 1937. Another was the increase of the discount rate in 1957. More will be said of these errors in discretionary monetary policy in subsequent sections of this chapter.

GENERAL MONETARY CONTROLS

The Reserve Requirement

The three basic instruments of monetary policy are all designed to manipulate the reserve position of the commercial banking system. An increase in member bank excess reserves expands the lending and investment capacity of the banking system. In the process, the ability of the banking system to create demand deposit money is increased. Conversely, a decrease in commercial bank excess reserves diminishes the ability of banks to lend, invest, and create money; a substantial deficiency of reserves can even force a contraction in the economy.

One of the policy instruments that the Federal Reserve System can use to affect commercial bank reserve positions is the reserve requirement. Changes in the reserve requirement cause changes in the composition of commercial bank reserves. With an increase in the reserve requirement, some reserves that were classified as excess become required reserves. A decrease in the reserve requirement, on the other hand, reduces required and raises excess reserves.

Table 12–1 lists the changes that have taken place in the reserve requirements of member banks. These reserve requirements were fixed by statute until 1935 when the Banking Act of 1935 gave the Board of Governors the authority to vary reserve requirements within legally prescribed limits. From 1935 to 1959 those limits for demand deposits were from 7 to 14 percent for country banks, 10 to 20 percent for reserve city banks, and 13 to 26 percent for central reserve city banks. Since that time the designation

TABLE 12–1. MEMBER BANK RESERVE REQUIREMENTS, 1917–1964 (PERCENT OF DEPOSITS)

EFFECTIVE DATE	NET DEMAND DEPOSITS* Central reserve city banks†	NET DEMAND DEPOSITS* Reserve city banks	NET DEMAND DEPOSITS* Country banks	TIME DEPOSITS Central reserve and reserve city banks‡	TIME DEPOSITS Country banks
1917—June 21	13	10	7	3	3
1936—August 16	19½	15	10½	4½	4½
1937—March 1	22¾	17½	12¼	5¼	5¼
May 1	26	20	14	6	6
1938—April 16	22¾	17½	12	5	5
1941—November 1	26	20	14	6	6
1942—August 20	24				
September 14	22				
October 3	20				
1948—February 27	22				
June 11	24				
September 16			16		7½
24	26	22		7½	
1949—May 1			15		7
5	24	21		7	
June 30		20		6	
July 1			14		6
August 1			13		
11	23½	19½		5	
16			12		5
18	23	19			
25	22½	18½			
September 1	22	18			
1951—January 11	23	19		6	
16			13		6
25	24	20			
February 1			14		
1953—July 1			13		
9	22	19			
1954—June 16					5
24	21			5	
July 29	20	18			
August 1			12		
1958—February 27	19½	17½			
March 1			11½		
20	19	17			
April 1			11		
17	18½				
24	18	16½			
1960—September 1	17½				
November 24			12		
December 1	16½				
1962—October 25				4	
November 1					4
In effect December 31, 1964		16½	12	4	4
Present legal requirements					
Minimum		10‡	7	3	3
Maximum		22‡	14	6	6

TABLE 12–1. (*Continued*)

Source: Board of Governors of the Federal Reserve System, *Annual Report* (1962), Table 15, p. 161, and *Federal Reserve Bulletin*, 1964.

* Net demand deposits are demand deposits subject to reserve requirements which, beginning with August 23, 1935, have been total demand deposits minus cash items in process of collection and demand balances due from domestic banks (also minus war loan and Series E bond accounts during the period April 13, 1943–June 30, 1947).

† Authority of the Board of Governors to classify or reclassify cities as central reserve cities was terminated effective July 28, 1962.

‡ From August 23, 1935, to July 28, 1959, the minimum and maximum legal requirements against net demand deposits of central reserve city banks were 13 and 26 percent respectively, and the maximum for reserve city banks was 20 percent.

All required reserves were held on deposit with Federal Reserve banks from June 21, 1917, until late 1959. Since then, member banks have also been allowed to count vault cash as reserves, as follows: (1) country banks—in excess of 4 and 2½ percent of net demand deposits effective December 1, 1959, and August 25, 1960, respectively; (2) central reserve city and reserve city banks—in excess of 2 and 1 percent effective December 3, 1959, and September 1, 1960, respectively; effective November 24, 1960, all vault cash.

"central reserve city bank" has been eliminated. As the commercial banking system has developed, financial centers other than the former central reserve cities have assumed greater responsibility in the finances of the nation. Thus, member banks are now either reserve city or country banks. The legally prescribed limits for the reserve requirements on demand deposits for country banks are still 7 to 14 percent, but for reserve city banks they are now 10 to 22 percent. The reserve requirement limits for time deposits are 3 to 6 percent for all classes of banks.

The Board of Governors has generally exercised its authority to vary reserve requirements in a manner that would be considered appropriate in terms of the preceding policy discussion. Manipulation of reserve requirements, however, is an instrument of policy that is infrequently utilized, particularly for curbing inflation.

Increases in reserve requirements. The first case of a discretionary increase in reserve requirements occurred in 1936–1937. This particular use of the reserve requirement instrument has evoked considerable controversy. From August of 1936 to May of 1937, all reserve requirements were raised to their legally permissible maximum. This amounted to a doubling of the requirements as they existed on August 15, 1936. Looking back from the perspective of today, many economists regard this doubling of reserve requirements as an inappropriate exercise of monetary policy by the Board of Governors. The U.S. economy had improved relative to the depression depths of 1932 and 1933 when there were in excess of twelve million unemployed workers. It was still not a full employment economy, however. In 1936, there were nine and one-half million unemployed, close to eight million in 1937, and in excess of ten million in 1938.[3] It is entirely possible that the increases in the reserve requirements in 1936 and 1937 aggravated, if not

[3] U.S. Department of Commerce, *Statistical Abstract of the United States* (Washington, D.C.: 1953), p. 186.

caused, the 1937–38 recession that occurred in the midst of the depression of the 1930's.

The official justification for the reserve requirement increases in 1936 and 1937 was that the "Board's action was in the nature of a precautionary measure to prevent an uncontrollable expansion of credit in the future."[4] Commercial banks had accumulated $3 billion in excess reserves by the mid-thirties, and the Board of Governors feared that commercial bank use of these excess reserves to expand credit in the economic upswing then under way might cause a price inflation. Hence, the Board of Governors took restrictive action and this was soon followed by a substantial decline in the stock of money.

It is difficult to appraise the wisdom of this action. If one views this large volume of excess reserves as balances that existed because of a lack of demand for bank loans, then the restrictive action had little direct effect on bank money creation and the 1937–38 recession, and the Federal Reserve was possibly correct in reducing the inflationary potential of unused reserves. Proponents of this view at most concede that "the timing of the increase in requirements proved unfortunate. For various extraneous reasons, there followed a sharp decline in business and prices."[5]

On the other hand, if one accepts the view that the banking system did not regard these reserves as excess reserves available for credit expansion, then the restrictive action was a significant factor in the 1937–38 contraction. It has been argued, for example, that

experience during the years from 1929 to 1933 had taught banks that it was not enough to keep in the form of high-powered money only the minimum amount required by law; legally required reserves could not be drawn on to meet emergency demands without the banks being liable to closure. . . . Doubling of required reserves . . . reduced drastically the cushion of effective reserves, as the banks viewed them, available against liabilities needing protection . . . the result was to induce banks to seek to rebuild their so-called excess reserves, thereby producing downward pressure on the money supply.[6]

The years 1936 and 1937 then offered us our first experiences with increases in the reserve requirement. Other increases occurred in 1941, 1948, and 1951. The increases in 1941 and 1951 were designed to help restrict credit extension in the private economy during a period of impending war in the first instance, and actual war in the second. The 1948 increase was intended to help restrain inflationary forces already at work in the economy. The effects of the 1948 and 1951 actions, however, were in part cancelled out by another Federal Reserve policy, support of the government securities market. During this same period commercial banks were selling securities to

---

[4] Board of Governors of the Federal Reserve System, *Annual Report* (1936), p. 2.

[5] E. A. Goldenweiser, *American Monetary Policy* (New York: McGraw-Hill, 1951), p. 180.

[6] Milton Friedman, *A Program for Monetary Stability* (New York: Fordham University Press, 1960), p. 46.

the Federal Reserve banks, thereby adding to member bank reserves. It will be recalled that the sale of government securities by the Federal Reserve causes member bank reserves to decline. Aside from the conflicting effects of other Federal Reserve actions, however, these three reserve requirement increases were economically appropriate and timely.

Since 1951 there has only been one increase in reserve requirements, and this increase was not intended as a contracyclical measure. In November of 1960, the reserve requirement for the demand deposit liabilities of country banks was increased from 11 to 12 percent. Simultaneously, it was announced that all member banks were permitted to count vault cash as part of their legal reserves. Country banks had substantial volumes of vault cash; therefore, the increase in reserve requirements was needed to avoid a substantial increase in country bank excess reserves.

In recent years, the Federal Reserve System has apparently been very reluctant to use increases in reserve requirements as an instrument to combat expansive forces in the economy. There are several reasons for this attitude. First, commercial bankers feel the direct impact of reserve requirement increases and are forced to readjust their loan and investment activities. Other tools of Federal Reserve policy, such as open market operations, do not have this direct impact. A sale of securities by the Federal Reserve banks reduces total and excess reserves, but no one commercial bank can directly blame the Federal Reserve banks for the stringency of its reserve position. Rather, it is the purchase of securities by bank customers that affects the reserve position of the bank directly, not Federal Reserve sale. A bank adjusts to customer actions of this sort in the course of everyday business. Furthermore, reserve requirement increases may encounter substantial resistance from bankers. Political pressure may be exerted to cause a reversal of policy, particularly if member bank profit positions are threatened.

Second, frequent reserve requirement changes can create difficulties for the managers of small banks. These banks are not equipped to make the rapid changes in the composition of their portfolios that such changes necessitate. In addition, changes in reserve requirements are announced in advance of the date on which they are to become effective. This causes a simultaneous attempt by all to adapt in advance, further complicating the adjustment process. For example, an announced increase in reserve requirements may induce many banks to sell U.S. government securities immediately to get additional reserves before the increase takes effect. This may cause a sharp drop in the price of those securities and substantial capital losses for the selling banks. The adjustment process is difficult for banks when the reserve requirement increases or decreases, but the increases cause more difficulty. Decreases are usually favorably received by banks.

Third, the most important reason that reserve requirement increases are used infrequently is because of their extraordinarily strong contractionary effect. The Federal Reserve has never raised reserve requirements less than $\frac{1}{2}$ percent. Offhand, this amount may seem minimal, but even such a small increase has a significant impact upon commercial bank money-creating potential.

Effects of a ½ percent increase in reserve requirements. Assume, for example, that a ½ percent increase in the reserve requirement for demand deposits is contemplated. By how much would this reduce the money-creating ability of the member banks? To solve this problem we use the following equation, developed in Chapter 7:

$$D = \frac{R - r'(TD)}{r + i} \qquad [7\text{--}5]$$

The factors included in equation 7–5 as applied to our problem are D, the amount of demand deposits the member banks are capable of supporting, given the other factors; R, the volume of member bank reserves; r, the reserve requirement for demand deposits; r', the reserve requirement for time deposits; TD, the volume of member bank time deposits; and i', the ratio of excess reserves to demand deposits that member banks wish to maintain.

Assume that prior to any change in the reserve requirement, the following situation prevails:

$$
\begin{aligned}
\textit{If:} \quad R &= \$20.140 \text{ billion} \\
r' &= .04 \\
TD &= \$89.361 \text{ billion} \\
r &= 0.1475 \\
i' &= 0.0037 \\
\textit{Then:} \quad D &= \$109.563 \text{ billion}
\end{aligned}
$$

If the actual volume of commercial bank demand deposit liabilities is equal to D—the volume that commercial banks can support—then the member banks have no room for an expansion of loans, investments, and demand deposit money. This does not mean that the member banks have no excess reserves, however. The fact that i' is greater than 0 shows that in fact they do; actually, under our assumptions, the member banks have $409 million in desired excess reserves. Banks cannot expand without switching some excess reserves needed to cover c and i to required reserves.

Now suppose there is a ½ percent increase in required reserves and r becomes .1525. Further assume that there is no cash drain or inflow. This results in a decreased D of $106.056 billion. In other words, an increase of ½ percent in the reserve requirement for demand deposits would lead to a $3.507 billion reduction in the money supply. In percentage terms, the forced contraction is equal to more than 3 percent of the original volume of demand deposits. This constitutes a rather sharp contraction in the money supply, and it is induced by only a small change in the reserve requirement.

Equation 7–5 is useful largely for pedagogical purposes, but it does bear a strong relationship to reality. The values chosen for r, r', and TD are those that applied for member banks during the four-week period ending October 16, 1963. Although the value .1475 for r differs somewhat from the 16½ and 12 percent reserve requirements prescribed for reserve city and country banks at that date, the figure was calculated as the combined ratio of required reserves for demand deposit liabilities to the sum of demand deposit liabilities for both reserve city and country banks. Thus, 14.75 percent represents the actual average reserve requirement for demand deposit liabilities of all member banks during this period.

One unrealistic assumption included in this equation was that the $409 million in excess reserves was not usable because of constancy in i'. This was done to simplify the example. A much more significant objection to this example would be that the period chosen was not one that might justify this sharp a contraction in credit. Most economists would agree that some tightening of credit in late 1963 was desirable, but not the $3.5 billion reduction in member bank demand deposit liabilities that a ½ percent rise in reserve requirements would have necessitated. Smaller increases in the reserve requirement are feasible, but the Federal Reserve System does not normally change reserve requirements by less than ½ percent. Thus, even small increases in the reserve requirement can exert a strong contractive force on the economy. If excess reserves are not large, this small increase can lead to a sharp contraction of loans and investments, and consequently (as Chapter 7 demonstrated) to a sharp reduction in the volume of demand deposit money.

It is for these reasons—(1) the disproportionately heavy impact upon banks, (2) the portfolio adjustment difficulties for banks, and (3) the severity of the resultant contractionary forces—that the Board of Governors makes infrequent use of reserve requirement increases. The Board could soften the overall impact of this device by simultaneously purchasing U.S. government securities, but this suggests that the open market operations are a superior anti-inflationary measure in the first place.

Decreases in reserve requirements. Decreases in reserve requirements have been more frequent than increases. The first decrease occurred in 1938. This action was clearly appropriate in light of the depressed condition of the economy at the time.

The next decrease occurred in a war year, 1942, and was limited to central reserve city banks. This action was not contracyclical. The New York and Chicago banks had been experiencing reserve drains as large volumes of government securities were sold by the Treasury in Chicago and New York. As depositors drew down their accounts to buy these securities, reserves were lost. The proceeds of the security sales were then used to make defense purchases throughout the country. To compensate, the government reduced the reserve requirements for central reserve city banks.

Since the end of World War II, reserve requirements have been reduced only in periods of recession or periods of less than full employment. Thus, reductions were made in the 1949, 1953–54, and 1957–58 recessions. During the 1960–61 recession, however, there was no general lowering of reserve requirements for demand deposits; instead, banks were supplied with additional lending capacity by being allowed to count vault cash as part of their reserves. In the fall of 1962 there was a reduction in the reserve requirement for time deposits. The economy was expanding at this time, but there was still a substantial amount of unemployment. (The purpose of this reduction was to provide reserves for long-term growth in deposits, however.)

How effective have reductions in reserve requirements been as a contracyclical monetary technique? It would appear that the measures taken in 1949, 1953–54, 1957–58, and 1962 were in the right direction. Periods of less than full employment and recessions call for increased lending capacity, as previously indicated. These decreases in reserve requirements were frequently accompanied by Federal Reserve bank sales of U.S. government securities, however. This tended to offset the expansive effects of the reserve requirement decrease. Apparently the Board of Governors felt that the excess reserve increases caused by the reserve requirement decreases were too great. Subsequently, there were open market purchases of U.S. government securities, so that additional reserves could be released gradually to the banking system. Again the point could be made that open market operations might have been a superior policy instrument in the first place.

To further illustrate how small decreases in reserve requirements lead to large increases in the ability of banks to expand deposit money, the formula used in the preceding section may be reversed. If r were initially 15.25 percent, then D could not exceed $106.056 billion. If r were subsequently reduced to 14.75 percent, then D could expand to $109.563 billion. Thus, if banks utilized all of their increased lending capacity, a $3.5 billion increase in the money supply would take place, which is a substantial increase in any type of economic situation.

Evaluation of the reserve requirement policy instrument. There is considerable doubt as to the merits of using variable reserve requirements as an instrument of economic policy. Contracyclical increases are unpopular, create management difficulties for bankers, and force banks to contract sharply in the absence of offsetting open market operations. Contracyclical reductions may not prove to be dependable in economic crisis. For example, it is often argued that banks cannot be forced to expand loans and investments; hence almost any type of central bank action designed to expand reserves, and thereby economic activity, will be ineffectual. The adage that you can bring a horse to water but cannot make him drink is often cited at this point as evidence of the weakness of all forms of monetary action. The economic history of the postwar period seems to put the lie to this adage, however. The cold war situation and an awareness of the economic and human loss associated with depression have helped to sustain comparatively high levels of employment and output. Our recessions have been mild. Banks have typically operated with small margins of excess reserves. Thus, it is reasonable to assume that, at least for mild recessions, banks will shortly make use of an increase in their money-creating abilities.

On the other hand, a reduction in reserve requirements is a powerful means of increasing bank lending ability. In the preceding illustration, a full utilization of a $3 billion increase in the loan and investment potential of the banking system over a short period of time could create undesired inflationary pressures in our postwar economy. Offsetting open market operations would be necessary.

Is there then no justification for using reserve requirements as an instrument of economic policy? The Board of Governors recognizes the difficulties inherent in the use of this policy instrument when it argues that "As an instrument of monetary management, changes in required reserve percentages are less flexible and continuously adaptable than the open market and discount instruments."[7] Nevertheless, the Board believes that reserve requirement reductions have a place among monetary management techniques in our postwar economy. Reserve requirement decreases immediately increase the excess reserves of *all* member banks, whereas open market operations first affect the reserve position of banks in New York City, where the U.S. government securities market is concentrated. Thus, the Board believes that the effects of a reduction in reserve requirements will be more quickly felt throughout the country than a purchase of U.S. government securities by the Federal Reserve Bank of New York. The fact that the Federal Reserve often sells securities at the same time that it lowers reserve requirements seems to cast suspicion on this line of reasoning, however. If the immediate effects of a sale of government securities is, in fact, concentrated in New York City, then how can this action act to offset a reduction of reserve requirements? Nothing has been done to reduce the full expansion capabilities of the non-New York banks. Only if the non-New York banks adjusted to their increased excess reserves much more slowly than the New York banks would a countermeasure directed towards the New York banks alone be acceptable.

Thus, it would seem that open market operations are more flexible than reserve requirement adjustments as an instrument of monetary policy. Only if variations in reserve requirements were substantially less than ½ percent could they be used without offsetting open market operations.

---

[7] Board of Governors of the Federal Reserve System, *The Federal Reserve System: Purposes and Functions* (Washington, D.C.: 1961), p. 54.

FIGURE 12–1. Short-term interest rates, 1919–64.

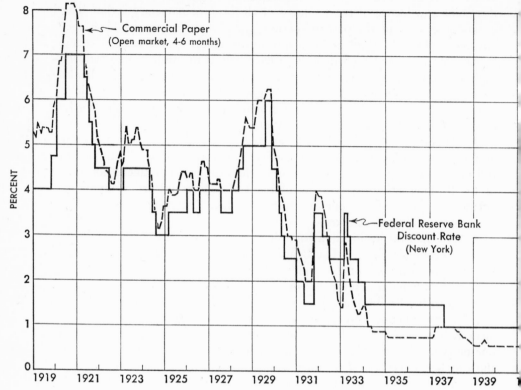

Source: Board of Governors of the Federal Reserve System, *Federal Reserve Historical*

The Discount Rate

The discount rate is the "price" that a district Federal Reserve bank charges member banks for lending them reserves.[8] Such borrowing is generally for a short period of time, about fifteen days. Each Federal Reserve bank sets the discount rate for its district although this is subject to review by the Board of Governors. Although changes in the rate do not occur frequently, the rate is reviewed by the Federal Reserve every fourteen days.

When changes are announced, the new rates are usually the same among the various Federal Reserve banks. This tendency has become more pronounced in recent decades as various sections of the nation have lost their regional character and, in financial matters, have become part of the national money market.

As pointed out earlier, member banks borrow to meet temporary shortages of reserves or to build up reserves prior to increasing their lending

---

[8] When the term "discount rate" is used, it is understood to include all three rates described in Chapter 11.

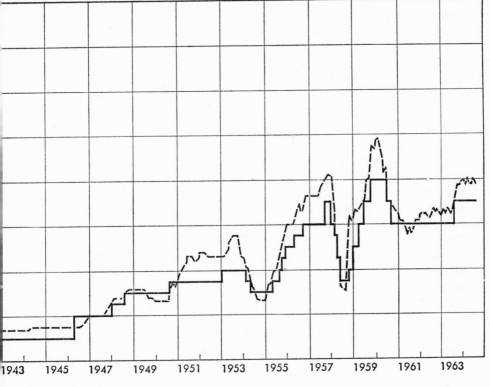

Chart Book, 1964, pp. 26–27.

activity. The Federal Reserve banks and the Board of Governors change discount rates in order to affect member bank lending activity. Theoretically, increases in the rate restrict member bank borrowing of reserves and hence bank lending activity; and conversely, decreases in the rate encourage member bank borrowing of reserves and lending activity.

Unfortunately, matters are not quite that simple. The data shows that Federal Reserve bank discounts and advances move in the same direction as the discount rate. Logically they should move in opposite directions if discount rate manipulations are to have their intended contracyclical effects. Banks, however, borrow additional reserves on the upward part of the cycle, even with high discount rates, partly because of increased business and consumer demand for funds and partly because the earnings possible on loans exceed the discount costs. On the downward side of the cycle, however, the situation is reversed.

The behavior of discount rates and discounts and advances from 1917 through 1964. Figure 12–1 shows the movement in the discount rate of the Federal Reserve Bank of New York and the numerous commercial paper rates from 1919 to mid-1964. The discount rate depicted on this graph represents advances secured by U.S. government securities and discounts and advances secured by eligible paper. Table 12–2 shows the present structure of discount rates, and Table 12–3 gives the volume of Federal Reserve bank discounts and advances from 1917 to 1964. This data seems to support our previous contention that the volume of discounts and advances fluctuate in the same direction as discount rates.

1. *1917–1932.* There were five periods of economic decline from 1917 to 1932: late 1918 to early 1919, 1920 to mid-1921, mid-1923 to mid-1924, 1927, and late 1929 through 1932. The remaining intervals were periods of economic expansion. Theoretically, periods of economic decline call for discount rate decreases. Only in the first recession, 1918–19, were there no discount rate decreases, and there were good reasons for not altering the rates at that time. For one thing, the recession was very short-lived. For another, discount rates were already abnormally low relative to the rates commercial banks could earn on their loans and investments. The Federal Reserve had assisted the U.S. Treasury in financing the war effort by keeping discount rates low. This had facilitated the purchase of U.S. government securities with borrowed funds by both commercial banks and the nonbank public at comparatively low interest costs. It also enabled the Treasury to market securities with lower interest rates than would have been possible in a government bond market not supported by the Federal Reserve banks. As a result of these wartime policies, we entered the short postwar recession with a discount rate structure that was already low.

The mere fact that discount rates were lowered in four of the five past recessions should not be taken as conclusive evidence that central bank policy was correct during all of those periods, however. Federal Reserve discount policy in 1920–21 seems to have been inappropriate, for example. Discount rates were raised sharply in late 1919 to counteract that year's price rises. They were again increased, however, in the first half of 1920. They were then maintained until well into 1921, when they were finally lowered. Thus, during most of this severe contraction, discount rates were at very high levels.

Viewed from a present-day perspective, this was clearly inappropriate monetary action. Viewed from the perspective of 1920–21, however, it may have appeared to be appropriate action, since the Federal Reserve System at that time was not so concerned with maintaining domestic economic stability as with maintaining our international gold position. The high discount rates of the period did help stem the outflow of gold. When a nation's internal rate of interest is low relative to those abroad, it tends to lose gold as its citizens purchase securities abroad rather than at home. On the other hand, when internal interest rates are high relative to those abroad, foreigners purchase the nation's securities and its own citizens tend to increase domestic security investments. This leads to an influx of gold.

TABLE 12–2. FEDERAL RESERVE BANK DISCOUNT RATES, IN EFFECT NOVEMBER, 1964

(PERCENT PER ANNUM)

FEDERAL RESERVE BANK	DISCOUNT FOR AND ADVANCES TO MEMBER BANKS						ADVANCES TO ALL OTHERS UNDER LAST PARAGRAPH, SECTION 13‡		
	Advances and discounts under Sections 13 and 13a*			Advances under Section 10b†					
	Rate on November 30	Effective date	Previous rate	Rate on November 30	Effective date	Previous rate	Rate on November 30	Effective date	Previous rate
Boston	4	Nov. 24, 1964	3½	4½	Nov. 24, 1964	4	5½	Nov. 24, 1964	4½
New York	4	Nov. 24, 1964	3½	4½	Nov. 24, 1964	4	5	Nov. 24, 1964	4½
Philadelphia	4	Nov. 24, 1964	3½	4½	Nov. 24, 1964	4	5	Nov. 24, 1964	4½
Cleveland	4	Nov. 27, 1964	3½	4½	Nov. 27, 1964	4	5½	Nov. 27, 1964	5
Richmond	4	Nov. 27, 1964	3½	4½	Nov. 27, 1964	4	5	Nov. 27, 1964	4½
Atlanta	4	Nov. 25, 1964	3½	4½	Nov. 25, 1964	4	5	Nov. 25, 1964	5
Chicago	4	Nov. 24, 1964	3½	4½	Nov. 24, 1964	4	6	July 19, 1963	4½
St. Louis	4	Nov. 24, 1964	3½	4½	Nov. 24, 1964	4	5	Nov. 24, 1964	4½
Minneapolis	4	Nov. 30, 1964	3½	4½	Nov. 30, 1964	4	5	Nov. 30, 1964	4½
Kansas City	4	Nov. 30, 1964	3½	4½	Nov. 30, 1964	4	5	Nov. 30, 1964	4½
Dallas	4	Nov. 27, 1964	3½	4½	Nov. 27, 1964	5	5	Nov. 27, 1964	4½
San Francisco	4	Nov. 27, 1964	3½	4½	Nov. 27, 1964	4	5	Nov. 27, 1964	4½

Source: *Federal Reserve Bulletin*, December, 1964, p. 1545.

* Advances secured by U.S. government securities and discounts and advances secured by eligible paper. Rates shown also apply to advances secured by securities of federal intermediate credit banks maturing within six months. Maximum maturity: ninety days, except that discounts of certain bankers' acceptances and of agricultural paper may have maturities not over six months and nine months, respectively, and advances secured by FICB securities are limited to fifteen days.

† Advances secured to the satisfaction of the Federal Reserve bank. Maximum maturity: four months.

‡ Advances to individuals, partnerships, or corporations other than member banks secured by U.S. government direct securities. Maximum maturity: ninety days.

Federal Reserve discount rate manipulation in 1920 was thus designed to protect our gold reserves.

Following the events of 1920 and 1921, Federal Reserve changes of discount rates during recession were in the appropriate direction until 1929 and 1931. During the interval, 1922–29, the Federal Reserve came to adopt the policy position that the instruments of monetary policy should be used to help promote price stability and a high level of business activity. This policy was abandoned in 1929 and 1931, however. In an attempt to stem excessive stock market speculation, the Federal Reserve raised discount rates

TABLE 12–3. FEDERAL RESERVE DISCOUNTS AND ADVANCES,
ANNUAL AVERAGES OF DAILY FIGURES, 1917–1964
(IN MILLIONS OF DOLLARS)

YEAR	AMOUNT	YEAR	AMOUNT	YEAR	AMOUNT
1917	376*	1933	283	1949	231
1918	1,134	1934	36	1950	129
1919	1,906	1935	7	1951	293
1920	2,523	1936	6	1952	801
1921	1,797	1937	14	1953	777
1922	571	1938	9	1954	217
1923	736	1939	5	1955	666
1924	373	1940	4	1956	833
1925	490	1941	5	1957	850
1926	572	1942	7	1958	295
1927	442	1943	25	1959	812
1928	840	1944	135	1960	436
1929	952	1945	376	1961	83
1930	272	1946	310	1962	136
1931	327	1947	219	1963	269
1932	521	1948	331	1964	289†

Source: 1917–60, Board of Governors of the Federal Reserve System, *Supplement to Banking and Monetary Statistics*. Section 10 (Washington, D.C.: 1962), p. 14; 1961–63, computed from *Federal Reserve Bulletin*, various issues, 1961–64.
* Based on data for August–December.
† Based on data for January–September.

in mid-1929. Actually other economic indicators had already turned down. Following the stock market crash of October, 1929, discount notes were quickly reduced, reaching their historical low to that date in mid-1931. This was appropriate. In October of 1931, however, there was another discount rate increase, this one designed to offset another drain of gold. There were about eight million people unemployed in the United States at the time—no time to restrict credit! Subsequently, rates were reduced in 1932.

What was the behavior of discount rates during the other years between 1918 and 1929? Increases in the rates were made in 1919, 1920, 1923, 1925, 1926, and 1928. With the exception of 1920, they were all years of economic expansion, and the increases in the discount rate were called for.

In general, therefore, it appears that during the period from 1917 to 1932, the Federal Reserve banks usually moved discount rates in an appropriate contracyclical manner. The principal exceptions were the low rates of World War I, the maintenance of high rates through much of 1921, and the increases of 1929 and 1931. However, in spite of discount rate increases at both appropriate and inappropriate times, most of the period was characterized by an easy money situation. As is illustrated in Figure 12–1, discount rates were typically below what the commercial banks could earn on commercial paper.

Although the manipulation of discount rates was generally appropriate in this period in terms of the national economy, the movement of discounts and advances was not in the right direction. In every year when discount rates were increased, discounts and advances to member banks increased. In every year, except 1932, when discount rates were decreased, discounts and advances to member banks decreased. This is exactly the opposite of what is supposed to happen; a discount rate increase should *decrease* member bank borrowing of reserves and a discount rate decrease should *increase* member bank borrowing. Yet this did not occur.

It is usually argued, however, that discount rate increases and decreases are not intended to bring about absolute decreases and increases, respectively, in member bank borrowing of reserves. Instead, the increased cost of borrowing reserves that comes with increases in the discount rate during economic expansion is simply intended to hold down the increase in reserve borrowing that would have taken place in the absence of the rate increase. In economic expansion there is a strong demand for funds by the nonbank public. Banks, as profit-seeking business enterprises, are anxious to satisfy that demand by expanding loans and investments. Thus, they tend to utilize their existing reserves more intensively at such a time and expand their reserve base with borrowings from the Federal Reserve banks. Thus, discount rate increases had little apparent effect on borrowings because the high return on commercial bank alternative investment opportunities relative to discount rates during most of the period from 1919 to 1929 tended to sustain member bank borrowing. In such a situation, discount rate increases at best only hold down the amount of member bank increased borrowing.

It is also argued that the decreased cost of borrowing reserves that comes with decreases in the discount rate is simply intended to minimize the decrease in reserve borrowing that is expected to take place in recession in the absence of the rate decrease. With decreased profit opportunities in recession, banks are anxious to repay borrowed reserves. The demand for loans by the nonbank public is weak in such periods, and it does not usually pay for banks to hold borrowed reserves that are not being utilized in profitable loan expansion. Discount rate decreases, therefore, only serve to minimize the decrease in the amount of member bank borrowing.

The preceding analysis is persuasive but difficult to establish empirically, since it posits a knowledge of how banks would have reacted in the absence of the rate changes that actually took place. It is extremely difficult to predict how banks will react to changes in the discount rate; it is even possible that an increase in rates can encourage banks to increase borrowings and, accordingly, their own loans and investments, as shall be pointed out in our subsequent evaluation of discount rate policy. On the other hand, a decrease in rates may even speed up repayment of borrowed reserves.

2. *1933–1951.* Member bank borrowing of reserves declined to insignificant proportions in the 1930's. Throughout the thirties member banks had substantial volumes of excess reserves and, as a result, there was no need to borrow reserves. Following a temporary rise in discount rates coincident with the nationwide closing of the banks from March 6, 1933, to March 13, 1933, there were reductions in the rates in April, May, and October of 1933, and further decreases in 1934, 1935, and 1937. From 1937 to 1942 there were no changes in discount rates; the rate on advances secured by U.S. government securities was at a historic peacetime low of 1 percent.

Although this rate was very low in the 1930's, it does not necessarily follow that it was a period of easy money. Since banks had substantial volumes of excess reserves and few lending and investment opportunities, there was no serious need to go to the discount window. The criterion of ease or restrictiveness of central bank policy should not be the absolute level of discount rates, however; it should be the level of discount rates relative to what banks can earn on their investment and lending opportunities. "The New York discount rate was never below the average 4- to 6-month commercial paper rate in any week in the eight years from 1934 through 1941. The result, of course, was negligible use of rediscounting facilities."[9] As Table 12–3 shows, Federal Reserve bank discounts and advances reached a low of $4 million in 1940. From this perspective, a policy of apparent monetary ease may actually be viewed as one of restriction. Many economists would disagree with this view, but it merits some thought, nevertheless.

Discount rates remained stable during World War II and the early postwar years. The discount rate on advances secured by U.S. government securities, however, was dropped to $\frac{1}{2}$ percent in 1942 and returned to 1 percent in 1946. These changes were the only ones made in this rate from 1937 to 1948. The main reason for this stability in discount rates is that decreases in rates during wartime are inappropriate from a contracyclical point of view. They encourage borrowing of reserves and credit expansion during a period of full employment, thus causing inflation.

On the other hand, to the extent that a war effort is financed through borrowing, a decrease in discount rates will encourage investment in government securities. As we shall see later, this type of financing effort is open to harsh criticism. A low discount rate was one means employed to assist

---

[9] Milton Friedman and Anna Jacobson Schwartz, *A Monetary History of the United States, 1867–1960* (Princeton, N.J.: Princeton University Press, 1963), p. 514.

the U.S. Treasury in financing American participation in World War II. Another was the support of the government bond market—a policy that is discussed in more detail in the next chapter.

The volume of discounts and advances made by the Federal Reserve banks increased gradually during the war. From a prewar low of $4 million in 1940, they increased to an average of $376 million in 1945. Following the war, commercial banks continued to use the "discount window" with substantially greater frequency than they had during the depressed thirties, but discounts and advances never approached the volume of the 1920's. A tendency on the part of banks to avoid borrowing reserves has always been part of our banking heritage. The 1930's merely reinforced this tradition and, except for our most prosperous postwar years, this tendency has remained evident to the present day. Another factor contributing to the small volume of discounting in the years 1933–51 was the open market policy of the Federal Reserve System. As previously mentioned, the Federal Reserve System had committed itself to supporting the government bond market during World War II. This policy of support continued through early 1951. One way in which commercial banks may provide themselves with additional reserves in order to expand loans is to sell some of their holdings of U.S. government securities. Normally, at such a time this would lead to a capital loss, since the increased supply of bonds would depress bond prices. The Federal Reserve was committed to maintaining the prices of U.S. government securities, however. Thus, when there were substantial decreases in government bond prices, the Federal Reserve bought government securities, thereby maintaining bond prices and providing commercial banks with reserves. This meant that commercial banks had little need to get additional reserves through discounts and advances. Also, to the extent that banks refrained from borrowing because of this open market policy, the effectiveness of contracyclical discount rate changes was reduced.

3. *1951–1964.* Support of the government bond market by the Federal Reserve System ended with the Treasury–Federal Reserve Accord in March of 1951. Since that time discount rate changes have been frequently used to promote economic stability. There has also been an increase in the use of the "discount window" by commercial banks during periods of economic upswing.

Discount rates were lowered in the contractions of 1953–54, 1957–58, and 1960–61 and raised in the expansions of 1950–53, 1954–57, 1958–60, and 1961–64. For the most part, these contracyclical adjustments appear to have been in the right direction. Nevertheless, in only one year, 1953, did discount rates and the volume of discounts and advances move in opposite directions. On the other hand, in 1955—a boom year—discounts and advances rose by more than $400 million. In 1956 they were further increased by almost $200 million. In fact, discounts and advances rose from a low of $217 million in 1954, the trough of the 1953–54 recession, to $850 million in 1957. In the same period, the discount rate for advances secured by U.S. government securities and for discounts and advances secured by eligible paper at the Federal Reserve Bank of New York, rose from 1½ to 3½ percent.

Furthermore, as Figure 12–1 shows, in periods of upswing, the discount rate was always below the rate for four- to six-month commercial paper, even when discount rates were being increased. And at the bottom of each contraction the rate for four- to six-month commercial paper was less than the discount rate, even after discount rate decreases. Thus it appears that, in spite of the correct direction of discount rate changes, these changes in themselves have not been big enough to have the desired economic effect. At best, as in the 1920's, they may have decreased the volume of increased borrowings in economic expansion, and minimized the decrease in borrowings in contraction. This, of course, is a contribution to maintaining economic stability, but it is very difficult to establish quantitatively that this is actually what occurred.

There is only one instance of a discount rate change in the 1950's that now appears to have been clearly inappropriate. The increases of August, 1957, were probably a miscalculation. The economy had reached its peak in June of 1957; a tightening of credit conditions in August would appear not to have been necessary. However, it could be pointed out in defense of these changes that the rate on four- to six-month commercial paper at that time was substantially above the discount rate. In any case, in November, 1957, several months after the recession of 1957–58 was well under way, the Federal Reserve banks reversed themselves and lowered discount rates.

The rate movements described for the period 1951–64 were nearly all designed to help stabilize the economy. The main exceptions to this were the rate increases of July, 1963, and November, 1964. These actions were taken principally to help reduce the adverse U.S. balance of payments and to protect the dollar against a gold outflow. Short-term interest rates abroad were higher than in the United States, thereby inducing an outflow of funds from the United States. By raising discount rates, it was hoped that this outflow would decrease because of increases in domestic interest rates.

Evaluation of the discount rate policy instrument. In general, discount rate manipulation does not appear to have been a particularly successful tool of economic policy. The contracyclical uses made of this instrument in the 1920's and since 1951 have, for the most part, been in the right direction. The ameliorative effects of these discount rate changes have not been quantitatively observable, however; discounts and advances have usually moved in the same direction as discount rates. This is largely due to the fact that the rate on four- to six-month commercial paper was usually above discount rates in periods of economic expansion, and below those rates in recession. When discount rates are below market yields on assets such as commercial paper, on which commercial banks are able to make substantial earnings, then commercial banks are encouraged to borrow reserves to expand their investment in these assets. Thus, in economic upswing, when this type of differential has tended to exist, Federal Reserve discounts and advances increased. One way in which the Federal Reserve could avoid this contradictory effect would be to make larger increases in the discount rates. On the other hand, when discount rates are above market yields on assets such as commercial paper, then banks are discouraged from borrowing reserves and expanding loans and investments. This type of differential has existed in recession, and thus Federal Reserve discounts and advances have decreased. They may well have decreased anyway in recession because of a lack of demand for loans from commercial banks. One must still raise the question, however: did the fact that market rates were below discount rates in recession aggravate the cyclical decline? Although discount rates were lowered, should they not have been reduced still further to bring them beneath market rates? The answers to these two questions is probably yes.

Thus, previous experience indicates that *discount rate changes, by themselves, have not been an effective instrument of monetary policy*. This conclusion is based primarily upon the movement of market rates, discount rates, and the volume of discounts and advances.

There are other factors that tend to work against the success of discount rate policy too, but these factors are largely nonquantitative:

1. The volume of discounts and advances are directly determined by member bank demands, not by Federal Reserve bank control.

2. Many member banks have a reluctance to borrow reserves.

3. Announced discount rate changes may have adverse effects on member bank borrowing.

4. A change in the discount rate may not be a signal for a change in Federal Reserve policy.

5. No change in discount rates may become a policy tending to restrict or encourage credit changes.

First, the Federal Reserve banks have no direct control over the volume of discounts and advances. If banks meet the prescribed qualifications for borrowing, they can almost always borrow reserves from their district Federal Reserve bank. This provides an escape for banks that wish to expand loans and investments in periods of full employment, rising prices, and a restrictive monetary policy. Even with large discount rate increases, banks that choose to pay the price for additional reserves can usually obtain them, and thereby circumvent Federal Reserve policy.

The Federal Reserve banks cannot directly change member bank reserves through discount rate policy. The most they can do by discount rate manipulation is to encourage or discourage banks to borrow reserves. Commercial banks may decide for themselves how much in reserves they wish to have. Thus, discount rate changes can only have the desired effect upon member bank reserve positions when the Federal Reserve System has guessed correctly about member bank reserve borrowing intentions. When the Federal Reserve System has guessed incorrectly, it must utilize other instruments of policy to offset the undesired movements of member bank borrowings. Typically, in such a situation, the Federal Reserve System resorts to open market operations to change member bank reserve positions. Thus, just as with reserve requirement changes, one wonders why open market operations are not used in the first place to bring about the desired change in member bank reserve positions.

This should not be taken to mean that there is no need for the discounting mechanism, of course. Open market operations cannot take care of the short-run needs for additional reserves by specific banks in specific communities. Yet,

. . . through the discount mechanism, individual member banks, especially in communities subject to unusually wide seasonal fluctuations in business payments, may cushion or spread out somewhat the reserve adjustments they find it necessary to make. In coping with short-term instabilities in bank reserve positions, open market operations and discount operations are complementary tools of monetary policy.[10]

Second, many member banks are apparently reluctant to borrow reserves. These banks usually maintain large volumes of excess reserves. Thus, if they wish to increase their credit holdings, they can do so even if the Federal Reserve banks raise discount rates in an economic upswing to levels above market rates. Thus, changes in the discount rate cannot restrict the lending operations of these banks; only the other two tools of monetary policy can do that.

On the other hand, banks that typically operate with a narrow margin of excess reserves may be seriously affected by discount rate increases. To the extent that discount rates are raised sharply because of increasing bank loans (made by the banks with large excess reserves and a reluctance to borrow), the brunt of the contractionary policy is borne by the banks operating with the narrow margin of excess reserves. A discount rate increase, therefore, can be discriminatory and unwittingly enhance the competitive position of one group of banks at the expense of another. Eventually, however, a contractionary discount rate policy will affect all banks; as the banks with excess reserves expand their loans and investments, their excess reserves will dwindle. Open market operations could bring this about a good bit sooner, however.

Generally it is the smaller "country" banks that are reluctant to borrow reserves and the large reserve city banks that most often go to the "discount window" of the Federal Reserve. In June of 1964, reserve city banks had $65 million in excess reserves, whereas country banks had $312 million. Of the $312 million in country bank excess reserves, only $76 million were borrowed, leaving them with $236 million in "free reserves" (excess reserves minus borrowings at the Federal Reserve banks). Reserve city banks, on the

---

[10] Board of Governors of the Federal Reserve System, *The Federal Reserve System: Purposes and Functions*, 1961, p. 58.

other hand, had $194 million in borrowings and —$129 million in free reserves.[11] This difference in reserve positions is not attributable to the difference in size between country and reserve city banks, since total reserve city bank assets were only about 1.7 times those of country banks.

To some extent the reluctance of country banks to borrow may be explained by their lack of investment opportunities. Reserve city banks are usually located in centers of financial importance and have investment opportunities not available to the country banks. Furthermore, the smaller average size of the country banks precludes them from extending loans to businesses of a large size. Finally, the reserve city banks, operating on a larger scale than the country banks, have large staffs that are specialized in each of the many different facets of banking activity. This enables the reserve city banks to gauge their reserve positions more accurately and thus to be more economical in their use of reserves. All of this suggests that country banks do not in fact have a built-in reluctance to borrow reserves; instead, it is their smaller size and less efficient operations that force them to maintain relatively large volumes of excess reserves as safeguards. In addition, there is a return to be earned upon these excess reserves, because country banks frequently lend reserves to reserve city banks in the federal funds market. Finally, the fact that country bank borrowing of reserves actually increases during periods of strong cyclical upturn also supports the notion that the reluctance of country banks to borrow is forced on them by the limitations of size and by lack of efficiency.

Whether small bank reluctance to borrow is "built-in" or "forced," however, in no way alters the conclusion that this reluctance to borrow weakens the use of discount rate manipulation as an instrument of contracyclical economic policy. Increased discount rates cannot force banks with excess reserves to reduce borrowings, and hence loans and investments.

Third, announced discount rate changes may have undesired effects on member bank borrowing. For example, an increase in rates should normally discourage borrowing of reserves. If expectations concerning future economic trends are such that the announcement of a rate increase leads to the anticipation of further interest rate increases, however, there may then be an increased demand for loans by borrowers before future discount and market interest rate increases take place. Commercial bankers may then have to expand their borrowings in order to meet the increased demands for credit.

Similarly, a decrease in rates should encourage bank borrowing of reserves, but if expectations are such that future rate decreases are anticipated, then the demand for bank loans may decrease and bank borrowing of reserves decline.

Fourth, a change in the discount rate may not be a signal for a change in Federal Reserve policy. For example, "when market rates of interest have moved away from close relationship with the existing discount rate, a

---

[11] *Federal Reserve Bulletin,* July, 1964, pp. 854–55.

change in the level of rates may represent merely a technical adjustment of discount rates to market rates so that the system's discount mechanism will function effectively in line with current policy."[12] If technical adjustments in discount rates are thought to be signs of a change in Federal Reserve policy, this misinterpretation may cause some degree of economic uncertainty. Suppose, for example, that a business contemplating expansion considers a decrease in the discount rate as a signal that the Federal Reserve System believes an economic slump imminent. The business may decide to postpone its expansion until the economic outlook is more favorable. A decrease in expenditures for expansion may then actually contribute to an economic downturn never anticipated by the Federal Reserve.

And fifth, no change in discount rates may become a policy tending to discourage or encourage credit changes. As indicated in the earlier historical discussion of this chapter, the difference between market and discount rates influences bank lending activity. If discount rates remain unchanged while market rates change, then, depending on the nature of the change in market rates, member bank borrowing and lending activity will either increase or decrease. The implication of this fifth factor is that, if discount rate changes are to be effective as an instrument of contracyclical economic policy, they must be utilized frequently in light of changing market rates of interest and the current economic situation.

Supplementary Readings
See the end of Chapter 13.

---

[12] *The Federal Reserve System: Purposes and Functions*, p. 47.

The Development
of Federal Reserve Instruments
# of Monetary Control, Part II

GENERAL MONETARY CONTROLS (CONTINUED)

Open Market Operations

The most potent instrument of monetary policy that the Federal Reserve System has at its disposal is its ability to engage in open market operations. By purchasing U.S. government securities and bankers' acceptances from the nonbank public it can directly increase both commercial bank reserves and the volume of demand deposit money. By selling U.S. government securities and bankers' acceptances to the nonbank public it can directly decrease both commercial bank reserves and the volume of demand deposit money.

When properly utilized, open market operations can be of great help in stabilizing the economy. Since the purchase and sale of securities can be done in small amounts or large amounts, it is possible to change the excess reserve position of the commercial banking system quickly or gradually and in limited amounts. As noted earlier, this is not the case with respect to reserve requirement changes.

Open market operations are not subject to the shortcomings of discount rate changes, either. Open market operations change reserve positions directly. Therefore, the effectiveness of this instrument is not dependent upon the demands of the commercial banking system for reserves. In addition, open market operations do not generally suffer from the "announcement" shortcomings of the discount mechanism. The FOMC continually engages in open market operations. As a consequence, commercial banks find it difficult to interpret whether an increase in Federal Reserve holdings of securities is a normal adjustment to a seasonal need for additional bank reserves or an actual change in Federal Reserve contracyclical monetary policy. Although this may cause some difficulty with respect to the use of the open market instrument, the absence of a clear-cut announcement of change in Federal Reserve open market policy does lessen the probability of adverse bank borrowing action like that which sometimes occurs when discount rate changes are announced.

The Use of the Open Market Instrument of Policy

1. 1917–1935. The use of open market operations as an instrument of economic policy is comparatively recent. When the Federal Reserve System was set up in 1913, it was expected that holdings of U.S. government securities would simply be a source of earnings for the Federal Reserve banks. Although some open market operations in bankers' acceptances was envisioned, the initial purpose of this instrument was to help facilitate the role of the United States in international trade through the development of a bankers' acceptance market.

In practice, however, open market operations in bankers' acceptances have never played a significant role in the implementation of monetary policy, whereas those in government securities have assumed ever-increasing importance. Initially, each Federal Reserve bank was permitted to carry on its own open market operations. This was but one aspect of the initial intention that each Federal Reserve bank should have a substantial amount of local autonomy in the regulation of banking in its own district. It was soon discovered, however, that independent operations in government securities tended to have destabilizing effects on the economy. For example, if the Federal Reserve bank in one district sold securities that were purchased in another district, the result would be a movement of reserves to the selling district. Banks in the district where the securities were purchased would correspondingly lose reserves, thereby leading to an unanticipated and frequently undesirable tightening of credit conditions.

In addition, it was soon recognized that if open market operations were undertaken by the Federal Reserve purely for the purpose of making a profit, this could have a destabilizing effect not on regional economies alone but on the national economy as well. In the early 1920's, for example, it was discovered that Federal Reserve bank purchases of U.S. government securities reduced the borrowing of reserves by member banks, and that sales of securities increased the use of discounting. Hence, a contracyclical discount rate policy could be undermined by individual Federal Reserve banks as they purchased and sold government securities for earnings. Thus, the need for coordination between the discount mechanism, the principal instrument of monetary management in the 1920's, and open market operations was obvious.

In 1922 a committee composed of members from various Federal Reserve banks was set up to coordinate purchases and sales of U.S. government securities by Federal Reserve banks. The following year, this committee was disbanded and in its place the Federal Reserve Board formed the Open Market Investment Committee, which was to buy and sell securities for all Federal Reserve banks. Individual Federal Reserve banks technically still had the power to buy and sell securities, but this was done in very limited amounts.

One shortcoming of the Open Market Investment Committee was that its membership did not include representatives from all of the Federal Reserve banks. Accordingly, in 1930, membership in the committee was broadened to include a representative from each bank. At the same time it was renamed the Open Market Policy Conference. The Banking Act of 1933 formalized this arrangement and renamed the conference the Federal Open Market Committee. It also denied each Federal Reserve bank the right to engage in open market operations on its own account, although an individual bank could still refrain from participation in FOMC operations if it wished. The Banking Act of 1935 removed this last right of individual Federal Reserve banks and established the FOMC in its present form.

Thus, it has only been since 1935 that open market operations have been carried on as they are at present. Throughout most of the 1920's and early 1930's, however, there was some attempt made to coordinate the administration of policy instruments. The various committees in charge of security purchases and sales attempted to avoid conflict with discounting policy.

How effective were open market operations as a contracyclical device during the period prior to 1935? This is a tricky question. It must be remembered that we tend to judge the use of this policy instrument in terms of our current policy that security purchases and sales should be utilized to influence the expansion and contraction of the economy. During the early part of the period being considered, however, this was not an objective of open market policy. Instead, the policy was simply to co-ordinate discounting and open market operations. In addition, most of the security sales and purchases during this period were primarily aimed at adjusting bank reserve positions to seasonal and temporary reserve needs. This is true even today; it is the main reason why the account manager buys and sells securities on a daily basis. Contracyclical purchases and sales of securities are only a small part of overall market operations. In the 1920's and early 1930's they were even less significant.

Nevertheless, small variations in Federal Reserve security purchases and sales can have a contracyclical effect, even though the bulk of the operations have no contracyclical purpose. Table 13–1 shows the annual average amount of U.S. government security and bankers' acceptance holdings by the Federal Reserve banks from 1917 through 1964. During the period ending in 1935, there was an increase in Federal Reserve bank security holdings (U.S. government securities plus acceptances) in every year except 1921, 1923, 1926, 1928, 1929, and 1935. There were business contractions from late 1918 to early 1919, 1920 to mid-1921, mid-1923 to mid-1924, in 1927, and from late 1929 onward. Of the six years in which Federal Reserve bank security holdings decreased, four were years of economic contraction, 1921, 1923, 1929, and 1935; these would appear to have been incorrect applications of contracyclical monetary policy. However, the action of 1921 may be excused on the grounds that it was not until 1922 and 1923 that the Federal Reserve System acknowledged some responsibility for maintaining

TABLE 13–1. FEDERAL RESERVE HOLDINGS OF U.S. GOVERNMENT
SECURITIES AND ACCEPTANCES, 1917–1964
ANNUAL AVERAGES OF DAILY FIGURES
(IN MILLIONS OF DOLLARS)

YEAR	U.S. GOVERNMENT SECURITIES	ACCEPTANCES	YEAR	U.S. GOVERNMENT SECURITIES	ACCEPTANCES
1917*	100	188	1942	3,191	—
1918	134	287	1943	7,724	—
1919	254	324	1944	14,772	—
1920	324	385	1945	21,363	—
1921	254	91	1946	23,250	8
1922	455	159	1947	22,330	—
1923	186	227	1948	21,511	—
1924	402	172	1949	19,560	—
1925	359	287	1950	18,410	—
1926	350	281	1951	22,756	—
1927	417	263	1952	23,066	—
1928	297	328	1953	24,661	—
1929	208	241	1954	24,646	—
1930	564	213	1955	23,891	13
1931	669	245	1956	23,709	23
1932	1,461	71	1957	23,345	27
1933	2,052	83	1958	24,654	40
1934	2,432	25	1959	26,194	35
1935	2,431	5	1960	26,373	39
1936	2,431	4	1961	27,393	—†
1937	2,504	3	1962	29,522	—†
1938	2,565	1	1963	31,764	—†
1939	2,584	—	1964	34,065‡	—†
1940	2,417	—			
1941	2,187	—			

Source: 1917–60, Board of Governors of the Federal Reserve System, *Supplement to Banking and Monetary Statistics:* Section 10, (Washington, D.C.: 1962), p. 14; 1961–64, computed from *Federal Reserve Bulletin*, various issues, 1961–64.
* Based on data for August–December.
† Not shown separately in data source.
‡ Based on data for January–September.

economic stability. Not until 1923 did the Federal Reserve System attempt to centralize open market security purchases by the Federal Reserve banks. It may also be claimed that 1935 was not a year of contraction, but one of business expansion. This is true, but it was a business expansion in the midst of a deep depression, and some expansion in security holdings was called for rather than the contraction that actually took place, even if the latter only amounted to $21 million.

In terms of our current conception of the function of open market operations, the decreases in Federal Reserve bank security holdings were inappropriate in four of the six years in which they occurred between 1917 and 1935. Only in two years, 1926 and 1928, did the decrease in security holdings coincide with business expansion, and in both cases the reduced security holdings were comparatively small—$15 and $55 million respectively.

Were the increases in Federal Reserve bank security holdings during this period any more meaningful? Security holdings were increased in twelve of these years. Five increases took place in the depression years of 1930 through 1934; of the remaining seven increases, four occurred in years that were primarily ones of business contraction—1918, 1920, 1924, and 1927. The beneficial effects of the 1924 and 1927 increases, however, were offset by discount and advance decreases. On three occasions increases took place during economic expansion, an inappropriate time for the monetary authorities to expand security holdings. These occurred in 1919, 1922, and 1925. The 1922 increase, however, was accompanied by discount and advance decreases that more than offset the expansion in security holdings.

In general, in the eighteen years from 1918 to 1935, security purchases moved in the wrong direction seven times. The contracyclical action associated with security purchases for the period 1930 to 1934 was quite impressive, however. Security holdings increased from $449 million in 1929 to $2.457 billion in 1934. Unfortunately, other monetary actions of this period offset the effects of these vigorous and appropriate purchases. Actually, to reach a judgment concerning the merits of Federal Reserve monetary actions, the net effect of all instruments of policy upon commercial bank reserve positions must be considered. In this section, however, we have only discussed whether or not Federal Reserve security purchases and sales, by themselves, were in the correct contracyclical direction.

2. *1935–1945.* Federal Reserve System open market operations in the 1920's and early 1930's had developed into an important instrument of contracyclical monetary policy. Starting in 1935, however, with a slight decrease in Federal Reserve bank security holdings, this policy was abandoned, and from 1935 through 1940, the level of securities held by the Federal Reserve banks was stabilized. There were some year-to-year variations, but these were relatively insignificant when compared with the substantial increases of the early 1930's. The apparent goal of policy during this period was to maintain an orderly market for government securities.

Beginning in 1937, the maintenance of an orderly government securities market became an increasingly important goal of open market operations. Maintaining an orderly market meant stabilizing U.S. government security prices. The first direct action of this sort came in 1937 when the Federal Reserve System began buying long-term securities to prop up their declining prices. Short-term securities were sold at the same time so that member bank reserve positions would not be increased by the purchase of the long-term securities. The next time the Federal Reserve entered the market with a view to propping up government bond prices was in September of 1939, when World War II started. Subsequent entries were made in early 1940 and immediately after Pearl Harbor in 1941.

With the start of World War II, the Federal Reserve System firmly committed itself to the policy of supporting the government bond market. The *Annual Report* of the Board of Governors of the Federal Reserve System for 1941 stated: "The System is prepared to use its powers to assure that an ample supply of funds is available at all times for financing the war effort and to exert its influence toward maintaining conditions in the United States Government security market that are satisfactory from the standpoint of the Government's requirements."[1]

To implement this policy, the Federal Reserve System stood ready to buy any amount of government securities that commercial banks and the nonbank public wished to sell. The U.S. government was issuing large volumes of securities to finance the deficit created by our huge armament expenditures. Usually, in such a situation, bond prices would decline because of the increased supply. Without Federal Reserve support, the increased supply would have forced the Treasury to offer higher interest rates in order to sell additional securities. This, in turn, would have meant increased government expenditures in the form of interest payments. These funds would have had to come either from taxes or from additional bond sales. Funds would have had to be diverted from armament expenditures so as to increase interest expenditures. Hence, the Federal Reserve System committed itself to the policy of supporting the government bond market. In effect, it increased the demand for the securities and thereby helped to maintain their price and hold down the interest burden of the Treasury. The effects of this policy may readily be seen in Table 13–1. U.S. government security holdings increased from $2.187 billion in 1941 to $21.363 billion in 1945.

The money supply also increased from $45.5 to $94.2 billion in the same period.[2] The result of this policy, therefore, was a substantial increase in the money supply. This occurred in the following fashion: The U.S. government sold securities to the nonbank public and the commercial banking system. To the extent that the nonbank public purchased the securities, there was no money creation. The Treasury simply received the money balances of the nonbank public and then spent those funds for wartime armaments, thereby returning the balances to the nonbank public. When members of the nonbank public decided to sell their security holdings, however, there was an increase in demand deposit money when either the Federal Reserve or the commercial banks purchased them. Furthermore, to

---

[1] *Annual Report* (1941), p. 1.

[2] The data are for June 30, 1941, and June 30, 1945. Data source: Board of Governors of the Federal Reserve System, *Supplement to Banking and Monetary Statistics:* Section 1 (1962), p. 15.

the extent that the securities sold by the Treasury were purchased by the commercial banking system, there was also an increase in the money supply. Initially there was an increase in Treasury demand deposits. As the proceeds of the security sales were spent by the Treasury, the funds were received by the nonbank public, thereby increasing the money supply.

The commercial banking system was an important cog in this process. Whenever it purchased securities, deposit liabilities increased. As deposit liabilities increased, however, excess reserves decreased and so did the lending ability of the banking system. This could well have been a serious problem. During World War II, however, the commercial banks did not run into this limitation of their money-creating powers. The FOMC, by buying securities, created the reserves that the commercial banks needed for expansion.

3. *1946–1951.* The Federal Reserve continued its open market policy of support for the government bond market during the early postwar years. The Treasury was no longer confronted with finding a market for an expanding government debt; the war was over and government expenditures had decreased. The Treasury was confronted with the problem of refunding the large national debt built up during the war, however. Large volumes of new securities had to be sold in order to get the funds needed to retire old securities as they came due. After the war people demanded goods and services they had long been denied during the war. They neither wanted nor demanded government bonds. As a result, without Federal Reserve support, bond prices would have dipped and interest costs increased.

The economy showed inflationary tendencies during the years 1946 through mid-1948. The commercial banking system tended to abet the price rises of these years by actively expanding loans, although deposit money increased only in 1946 and 1947. It was the security price support program of the Federal Reserve System that supplied commercial banks with the reserves needed to support this expanding loan activity.

One would imagine, therefore, given this set of circumstances, that the Federal Reserve would have sharply increased its security holdings from 1946 to 1948. Actually, however, these holdings only increased in 1946; decreases occurred in 1947 and 1948. These decreases stemmed in large part from Treasury debt retirement practices. Federal government tax receipts exceeded expenditures in these years and yielded a large cash surplus. This surplus was used to retire federal debt, much of which was held by the Federal Reserve banks. Thus, although actual Federal Reserve open market policy during these years of inflation was basically expansive, nevertheless, in 1947 and 1948, debt retirement induced a decrease in Reserve bank security holdings—the right direction for Federal Reserve security holdings to move in periods of full employment and inflation. Had the Federal Reserve System followed the aggressive contracyclical monetary policy that would seem to have been appropriate, there would have been significant additional decreases in Federal Reserve bank security holdings. In practice, however, the Treasury surplus was the principal deflationary force at work in the economy; Federal Reserve policy was expansive. Therefore, there was inflation. Actual commercial bank reserves rose from $16 to $18 billion from 1946 to 1948, and excess reserves, despite the reserve requirement increase of 1948 previously noted, were never under $740 million in any month of the three-year period.[3]

In 1949, the situation was substantially different. Businesses found that their inventories were excessive and proceeded to reduce them. This helped set contradictionary forces to work and a recession developed. Open market operations at this time were again perverse. Instead of buying more of government securities, the Federal Reserve sold them. Federal Reserve holdings of government securities decreased by $4 billion in 1949, causing member bank reserves to fall by $2.6 billion.[4] In a recession, there is generally a strong demand by commercial banks and financial investors for U.S. government securities because they represent a safe investment. This increased demand usually causes government bond prices to rise. Federal Reserve sales of securities in 1949 prevented these price rises from taking place.

The beginning of the Korean conflict in June, 1950, triggered a sharp economic expansion. The Federal Reserve System attempted to restrain these inflationary forces by raising reserve requirements and discount rates. The commitment to support government bond prices interfered with these contracyclical moves, however. From June, 1950, to March, 1951, Federal Reserve holdings of government securities actually expanded by $4.5 billion; member bank reserves rose by $3 billion.[5] The money supply also rose by $3 billion.[6]

Throughout most of the 1940's, the members of the FOMC had generally agreed with the policy of supporting the price of government bonds. By 1950, however, many of the members became quite dissatisfied with the policy. This produced some dissension between the Federal Reserve System and the U.S. Treasury. The FOMC felt that it was unwise to continue supporting government bond prices; the Treasury, on the other hand, wanted this easy money policy continued so as to keep the interest burden of the national debt low. After considerable controversy, which even involved President Truman, the Federal Reserve and the U.S. Treasury reached an accord in March of 1951. The issue was resolved in favor of the position of the Federal Reserve. For the first time in almost ten years, the Federal Reserve was allowed to follow a restrictive monetary policy without having to undercut that policy by buying government securities at fixed prices whenever commercial banks were short of reserves.

4. *March 1951-1964.* Since the Treasury–Federal Reserve Accord of

---

[3] Board of Governors of the Federal Reserve System, *Supplement to Banking and Monetary Statistics:* Section 10 (1962), p. 16.
[4] *Ibid.,* p. 17.
[5] *Ibid.,* p. 17.
[6] *Ibid.,* p. 15.

1951, Federal Reserve use of open market operations has, for the most part, been in an appropriate contracyclical direction. Federal Reserve bank holdings of securities expanded in 1951, 1952 and 1953 and remained roughly constant in 1954. Of these increases, those of 1951 and 1952 would appear at first glance to have been inappropriate. After more careful consideration, however, it becomes apparent that they may have been appropriate after all. Most of the increase of 1951 occurred prior to the Treasury–Federal Reserve Accord, and it was timed to coincide with the 1951 reserve requirement increases. The overall increase in security holdings from 1951 to 1952 was only $300 million, in any case.

The increase of 1953 was an appropriate contracyclical action. The large volume of security purchases coincided with the first six months of the 1953–54 recession. Following this recession the nation experienced the sharp economic upturn of 1955–57. Federal Reserve policy then changed to one of increasing restraint. Security holdings decreased somewhat in 1955, remained roughly constant during 1956, and decreased again in early 1957. In addition, restraint was simultaneously applied through increased discount rates.

The 1957–58 recession was sharp, but comparatively short-lived. Open market operations did not begin to function contracyclically until March, 1958, just prior to the economic upturn. Reserve requirements and discount rates had been reduced earlier. Once the purchase of government securities by the account manager began, it continued each month, except for a seasonal adjustment in January and February, 1959, straight through December, 1959. These purchases, by themselves, were not contracyclical because there was no longer a recession. There followed significant sales of securities in early 1960. In midyear there came another reversal of policy: security purchases resumed. Discount rates were lowered at the same time. Since this occurred just prior to the onset of the 1960–61 economic downturn, it appears that the Federal Reserve may have attempted to anticipate the downturn by returning to a policy of monetary ease.

The easing of monetary conditions that started in 1960 continued through 1964. Aside from seasonal decreases in early 1961, 1962, 1963, and 1964, Federal Reserve bank holdings of securities increased in every month except December, 1960, September, 1962, and November, 1962. The decrease that occurred in December, 1960, was in part designed to offset the substantial increase in member bank reserves that resulted from the new Federal Reserve ruling that all vault cash could be counted as part of reserves from November 24, 1960, onward. The two decreases in 1962 were in very small amounts, $67 and $46 million for September and November, respectively.[7]

The recession of 1960–61 ended in May, 1961. Logically, it would seem that there should then have been a decrease in Federal Reserve bank holdings of securities. The economy seemed to be improving rapidly throughout

---

[7] *Federal Reserve Bulletin*, February, 1963, p. 206.

the period 1961–64. Gross national product increases were substantial and there were significant increases in the stock of money as a result of the easy Federal Reserve monetary policy. Unemployment was persistent, however. Although employment was at a record level, the civilian work force was growing so rapidly that the unemployment rate during this period was usually just slightly less than 6 percent of the work force. Unemployment did not begin to approach 5 percent until mid-1964. Apparently the Board of Governors and the FOMC considered this statistic important enough to warrant a continuation of moderate ease in the money markets.

Evaluation of the open market policy instrument. The open market policy instrument came to be used increasingly in a contracyclical manner in the 1920's and early 1930's. This policy changed abruptly in 1937, when the Federal Reserve attempted to support the government securities market for the first time. Early in World War II the FOMC firmly committed itself to this policy, which continued until the Treasury–Federal Reserve Accord in March, 1951. The policy of supporting the price of government securities caused an expansion of bank reserves and the money stock during World War II and also permitted commercial banks to evade the postwar policy of restriction during periods of inflation. Since 1951, however, the open market instrument has generally been used in the appropriate contracyclical direction.

There are *four principal advantages to the open market instrument.* Increases or decreases in Federal Reserve bank security holdings may (1) be made slowly or rapidly, and (2) be made in limited or in large amounts. In addition, these open market operations (3) directly manipulate the reserve positions of member banks on the initiative of the FOMC and (4), when involving the nonbank public, directly affect the stock of money. These four factors make open market operations a swift and flexible corrective for economic instability. They also permit the Federal Reserve to correct an inappropriate use of policy instruments, including the open market instrument itself.

This does not mean, however, that it is easy to use open market operations as an instrument of monetary policy. Just as reserve requirement changes and discount rate manipulation pose problems for the monetary authority, so does the purchase and sale of securities. Fortunately, however, the problems posed by the open market instrument are not as great as those of the other policy instruments.

Problems posed by the use of open market operations. First, we may be attempting to accomplish too much by using open market operations in both a dynamic and defensive manner. We use open market operations "defensively" to make adjustments for seasonal or unanticipated changes in commercial bank reserves. We use open market operations "dynamically" as a contracyclical instrument of economic policy. This often complicates the job of the account manager. For example, there is normally an influx of currency into the banking system from the nonbank public at the first of each year. Since this tends to increase bank reserves and lending ability, and since such large increases in lending capacity are considered undesirable by the FOMC, the account manager sells securities.

This appears simple enough. The sale of securities must be sufficiently high to offset the amount of the reserve increase that is deemed undesirable. This operation should have a neutral effect on the degree of ease or tightness that is prevalent in the money markets. It is very easy to miscalculate the dollar amount involved, however. The account manager may over-estimate the extent of the cash inflow expected to take place and, as a result, sell too many securities. The result will be an unintended tightening of credit conditions. Banks may interpret the tightness of their reserve positions as a sign of a change in Federal Reserve policy, and accordingly re-examine their lending and investment policies.

To avoid miscalculations of this kind, the account manager has available to him a great deal of statistical information. He has detailed records of how the forces over which the Federal Reserve usually has no direct control (e.g. changes in vault cash, foreign accounts, or the balance of payments) have behaved in the past. He has been informed by the Treasury of impending security sales, tax receipts, and the expected future rate of government expenditures. He knows the extent to which banks have been borrowing reserves, either from the Federal Reserve banks or in the federal funds market. All of this information helps him reach his daily decision on security purchases and sales for defensive purposes. Various statistical indicators such as changes in the stock of money, the unemployment rate, or the gross national product also help him decide how much dynamic action is required to carry out the FOMC current directive. In addition, of course, his long experience in the securities market gives him a "feel" for market conditions. Thus, he combines the quantitative and qualitative information available to him and makes his overall decision on whether to buy or sell Federal Reserve bank security holdings.

Nevertheless, miscalculations can happen. The data may have been interpreted incorrectly. Knowledge of the past is usually reliable for future prognostication, but each new statistic has a way of altering past performance records. All of this suggests that it might be simpler to use open market operations for dynamic purposes alone. Commercial banks would be forced to resort to the "discount window" and the federal funds market to get the reserves needed to meet seasonal and unanticipated shortages in reserves. These borrowings could be repaid when seasonal and unanticipated reserve increases occurred. This is not a specific policy recommendation; it is merely one of a number of alternative ways of handling Federal Reserve policy that should be considered if the Federal Reserve is to be the viable and adaptive institution it has striven to be since the Accord of 1951.

Second, the variety of purposes for which we use open market operations makes it difficult to interpret the significance of open market transactions. The defensive measures just mentioned, for example, could lead to decreases in the quantity of securities held by the Federal Reserve in a period when dynamic action calls for an increase in security holdings. The actual movement of total security holdings may be quantitatively correct, but imply, from a reading of the data change, a modification in policy that has not actually taken place. This, in turn, may set off the type of change in bank expectations previously mentioned. *Changes in the absolute level of reserves and Reserve security holdings, therefore, are difficult to interpret and should not necessarily be taken as indicative of the degree of tightness in monetary policy.*

In addition, since the Accord of 1951, Federal Reserve use of open market operations has been coordinated, for the most part, with other policy instruments, discount rate and reserve requirement changes. This further complicates the task of interpreting Federal Reserve policy from its open market operations. It is not possible to look at open market operations in isolation and determine whether or not they were appropriate. The purchase or sale of securities may have been made to compensate for undesired changes in commercial bank reserves resulting from incorrect applications of other instruments of policy. Reserve requirement changes, for example, can lead to changes in member bank reserve positions that are excessively large; open market operations may be used to correct this situation.

Thus, to evaluate the open market instrument properly, we must consider it within the context of all Federal Reserve policy actions.

Third, the fact that the federal debt is composed of varying maturities complicates the open market policy of the Federal Reserve. Not only must decisions be made concerning the amount of securities to be held, but also concerning their maturity distribution.

Shortly after the Treasury–Federal Reserve Accord of March, 1951, the Federal Reserve System made a decision concerning the maturity distribution of the purchase and sale of government securities. It was decided that the FOMC should confine its intervention in the securities market to a minimum, that it was preferable to allow the forces of a free competitive market to set the price and interest rates for both private and government securities. Nevertheless, it was emphasized that some intervention would be necessary since open market operations were our most flexible policy instrument. Thus, the question was how best to keep intervention in free market forces to a minimum and simultaneously stabilize the economy through bank reserve manipulation. The solution that was decided upon was to confine open market operations to only one portion of the government securities market, short-term securities. The practice developed, therefore, in 1952 and 1953, of restricting open market operations principally to Treasury bills.

Treasury bills are obligations of the U.S. Treasury that have maturities from three months to one year. Most Treasury bills, however, are restricted to issues of ninety-one and 182-day bills. Because of the shortness of maturity, there is a continual market for these securities. Trading in Treasury bills is more active than it is for any other type of securities. As a result, the FOMC believed that open market operations could be conducted with the "least impact" in this part of the government securities market.

This policy of confining open market operations principally to Treasury bills was known as the "bills only" policy. Actually, the FOMC did not confine itself entirely to Treasury bills. Other government securities that had a maturity of less than fifteen months were also bought and sold, and, on a few occasions, the Federal Reserve was again called upon to support the government securities market. This occurred briefly in December, 1955, and July, 1958.

Apparently, it was felt that restricting security purchases to short-term government securities would be an important step toward simplifying the decision-making process. The FOMC had to be concerned only with the volume of open market operations and their influence on bank reserve positions. It no longer had to worry about choosing among a variety of maturities for its purchases and sales. Staying out of the longer-term securities market would permit private demands for government securities to determine their prices and interest yields. The Federal Reserve purchases and sales of short-term securities would not have a particularly destabilizing effect on security prices because of the large volume of private dealings in this market. In addition, much was made of the point that if

. . . Federal Reserve operations were regularly conducted in all maturity sectors of the Government securities market, the portfolio managers of financial institutions, other investors, and professional traders might well become unduly sensitized to possible changes in monetary policy. A particular hazard, for instance, would be that the trading in the longer term area of the market, which normally experiences the widest price swings, might become overly influenced by guesses about the maturities that might be involved in System operations.[8]

There was considerable opposition to this "bills only" policy. There were many within the Federal Reserve System and the U.S. Treasury who felt that the FOMC should not manipulate the economy only by influencing member bank reserve positions, but that it should also help set short-term and long-term rates of interest. This could only be done, it was thought, if the FOMC dealt with all of the maturities in the government securities market. Was it not desirable on occasion that long-term interest rates be reduced by the Federal Reserve's buying long-term governments, for example? Would this not induce decreases in private long-term rates and thereby serve to stimulate business investment in plant and equipment?

Changes in economic conditions have a way of forcing changes in the

---

[8] Board of Governors of the Federal Reserve System, *The Federal Reserve System: Purposes and Functions* (Washington, D.C.: 1961), pp. 40–41.

techniques of policy instrument utilization. An adverse U.S. balance of payments developed in the late 1950's and early 1960's. This led to a reduction of U.S. gold reserves as foreigners chose to take gold instead of building up their claims to American dollars. The Federal Reserve increased its holdings of securities in the 1960–61 recession. Under a "bills only" policy, these purchases were heavily concentrated in short-term securities. With increased demand, short-term interest rates tended to go down. Part of the adverse balance of payments of this period was due to the difference between U.S. and foreign short-term rates of interest. Higher short-term yields abroad induced individuals, businesses, and financial institutions in the United States to invest idle funds in foreign short-term securities rather than in U.S. securities. Foreigners were also induced to restrict their purchases of U.S. securities. As a result, there was an increased short-term capital outflow from the United States. Thus, the claims to U.S. dollars and gold rose. It was decided that heavy Federal Reserve purchases of short-term government securities aggravated this situation inasmuch as they tended to hold down our short-term interest rates.

As a consequence, the "bills only" policy was abandoned in favor of a new policy that might at once induce easy credit conditions in the U.S. by providing banks with ample lending capacity and also lead to short-term interest rate increases, thereby reducing the gold outflow. The new policy dictated that the Federal Reserve should sell some short-term U.S. government securities so as to raise the yields and thus eliminate short-term capital outflows, and that it should buy long-term Government securities so as to provide banks with greater lending ability. The purchase of long-term securities would also depress long-term interest rates and thereby possibly lead to investment demand increases domestically, which could help sustain domestic employment levels. The new policy is known as "operation twist."

Officially, the "bills only" policy was abandoned in February, 1961. Since then open market policy has had a twofold function: to maintain a stable but growing domestic economy and to improve the U.S. balance of payments situation. The decision-making process of the account manager has become quite complicated again. He must operate with possibly conflicting objectives in mind (domestic stability and a favorable balance of payments) and he must determine not only the amount but also the kind of securities that he is to purchase.

Evaluation of General Monetary Controls

Have general monetary controls been used in a contracyclical manner? The preceding discussion has reached the following broad conclusions concerning the historical effectiveness of each of the three instruments of monetary policy:

First, the Federal Reserve System has had the power to change reserve requirements only since 1935. From 1935 through 1963, only the doubling of reserve requirements from 1936 to 1937 was a move in the wrong direction. Other changes in the reserve requirement seem to have been correct in light of the prevailing economic conditions.

Second, discount rate changes have generally been in the right contracyclical direction also. This has been particularly evident since 1951. However, the movement of discounts and advances, and the relationship between the discount rate at the Federal Reserve Bank of New York and the interest rate on four- to six-month commercial paper, seem to indicate that frequently the discount rate changes made were too mild.

Third, open market operations have been a formal instrument of policy only since 1935. They were used to some extent, however, in the 1920's and early 1930's. Movements in security holdings of the Federal Reserve banks, although inappropriate in much of the period of the twenties, were definitely used in an appropriate contracyclical manner in the early thirties. The commitment to support prices in the government bond market eliminated open market operations as an instrument of contracyclical policy from 1935 through March, 1951, however. Since March, 1951, open market operations have resulted in correct contracyclical movements of Federal Reserve bank holdings of securities in all years except 1952 and 1959. References made earlier to monthly movements in Federal Reserve security holdings indicate that our use of this instrument has become increasingly skillful. The security purchases of mid-1960 were particularly well timed, for example.

The preceding evaluation of the three policy instruments was made by studying each one separately. How well do these instruments work together, however? Table 13–2 summarizes all of the various uses made of the policy instruments in recent years. In addition to the policy instruments already discussed, this table shows the direction of movements in Federal Reserve credit, which is sometimes regarded as an important indicator of the ease or restrictiveness of Federal Reserve policy. (The actual behavior of Federal Reserve credit is given in Figure 13–1.) The last column of Table 13–2 is a comment on the overall ease or tightness of Federal Reserve policy during each of the economic expansions and contractions of the period since October, 1949.

Federal Reserve credit. Before evaluating the general implementation of monetary policy, some comment on Federal Reserve credit is in order. Federal Reserve credit is a collective term encompassing such Federal Reserve bank balance sheet items as U.S. government securities, discounts and advances, acceptances, float, and such minor items as funds "due from" foreign banks. These are almost all items over which the Federal Reserve has some form of control. Increases of Federal Reserve credit must directly lead to increases in member bank reserves; conversely, decreases in Federal Reserve credit must directly lead to decreases in member bank reserves. Quantitatively, this item is the single most important determinant of the volume of member bank reserves. A change in any or all policy instruments usually

TABLE 13-2. THE USE MADE OF MONETARY INSTRUMENTS OF POLICY, 1949-64

REFERENCE DATES FOR UNITED STATES BUSINESS CYCLES	USE OF RESERVE REQUIREMENTS	USE OF DISCOUNT RATES	DISCOUNTS AND ADVANCES	FEDERAL RESERVE BANK SECURITY HOLDINGS	FEDERAL RESERVE CREDIT	OVERALL EASE OR TIGHTNESS OF POLICY
Expansion following October, 1949 trough, through July, 1953 peak	+January, February, 1951	+August, 1950, January, 1953	−1950 +1951 through July, 1953 peak	+through whole expansion	+through whole expansion	Ease
Contraction through August, 1954 trough	−July, 1953; June, July, August, 1954	−February, April, May, 1954	−through whole contraction	−gradual decline in contraction	−gradual decline in contraction	Ease
Expansion through July, 1957 peak		+April, May, August, September, November, 1955; April, August, 1956	−remainder 1954 +1955–1956	−1955; February–June, 1957		Increasing tightness
Contraction through April, 1958 trough	−February, March, April, 1958	+August, 1957 −November, December, 1957; January, March, April, 1958	−through whole contraction	+March–April, 1958		Tight in early part, ease in latter part
Expansion through May, 1960 peak	−December, 1959	+September, October, November, 1958; March, May, June, September, 1959	−remainder 1958 +1959 −March to May, 1960	+May, 1958–December, 1959 −January, 1960	+May, 1958–December, 1959	Tight
Contraction through February, 1961 trough	−August, September, November, December, 1960	−June, August, September, 1960	−through whole contraction	+through whole contraction	+through whole contraction	Ease
Expansion through 1964	−October, November, 1962	+July, 1963; November, 1964;	−remainder 1961 +1963	+through 1964	+through 1964	Ease

results in a change in Federal Reserve credit and member bank reserves.

Because of the direct connection between Federal Reserve credit and member bank reserves, it is sometimes thought that the movements of Federal Reserve credit provide the best measure of the nature and effectiveness of Federal Reserve policy. This, however, reveals an oversimplified view of the mechanics of policy implementation.

The reserve requirement and Federal Reserve credit frequently change in the same direction, for example. This does not necessarily mean that Federal Reserve policy is contradictory, however. For instance, reserve requirements were increased in January and February of 1951; the total

FIGURE 13–1. Member bank reserves and related items, 1941–64.

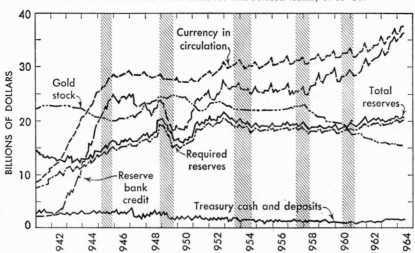

Source: Board of Governors of the Federal Reserve System, *Federal Reserve Historical Chart Book*, 1964, p. 3.

Shaded areas refer to periods of economic contraction: February, 1945–October, 1945; November, 1948–October, 1949; July, 1953–August, 1954; July, 1957–April, 1958; and May, 1960–February, 1961.

amount of the increase was 2 percent, a very substantial increase. In the absence of offsetting forces, this would have resulted in a substantial reduction in excess reserves. As can be seen from the narrowed spread between total and required reserves in Figure 13–1, excess reserves were reduced, but not substantially. Member banks increased their borrowings and sold some government securities. There was a marked increase in Federal Reserve credit. Thus, member bank total and required reserves both increased. It appears that the movement of Federal Reserve credit reflects an effort by the Board of Governors to offset the effects of the very large increase in reserve requirements by means of security purchases. Most of the Reserve credit increase of this period was attributable to open market purchases and increased float.

Similarly, there are frequently parallel decreases in reserve requirements and Federal Reserve credit. Reserve requirements were decreased in July, 1953, June and July, 1954, February, March, and April of 1958, September and December of 1960, and October, 1962 (on time deposits alone). In addition, part of vault cash was permitted to satisfy the reserve requirement in 1959, and all vault cash was counted after November 24, 1960. These last two changes amounted to reserve requirement decreases. There were several corresponding movements in Federal Reserve credit during these periods: an increase in mid-1953, a decrease in mid-1954, stability from February through April, 1958, a less than normal seasonal increase in December, 1959, and a larger than normal seasonal decrease in January, 1960, an overall increase in the last third of 1960, and increases in the last part of 1962. In short, Reserve credit moved in the same direction as reserve requirements in all periods except for mid-1953, late 1960 and late 1962. Here again, most of the movement in Federal Reserve credit for these periods resulted from open market operations designed to offset the effects of reserve requirement changes.

This type of behavior of Federal Reserve credit has prompted some economists to conclude that "until 1951, the change in Federal Reserve credit outstanding was a consequence of the bond support program; thereafter, of a deliberate policy on the part of the System to use open market operations to spread out the effects of discontinuous changes in reserve requirements."[9]

Movements in Federal Reserve credit are not an altogether reliable measure of the ease or restrictiveness of Federal Reserve monetary policy. Federal Reserve credit holdings may be shifted to soften the impact of the reserve requirement instrument or to offset the movements of other determinants of member bank reserves. For example, the increase in Reserve credit in 1959 may be viewed as inappropriate in itself. As Reserve credit increased, however, our gold stock dwindled. It will be recalled from Chapter 11 that gold stock and member bank reserve changes are positively related. Thus, some of the Reserve credit increase may be viewed as an attempt to offset the drain on reserves caused by the outflow of gold from the U.S. economy.

Reserve credit movements tend to reflect Federal Reserve manipulation of discounts and advances, open market operations, and float. Open market operations are usually the adjusting force. Thus, when discounts and advances increase in the face of discount rate increases, in the absence of open market operations, Federal Reserve credit and hence member bank reserves increase. With open market sales, however, the increase in Federal Reserve credit and member bank reserves may be kept to a minimum.

In addition, it appears that the Federal Reserve System is increasingly allowing float to function as a source of reserves for member banks. From the end of 1959 to the end of 1963, Federal Reserve holdings of U.S. gov-

---

[9] Milton Friedman and Anna Schwartz, *A Monetary History of the United States, 1867–1960* (Princeton, N.J.: Princeton University Press, 1963), p. 604.

ernment securities increased $6.7 billion, float $1.0 billion, and Federal Reserve credit $7.2 billion. In the same period, discounts and advances decreased more than $500 million.[10] It would appear that the Federal Reserve System is supplementing its use of open market operations with variations in float as a means of providing commercial banks with additional reserves. All of these operations influence the movement of Federal Reserve credit.

Evaluation of Federal Reserve policy since 1951. Our previous analysis of the use of each individual policy instrument indicates that during the years since 1951, the Federal Reserve has frequently followed a correct contracyclical monetary policy. Since the Accord of March, 1951, occurred in the midst of economic expansion, the discussion starts with an earlier reference point, the beginning of the expansion period in which the Accord was made, October, 1949.

Normally, economic expansion during periods of high employment levels calls for a restrictive monetary policy, and economic contraction calls for monetary ease. In terms of the reference dates for United States business cycles listed in Table 13-2, this means that there should have been monetary ease in the contractions of 1953-54, 1957-58, and 1960-61. The expansions of 1949-53, and 1955-57, called for some tightening of money and credit conditions. On the other hand, much of the expansions of 1958-60 and 1961-64 called for some ease in money and credit conditions, since the unemployment rate had continued high after the 1957-58 recession.

Table 13-2 shows that our experience with Federal Reserve policy has been mixed. During the *expansion following the October, 1949, trough through the cyclical peak reached in July, 1953,* Federal Reserve policy was generally one of monetary ease. True, reserve requirements were raised in early 1951, and discount rates increased in August of 1950, but these movements, as previously noted, were offset by Federal Reserve security purchases. Although 1952 was a year of monetary ease, open market purchases rose only $300 million above the 1951 levels, but Federal Reserve credit rose $730 million, most of this occurring because of increased discounts and advances. Member bank reserves increased $1 billion in the same year.[11] Late in this period, however, there was some restraint by the Federal Reserve System as the threat of inflation became apparent.

The expansion of this period had been unique until early 1953. Employment levels were extremely high and price levels very stable. Prices had not yet increased, but the Federal Reserve feared that they would. Member bank borrowings had increased substantially in 1952; free reserves had become negative for the first time since 1932. As a consequence, the Federal Reserve sought to halt the incipient price inflation that might have started

---

[10] *Federal Reserve Bulletin,* January, 1964, p. 48.
[11] *Supplement to Banking and Monetary Statistics:* Section 10, p. 14.

from bank credit expansion in a period when industry was operating close to capacity. The action taken was to raise discount rates and so pressure banks into reducing their borrowings. Interest rates increased and member banks attempted to improve their reserve position by reducing their investments. This reaction of the banking system led the Federal Reserve to believe that its restrictive action had been too severe. A quick reversal of policy was made in May, 1953, when the Federal Reserve increased its holdings of government securities. This action did not immediately result in a substantial easing of credit conditions. Member bank free reserves did decrease from —$631 to —$303 million from April to May, 1953.[12] The normal seasonal decline in total member bank reserves was permitted to take place, however. Federal Reserve security holdings did increase, but total Federal Reserve credit decreased.

How effective was Federal Reserve policy in controlling the expansion just discussed? In isolation, the use made of the reserve requirement and discount rate mechanisms was appropriate through the whole period; the actions taken were in the right direction. In sum, however, the movement of Reserve credit and member bank reserves show that we had monetary ease through almost the whole expansion. It is surprising that this policy of ease did not result in price inflation in 1952. A policy of monetary ease was clearly inappropriate throughout most of this period of high employment levels. The restrictive action of early 1953, late in the expansion, was also inappropriate. On the other hand, the rapid change in policy from restriction to ease in May, 1953, was clearly correct because it preceded the cyclical peak of July, 1953, and subsequent economic contraction.

The Federal Reserve followed a policy of monetary ease throughout the *1953–54 contraction*. Reserve requirements and discount rates were lowered. There was a very small contraction in Federal Reserve bank security holdings and Reserve bank credit, but it was not restrictive in character, because the decrease in credit was primarily coincident with the 1954 rather than the 1953 reserve requirement decreases. Thus, the impact of the July, 1953, reserve requirement decrease was not undermined by offsetting reserve credit decreases. As a consequence, credit conditions remained easy through the 1953–54 contraction.

Federal Reserve policy was one of increasing restrictiveness through the *1955–57 economic expansion*. Discount rate increases and Federal Reserve bank security holding decreases took place. Federal Reserve credit, however, was virtually constant through the period. In economic expansion and boom, commercial banks need additional reserves in order to support the additional demand deposits that are created as bank lending activity increases. When those reserves are not provided by the Federal Reserve System, member banks are forced to borrow reserves. This occurred in 1955–57; starting in early 1955, member bank borrowings increased sharply. Free reserves dropped, becoming negative in August, 1955, and remaining that

_____
[12] *Ibid.*, p. 58.

way through the remainder of the boom, except for one month, January, 1957. Member bank reserves, of course, did not increase. The borrowing of reserves and some increase in float served simply to offset the decrease in member bank reserves and Federal Reserve credit that would have occurred as a result of the open market sales that were taking place. Member bank reserves, therefore, were not permitted to increase.

Without the additional reserves needed to meet the demand for funds, banks reduced their investments and increased their lending activity. The net result of this action, as explained in Chapter 6, was a transfer of money balances from the less active part of the nonbank public to the more active borrowing and spending part. At the same time the banking activity of nonbank financial institutions increased. Increased inflationary pressures were thereby at work in the economy.

The period of the 1955–57 expansion was one of high employment levels, rising prices, increasing private investment outlays, and rapidly increasing gross national product. The monetary policy of the period, as we have seen, was one of restraint, appropriate for such a period. It is ironic that prices increased in this expansion in the face of an appropriately restrictive monetary policy. The aforementioned lending activity as well as price and cost increases in the automobile and durable investment goods industries helped overcome the restrictive monetary policy.

The *contraction* that followed the 1955–57 boom was short, but sharp. Unemployment increased substantially. Our monetary authorities were slow to respond to this contraction. Discount rates were increased in August of 1957, and were not reduced until November. Reserve requirements were reduced in early 1958 and some open market purchases were made in March of 1958. In addition, Federal Reserve credit did not expand, but free reserves did increase as reserve requirements were lowered. Thus, when the Federal Reserve finally did respond to this contraction, it was in the latter stages of the recession. Monetary policy for this period, therefore, does not appear to have been appropriate.

Federal Reserve monetary action during the *1958–60 expansion* is more difficult to interpret. Discount rates were increased three times in 1958 and four times in 1959. This action was restrictive, which often is appropriate policy for a period of business expansion. At the same time, however, the unemployment rate was in excess of 5 percent in all but four months of the expansion; the lowest average unemployment rate for any full year, 5.5 percent, came in 1959.[13] On the basis of the unemployment statistics, a policy of monetary ease would probably have been preferable, assuming that monetary forces can actually have an effect on demand and spending.[14]

---

[13] *Federal Reserve Bulletin,* January, 1960, p. 78, and January, 1961, p. 88.

[14] It must be recognized, however, that if an easy money policy leads to demand increases in those sectors of the economy that have full employment, price inflation will follow. It is important that spending increases where unemployment exists. If many people are permanently unemployed due to a lack of proper job skills, then inflation and less than full employment may exist simultaneously.

Discount rates were increased, however. Their increases were so prompt and strong that, at the time of each of the increases, the discount rate for the Federal Reserve Bank of New York almost equaled the prime rate on four- to six-month commercial paper. This was as close as the Federal Reserve System had come in the post-Accord period to pushing the discount rate above the commercial paper rate in economic expansion. This was done, however, when we still had a large volume of unemployment! In addition, the high discount rate set in September, 1959, was kept for nine months, six months after the commercial paper rate had begun to decrease.

The behavior of Federal Reserve security holdings and Federal Reserve credit was significantly different from discount rate changes. Security purchases began in May of 1958 and continued through December, 1959. Federal Reserve credit simultaneously increased. This would indicate that there was a policy of monetary ease in open market operations and Federal Reserve credit. Such was not the case, however. Most of the large increases in Federal Reserve security holdings and Federal Reserve credit were made merely to offset other forces that were tending to decrease member bank reserves—namely, increases in currency in circulation and decreases in our gold stock. Federal Reserve credit increased from May, 1958, through December, 1959, by $4.5 billion, whereas the increase in currency in circulation and the decrease in gold stock were $2.0 and $2.3 billion respectively. Member bank reserves in the same period increased by only $0.7 billion.[15]

The subsequent security and Reserve credit reductions in early 1960 tended to restrict commercial bank lending activity even further. During this entire expansion from May, 1958, through May, 1960, Federal Reserve credit increased $2.5 billion, while member bank reserves remained almost constant.[16] With economic growth, a larger population, and increased real output in the economy, some expansion of commercial bank reserves was surely needed. Federal Reserve policy, however, called for limiting the availability of new reserves to member banks. This policy was apparently based on the assumption that this expansion was much like earlier expansions, with comparatively high employment levels and potential price level increases.

Here it can readily be seen why the policies of this period are difficult to interpret. First, it was a period of expansion, which theoretically calls for monetary restriction if inflation is to be avoided. Second, discount rates were increased, which is an appropriate action in light of the first point. Third, the Federal Reserve purchased securities and expanded Reserve bank credit, which are expansionary actions. Fourth, these increases in Reserve credit and security holdings, however, merely served to offset forces tending to decrease member bank reserves. Hence, open market policy and Reserve credit changes were basically restrictive, which is appropriate in terms of the first point. Fifth, unemployment in this period was usually in excess of

---

[15] *Supplement to Banking and Monetary Statistics*, Section 10, p. 19.
[16] *Ibid.*

5.5 percent, which theoretically calls for credit expansion and monetary ease. Hence, our restrictive policies of this period were inappropriate in light of the employment situation.

The *contraction* that continued through *February, 1961,* and the *expansion* that continued through *1963* and into *1964* are much easier to interpret in terms of Federal Reserve policy actions. Both of these periods were characterized by monetary ease. Reserve requirements were lowered both in the contraction and the expansion. Discount rates were lowered in the contraction, but raised slightly in the expansion for purposes of reducing our gold outflow. Federal Reserve bank security holdings and Federal Reserve credit both increased during the contraction and expansion. Reserve credit expansion, however, was greater than the increase in member bank reserves. As in preceding periods, decreases in gold stock and currency in circulation increases tended to absorb some of the reserve-creating potential of Reserve credit increases. At no time, however, did it appear that member banks were deficient of reserves. From June, 1960, through December, 1964, member bank free reserves were positive, although they were becoming comparatively low at the end of 1963. All of these forces show that monetary policy was expansive through both the first contraction and the first expansion of the 1960's. In light of continued high unemployment levels this was appropriate policy.

In general, an assessment of the appropriateness of Federal Reserve monetary policy since the Treasury–Federal Reserve Accord yields mixed results. In the seven expansions and contractions studied, Federal Reserve policy was appropriate for the most part, in four periods: the contraction of 1953–54, the expansion of 1955–57, the contraction of 1960–61, and the expansion of 1961–64. In the remaining three periods, the basic policy appears to have been incorrect. A number of monetary actions were taken during these periods that were correct, however, either on the basis of the prevalent national economic trends or in light of what the monetary authorities took to be the major economic problems of the period. *All of this should make us recognize that our use of general monetary instruments is imperfect because we have imperfect knowledge of the present status of the economy, of the probable course of economic events, and of the effect our use of the instruments of monetary policy will have on the behavior of the economy.*

Additional problems in the use of general monetary controls. The historical discussion thus far has tended to show that policy mistakes can occur, even when the use of policy at first appears to be correct. The *timing* of policy changes can be of great importance, for example. Thus, the timing of credit restrictions in early 1953 and the summer of 1957 was bad. On the other hand, the reversals of policy in 1953 and 1960, when the Federal Reserve began expanding security holdings, were well timed to precede the economic downturn. They may have helped lessen the extent of the downturn.

One thing that almost all economists agree upon is that *general monetary controls can break almost any inflation* provided it is not being stimulated by increases in bank reserves and the money supply because of an inappropriate expansionary policy. An increase in reserve requirements or a sufficiently large sale of government securities by the Federal Reserve banks can wipe out member bank excess reserves as quickly as they are created through discounts and advances. These techniques, however, must be used in moderation, since there is always the danger of causing a sharp economic contraction rather than merely stemming rising prices.

As noted earlier, however, economists are by no means in agreement that an easing of credit and money conditions will produce economic recovery. The general consensus is that, at best, monetary ease may encourage recovery, but that an increased desire to spend is the true source of a recovery. More is said of this in Parts III and IV where we consider monetary theory and alternative economic policies. This presumed inability of monetary instruments to cause an economic upturn is what most economists regard as the *principal shortcoming* of monetary policy as it is presently practiced.

There are other problems connected with the use of general monetary controls, too. An appropriate use of policy may be offset by other forces. For example, increased cold war pressures during a period of full employment may lead to an increase in government expenditures, a deficit, and rising prices, thereby offsetting a contractionary monetary policy. There may be little that can be done about such a situation in the absence of Congressional approval of needed tax increases. More unfortunate is the fact that an appropriate use of policy may be partly offset *by forces that are touched off by the use of the instruments themselves.* There are basically three such forces: (1) velocity offsets due to commercial bank lending and investing activity, (2) velocity offsets due to the lending activity of nonbank financial institutions, and (3) offsets attributable to nonmember bank lending and investing activity.

First, commercial bank lending and investing activity may induce undesired changes in the velocity of money that would tend to offset an appropriate use of the instruments of monetary policy. In periods of economic expansion, banks try to offset the restrictions placed on their lending abilities by reducing their investments. For the banking system as a whole, this draws down the comparatively idle demand deposits of the nonbank public as it purchases these securities. The banking system is then able to expand loans and create deposits in an amount equal to investment reduction. The funds received by borrowers are active money balances and will be spent. Thus, if there is no change in the money supply, its utilization will have increased. This velocity increase adds to demand for goods and services and, in a full employment economy, may lead to price inflation. The monetary authority could then follow a more restrictive monetary policy, but if it is applied too rigorously it may lead to an economic reverse. Furthermore, a tighter money policy may lead to an enhancement of the competitive position of nonbank financial institutions and, as some argue, further weaken the controls of the Federal Reserve System over the economy.

Second, velocity increases attributable to increased lending activity of nonbank financial institutions may also take place and thereby further weaken the effects of a restrictive monetary policy. Briefly, the funds that nonbank financial institutions attract come to them in the form of commercial bank demand deposits. When these funds are switched from inactive deposits at commercial banks to accounts of the nonbank financial institutions, these institutions will activate the money balances. The funds will be used to expand mortgage loans and corporate security holdings. Thus, there is increased spending of a given volume of money balances and a resultant increase in inflationary pressures.

It was previously mentioned that banks typically attempt to switch their assets from investments to loans during economic expansion so as to maximize their earnings. There is a limit, however, to the degree to which this switching may take place. For liquidity purposes, the Federal Reserve System insists that member banks maintain at least a certain amount of their assets in safe U.S. government securities in addition to required reserves. The limits imposed by the regulators of the nonbank financial institutions are much weaker, however. Savings and loan associations that are members of the Federal Home Loan Bank System are presently operating under a 7 percent reserve requirement, most of which may consist of U.S. government securities. Country banks, on the other hand, must maintain reserves equal to 12 and 4 percent of their demand and time deposits respectively, yet only vault cash or deposits at the Federal Reserve banks count as reserves. Therefore, the requirement that commercial banks must also maintain a large volume of safe U.S. government securities further restricts the shiftability of member bank assets. So long as nonbank financial institutions are able to attract deposits from commercial bank depositors and at the same time satisfy their own comparatively low reserve requirements, these institutions will be able to continue expanding the velocity of the money supply and thereby counteract a restrictive monetary policy.

Third, the regulations of the Federal Reserve System do not extend to all commercial banks, only to member banks. The deposit liabilities of the member banks constitute better than 85 percent of the deposits of all commercial banks, yet, in terms of total numbers, nonmember banks represent the majority. The nonmember banks are subject to state banking law, not the Federal Reserve Act. The state banking laws and regulations of most of the fifty states are somewhat laxer than the requirements of the Federal Reserve Act. As a result, the ratio of cash assets to deposits is almost always lower for state nonmember banks than for "country" member banks. Thus, nonmember bank loans increase proportionately more than those of "country" member banks during periods of monetary restriction. During periods of monetary ease, however, nonmember banks expand loans less than do member banks. This behavior pattern has led one economist to draw the "inference . . . that nonmember banks are less responsive than member banks to changes in the direction of Federal Reserve policy."[17]

This makes it possible for nonmember banks to offset the desired effects expected from a particular type of Federal Reserve monetary policy. If the lending activity of the member banks is being restricted by the Federal Reserve, it is possible that borrowers may be able to get loans from the nonmember banks. Increased loans lead to an increased money supply, and this will cause spending to rise. To offset this trend the Federal Reserve may have to tighten credit conditions even further for the member banks. This situation has not yet occurred to any measurable extent because the size of nonmember banks relative to member banks is still small. There is no guarantee that this will always be the case, however. This is one of the reasons that it is sometimes contended that all commercial banks should be required to become member banks.

Conclusion. Our discussion of the instruments of general monetary control has tended to emphasize the difficulties inherent in policy implementation. The three basic tools have sometimes been used correctly; other times there have been miscalculations. Rapid changes sometimes occur in the economy, and it is difficult to predict both the course of economic fluctuations and the response of consumers and business to policy changes. The monetary instruments of policy discussed in Chapters 12 and 13 have been our principal weapons in combating cyclical movements since 1951. The Federal Reserve System is constantly seeking to develop measures superior to those presently being used to forecast the future performance of the economy and its reaction to our discretionary instruments of monetary management.[18] Possibly the Federal Reserve should even consider entirely new techniques of monetary management. Some of the possible alternative policy instruments will be considered in Part IV of this text.

SELECTIVE CREDIT CONTROLS

The Federal Reserve also makes use of one instrument of selective credit control. *Selective credit controls* regulate the terms on which one may borrow for specific spending purposes. The presumption on which these

---

[17] Clark Warburton, "Nonmember Banks and the Effectiveness of Monetary Policy," in the Commission on Money and Credit, *Monetary Management* (Englewood Cliffs, N.J.: Prentice-Hall, 1963), p. 337.

[18] For example, the measure "free reserves" has sometimes been used by the FOMC as a guide to open market operations. A large volume of free reserves is interpreted as being indicative of an easy money policy. Negative free reserves is taken as a sign of a tight money policy. Actually a given level of free reserves can produce either easy or tight money conditions. See: William G. Dewald, "Free Reserves, Total Reserves, and Monetary Control," *The Journal of Political Economy* (1963), pp. 141–53; and A. J. Meigs, *Free Reserves and the Money Supply* (Chicago: University of Chicago Press, 1962).

controls are based is that certain types of spending are relatively more important as sources of economic instability than other types of spending. Thus, it is thought that by regulating the comparative ease of borrowing for these spending purposes in recession or inflation, undesired cyclical instability will be dampened. For example, selective credit controls may be imposed on borrowing for residential construction purposes. The amount of down payment required may be manipulated; the interest rates charged for mortgage loans may be varied, and the length of the repayment period may be changed. For example, if it were believed that increased expenditures on residential construction during a period of full employment represented a primary source of rising prices, then repayment periods could be shortened for new construction loans and interest rates and required down payments increased. This should cause spending on residential construction to decrease and the inflationary forces extant in the economy to diminish.

Controls over borrowing for residential construction purposes are only one set of selective credit controls that have been designed to regulate specific forms of spending. In addition to real-estate credit controls, we have also had experience with consumer credit and stock market credit controls. Consumer credit controls are usually designed to regulate spending on consumer durable goods because this type tends to fluctuate with the business cycle. Normally the purchase of such consumer durables as refrigerators and washing machines increase during the upward part of economic fluctuations and decrease during the downward part. This type of spending behavior in itself, will tend to intensify whatever type of economic fluctuation is current. To the extent that consumers borrow to make these purchases and are sensitive to changes in the terms on which they may borrow, the use of consumer credit controls may tend to lessen economic instability.

Regulations over stock market credit are not designed to affect the volume of spending on real economic goods as are consumer and real estate credit controls. Instead, selective credit controls over the purchase and sale of stock are designed to lessen speculation in stocks. For example, a margin requirement of 50 percent means that a lender may lend an amount up to 50 percent of the current market value of the stock that the proceeds of the loan will be used to purchase. Therefore, an increase in the margin requirement will decrease the amount that may be loaned for the purchase of stock. Theoretically, this should reduce the amount of borrowing for the purpose of purchasing stock and at the same time reduce speculation in securities. Furthermore, a reduction in borrowing to acquire stock should tend to reduce the demand for stocks, and, consequently, reduce upward pressures on stock prices. This is regarded as a significant move in a period of high stock speculation such as occurs in an inflation, since rising stock prices increase the amount that can be borrowed for stock purchase purposes, given a fixed margin requirement. Increased borrowing can then lead to additional increases in the price of stock and a "pyramiding" of borrowing can take place.

Stock speculation, in itself, has little direct effect on spending for real goods and services in the economy. The danger of stock speculation lies in its influence on expectations. Rising stock prices may lead to favorable expectations concerning the economic outlook that are wholly unwarranted. Those whose stock holdings have sharply increased in value on paper may be induced by this to increase their borrowings and spendings on real goods and services. In a period of full employment, this can contribute to price inflation. In addition, suppose that many holders of stock then decide to take their profits. This might cause a collapse of stock prices. Those who borrowed to purchase stocks or goods and services will be forced to liquidate asset holdings to repay their loans as they come due. This will cause stock prices to fall even further; lower stock prices and credit reduction may then lead to the expectation of an economic decline. If this occurs, spending plans will be re-examined and actual spending, income, and output will decline. Hence, there is a definite need for controls designed to lessen stock speculation.

All forms of selective credit controls, however, suffer from one main defect. *In the absence of direct controls on the manner in which individuals may spend their funds, there is almost no way in which credit controls can be made to produce the desired type of spending restriction.* It is always possible to borrow for one purpose and use the proceeds of the loan for some other purpose. When an individual borrows, the funds are simply placed in his checking account. No distinction is made between the borrowed funds and the other funds in the deposit account. Thus, it would be possible to get an unsecured consumer loan and to use the entire proceeds of this loan for the purchase of stock. Even if the proceeds of the loan are actually used for some specified purpose such as debt consolidation, the loan may still result in the freeing of other funds for use in activities such as stock purchases or real-estate speculation.

This shortcoming inhibits the effectiveness of most selective credit controls. Nevertheless, we continue to use some form of selective credit control. At present, however, these controls function as a minor tool of general monetary policy. Manipulation of the margin requirements for the purchase of stock is the only form of selective credit control still at the disposal of the Board of Governors.

Margin Requirements

Margin requirements are set by the Board of Governors in accordance with the Securities Exchange Act of 1934. Their purpose is to limit the amount of credit that may be extended on a security by prescribing its maximum loan value, which is calculated as a specified percentage of its market value at the time of credit extension. The margin requirement is thus the difference between the market value of the security and its maximum loan value. For example, if the security has a market value of $100, and if the margin requirement is 70 percent, then $30 is the maximum amount that may be loaned for the purchase of the security.

Margin requirement control was given to the Federal Reserve to avoid the recurrence of stock market speculation such as that which occurred in the late 1920's. It was common practice during this period to purchase stocks almost entirely with borrowed funds. This technique created a strong demand for stocks and it buoyed up their prices. Once stock prices broke, however, those who had borrowed were unable to cover their debts. If the value of stock fell beneath the volume of borrowings, the borrower could no longer get enough funds from the sale of stock to cover his debt. With the stock market crash of 1929, stock values declined so markedly that hundreds of thousands of people were financially ruined. Borrowers could not repay their loans, and lenders were unable to collect. The outcome of this financial chaos was a complete revamping of our laws governing the sale of stocks, the establishment of the Securities and Exchange Commission, and the granting of margin requirement control to the Federal Reserve.

Two specific regulations cover the extension of credit for the purchase and carrying of securities, Regulations T and U. Regulation T applies to lending by brokers and dealers in corporate securities; Regulation U applies to lending by commercial banks on stocks listed on the national stock exchanges. The margin requirements for both types of lenders are the same.

These margin requirements are only applicable when the borrowing is for the purpose of purchasing or carrying stock. Margin requirements do not come into effect when a security already owned by the borrower is used as collateral on a loan for other purposes. The amount borrowed may then exceed the loan value of the security. Furthermore, as previously indicated, once the borrowed funds have entered a checking account, it is difficult to trace the precise use to which they are put. They may be used for the ostensible purposes of the loan, or for other purposes, including the purchase of stock.

In addition, not all stocks fall under Federal Reserve regulations. Only those stocks listed on the national exchanges, such as the New York Stock Exchange and the American Stock Exchange, come under Regulation U. Thus the scope, as well as the effectiveness, of our present margin requirements is limited.

In spite of these shortcomings, however, the Federal Reserve System frequently employs margin requirements as a contracyclical instrument of economic policy. Table 13-3 shows the use made of margin requirements since the end of World War II. They have been increased eight times and each increase occurred during a period of economic upturn. They have been decreased six times, and all decreases except those of 1947 and 1962 approximately coincided with an economic downturn. The 1947 decrease followed an earlier 1946 increase to 100 percent. The 1962 decrease followed a sharp break in the price of stocks on the various U.S. stock exchanges in May of 1962. Stock market credit decreased markedly following the break in stock prices, and this led the Board of Governors to conclude that "a 70 percent margin requirement was not necessary to prevent the excessive use of credit for the purchase or carrying of securities."[19]

TABLE 13–3. MARGIN REQUIREMENTS, 1945–64*
(PERCENT OF MARKET VALUE)

REGULATION	2/5/45	7/5/45	1/21/46	2/1/47	3/30/49	1/17/51	2/20/53
Regulation T							
For extension of credit by brokers and dealers on listed securities	50	75	100	75	50	75	50
For short sales	50	75	100	75	50	75	50
Regulation U							
For loans by banks on stocks	50	75	100	75	50	75	50

	1/4/55	4/23/55	1/16/58	8/5/58	10/16/58	7/28/60	7/10/62	11/6/63
Regulation T								
For extension of credit by brokers and dealers on listed securities	60	70	50	70	90	70	50	70
For short sales	60	70	50	70	90	70	50	70
Regulation U								
For loans by banks on stocks	60	70	50	70	90	70	50	70

Source: Board of Governors of the Federal Reserve System, *Annual Report* (1960), p. 160; and *Federal Reserve Bulletin*, October, 1964, p. 1280.

* Regulations T and U, prescribed in accordance with Securities Exchange Act of 1934, limit the amount of credit that may be extended on a security by prescribing a maximum loan value, which is a specified percentage of its market value at the time of extension; margin requirements are the difference between the market value (100 percent) and the maximum loan value. Changes on February 20, 1953, and January 4, 1955, were effective after close of business on these dates. For earlier data, see *Banking and Monetary Statistics*, Table 145, p. 504.

Other Forms of Selective Credit Controls

In addition to margin requirements, we have also had experience with the selective control of consumer and real-estate credit. Consumer-credit controls were imposed in World War II between 1948 and 1949, and during the Korean conflict. Real estate credit controls were imposed for the first time during the Korean conflict. These forms of control are no longer in effect.

[19] Board of Governors of the Federal Reserve System, *Annual Report* (1962), p. 114.

Our experience with these forms of credit management was quite mixed. Consumer credit controls were instituted to relieve the inflationary pressure of increased expenditures on consumer durables. Minimum down payments were fixed and the term of installment contracts limited. During World War II, the volume of consumer credit decreased, but this might have occurred even if there had been no controls. Increased incomes during the war encouraged debt repayment, and the lack of available consumer durables naturally restricted the total volume of consumer durable expenditures. One of the principal difficulties with this form of control was the enforcement problem; the number of business establishments and the variety of goods covered by the controls was enormous.

Real-estate credit controls operated much like consumer credit controls. Minimum down payments and the maximum maturities of mortgage loans were fixed. It was hoped that higher down payments and shorter maturities would restrict the expansion of real estate credit that had been taking place in 1950. These controls encountered considerable resistance from builders, the public, and veterans' groups, however. Their effectiveness was further hampered by the backlog of construction orders that had been placed prior to the time when controls were to take effect.

Supplementary Readings for Chapters 12 and 13

Board of Governors of the Federal Reserve System. *The Federal Reserve System: Purposes and Functions.* Washington, D.C., 1963, Chapter 3.

Friedman, Milton. *A Program for Monetary Stability.* New York, Fordham University Press, 1960, Chapter 2.

Friedman, Milton, and Anna Schwartz. *A Monetary History of the United States, 1867–1960.* Princeton, N.J., National Bureau of Economic Research, 1963, Chapters 6, 7, and 11.

Goldenweiser, E. A. *American Monetary Policy.* New York, McGraw-Hill, 1951, Chapters 8, 9, 10, and 11.

Roosa, Robert V. *Federal Reserve Operations in the Money and Government Securities Markets.* New York, Federal Reserve Bank of New York, 1956.

Smith, Warren L. "Reserve Requirements in the American Monetary System." In Commission on Money and Credit, *Monetary Management,* Englewood Cliffs, N.J., Prentice-Hall, 1963, pp. 175–315.

————. "The Instruments of General Monetary Control." *The National Banking Review* (1963), pp. 47–76.

Warburton, Clark. "Nonmember Banks and the Effectiveness of Monetary Policy." In Commission on Money and Credit, *Monetary Management,* Englewood Cliffs, N.J., Prentice-Hall, 1963, pp. 317–60.

Chapter 14

Monetary Powers
of Other Government Agencies

The Federal Reserve System is the only government agency that is directly charged with the responsibility of promoting general economic growth and stability. It performs this task by regulating the U.S. monetary system through manipulation of commercial bank reserve positions. Other federal agencies possess monetary powers too, but none has as its primary task the regulation of the entire economy.

The Treasury, for example, implements the fiscal policies articulated by Congress and the President. The extent to which the Treasury can operate independently of Congress and the President is very limited, however. It cannot increase spending or reduce tax rates in order to stimulate the economy, in the same way that the Board of Governors can manipulate discount rates, reserve requirements, and open market operations. Other government agencies, like the Federal Housing Administration or the Commodity Credit Corporation, have the power to affect specific types of credit extension. These agencies do not operate to promote general economic stability and growth, however. Only to the extent that their operations in one specific area of credit extension are contracyclical do they contribute to economic stability.

This chapter briefly examines the monetary powers of various federal agencies. Our discussion considers the powers of these agencies to affect money, even though some of these powers may not be exercised. Previously discussed agencies such as the Federal Reserve System, the Federal Home Loan Bank Board, and the FDIC are not re-examined at this point.

THE U.S. TREASURY

There are several ways in which the Treasury may influence commercial bank reserves and the money stock: (1) by buying and selling gold and silver, (2) by issuing coin and currency, (3) by moving its balances at commercial banks, and (4) by using various debt management techniques.

It must be emphasized, however, that the power to create deficits or tax surpluses is *not* among the powers available to the Treasury. Congress and the President determine deficits and surpluses. The Treasury, through its debt management operations, merely determines how deficits will be financed and how tax surpluses will be used in debt retirement.

The Purchase and Sale of Gold and Silver

The influence of gold purchases on bank reserve positions was discussed in Chapter 11. It will be recalled that when the Treasury uses its funds at the Federal Reserve banks to purchase gold, there is an increase in member bank reserves and demand deposit liabilities. Conversely, the sale of gold by the Treasury tends to decrease member bank reserves and demand deposit liabilities. The purchase or sale of silver by the Treasury has identical results.

If these transactions in gold and silver have any impact on commercial bank reserve positions, it is unplanned. The Treasury does not normally sell gold and silver unless it is first approached by legitimate purchasers. It does not normally enter the market to buy gold and silver; it purchases these money metals at the legally prescribed price only when it is approached by legitimate sellers. Thus, the volume of Treasury gold and silver holdings does not depend upon independent Treasury action. The Treasury is simply an involuntary agent in these transactions.

The Issue of Coin and Currency

When the Treasury issues coin and currency, Federal Reserve holdings of Treasury coin and currency increase, as do the Treasury deposit accounts at the Federal Reserve banks. As the Treasury utilizes its increased balances in the purchase of goods and services from the nonbank public, commercial bank reserves and the demand deposit component of the money supply increase. As the Federal Reserve banks put the currency into circulation, demand deposit money is reduced. Thus, only when the Treasury spends the proceeds from the sale of coin and currency to the Federal Reserve banks, is there a direct effect upon the stock of money.

The Treasury puts additional coin and currency into circulation as it is needed by the public. In recent years, the demand for coins, in particular, has been running ahead of the ability of the Treasury mints to produce. There is almost never a reduction of the total volume of Treasury coin and currency in circulation, although, as noted in Chapter 11, in 1963 the Treasury began withdrawing its silver certificates in order to economize on its silver holdings. Federal Reserve notes are now being used to replace the low denomination Treasury notes.

As in the case of gold and silver acquisitions and sales, the Treasury does not manipulate the volume of Treasury coin and currency outstanding so as to affect the volume of bank reserves and the money stock.

Location of Treasury Balances

The Treasury does have full control over the location at which it keeps its funds. They may be held in tax and loan accounts at commercial banks, in the general account with Federal Reserve banks, or in the Treasury's own vaults. As noted in Chapters 5 and 11, the Treasury usually makes payments out of its general account, places payments received into tax and loan accounts, and transfers funds from tax and loan accounts to the general account as expenditures come due.

The purpose of the tax and loan accounts is to soften the economic repercussions of Treasury tax collections and bond sales. If such receipts were to be placed immediately in the general account and held idle until such time as the Treasury needed them, serious deflationary forces would be set to work. By keeping tax and bond sale receipts in tax and loan accounts, bank reserve positions and total commercial bank demand deposit liabilities are left unaffected. The deposits are merely redistributed from the taxpaying public to the U.S. Treasury.

Although it is evident that the Treasury manipulates its balances so as to avoid affecting commercial bank money-creating abilities adversely, still, the location of Treasury balances is a potential tool of monetary control. In the past the Treasury has usually left adjustment of commercial bank reserve positions to the Federal Reserve System. However, if the Treasury decided to, it could exert a powerful force on bank reserves by changing the location of its funds. By transferring $1 million from its general account to tax and loan accounts, for example, it would increase commercial bank reserves by $1 million. Assuming a 12 percent reserve requirement, commercial bank required reserves would increase by $120,000 because of the increase in demand deposit liabilities owed to the Treasury. Excess reserves, however, would increase by $880,000. In terms of the simple money expansion formula introduced in Chapter 7,

$$D = \frac{R}{r} \qquad [7\text{--}1]$$

We have

$$D = \frac{\$880,000}{.12} = \$7,333,333$$

Thus, on the basis of a $1 million transfer of Treasury deposits to commercial banks, the lending and money-creating abilities of the commercial banking system would increase by $7,333,333.

A transfer of deposits in the opposite direction—from tax and loan accounts to the general account—would have a strong contractionary effect. Total reserves, required reserves, and excess reserves would decrease by $1 million, $120,000, and $880,000 respectively. The demand deposit supporting ability of the banking system would thus be reduced by $7,333,333.

Similarly, if the Treasury decreased the amount of cash in its own vaults by $1 million and placed these funds in tax and loan accounts, there would be an increase in commercial bank reserves of $1 million with the previously described multiple increase in the lending ability of the banking system. On the other hand, if the Treasury demanded cash in exchange for balances in its tax and loan accounts, the process would take place in reverse.

Debt Management

Manipulation of the composition of the national debt is termed debt management. Our present federal debt is in excess of $300 billion and almost one-third of this amount is held by various federal agencies. The Federal Reserve banks alone held $33.6 billion in U.S. government securities at the end of 1963. Over $200 billion, however, is owned by the public. Table 14–1 gives a more complete picture of the ownership of the federal debt.

TABLE 14–1. OWNERSHIP OF DIRECT AND FULLY GUARANTEED
SECURITIES
(PAR VALUE IN BILLIONS OF DOLLARS)

HOLDER	AMOUNT, END OF DECEMBER, 1963
U.S. government agencies and trust funds	58.0
Federal Reserve banks	33.6
Commercial banks	64.1
Mutual savings banks	5.8
Insurance companies	11.0
Other corporations	20.7
State and local governments	20.8
Individuals	
Savings bonds	48.1
Other securities	18.8
Foreign and international	15.9
Other miscellaneous investors	13.3
Total gross debt	310.1

Source: *Federal Reserve Bulletin*, March, 1964, p. 264.

Important decisions must be made periodically by the Treasury with respect to the handling of this enormous debt. Refunding decisions have to be made. If there is a surplus in the budget, the Treasury must decide how to handle the surplus. If there is a deficit, the financing of this deficit needs Treasury attention. These decisions will have a significant effect on the banking system and economic activity.

Refunding. By "refunding" we mean the issuance of new debt and the use of the proceeds to retire old debt. More than 40 percent of U.S. government marketable securities have a maturity of less than one year.[1] As a consequence, a large volume of debt needs to be refunded annually. The Treasury must decide what type of security is to be used to replace old debt as it comes due. Since the ownership distribution of securities may be affected by the refunding decision, bank reserve positions may also be affected. For instance, if new issues are sold to the commercial banks, and the proceeds used to retire securities held by the Federal Reserve banks, there will be a loss of commercial bank reserves. The balance sheet changes for such a transaction are as follows:

BALANCE SHEET CHANGES FOR THE COMMERCIAL BANKING SYSTEM

ASSETS	LIABILITIES + CAPITAL ACCOUNTS
U.S. government securities +$1,000,000 (a)	U.S. government demand deposits +$1,000,000 (a)
Reserves −$1,000,000 (b)	U.S. government demand deposits −$1,000,000 (b)

BALANCE SHEET CHANGES FOR THE FEDERAL RESERVE SYSTEM

ASSETS	LIABILITIES + CAPITAL ACCOUNTS
U.S. government securities −$1,000,000 (b)	Member bank reserves −$1,000,000 (b)

Entries a show the effects of the sale of the securities; entries b show the effects of the retirement of securities held by the Federal Reserve banks.

On the other hand, if the new securities had been sold to the Federal Reserve System and the proceeds used to retire old securities held by the commercial banking system, then the situation would have been reversed. Commercial bank reserves would have increased and there would have been an expansion in their ability to lend and create money.

In general, if new securities are sold to the commercial banking system or the nonbank public and the proceeds are used to retire debt held by governmental agencies, the result will be a decrease in commercial bank lending ability. If, however, new securities are sold to the Federal Reserve banks (this can be done only in very limited quantities) and the proceeds used to retire debt held by the nonbank public or the commercial banking system, then commercial bank reserve positions will be improved.

Surpluses. When the federal government collects more in taxes than it spends, a surplus is created. It is up to the Treasury to decide whether to hold the surplus idle or to use it to retire part of our debt. If it decides to retire debt, then commercial bank reserves will be affected, depending on whose debt holdings are retired.

---

[1] *Federal Reserve Bulletin*, March, 1964, p. 365.

The surplus itself represents a decrease in nonbank public demand deposit holdings and an increase in Treasury accounts. If the debt retired is held by the nonbank public, then the surplus and debt retirement will have no effect upon bank lending positions. Demand deposits will simply have been redistributed from the taxpaying part of the nonbank public to the bond-holding part.

On the other hand, if the debt retired is held by the Federal Reserve banks, commercial bank reserves will be reduced. If the debt retired is held by commercial banks, however, then there is no change in total bank reserves. Excess reserves are increased, however, because of an overall decrease in commercial bank demand deposit liabilities:

BALANCE SHEET CHANGES FOR THE COMMERCIAL BANKING SYSTEM

ASSETS	LIABILITIES + CAPITAL ACCOUNTS
	Nonbank public demand deposits −$1,000,000 (a)
	U.S. government demand deposits +$1,000,000 (a)
U.S. government securities −$1,000,000 (b)	U.S. government demand deposits −$1,000,000 (b)

Entries a show the effects of the tax surplus; entries b show the effects of the security retirement on commercial banks.

Deficits. When the federal government spends more than it collects in taxes, funds must be found to meet the excess of expenditure. Two alternatives exist. The Treasury may print more currency and use it to meet the deficit, or it may borrow the funds. In the United States the first alternative has not been considered acceptable. Therefore, the Treasury resorts to borrowing. It does this by issuing new government securities. The principal purchasers of new securities are the nonbank public and the commercial banking system.

When the funds are borrowed from the commercial banking system, there is initially an increase in commercial bank holdings of U.S. government securities and an equal increase in Treasury tax and loan deposit accounts because banks pay for the securities by increasing Treasury tax and loan accounts. This act lowers the ability of the banking system to lend to the nonbank public, since the banks used some of their capacity for loan and investment expansion to buy government securities. Subsequently, as the Treasury spends the proceeds of the loan, the newly created balances will be transferred to the nonbank public. The net effect is that the demand deposit money holdings of the nonbank public will increase as a result of the method used by the Treasury to finance the deficit.

A deficit need not always result in an increase in the stock of money, however. If the Treasury were to sell the securities to the nonbank public, for example, then there would be no change in the stock of money. Instead, demand deposits would be transferred from the bond-buying part of the nonbank public to the U.S. Treasury, and then in turn to that part of the nonbank public which sells goods and services to the Treasury. Thus, money balances would simply be redistributed among the members of the nonbank public. The impact of this redistribution of deposit ownership, however, is not likely to be neutral. Those who produce goods and services for sale to the Treasury generally utilize their money balances more intensively than those who purchase securities. As a result, the velocity of the money supply will increase, thereby leading to increased expenditures in the economy.

It is very dangerous to finance a deficit in an inflatory period by selling new securities to the central bank. If the Treasury were to sell securities to the Federal Reserve banks, and then spend the proceeds, the effect would be an equal increase in commercial bank reserves and demand deposit liabilities initially. Without offsetting action by the central bank, the banking system could then create deposits by a multiple of the volume of excess reserves created by the above procedure. This would simply set in motion more inflationary forces. It is equally dangerous to finance the deficit by directing the central bank to support the government bond market by purchasing securities previously purchased by the nonbank public and the commercial banking system. The results are the same as if the central banking system bought the securities in the first instance. Commercial bank reserves increase. It was in precisely this manner that a large part of our World War II deficits were financed. The result was continued inflationary pressures in the economy.

Debt management and economic fluctuations. In short, Treasury debt management techniques can affect commercial bank reserve positions and money-creating abilities in a variety of ways. Refunding may expand or contract reserves, depending on whose securities are retired and who purchases the new securities. To the extent that the central banking system buys new securities, bank reserves will probably increase. To the extent that the central banking system has its security holdings retired, bank reserves will probably decrease. The exception to this occurs when the Federal Reserve buys new securities and has its holdings retired. In addition, a Treasury surplus reduces bank reserves when it is used to retire securities held by Federal Reserve banks. A deficit expands reserves when the Federal Reserve banks buy the new government securities.

Normally, however, the Treasury does not make debt management decisions for the specific purpose of regulating the economy through the banking system. Instead, it uses debt management to complement the activities of the Federal Reserve, not to interfere with them. *The principal job of regulation is left to the Board of Governors of the Federal Reserve System.* This is not to say, however, that there is never any Treasury interference. The support of the government bond market by the Federal Reserve System during and after World War II is an excellent example of how a decision to manage the debt in a particular way—in this case to keep the interest burden of the debt low—can interfere with Federal Reserve control of the banking system.

As a general rule, it would be advisable for the Treasury to make its debt management decisions so that changes in the maturity, ownership, and interest yields of the federal debt do not react on the economy in a procyclical manner. If possible, these changes should be contracyclical.

What would be appropriate contracyclical Treasury debt management policy? In a *recession* the following guidelines might be used: First, if there is a deficit and the recession is severe, then the debt should be financed through the sale of securities to the central banking system.[2] If the recession is mild, however, then the securities should be sold either to the commercial banks or the nonbank public. In a mild recession, the economy may be overstimulated by the sharp increase in reserves that arises from central bank security purchases. Second, if there is a tax surplus, then it should not be used to retire securities held by the central banking system, since this would reduce commercial bank reserves. Instead it should be employed to retire securities held by either commercial banks or the nonbank public. This helps reduce somewhat the deflationary effects of the surplus itself. Third, new security issues and debt retirement should be manipulated in such a way that the maturity structure of the debt is shortened. The growth and prosperity of the economy are in large part dependent upon business investment expenditures. If the Treasury lengthened the maturity of the debt by selling long-term securities in a recession, it is possible that there would be a reduction of funds available for business investment. Government debt is virtually riskless in terms of the ability of the government to repay debt, but business is not so fortunate. Lenders may therefore be more inclined to purchase long-term government securities in a recession than corporate bonds. It is therefore advisable for the Treasury to shorten the maturity of the debt and permit long-term funds to be channeled into business investment.

In an inflation, these policies should be reversed. First, if there is a deficit, it should not be financed by selling securities to the central bank. Such a procedure is extremely inflationary. Second, if there is a surplus, it should be used to retire securities held primarily by the central bank. Such a procedure will draw down the reserves of commercial banks and thus reduce

---

[2] An even more efficient way of financing increased government expenditures during severe recession would be pure money creation. Let the central bank finance the increased expenditures by creating money without the simultaneous purchase of a new Treasury security. In this way there would be no increased interest burden on taxpayers, and no accompanying problem of the deflationary aspects of possible future debt retirement. This is a policy that I would be willing to advocate only for depressions of the magnitude we experienced in the 1930's, however. Given an irresponsible legislature and executive, this policy could be disastrous if carried into periods of full employment.

their money-creating potential. Third, the maturity structure of the debt should be lengthened. If the Treasury concentrates on the sale of long-term securities, long-term funds may be drawn away from business investment, thereby reducing inflationary pressures. Unfortunately, this is precisely the period in which the Treasury may find it difficult to market long-term securities. During periods of full employment and inflation, interest rates are bid up by competitors for funds. The Treasury is one such competitor. It is prohibited by law, however, from marketing issues maturing in five or more years at interest yields in excess of 4¼ percent. This interest limitation makes it difficult for the Treasury to compete with private enterprise for long-term funds.

OTHER FINANCIAL PROGRAMS

The list of government agencies engaged in lending and debt-insuring activity is almost too long to enumerate. Federal lending and insurance programs are concentrated in three principal fields: agriculture, business, and housing. Federal activity in these fields involves loaning directly, participating in private loans, and insuring parts of private loans. Table 14–2

TABLE 14–2. SUMMARY OF LOANS OUTSTANDING,
DECEMBER 31, 1958, IN ALL FEDERAL LOAN AND
INSURING PROGRAMS
(IN MILLIONS OF DOLLARS)

TYPE OF PROGRAM		AMOUNT
Agricultural loans	12,244	
Business loans	1,469	
Housing loans	67,060	
Miscellaneous loans	432	
Total		81,205
Subtractions to eliminate double counting		
Agricultural loans	−1,197	
Housing loans	−3,901	
Total subtractions		−5,098
Net total		76,107

Source: Stewart Johnson, "Statistics on Federal Lending Loan Insurance Programs in the United States, 1929–1958," in Commission on Money and Credit, *Federal Credit Programs* (Englewood Cliffs, N.J.: Prentice-Hall, 1963), Summary Table I–A, p. 3.

gives an indication of the enormity of federal activity in the lending field. The data include both the federal loans made and the value of the private loans that are insured by the various government agencies. This clearly demonstrates the overwhelming importance of federal lending and insuring activity in housing and agriculture.

How important is this type of federal activity for monetary stability? These programs are designed to help specific industries, individual home purchasers, and specific firms. Normally, the agencies that regulate these loan and insurance programs do not have the additional function of regulating their activities in a contracyclical manner. Occasionally, therefore, these agencies act in a procyclical manner. For example, in periods of full employment and rising prices, it frequently becomes difficult for small businesses to borrow for purposes of expansion. The Federal Reserve System is making it increasingly difficult for commercial banks, which are an important source of funds for small business, to lend. As a result, banks will lend only to their larger and, presumably, more credit-worthy customers. Small businesses then turn for funds to the Small Business Administration, an independent agency of the federal government. As its lending activity expands in this period, total lending in the economy increases. Thus, by providing additional funds in a period of inflation, a federal agency may make it more difficult for the Federal Reserve to regulate economic activity.

On the average, it appears that the various federal credit programs have behaved perversely relative to economic activity. "Since World War II they have created inflationary pressures in every year . . ."[3] As Table 14–3

TABLE 14–3. FEDERAL CREDIT EXTENDED, 1950–58
(IN MILLIONS OF DOLLARS)

YEAR	NET CHANGE IN CREDIT EXTENDED TO				
	Housing	*Agriculture*	*Business*	*Miscellaneous*	*Total*
1950	4,955	(415)	(117)	15	4,438
1951	4,555	330	521	31	5,437
1952	3,318	993	171	23	4,505
1953	3,512	1,845	(200)	28	5,185
1954	2,802	179	(528)	11	2,464
1955	5,568	69	(203)	16	5,450
1956	3,919	620	93	9	4,641
1957	4,068	(244)	58	32	3,914
1958	4,403	2,210	61	40	6,714

Source: Computed from Warren A. Law, "The Aggregate Impact of Federal Credit Programs on the Economy," in Commission on Money and Credit, *Federal Credit Programs*, Tables II–9, 10, 11, and 12, pp. 312–15.

shows, during the 1950's the net change in total credit extended by the federal credit programs was positive in each year. Except for the recession periods of 1953–54 and 1957–58, however, at least some decrease in credit

---

[3] Warren A. Law, "The Aggregate Impact of Federal Credit Programs on the Economy," in Commission on Money and Credit, *Federal Credit Programs* (Englewood Cliffs, N.J.: Prentice-Hall, 1963), p. 310.

extended was called for on contracyclical grounds. Thus, it seems reasonable to conclude, at least for the period for which data has been compiled, that federal credit programs have acted perversely during periods of rising prices and full employment.

SUMMARY

The U.S. Treasury and other government agencies are not charged with the responsibility of regulating the stability of the economy. Their actions may affect credit conditions and the ability of commercial banks to lend, however. On a contracyclical basis it would seem to be prudent for the Treasury to coordinate its debt management activities with current Federal Reserve policy. Although the Treasury normally attempts to do this, other federal agencies do not usually coordinate their policies with those of the Federal Reserve.

Supplementary Readings
Commission on Money and Credit. *Fiscal and Debt Management Policies.* Englewood Cliffs, N.J., Prentice-Hall, 1963.
———. *Federal Credit Agencies.* Englewood Cliffs, N.J., Prentice-Hall, 1963.

Chapter 15

Commercial Bank Reserves
and the Money Supply

Variations in the money stock have an effect on economic activity. As succeeding chapters will demonstrate, there is some controversy among professional economists as to the precise nature of the relationship. The following basic statement is generally considered axiomatic, however. If an increase in the desire to spend is accompanied by either an increase in the stock of money or an increased turnover of a given money stock, then spending will rise and so will the level of general economic activity. On the other hand, if a decreased desire to spend is accompanied by a decrease in the stock of money or its turnover, spending will decline and an economic recession will occur. Whether monetary changes *cause* spending changes or merely *accompany* them, variations in the money supply are clearly related to the level of economic activity. The volume of money is primarily dependent upon commercial bank reserve positions. The Federal Reserve, therefore, seeks to stabilize the economy by regulating the reserve position of the commercial banking system.

Subsequent chapters in Part III will examine the influence of the money supply on the economy. To understand this influence, however, certain basic points on money supply determination need to be studied first.

In this chapter there is a brief review of money supply determination as developed in Part I. Second, the determination of member bank reserves is reconsidered in quantitative terms. Third, the quantitative determination of the money stock is examined. Finally, there is some discussion of the theory of money supply determination. Subsequent chapters in Part III will examine the influence of the money supply on the economy. The demand for money is discussed at length in Chapter 20.

REVIEW

We have said that money is anything generally acceptable as a means of extinguishing debt. It facilitates the exchange of goods and services and acts as a store of value. In the United States, money consists of currency and demand deposits owned by the nonbank public. Other liquid assets perform *some* of the functions of money, but none of them are as convenient for use in transactions or as completely free from the possibility of default.

The volume of currency depends largely upon the demands of the public, since our central bank, the Federal Reserve System, is willing to supply almost any amount of currency demanded. Changes in the amount of currency outstanding are usually accompanied by opposite changes in the volume of demand deposit money. The U.S. government does not normally create currency to meet its own obligations. Therefore, increases in the volume of currency occur when individuals and businesses demand currency in exchange for demand deposit money. Commercial banks use their reserve accounts at the Federal Reserve banks to acquire the additional currency to meet these demands. Conversely, the amount of currency in circulation decreases when currency is exchanged for demand deposits. Commercial banks deposit their excess currency holdings with the Federal Reserve banks and their reserve accounts are increased.

Shifts in the volume of demand deposits are more significant than currency changes. The largest increases in demand deposit money take place when commercial banks extend loans and make investments. In turn, demand deposits contract when loans and investments are retired.

The ability of the individual bank to create money (demand deposits) is limited by the volume of its excess reserves. The ability of the commercial banking system to create money also depends upon its excess reserve position. Because of a fractional reserve requirement, however, the banking system can create a volume of deposits that is a multiple of its excess reserves. Similarly, when there is a deficiency of reserves, the banking system must contract deposits by a multiple of the reserve shortage.

Thus, the banking system's reserve position and its ability to create money depend upon (1) R, the volume of its reserves, (2) r, the reserve requirement for demand deposits, (3) TD, the volume of time deposits, (4) r', the reserve requirement for time deposits, (5) c, the ratio of currency to demand deposits that is currently desired by the public, and (6) i', the ratio of working balances of excess reserves to demand deposits that is desired by the banking system. Of these various factors, R, r, and r' depend upon Federal Reserve policies or, in the case of nonmember banks, upon state banking authorities. TD and c, on the other hand, depend upon the desires of the public. Only i' depends directly upon commercial bank policy. In Chapter 7 all these factors were combined into equations 7–4 and 7–5:

$$\Delta D = \frac{\Delta A}{r + c + i'} \qquad\qquad D = \frac{R - r'(TD)}{r + i'} \qquad [7\text{--}4, \ 7\text{--}5]$$

D is the volume of demand deposits the commercial banking system can support, given the other five factors; ΔD is the potential change in D given c and some change in reserves, ΔA. Note that D refers to the volume of demand deposits the system *can* support, not the volume it will actually create.

To determine just how much money (currency and demand deposits) the economy has, it is not enough that we have information on just those factors that affect reserve positions. The amount of money in the economy actually depends on the interaction of the public's demand for money and the willingness and ability of the banking system to supply money.

THE QUANTITATIVE DETERMINATION
OF MEMBER BANK RESERVES

Bank reserve positions cannot be considered the *sole element* determining the volume of demand deposit money in the economy. Nonetheless, *bank reserve positions are generally regarded as the most critical part of money supply determination.*

As noted in Chapters 10 through 13, the Federal Reserve System is held responsible for promoting a stable and growing economy by manipulating member bank reserve positions. This is done by means of open market operations, reserve requirement changes, and discount rate manipulations. Of these techniques, open market operations are employed the most frequently. They are used to augment or decrease member bank reserves for dynamic contracyclical purposes and also for defensive purposes to cover seasonal or unanticipated bank reserve difficulties.

There are many forces that directly affect the volume of member bank reserves. This section summarizes *all* those forces which quantitatively determine the volume of member bank reserves, forces that the Federal Reserve must consider when engaging in open market operations. The focus is on member bank reserves. This does not mean that nonmember banks are unimportant; they are very important for the communities in which they are located. In the aggregate, however, the volume of demand deposits created by member banks is significantly larger. Similarly, member banks as a group carry on a larger volume of banking activity.

Factors Tending to Increase and Decrease Reserves

Table 15–1 lists all of the various factors that tend to increase or decrease member bank reserves. Those that supply reserves are called *sources of funds*. When these factors increase, member bank reserves with Federal Reserve banks tend to increase. When they decrease, they tend to decrease member bank reserves. This should not be taken to mean, however, that an increase or decrease in a source of funds *must* increase or decrease reserves. Other factors may act as an offset. For example, a gold stock increase should lead to an increase in reserves, but if the increased reserves are not desirable from a contracyclical view, the Federal Reserve may decide to sell government securities to depress reserves. In itself, an increase in a source of funds tends to increase reserves. However, since other sources *may* respond in an opposite direction, it is the *total* change in bank sources of funds that is important for the purpose of member bank reserve determination.

TABLE 15-1. FACTORS TENDING TO INCREASE OR DECREASE MEMBER BANK
RESERVES
MARCH, 1963, AND MARCH, 1964
(IN MILLIONS OF DOLLARS)

RESERVES AND RELATED ITEMS	MARCH, 1963*	MARCH, 1964*	CHANGES IN FACTORS FROM MARCH, 1963, TO MARCH, 1964
Factors supplying reserve funds (sources of funds)			
Federal Reserve credit			
U.S. government securities	30,613	33,389	+2,776
Discounts and advances	185	259	+ 74
Float	1,626	1,710	+ 84
Other	53	96	+ 43
Total	32,477	35,454	2,977
Gold stock	15,878	15,462	− 416
Treasury currency outstanding	5,576	5,579	+ 3
Total	53,931	56,495	+2,564
Factors absorbing reserve funds (uses of funds)			
Currency in circulation†	34,431	36,615	+2,184
Treasury cash holdings	446	434	− 12
Treasury, foreign, and other deposits with Federal Reserve banks	1,251	1,303	+ 52
Other Federal Reserve accounts	1,095	998	− 97
Total	37,223	39,350	2,127
Member bank reserves with Federal Reserve banks	16,707	17,146	+ 439
Total	53,930‡	56,496‡	+2,566‡
Addendum			
Member bank reserves			
With Federal Reserve banks	16,707	17,146	+ 439
Currency and coin	2,808	3,058	+ 250
Total	19,515	20,204	+ 689

Source: *Federal Reserve Bulletin*, April, 1964, pp. 452–53.
* Averages of daily figures.
† Includes currency and coin held as vault cash by commercial banks.
‡ Totals of sources of funds do not agree with totals of uses of funds because of rounding.

In addition to the sources of funds, there are *uses of funds*. These uses compete with reserves in that they tend to absorb and thereby reduce member bank reserves. When the uses of funds increase, member bank reserves with Federal Reserve banks tend to fall. When these factors decrease, they tend to increase member bank reserves with the Federal Reserve banks.

As is shown in Table 15–1, reserve sources of funds increased by $2.564 billion from March, 1963, through March, 1964. Uses of funds other than member bank reserves with Federal Reserve banks increased by $2.127 billion in the same period, however. Subtracting the increase in the factors absorbing reserves from the increase in the sources of funds leaves a $439 million increase in member bank reserves held with the Federal Reserve banks.[1]

The relationship between member bank reserves held with the Federal Reserve banks can conveniently be summarized in the following equation:

$$\text{Member bank reserves with Federal Reserve banks} = \text{sources of funds} - \text{uses of funds} \qquad [15\text{–}1]$$

Breaking this simple formula down into its component factors, we have:

$$\text{Member bank reserves with Federal Reserve banks} = \left\{ \begin{array}{c} \text{total Federal} \\ \text{Reserve credit} \\ + \\ \text{gold stock} \\ + \\ \text{Treasury currency} \\ \text{outstanding} \end{array} \right\} - \left\{ \begin{array}{c} \text{currency in circulation} \\ + \\ \text{Treasury cash holdings} \\ + \\ \text{Treasury, foreign, and} \\ \text{other deposits with} \\ \text{Federal Reserve banks} \\ + \\ \text{other Federal Reserve} \\ \text{accounts} \end{array} \right\}$$

$$[15\text{–}2]$$

Almost all of these factors were discussed in Chapter 11 where the influence of various Federal Reserve balance sheet items on member bank reserves was examined. Here, however, U.S. Treasury balance sheet items are considered in addition to the Federal Reserve balance sheet accounts.

Federal Reserve credit. The major source of funds is Federal Reserve credit. When the Federal Reserve purchases bankers' acceptances, makes discounts and advances, purchases U.S. government securities, and expands "float," there is a direct increase in member bank reserves. Conversely, when these sources of funds decrease, member bank reserves decrease.

Gold stock. The second most important source of funds is our gold stock. As the Treasury buys gold using its accounts at the Federal Reserve banks, member bank reserves are increased and vice versa. This factor, gold stock, differs somewhat in total from the gold certificate reserves of the Federal

---

[1] Subtracting $2.127 billion from $2.564 billion yields $437 million instead of $439 million. The difference in the two figures is attributable to rounding.

Reserve banks. When the Treasury buys or sells gold, it almost always issues or retires an equal amount of gold certificates. Not all Treasury gold holdings, however, are used as the basis of issues of gold certificates. The Treasury keeps a small volume of gold balances idle. For example, the gold stock at the end of March, 1964, was $15.462 billion, while total gold certificate reserves were $15.190 billion.[2]

Treasury currency outstanding. The third source of funds is Treasury currency outstanding, the total value of currency issued by the Treasury. As noted in Chapter 11, when the Treasury issues additional currency, the Federal Reserve banks purchase it by increasing the Treasury's general account. Member bank reserves then increase as the Treasury spends its increased deposit balances. Although this factor accounts for approximately 10 percent of all sources of funds, changes in Treasury currency are far less dramatic than either Federal Reserve credit or gold stock changes. Only $3 million out of the total $2.564 billion change in sources of funds from March, 1963, to March, 1964, was attributable to changes in Treasury currency outstanding, for instance.

Currency in circulation. Uses of funds work in the opposite direction from sources. As uses increase, member bank reserve deposits decrease. The most important use of funds is currency in circulation outside of the Treasury and Federal Reserve banks. This is currency held by both the nonbank public and the commercial banking system itself. As previously mentioned, commercial bank reserves move in the opposite direction from public currency holdings. However, commercial bank reserves need not vary in the opposite direction from currency in circulation. That part of currency in circulation which is held by commercial banks is actually part of their total reserves. Hence, only member bank reserves held with the Federal Reserve banks vary with currency in circulation. Other things being equal, if the public wants additional currency or commercial banks choose to hold a greater portion of their reserves in the form of vault cash, then member bank reserves with Federal Reserve banks must decline. On the other hand, a return of cash by the public to the banks or a decrease in the fraction of reserves banks wish to hold in the form of vault cash will increase member bank reserves with the Federal Reserve banks.

As can be seen in Table 15–1, currency in circulation is by far the principal competing use for funds. From March, 1963, to March, 1964, currency in circulation expanded by $2.184 billion; banks picked up $250 million of this increase as vault cash. This means that the currency holdings of the nonbank public increased by $1.934 billion. In the absence of Federal Reserve offsets, total member bank reserves would have been reduced by the same amount.

---

[2] *Federal Reserve Bulletin*, April, 1964, pp. 435, 459.

Treasury, foreign, and other deposits with Federal Reserve banks; other Federal Reserve accounts. The second most important factor that competes with reserves for funds consists of the sum of various Federal Reserve balance sheet liability and capital account items. These are Treasury, foreign, and other deposits with Federal Reserve banks and other Federal Reserve accounts. These factors and their effects on bank reserves were described in some detail in Chapter 11.

Treasury cash holdings. The final use that competes with reserves for funds is Treasury cash holdings. This simply consists of the cash held by the Treasury in its own vaults. If the Treasury draws down its cash holdings by increasing its cash payments, the nonbank public will receive the funds and part of them will find their way into the banking system, thereby building up commercial bank reserves. If the commercial banks do not wish to hold on to the increased amount of vault cash, they can send the cash to the Federal Reserve banks and have their reserve deposit accounts increased. In a similar manner, the increase of Treasury cash holdings will draw down member bank reserves with Federal Reserve banks.

Summary and Evaluation

As sources of funds increase, member bank reserves with Federal Reserve banks increase. As sources of funds decrease, member bank reserves with Federal Reserve banks decrease. In the absence of offsetting vault cash changes, when sources of funds change total member bank reserves move in the same direction as member bank reserves with Federal Reserve banks.

As uses of funds increase, member bank reserves with Federal Reserve banks decrease. As uses of funds decrease, member bank reserves with Federal Reserve banks increase. Again, in the absence of offsetting vault cash changes, total member bank reserves move in the same direction as member bank reserves with Federal Reserve banks when uses of funds change.

The quantitative determination of member bank reserves should not be viewed mechanically. Actual bank reserve positions are determined by the influence of all of the factors giving rise to or absorbing funds. In practice, a factor tending to increase reserves may well be offset by some factor tending to absorb reserves. Table 15–1 and equations 15–1 and 15–2 can be used to show the principal *quantitative reasons* for member bank reserve changes (Federal Reserve credit, gold stock, and currency in circulation changes). Pinpointing the quantitative reasons for reserve changes, however, is not the same as explaining *why* there was a change. To answer the question why, we need to explain the behavior of our monetary authorities (who determine Federal Reserve credit), our balance of payments (which helps determine the size of our gold stock), and the actions of the nonbank public (which determine the nonbank public part of currency in circulation). For example, from June, 1950, to June, 1951, member bank reserves increased $3.2 billion and the principal source was a $5.6 billion rise in Federal Reserve credit. A subsequent decrease in gold stock, however, absorbed $2.5 billion in funds.[3] Principally two forces lay behind these changes: (1) the Korean conflict, and (2) the Federal Reserve policy of continued support of the government bond market.

THE QUANTITATIVE DETERMINATION OF THE STOCK OF MONEY

Just as we can describe the quantitative determination of member bank reserves, so we can also describe the quantitative determination of the stock of money. The same note of caution, however, applies; showing quantitatively *how* money stock changes in response to various factors does not explain *why* the various factors and the money stock change.

Three institutions have the power to vary the money supply: the commercial banking system, the Federal Reserve System, and the U.S. Treasury. The components of our money supply—demand deposits, Federal Reserve notes, and Treasury currency—are liabilities of these three institutions. Hence, these liabilities are called *monetary liabilities.*

It will be recalled that assets must equal liabilities plus capital accounts. Thus, if liabilities are broken down into monetary and nonmonetary liabilities, we have

$$\text{Assets} = \text{Monetary liabilities} + \text{nonmonetary liabilities} + \text{capital accounts} \qquad [15\text{--}3]$$

and

$$\text{Monetary liabilities} = \text{Assets} - \text{nonmonetary liabilities} - \text{capital accounts} \qquad [15\text{--}4]$$

The quantity of the money stock is determined by subtracting the non-monetary liabilities and capital accounts from the assets of the three institutions that create monetary liabilities. This is shown in Table 15–2.[4]

---

[3] Board of Governors of the Federal Reserve System, *Supplement to Banking and Monetary Statistics:* Section 10, p. 17.

[4] This table is based upon, but not identical with, the "Consolidated Condition Statement" published monthly in the *Federal Reserve Bulletin.* The focus of Table 15–2 is upon demand deposits and currency, whereas the "Consolidated Condition Statement" emphasizes total deposits and currency. A description of the "Consolidated Condition Statement" is contained in the following: Board of Governors of the Federal Reserve System, *Supplement to Banking and Monetary Statistics:* Section 1—Banks and the Monetary System (1962). It should be noted that Table 15–2, like the "Consolidated Condition Statement," "is a consolidation rather than a combination of the accounts of the components. In the process of consolidation most of the relationships among the components are eliminated" (*Supplement,* p. 3).

From the relationships established in equation 15–4 and Table 15–2 it can be seen that the money stock will vary directly with changes in assets and inversely with nonmonetary liability and capital account changes. All of the factors that tend to increase or decrease the stock of money have al-

TABLE 15–2. FACTORS TENDING TO INCREASE OR DECREASE THE STOCK
OF MONEY,
MARCH, 1963, AND MARCH, 1964
(IN BILLIONS OF DOLLARS)

FACTORS	MARCH 27, 1963	MARCH 25, 1964	CHANGES IN FACTORS FROM MARCH, 1963, TO MARCH, 1964
Factors supplying money (*assets*)			
Gold stock	15.9	15.5	− 0.4
Treasury currency outstanding	5.6	5.6	—
Commercial bank loans and investments	234.9	253.5	+18.5
Federal Reserve loans and investments	31.0	33.8	+ 2.8
Total	287.4	308.4	+21.0
Factors absorbing funds supplying money (*liabilities and capital accounts*)			
Nonmonetary liabilities			
Time deposits at commercial banks	102.2	115.7	+13.5
Treasury cash holdings	0.4	0.4	—
Treasury deposits at Federal Reserve banks	0.9	1.1	+ 0.2
Treasury deposits at commercial banks	7.3	7.9	+ 0.6
Net foreign deposits	1.2	1.2	—
Other nonmonetary liabilities and capital accounts*	29.9	31.7	+ 1.8
Total	141.9	158.0	+16.1
Monetary liabilities			
Currency outside banks	30.1	32.0	+ 1.9
Demand deposits	115.4	118.4	+ 3.0
Total	145.5	150.4	+ 4.9
Total	287.4	308.4	+21.0

Source: *Federal Reserve Bulletin*, April, 1964, pp. 452, 453, 463, and 464.
* Computed as the difference between assets and the sum of all other nonmonetary liabilities and monetary liabilities.

ready been discussed in some other context, principally with respect to commercial bank reserve positions. As a result, the discussion at this point can be relatively brief.

Factors Tending to Supply Money

Commercial bank loans and investments are the greatest source of money. When commercial banks grant loans or make investments, they either create deposits or put currency into circulation. Conversely, as commercial bank loans are retired or holdings of investments reduced, commercial bank deposit liabilities are reduced. In addition, since some people repay loans with currency, currency outside banks may also be reduced.

The second largest source of money is Federal Reserve bank loans and investments. When the Federal Reserve buys bankers' acceptances and U.S. government securities from the nonbank public, the stock of money is directly increased. Bank reserves move in the same direction as the stock of money. On the other hand, when the Federal Reserve buys bankers' acceptances and U.S. government securities directly from commercial banks, only bank reserves are initially increased. Similarly, the extension of discounts and advances to commercial banks will only directly affect bank reserves, not the currency and demand deposit holdings of the nonbank public. This type of change in Federal Reserve loans and investments tends to affect "other nonmonetary liabilities and capital accounts" instead of monetary liabilities.

There is an indirect connection between Federal Reserve loans and investments and monetary liabilities even when the nonbank public is not directly involved in the loan and investment change. By purchasing securities from commercial banks or making discounts and advances, the Federal Reserve banks may prevent commercial banks from contracting their assets and, accordingly, the stock of money.

Changes in the gold stock and Treasury currency outstanding may also affect the stock of money. To the extent that the buyers and sellers of gold to the Treasury are members of the nonbank public, the money supply will vary in direct proportion to the gold stock. To the extent, however, that Treasury currency is issued in response to the need of the nonbank public for Treasury currency, there will be an increase in currency in circulation, but no change in the total money stock. Instead, Treasury deposits at Federal Reserve banks will probably increase.

All of the factors that tend to supply money expanded by $21 billion from March, 1963, to March, 1964, but the money stock rose by only $4.9 billion in the same period. This was due to the fact that there was a sharp rise in nonmonetary liabilities.

Factors Absorbing Funds Supplying Money; the Relationship between Assets and Nonmonetary Liabilities

The funds that are supplied when *assets supplying money increase* need not all go into monetary liabilities. They may also be absorbed by nonmonetary liabilities and capital accounts. As commercial bank loans and investments expand, for example, some borrowers may choose to increase their time deposit holdings instead of currency or demand deposits. It is quite probable that many of those who receive payment from borrowing businesses will also build up time deposits. For instance, if commercial banks lend $10 million to businesses so that these firms may meet their payrolls, the employees, upon receiving the $10 million, may decide to put $8 million in demand deposits, $1 million in currency, and $1 million in time deposits. This would cause the stock of money to increase by $9 million instead of $10 million. The balance sheet entries for this type of transaction are as follows:

BALANCE SHEET CHANGES FOR THE COMMERCIAL BANKING SYSTEM

ASSETS		LIABILITIES + CAPITAL ACCOUNTS	
Loans and investments	+$10,000,000 (a)	Demand deposits of borrowing businesses	+$10,000,000 (a)
		Demand deposits of borrowing businesses	−$10,000,000 (b)
Vault cash	−$1,000,000 (b)	Demand deposits of payroll recipients	+$8,000,000 (b)
		Time deposits of payroll recipients	+$1,000,000 (b)

Entries a show the effects of borrowing and entries b show what happens when these borrowed funds are spent by the borrowing firms.

Similarly, if commercial bank loans and investments expand as a result of the purchase of securities from the U.S. government, Treasury demand deposits rather than the demand deposits of the nonbank public increase. Only when the Treasury spends the proceeds of the security sale will monetary liabilities increase.

Asset decreases may also be accompanied by nonmonetary liability decreases. For example, an individual may choose to repay a consumer loan by drawing down his time rather than his checking account. Thus, changes in the factors supplying money may change either monetary or nonmonetary liabilities.

Changes in money-supplying assets are not the only factors that can cause a shift in monetary and nonmonetary liabilities. There is often a direct connection between monetary and nonmonetary liabilities that does not involve assets. As a rule, in the absence of asset changes, monetary liability increases tend to accompany nonmonetary liability decreases and vice versa. For example, as noted in Chapter 2, there are frequent transfers between time and demand deposits. A rise in interest rates payable on time and savings deposits will usually induce depositors to build up their time deposit accounts and to maintain lower demand deposit balances. On the other hand, when consumers anticipate large capital expenditures they will frequently transfer funds from time to demand deposit accounts.

As illustrated in Table 15–2, time deposits are the principal nonmonetary liability competing with monetary liabilities for funds. In the year from March, 1963, to March, 1964, time deposits expanded by $13.5 billion, whereas all other factors absorbing funds expanded by only $2.6 billion.

THE THEORY OF THE SUPPLY OF MONEY

In capsule form, most theories of money supply determination may be stated as follows: money consists of currency outside banks and demand deposits. Since variations in currency can occur only at the expense of demand deposits, the total volume of money primarily depends upon demand deposit variations. The ability of the banking system to create demand deposits depends on its reserve base, which in turn is controlled by the Federal Reserve System. Depending upon the required reserve ratios, the volume of demand deposits will be some multiple of the reserve base. The powers of the Federal Reserve are such that it can cause the reserve position of the commercial banks to be whatever it desires. Hence, it is argued, the volume of money depends upon central bank policy.

This line of analysis makes two rather untenable assumptions, however: (1) that the commercial banking system reacts passively to changes in its reserve base, and (2) that the Federal Reserve System selects a specific amount of money that it considers suitable for the economy and counters any move by commercial banks to create a different amount.

The discussions in Chapters 6, 12, and 13 show that these assumptions are not valid. First, commercial banks tend to economize on reserves during periods of economic upturn. They expand loans, investments, the turnover of money, and the money stock in order to take advantage of rising interest returns. The growth of loans, the turnover of money, and the volume of demand deposits are reduced during economic contraction as interest yields to banks on loans and investments drift downward. Thus, banks react quite vigorously to changes in reserve positions. Furthermore, the Federal Reserve System makes policy changes slowly, thereby allowing commercial banks substantial latitude in money supply creation within the context of a given reserve base. These considerations show that the commercial banking system attempts to vary the i' of equation 7–4, the ratio of working balances of excess reserves to demand deposits, *inversely* with the return to be earned on loans and investments. The higher the return, the lower the i' becomes, and the greater the money supply.

A First Approximation to the Theory of the Money Supply

As a first step toward a theory of money supply determination, it appears that, other things being given, the *money supply is a function of the reserve base and the return to be earned on loans and investments.* Let us call this return the *rate of interest, i.* Putting this into equation form we have

$$M_s = f(R, i, Z')$$

[15–5]

where M_s stands for the money supply, R, the reserve base of the banking system, i, the rate of interest, and Z', all other forces affecting the money supply. M_s is assumed to be an increasing function of both R and i; that is, the money supply will expand with increases in reserves and the rate of interest. The money supply will also decrease with declines in reserves and the rate of interest.

Figure 15–1 shows in diagrammatic form the relationship between i and M_s, given R. The money supply line is called *MM*. The reserve base, as noted, is not shown in the diagram. It is assumed that this is fixed by the central bank. Thus, the line *MM* shows how the money supply varies in response to interest rate changes, other things being given. The line slopes

FIGURE 15–1. The supply-of-money schedule.

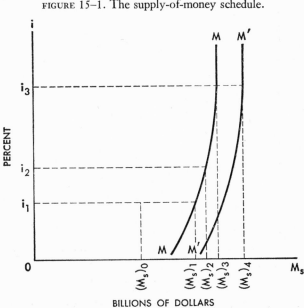

BILLIONS OF DOLLARS

upward and to the right, meaning that higher amounts of M will accompany higher values of i. Notice, however, that *MM* becomes steeper as the rate of interest rises higher. For example, as i increases from i_1 to i_2, the money supply increases only by a very small amount from $(M_s)_1$ to $(M_s)_2$. This indicates that the money supply is not very responsive to interest rate changes at very high rates of interest, which may be attributable to the fact that, given R and Z', as the money supply increases banks find it increasingly difficult to create money because of their rapidly diminishing margins of excess reserves. Eventually, with no change in R, the i' of equation 7–5 must become 0. At this point banks can no longer create money and the line *MM* becomes perfectly vertical. In our diagram this occurs at $(M_s)_3$ and i_3.

A Second Approximation to the Theory of Money Supply

The line *MM* assumes a given reserve level, *R*. In addition, other factors controlled by the central bank such as the *r* and *r'* of equation 7–5 are assumed unchanged. These forces are included in *Z'*. What happens if the various forces controlled by the central bank are permitted to change? If *R* increases because of open market operations, for example, or if *r* and *r'* decrease, then, at any given rate of interest, commercial banks have more excess reserves and consequently can create additional money balances. The line *M'M'* in Figure 15–1 shows the effects of such changes. The money

FIGURE 15–2. Changes in the supply-of-money schedule caused by discount rate changes.

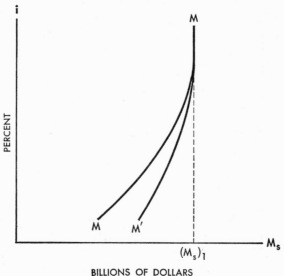

BILLIONS OF DOLLARS

supply line has shifted to the right from *MM*. If *R* should decrease, or *r* and *r'* rise, however, the banking system can no longer support as much money. The money supply schedule would shift to the left.

These changes will also affect the maximum amount of money that the economy can have. For example, a decrease in *r* and *r'*, or an increase in *R*, will expand the maximum amount of money. In Figure 15–1, this is demonstrated by the rise from $(M_s)_3$ to $(M_s)_4$.

If the discount rate decreases, the spread between the return to be earned by commercial banks on loans and investments and the cost of borrowing reserves widens. This may induce banks to lend more money. If the central bank does not simultaneously permit *R* to expand, however, then the maximum amount of money that can be created is not expanded. The results of a discount rate drop are shown in Figure 15–2 as a movement from *MM* to *M'M*. Conversely, a rise in the discount rate would cause a movement to the left without changing the maximum money supply figure, $(M_s)_1$.

Finally, two last elements in equations 7–4 and 7–5 must be considered— c and TD. These forces are included in Z'. They are not controlled directly by our monetary authorities. It will be recalled that as c, the ratio of currency to deposits, increases, the ability of the banking system to create money decreases. Although currency only replaces demand deposit money, currency drains reduce bank total reserves, R, and hence, in the absence of offsetting forces, reduce the potential amount of money that banks can create by a multiple of the currency drain. Thus an increase of c would lead to a reduction of R and hence shift the money supply line to the left, possibly from $M'M'$ to MM in Figure 15–1. Similarly, an increase of TD, time deposits, other things being equal, would reduce the amount of money that a given reserve base can support. The money supply line would again shift to the left. Another important factor in money supply determination, therefore, is the behavior of c, the demand for currency relative to demand deposits, and the demand for time deposits. Economic research in these areas has only been undertaken recently.[5]

Summary of forces affecting MM. All of these factors influence the MM line. An analysis of their combined impact will yield a theory of money supply determination:

1. The money supply schedule slopes upward and to the right with respect to the rate of interest; this means that the money supply and the rate of interest are directly related. The higher the rate of interest, the greater will be the potential supply of money; the lower the rate of interest, the lower will be the potential supply of money.

2. The money supply varies in direct proportion to R, the reserve base. As R increases and decreases, MM shifts to the right and left respectively.

3. The money supply varies inversely with r (the reserve requirement for demand deposits), r' (the reserve requirement for time deposits), and the discount rate. Increases in these variables will cause MM to shift to the left; decreases in these variables cause MM to shift to the right.

4. The money supply varies inversely with c and TD. Increases in c, the ratio of currency to deposits, and TD, time deposits, cause MM to move to the left. Decreases in these forces cause MM to move to the right.

The Theory of the Money Supply and Its Relation to the Actual Amount of Money

The MM line shows how much money it is *possible* to have at varying rates of interest (other things being given)—but how much money will

---

[5] For a recent study of the demand for currency see the article by Philip Cagan cited at the end of the chapter.

there *actually* be at a given time? This theory does not give us enough information to determine the actual amount. Earlier sections of this chapter explained the quantitative determination of member bank reserve positions and the stock of money. The values given for reserves and the stock of money, however, are merely the results of a whole set of forces, only some of which are the money supply forces discussed above. Other factors are yet to be discussed.

To determine the amount of money the economy has at any point in time, information about the demand for money as well as the money supply schedule is needed. For example, given MM, if at i_1 in Figure 15-1 people only want $(M_s)_0$ instead of $(M_s)_1$, there is an excess money supply situation. If at i_3, people want $(M_s)_4$ instead of $(M_s)_3$, there is an excess demand for money; that is, there is a shortage of money relative to individual and business demands.

So far, in Parts I and II, we have been primarily concerned with the roles that private financial institutions and the government play in money supply determination. The interaction of the supply and demand for money is first discussed explicitly in Part III, which deals with monetary theory, the study of the relationship of money to aggregate economic activity. Part III seeks to develop a basic understanding of contemporary monetary theory, so that we may see how the principal aggregate economic variables interact to determine income and output.

Supplementary Readings

Brunner, Karl. "A Schema for the Supply Theory of Money." *International Economic Review* (1961), pp. 79–109.

Cagan, Philip. "The Demand for Currency Relative to the Total Money Supply." *The Journal of Political Economy* (1958), pp. 303–28.

PART III Money and Aggregate
Economic Activity

Chapter 16

An Introduction
to Monetary Theory

OBSERVATIONS ON THEORY

Like most scientific theory, economic theory may function as a framework of analysis or simply as a series of hypotheses subject to empirical verification. As an analytical framework, economic theory attempts to provide a *measure* against which to observe the real world. As such, the framework may or may not correspond to the actual functioning of the economy. A set of economic hypotheses, on the other hand, attempts to *explain* how the world in which we live and work actually operates.

These two views of economic theory are obviously not completely distinct from one another. A set of hypotheses often leads to the formulation of a framework of analysis. Thus, in monetary theory, for example, what we now call the "Keynesian theory" led to the "Keynesian income–expenditure analytical framework," which any economist can use to help explain reality, no matter what set of hypotheses he tentatively accepts.

Most economists strive to make their framework of analysis correspond as closely as possible to reality. Thus, to some extent both the analytical framework and the hypotheses have the same ultimate goal. It could be argued, however, that it makes little difference whether or not economic theory bears a close relation to the real world, so long as it is useful in explaining and predicting economic behavior. This line of reasoning may be specious, however. It is somewhat like saying that we should continue to use the Ptolemaic system of explaining the movements of the planets and the stars because that system does a fairly good job of predicting the motions of some heavenly bodies. We have long since put Ptolemy aside because other systems seem to be closer to the reality of cause and effect and give even better results. Similarly, a particular economic theory may do an adequate job of predicting behavior, but it may be completely misleading about the causal forces behind the predicted economic events.

If economics is to have value, it must improve our understanding of the world. All science is dedicated to this end. Since economics is specifically concerned with the study of our economic and social environment, its framework of analysis and its hypotheses must continuously come closer and closer to an approximately correct interpretation of economic cause, effect, and interrelationship. This can be accomplished only by continual quantitative testing of hypotheses—testing designed not to prove a hypothesis but to disprove it. If a proposition is not disproved, then it is only tentatively accepted until a better explanation is offered. This scientific method of testing theories is sometimes called the falsification method.[1] It proceeds according to the following pattern: (1) formulate a theory; (2) deduce conclusions from the theory; (3) compare this theory with others; (4) quantitatively test its conclusions; and (5) accept the theory tentatively, if it has not been proven false by the test.

MONETARY THEORY

Monetary theory may be approached in this manner. Contemporary economists, when handling problems of income determination, economic fluctuations, and economic growth, treat those problems almost exclusively within the Keynesian income–expenditure analytical framework. Even those economists who reject many of the Keynesian hypotheses concerning money and income nevertheless use the general Keynesian framework as a tool of analysis.

Monetary theory studies the influence of the demand for and supply of money upon prices, interest, output, and employment. Actually, monetary theory is part of a broader area of study—the theory of output and employment determination, sometimes called *macroeconomic theory*. Our purpose here is to place money in its proper perspective within the broader study of macroeconomic analysis. In so doing we will have to spend some time developing that framework of analysis, but our emphasis will be upon money and its demand within that framework. A thorough treatment of aggregate economic activity is to be found in books on output and employment theory.

The role that money plays in the economy is a subject of great controversy among contemporary economists. The disputes concerning money are of a theoretical and empirical nature. Most economists would agree that money supply and demand changes can play a significant role in the determination of the level of economic activity. The disagreement is centered on the mechanism by which these changes influence the economy. Briefly, one position is that the interest rate will affect the demand for investment goods, which in turn helps determine income and employment. Variations in the stock of money and the demand for money change the

---

[1] Karl Popper, *The Logic of Scientific Discovery*, (New York: Basic Books, 1959), Chapter 4.

interest rate and hence affect income and employment in the economy. This is the view of many "Keynesian" theorists. Other economists, although they accept the view that money supply and demand determine the interest rate, believe in addition that a change in the money supply and demand may directly affect the demand for the various forms of liquid and real wealth, and hence indirectly affect aggregate economic activity. This is the view of many contemporary "quantity" theorists. Ultimately the differences may be resolved by empirical work.[2]

PREVIEW OF PARTS III AND IV

In Part III of this text we shall first be concerned with the historical development of monetary theory, referring briefly to several economists who have made significant contributions to the development of our contemporary theories and our framework of analysis. This will place our current state of knowledge in proper perspective. Subsequently we shall study the Keynesian framework of analysis, using it to examine various contemporary hypotheses concerning the role that money plays in the economy. With this knowledge in mind, we should then be able to come to grips with economic policy issues. This will be done in Part IV of this text, which examines (1) the various policy problems, (2) the alternative policies called for by the various monetary theories, and (3) some suggestions as to what seems to be appropriate monetary policy.

Supplementary Reading
Popper, Karl. *The Logic of Scientific Discovery*. New York, Basic Books, 1959.

---

[2] See Chapter 21 for a fuller exposition of these alternative theoretical positions.

Chapter 17

The Historical Development
of Monetary Theory

INTRODUCTION

In this chapter we shall attempt to summarize the historical development of monetary theory. The survey is necessarily incomplete. The emphasis is on a selected group of philosophers and economists whose work in some way constituted an advance in economic knowledge or synthesized a stream of analysis. Our purpose is to show how earlier theorists visualized the relationship between monetary phenomena and the state of economic activity. This will help to place our contemporary framework of analysis in perspective.

The philosophers of the sixteenth, seventeenth, and eighteenth centuries were concerned with economic problems much like those of today—less than full employment, inflation, and lack of growth in the level of aggregate economic activity. The policy recommendations made were ones that we still hear a great deal about today—expand bank credit and the money supply during periods of depression and restrict the expansion of the money supply during periods of full employment and rising prices.

On the other hand, most economists of the nineteenth and early twentieth centuries concentrated on problems of the pricing process. They wanted to know how best to allocate productive resources among competing uses. They were also concerned with how the prices of productive resources and final products are determined. These economists tended to neglect problems of the economy as a whole, largely because they assumed full employment of resources. Although they were aware that less than full employment situations existed, they accepted the view that production creates its own demand. Under this assumption, depression is conceived to be simply a temporary departure from normal full employment. Money supply and demand changes lead to price, but not output and employment, changes in the long run.

During the early part of the twentieth century there was a revived interest in the study of monetary economics and a renewed concern with crises affecting the level of economic activity. Economists sought to develop a framework of analysis that could help explain both price behavior and cyclical movements in the economy. Thus, Irving Fisher developed the equation of exchange. Alfred Marshall, John Maynard Keynes, D. H. Robertson, Leon Walras, A. C. Pigou formulated alternative cash balance equations. These equations, as we shall see, are still widely used by economists to help explain not only price level behavior but also output and demand for money changes. Other economists placed greater emphasis on explaining the volatile nature of the economy, its cyclical ups and downs. Irving Fisher wrote on this, as did Knut Wicksell, Ralph Hawtrey, and others. They sought a complete theory of the cycle. For the most part they focused on the interest rate as the prime mover. As an economic policy they advocated central bank control over the interest rate. This, it was felt, would eliminate recurrent inflations and recessions.

The depression of the 1930's demonstrated the inadequacies of these theories, however. The economic models of the early twentieth century were too elementary to handle the complex aggregate economic problems of our technically advanced society. The old theories reasoned much too simply from cause to effect, neglecting the manifold interrelationships between variables. As a result, we were ready for the "Keynesian Revolution" that completely changed our notions about the determination of overall economic activity. Chapters 18 through 21 will be concerned with these recent developments.

THE SIXTEENTH CENTURY

Jean Bodin (1530–1596)

Those who write on economic subjects tend to do so within the context of the problems of their age. The fifteenth, sixteenth, and seventeenth centuries were ones of price revolution. Thus, many economic philosophers of the time were largely concerned with explaining why prices had risen.

In his "Reply to the Paradoxes of Malestroit Concerning the Dearness of All Things and the Remedy Therefor," for example, Jean Bodin argued that there were a number of reasons for the rise in French prices during the sixteenth century, the principal ones being the abundance of gold and silver, monopolies, scarcity, the pleasure of princes, and coinage debasement.

Bodin's "Reply" was a rebuttal to Malestroit's contention that prices in France were no higher than in the past since goods cost no more gold and silver than formerly. Bodin countered this by citing evidence that wine and wheat were twenty times the cost of a hundred years previous and that land, which he assumed to be fixed in quantity and quality, was three times what it had been fifty years earlier. Bodin, however, was not content merely to cite statistics to prove that prices had risen in the French economy; he was fundamentally concerned with the *causes* of the price rise. He lists the five previously cited causes, the most important of which was the first, namely, the abundance of gold and silver. "I find that the high prices we see today are due to some four or five causes. The principal and almost the only one (which no one has referred to until now) is the abundance of gold and silver, which is today much greater in this Kingdom than it was four hundred years ago, to go no further back."[1]

Bodin goes on to state that the amount of gold and silver, which was used as currency in his time, had increased substantially and that, as a consequence, prices had risen. Here we have one of the first statements linking price movements to money stock movements. Bodin also raises this question: if it is the abundance of gold and silver that causes high prices, where do the gold and silver come from? They arise, he explains, from trade with foreigners who have mines of gold and silver at their disposal. Spain, for example, with gold and silver obtained from the mines of Peru, was able to demand increased quantities of goods and services produced in France— wheat, cloth, dyes, paper, and books. England had mines also, and, since she could not produce wine, prunes, and dye, bought them from France. Thus, as we would say today, the increased supply of money caused an increased demand for French goods. Prices responded by increasing at home and abroad.

THE SEVENTEENTH AND EIGHTEENTH CENTURIES

The economic problems of the late seventeenth and much of the eighteenth century were quite different from those of the preceding period in which Bodin wrote. Now the problems were boom and bust, economic distress, and less than full employment. In many ways these problems were much like those of the depression years of this century.

John Locke (1632–1704)

John Locke, writing in the 1690's, advanced monetary theory considerably beyond Bodin.[2] Bodin had been primarily concerned with the effects of money on prices. Locke expanded this discussion by studying the effects

---

[1] Jean Bodin, "La Réponse de Jean Bodin aux paradoxes de Malestroit touchant l'encherissement de toutes choses et le moyen d'y remedier," as reprinted in Arthur E. Monroe, Ed., *Early Economic Thought*, (Cambridge, Mass.: Harvard University Press, 1924), p. 127.

[2] See John Locke, *Consequences of the Lowering of Interest, and Raising the Value of Money*, 1692; and *Further Considerations Concerning Raising the Value of Money*, 1696. For an excellent discussion of Locke and other writers of the eighteenth century see Douglas Vickers' *Studies in the Theory of Money, 1690–1776* (Philadelphia: Chilton Company, 1959).

of money on trade, the role of the demand for money, and the importance of interest rates in the economy.

In Locke's opinion, money is necessary to carry on trade. If it is not generally available and in circulation, then it is difficult to purchase goods and services. As a result, there is a stoppage of trade. Locke here posited relationship between money and economic activity, but did not explain precisely how the relationship operates.

To Locke, money was important in another respect: a certain amount was needed to carry on a specific amount of trade. The amount needed depended upon the "quickness of circulation" of money. Today we would say *"velocity of circulation"* rather than "quickness of circulation." Both terms refer to the number of times that the money in the economy is spent or turned over during a particular period of time. The more often money is spent, the more economic activity takes place. The less often it is spent, the lower the volume of trade. To put it another way, the greater the amount of money people want to hold, the smaller its turnover (velocity) will be, and the greater the amount of money that will be needed to carry on a specific volume of trade.

The relative need of the community for the necessities of life and the activity of its commerce determined how much money was demanded and consequently, its quickness of circulation. Here, Locke made a significant advance in money analysis; this is one of the first formulations of the velocity and demand for money concepts.

Locke also had a relatively advanced notion of "interest." He defined interest as the price for the hire of money. Its level is determined by the relationship between the amount of money needed and the amount available. Thus, if the amount needed for trade was great relative to the supply, the interest rate would be high. Furthermore, if the rate of interest were legally to be forced beneath this high level, no additional borrowing could take place, because lenders would be unwilling to lend.

John Law (1671–1729)

John Law, aside from his reputation as a romantic adventurer, financier, and organizer of the Banque Royale in France, is best known as the author of *Money and Trade Considered* (1705). Writing in a period of high unemployment, Law argued that trade depends upon money. Hence, the more money there was in the economy, the more likely we are to have full employment.

In Law's time money consisted largely of gold and silver coin. Thus, the more money metal there was in circulation, the greater the employment. Law went further than this, however, and extended the argument to bank notes. The more "credit money" in circulation, he said, the more people will be employed. In a period of less than full employment, how would the monetary authority get more money into circulation and hence induce a higher level of employment? Law reasoned that the best way is through the issue of paper currency by banks.

He did not propose an unlimited issue of paper currency, but a limited one suited to the needs of trade. Thus, there would be no danger of over-extending currency. This argument is similar to the "commercial loan theory of banking" discussed in Chapter 3. It is also called the "real bills doctrine."[3] Law proposed that the notes issued be secured by the value of land. Thus, the maximum amount of notes that could be issued would be limited by the total value of land. The actual amount in circulation, so long as it is less than the value of land, would depend upon the need for money in trade. Hence there would be little change in the value of money and the amount of money would always be adequate to keep trade and employment active.

The flaw in the argument is that this system depends entirely upon a permanent valuation of land. If the price of land were to increase, then more currency could be issued. This would drive up the price of other goods and increase the need for additional money balances. Cumulative price inflation would follow. If on the other hand, the value of land decreases, there would be a need to reduce the amount of money in circulation, which in turn would reduce trade, the price of other goods, and the need for money. Cumulative price deflation would ensue.

Law's principal contribution to monetary analysis was his attempt to establish a positive relationship between employment, trade, and the amount of metallic and bank money in the economy.

Richard Cantillon (1680–1734)

Richard Cantillon, in his essay "On the Nature of Trade in General" (written in 1734 and published in 1755), went far beyond Bodin, Locke, or Law in his examination of monetary principles. He did not argue as directly as they from money changes to either price or employment changes, however. Instead he was concerned with the process by which money stock changes affect price. He was apparently one of the first to argue that an increase in the quantity of money raises prices through its prior effect of increasing demand. His contributions, however, valuable as they were, did not directly affect economic thought until the latter half of the nineteenth century, when Stanley Jevons rediscovered Cantillon's work.

Cantillon's theory of money was principally concerned with the relationship between money and prices, although he did discuss employment changes to some degree as well. He wanted to discover how the money-price relationship operates. "The great difficulty of this analysis consists in discovering by what path and in what proportion the increase of money

---

[3] See Lloyd W. Mints' *A History of Banking Theory*, (Chicago: University of Chicago Press, 1945) for the classic refutation of this doctrine, pp. 30–32.

raises the price of things."[4] His solution was: "I hold that in general an increase in the monetary stock causes in a State a proportional increase in consumption, which by degrees produces the rise of prices."[5] Thus, an increase in the money stock stimulates demand, which eventually leads to price increases.

How does this occur? Cantillon presents several examples, two of which are considered here. First, if the increase in money comes from mining, then the mine owners and those who work the mines will increase their expenditures on food, clothing, and other goods. This gives added employment to artisans, who, in turn, will increase their expenditures. Thus, there will be a multiple round of expenditure and employment increases. In the process, however, prices begin to rise and those people who did not participate in the initial round of expenditure and employment increases will suffer from higher prices. Cantillon regards these people as fixed income recipients; they must reduce their consumption or leave the country. "This, roughly, is how a considerable increase of money from Mines increases consumption; and while diminishing the number of inhabitants, brings about a greater expenditure among those who remain."[6]

The increased domestic price level would then induce people to make more purchases abroad where goods are cheaper. This would cause money to leave the economy, and a reverse cycle of lower money circulation, poverty, and misery would follow.

A second case discussed by Cantillon imagines an increased money stock resulting from a country selling more abroad than it purchases. This is what we now term a favorable balance of trade. With more money coming into the country than is leaving, there will be a gradual increase in expenditures, consumption, and prices. This time, however, the process will not reverse itself unless the favorable balance of trade turns unfavorable.

Cantillon developed a relatively sophisticated theory of how money affects the economy. He did not limit himself to a discussion of the supply of money; he also examined the velocity of money: "an acceleration, or a greater speed, in the circulation of money in trade amounts to the same thing as an increase in standard money . . ."[7] He showed that an increase in the velocity of money, given the money supply, would increase trade, just as an increase in the money supply, given constant velocity, would increase trade.

Summary

Writers of the seventeenth and eighteenth centuries argued that economic activity and trade depended upon money and its circulation. They concen-

---

[4] Richard Cantillon, "On the Nature of Commerce in General," as reprinted in A. E. Monroe, *op. cit.*, p. 264.
[5] *Ibid.*
[6] *Ibid.*, p. 265.
[7] *Ibid.*, p. 264.

trated on the interaction of the demand for goods and services, the stock of money, the quickness of circulation, the volume of employment, and the price level.

THE NINETEENTH CENTURY

There was relatively little development of monetary theory in the nineteenth century. Economists turned away from the study of the economy as a whole to a study of commodity pricing and resource allocation. When discussing monetary phenomena, they generally assumed a full employment economy. This led them to discuss money changes in terms of price level effects. As a consequence, many of these economists developed a monetary theory that today we would call a "crude quantity theory of money." In essence it maintained that money stock changes lead to proportionate price level changes. Although these economists were aware of the velocity concept, they usually assumed it to be constant.

Since they were primarily concerned with resource analysis, nineteenth-century economists did not often consider short-run unemployment problems. They usually accepted Say's law that "production creates its own demand." According to this theory, when people work and create goods, they receive income, most of which is spent. That which is not spent is saved, but this does not cause demand to fall off. Funds that are saved will eventually be channeled into investment demand for such goods as plant equipment. Therefore the demand for new goods is created by the supply. Demand is always sufficient to take goods off the market and therefore less than full employment cannot long persist. Today, of course, we only have to point to the depression of the 1930's to see the limitations of this concept.

Some nineteenth-century economists did write about money, however, and they made a number of contributions to monetary theory. These were men like Thornton, Ricardo, and Mill.

Henry Thornton (1760–1815)

Thornton wrote during the Napoleonic wars, when the Bank of England refused to convert paper currency into specie (metallic money). Prices rose because of "the restriction," as it was called, and a vigorous monetary debate followed. One group, the bullionists, argued that the value of paper currency had depreciated because it had been issued to excess. The other group, the antibullionists, did not believe that paper currency could be issued to excess if it were issued on the basis of the needs of trade. Here again is the real bills doctrine. Notice also how this debate centered around the relation between money and prices, not around the relation between money and employment.

Henry Thornton was a bullionist. Here is his view of how money stock changes lead to price change:

> Let us, now, trace carefully the steps by which an encrease of paper serves to lift up the price of articles. Let us suppose, for example, an encreased number of Bank of England notes to be issued. In such case the traders in the metropolis discover that there is a more than usual facility of obtaining notes at the bank. . . . Every trader is encouraged by the knowledge of this facility of borrowing . . . is rendered, by the plenty of money, somewhat more ready to buy, and rather less eager to sell. . . . Thus an inclination to buy is created in all quarters, and an indisposition to sell. Now, since the cost of articles depends on the issue of that general conflict between buyers and sellers . . . it follows, that any circumstance which serves to communicate a greater degree of eagerness to the mind of one party than to that of the other, will have an influence on price.[8]

In Thornton's opinion, an increased money supply will lead to increased demand and consequently higher prices.

Thornton does not say that price need rise proportionately to the money increase. He was well aware that an increase in money may lead to the employment of idle factors of production and hence to more output but not necessarily higher prices. He felt that the number of unemployed persons is limited. Hence, once the idle are employed, prices will rise as long as the stock of money continues to increase:

> An encreased quantity of articles can only arise from additional commodities either brought from abroad or produced at home through the exertion of new industry. . . .
> When the Bank of England, enlarges its paper, it augments, in the same degree, as we must here suppose, its loans to individuals. These favoured persons immediately conceive, and not without reason, that they have obtained an additional though borrowed capital, by which they can push their own particular manufacture or branch of commerce. . . .
> But, first, it is obvious, that the antecedently idle persons to whom we may suppose the new capital to give employ, are limited in number; and that, therefore, if the encreased issue is indefinite, it will set to work labourers, of whom a part will be drawn from other, and perhaps, no less useful occupations. . . .
> . . . whatever view we take of the subject, we seem obliged to admit, that although additional industry will be one effect of an extraordinary emission of paper, a rise in the cost of articles will be another.[9]

Another one of Thornton's contributions is the policy conclusion that he draws from his analysis. He argues that the amount of paper money should be limited, that money should neither be issued to excess nor allowed to diminish sharply, in order to limit price variation. As the economy grows in productivity, however, some increase of the money supply should be permitted.[10] Today, we are still discussing proposals of this sort.

---

[8] Henry Thornton, *An Enquiry into the Nature and Effects of the Paper Credit of Great Britain* (London: 1802), pp. 195–96.
[9] *Ibid.*, pp. 257–61.
[10] *Ibid.*, p. 295.

David Ricardo (1772–1823)

Ricardo, like Thornton, was a bullionist. His writing, however, is by no means as succinct as that of Thornton. If we were to judge Ricardo only on the basis of his work in *The Principles of Political Economy and Taxation* (1821) we would be forced to conclude that he was a crude quantity theorist. He argues that the value of paper money can be maintained by limiting its quantity.

In "On the High Price of Bullion," however, he introduces the notion of "rapidity of circulation."

"The value of the circulating medium of every country bears some proportion to the value of the commodities which it circulates. In some countries, this proportion is much greater than in others, and varies, on some occasions, in the same country. It depends upon the rapidity of circulation, upon the degree of confidence and credit existing between traders, and above all, on the judicious operations of banking.[11]

In other words, given a constant stock of money and no change in productivity, an increase in the rapidity of circulation (velocity) will lead to a price level increase. When velocity increases, the money supply is being used more often because people demand more goods and services. To get more goods each individual draws down his money holdings, but collectively money holdings remain the same. This is how velocity increases. People, however, do not get more goods, since more are not available. Hence the increased demand simply succeeds in bidding up the price of goods. Ricardo did not make this extension of the analysis, however. Like other bullionists, he assumed that velocity was as high as possible in Great Britain, and hence was a constant. Because of this erroneous assumption, his statement that the value of money depends on the rapidity of circulation is rendered meaningless.

With respect to economic policy, Ricardo also felt that paper money should be limited in quantity because its overissue would lead to price increases.

John Stuart Mill (1806–1873)

The works of John Stuart Mill provide us with a synthesis of the classical economics of the nineteenth century. Although well aware of unemployment and business crises, Mill accepted Say's law. As a consequence, his monetary analysis concentrated largely on the relation between money and prices.

Most of John Stuart Mill's monetary theory is developed in Book III of

---

[11] David Ricardo, "On the High Price of Bullion," reprinted in Piero Sraffa, *The Works and Correspondence of David Ricardo* (Cambridge: 1951), vol. III, p. 90.

his *Principles of Political Economy*. Here, he begins with a definition of money that is actually very close to the definition many textbooks use today.

Definition of money. Mill defines money as a medium of exchange and common measure of value. Money is useful because of the inconveniences of barter and the necessity of having something in circulation that has durability. Gold and silver, thought Mill, are particularly well suited to these purposes; they are portable, imperishable, divisible, and acceptable to all people. "Of all commodities they are among the least influenced by any of the causes which produce fluctuations of value."[12] Furthermore, any change in their value would not be sudden, since their quantity may not readily be diminished or increased.

Value of money. Mill considered money a commodity, the value of which was determined like that of other commodities—temporarily by supply and demand, and by the cost of production in the long run. Cantillon and Ricardo had held similar positions.

According to Mill, the value of money depends, other things being equal, upon its quantity and its rapidity of circulation. The purchasing power of money depends first on supply and demand.

The supply of money, then, is the quantity of it which people are wanting to lay out; that is, all the money they have in their possession, except what they are hoarding, or at least keeping by them as a reserve for future contingencies. The supply of money, in short, is all the money in circulation at the time.[13]

This concept of money supply differs from our current understanding of the term in that we include monetary hoards. The demand for money he defines as "all the goods offered for sale."[14]

It should also be remembered that our present definition of money includes demand deposits, whereas Mill considered only real commodities to be money.

How do demand and supply determine the value of money? "An increase of the quantity of money raises prices, and a diminution lowers them . . ."[15] Thus, if other things remain unchanged, an increase in the supply of money will increase the demand for goods by an equal amount and this will lead to a universal rise in prices.

The rapidity of circulation also helps determine the value of money. Mill defines it as "the average number of purchases made by each piece in order to effect a given pecuniary amount of transactions."[16] If the amount of transactions and the amount of money is fixed, then the value of money

---

[12] John Stuart Mill, *Principles of Political Economy*, Ashley Edition (London: Longmans, Green and Co., 1909), p. 485.
[13] *Ibid.*, p. 490.
[14] *Ibid.*
[15] *Ibid.*, p. 495.
[16] *Ibid.*

varies inversely with the rapidity of circulation. That is, the higher the rapidity of circulation grows, the less the purchasing power of a particular amount of money will be and the higher the price of goods and services. This is a velocity concept very much like that later used by Irving Fisher. The basic concept is that the more often money changes hands in the purchase of goods and services, given the amount of goods available, the greater the demand for goods will be and the higher the price of those goods.

In general, Mill formulated what amounts to a relatively crude quantity theory of money. Mill's other theory of the value of money—the cost of production theory—has been almost universally abandoned.

Credit. Mill does not ignore the importance of credit; he conceives of it as an important determinant of the price level. He feels that credit, no matter what form it takes (bank notes, bills of exchange, promissory notes, or deposits and checks), has an influence on the price level. In fact, it has the same influence on the price level as gold and silver money itself. An increase in the volume of credit extension increases the demand for goods, and, accordingly, prices rise. Similarly, an increase in the amount of inconvertible paper currency (paper money that is not convertible on demand into gold and silver coin) causes price increases.[17]

THE EARLY TWENTIETH CENTURY

Economists of the early twentieth century continued in the tradition of nineteenth-century classical economics. They believed the price level to be determined by the volume of money, that relative prices are determined by the supply of and demand for commodities, and that full employment is the normal state for the economy. These scholars did advance the development of monetary theory in two areas, however. First, they formulated alternative analytical approaches to explaining the economic role of money. The *Fisher transactions equation of exchange* and the various *Cambridge cash balance equations* are examples of this development of monetary theory as a framework of analysis. Second, there was renewed study of the role of money in short-term cyclical fluctuations. Here, however, there was usually little attempt at empirical verification of hypotheses. The remainder of this chapter examines these early twentieth-century contributions to monetary theory.

Irving Fisher (1867–1947)

Irving Fisher, an American mathematician and economist, formulated *the equation of exchange*, attempted a statement of the quantity theory of

---

[17] *Ibid.*, Chapters 12 and 13.

money in the early twentieth century, and developed a theory of the cycle that was designed to explain economic fluctuations during those periods of transition when prices are rising or falling.

The Equation of Exchange. The equation of exchange as formulated by Irving Fisher is stated as

$$MV + M'V' = \Sigma pQ \qquad [17\text{--}1]$$

where M is the amount of currency in the economy during a given year, V the velocity of circulation (turnover) of this currency, M' the volume of demand deposits in the economy during the year, V' the velocity of circulation of these demand deposits, and ΣpQ the sum of (1) the average price, p, of a commodity purchased in the economy during the given year multiplied by the quantity, Q, of it purchased, (2) the average price, p', of some other commodity purchased during the given year multiplied by the quantity, Q', of it purchased, and (3) so forth for all other goods exchanged. In other words, equation 17–1 is a simplified way of expressing the following equation:

$$MV + M'V' = pQ + p'Q' \cdots \qquad [17\text{--}2]$$

Fisher himself further simplified this equation to

$$MV + M'V' = PT \qquad [17\text{--}3]$$

where P is a weighted average of prices and T is the sum of all the Q's. Strictly speaking, this simplification is not legitimate, since it implies that one can add together such diverse commodities as eggs, guns, and oranges. If each of the symbols in 17–3 is expressed as an index number, however, then this criticism no longer applies. P and T would then be indices of prices and quantities respectively. The equation would then show the relative change in each of the magnitudes rather than their absolute values.

Contemporary Versions of the Equation of Exchange. Today many variants of equations 17–1, 17–2, and 17–3 are used by economists. One particularly popular version is

$$MV = PQ \qquad [17\text{--}4]$$

where M is the average amount of money in the economy during a specified period of time such as a year, V is the number of times this money is spent on PQ, which is the sum of the values of a specified group of goods.[18]

There are two principal differences between Fisher's equation of exchange and this contemporary formulation. First, the contemporary definition of M includes both currency and demand deposit money, whereas Fisher's M includes only currency. Second, Fisher's PQ includes all goods and services exchanged during a given period of time, whereas contemporary economists

---

[18] See Chapter 18 for a complementary discussion.

usually define PQ in terms of the specific problem they are considering. When the relation between money and gross national product is being considered, for example, PQ refers to gross national product, the value of newly produced final goods and services. V, in this instance, is an *income velocity* concept, showing the number of times that the volume of money, M, is spent on gross national product. When used in this manner, equation 17–4 is sometimes restated as follows:

$$MV = Y \hspace{3cm} [17\text{--}5]$$

where Y is gross national product.

On the other hand, when economists study the relation of the expenditure of money to all goods and services bought and sold, all transactions are considered—dealings in new goods and services, the resale of used goods, financial transactions, and so on. In this case, PQ is much larger than gross national product, and V represents *transactions velocity*, the number of times money is spent on *all* types of goods and services during a given time period. This type of velocity figure, of course, is much larger than the figure for income velocity. Fisher's V and V' both represent transactions velocity. Sometimes, when economists wish to emphasize the fact that they are concerned with transactions velocity they will use the following type of Fisher equation:

$$MV = PT \hspace{3cm} [17\text{--}6]$$

where M is the average amount of money in circulation during the given time period, V is the number of times that M is used in the purchase of PT, and PT is the monetary value of all transactions in the economy during the time period in question.

The difference between 17–5 and 17–6 can be illustrated as follows. Assume that the average amount of money in a given year, t, is $150 billion, and that gross national product, Y, is $600 billion. Then, since $MV = Y$, and $150 billion $\times V$ = $600 billion, V (income velocity) must equal 4 in terms of equation 17–5. Thus, the money stock was used four times in the purchase of gross national product. If in some subsequent time period, $t + 1$ M rises to $175 billion and Y to $787.5 billion, then V must also have increased to 4.5.

On the other hand, if M is $150 billion in time period t, and the value of all transactions is $3,750 billion, then, since $MV = PT$, V must equal 25 in terms of equation 17–6. If M rises to $175 billion and PT to $4,000 billion, then V must have declined to 22.86.

One factor that should be stressed concerning the equation of exchange is that the equation itself is a mere truism. This applies no matter what variant of the equation is being used. The equation merely summarizes what has occurred. The left-hand side, the money side of the equation, must always equal the right-hand side, the goods side. Thus, each side is simply a different manner of describing the same phenomena, expenditures. The goods side expresses the value of expenditures; the money side expresses the volume of money multiplied by the number of times it is used so as to lead to the value of expenditures.

The equation itself contains no statement of causality. In equation 17–4, for example, the *equation does not explain why* M, V, P, and Q possess certain values. It does not state how, in reality, a change in one of the four magnitudes will cause a change in the others. The equation of exchange merely summarizes in convenient form the resultant values of M, V, P, and Q. It is the function of theory, however, as hypothesis, to explain cause and effect. One of the functions of contemporary monetary theory, for example, as developed in Chapter 21, is to explain why velocity changes— whether it is a mere residual caused by changes in the right-hand side of the equation of exchange, or whether it may vary independently of the right-hand side and thereby directly determine PQ changes. Thus, monetary theory seeks to define causality. Does changed V lead to changed PQ, or does change in PQ determine the change in V? The equation of exchange does not resolve these questions for us, however.

Fisher's Use of the Equation of Exchange. An equation of this sort is merely a *tool* that economists use to help explain economic change. Thus, Irving Fisher, having formulated his equation of exchange 17–3, proceeded to use it to explain economic relationships.

On the basis of the equation of exchange, he gave a precise statement of the *quantity theory of money:* "The price level varies (1) directly as the quantity of money in circulation (M), (2) directly as the velocity of its circulation (V), (3) inversely as the volume of trade done by it (T). The first of these three relations is the most important. It constitutes the 'quantity theory of money.' "[19] This statement is carefully hedged by Fisher, however:

> The quantity theory . . . does not claim that while money is increased in quantity, *other* causes may not affect M', V, V', and the Q's, and thus aggravate or neutralize the effect of M on the p's. But these are not the effects of M on the p's. So far as M *by itself* is concerned, its effect on the p's is strictly proportional. . . .
> We have emphasized the fact that the strictly proportional effect on prices of an increase in M is only the *normal* or *ultimate* effect after transition periods are over. The proposition that prices vary with money holds true only as between two imaginary periods for each of which prices are stationary or are moving alike upward or downward and at the same rate.[20]

Thus, it would appear that the quantity theory of money, as formulated by Fisher, is only valid in the long run and when all quantities in the equation of exchange except M and P are constant.

---

[19] Irving Fisher, *The Purchasing Power of Money* (New York: The Macmillan Company, 1911), p. 29.
[20] *Ibid.*, pp. 158–59.

Fisher, as the above quote shows, was well aware of how *other causes* could disturb the relationship between money and prices. Factors that he felt would influence the volume of trade, *T*, are listed in Table 17–1. Historically, Fisher felt that these outside influences had usually tended to increase *T* and to decrease *P*. They were looked upon largely as long-run sources of change in *T*. Population, technical knowledge, and capital accumulation changed slowly and over time would lead to increased *T* and possible price declines.

TABLE 17–1. FISHER'S OUTSIDE
INFLUENCES ON THE VOLUME OF TRADE

Conditions affecting producers
　Geographical differences in natural resources
　The division of labor
　Knowledge of the technique of production
　The accumulation of capital
Conditions affecting consumers
　The extent and variety of human wants
Conditions connecting producers and consumers
　Facilities for transportation
　Relative freedom of trade
　Character of monetary and banking systems
　Business confidence

Source: Irving Fisher, *The Purchasing Power of Money* (New York: The Macmillan Company, 1911), pp. 74–75.

Fisher also examined the outside causes that affect the velocities of circulation of money and deposits. His classification of these factors is given in Table 17–2. Fisher believed that three sets of forces—individual habits (thrift habits, the habit of charging, and the habit of using checks), the systems of payments in the community, and general causes (density of population and rapidity of transportation)—had tended historically to increase the velocity of circulation of money, and hence to increase prices. As in the case of *T* variations, Fisher saw these as long-run influences on velocity. Although Fisher seems to have been correct in observing the increase of *T*, some economists today believe that velocity has tended to decrease in the long run rather than increase. In short-run periods of transition, however, Fisher believed that there could be substantial variation in velocity.[21]

With respect to outside influences on the volume of deposits, *M′*, Fisher felt that the substitution of checks for cash payments had exerted a powerful

[21] Some of the sources of this short-run change in *V* are mentioned in our subsequent discussion of Fisher's transition period theory of the cycle. Some contemporary sources of velocity change have already been discussed: (1) commercial bank loan and investment behavior, and (2) the development of nonbank financial intermediaries. There is additional discussion of these points in Chapter 21.

influence in the direction of raising prices. Since, today, we count demand deposits as part of money stock, Fisher's argument, in modern terms, simply amounts to a statement that an increase in the money stock tends to increase prices, which is another way of stating the Fisher version of the quantity theory.

Fisher concluded that the long-run behavior of T tended to lower prices, but that the long run effects of V, V', and M' changes were to raise prices. The cumulative effects of these influences over time could well be significant for price level variation, but in the short run their effects would tend to be negligible. This does not mean that he believed that M and P must always move proportionately in the short run; as previously shown, Fisher felt that M and P need not be proportional in periods of transition.

TABLE 17–2. FISHER'S OUTSIDE INFLUENCES ON THE VELOCITIES
OF CIRCULATION OF MONEY AND DEPOSITS

Habits of the individual
  As to thrift and hoarding
  As to book credit
  As to the use of checks
Systems of payments in the community
  As to frequency of receipts and of disbursements
  As to regularity of receipts and disbursements
  As to correspondence between times and amounts of receipts and disbursements
General Causes
  Density of population
  Rapidity of transportation

Source: Irving Fisher, *The Purchasing Power of Money*, p. 79.

Fisher's Theory of the Cycle. Fisher recognized that the relationship between money and prices was not rigid and that the economy is generally in a period of transition. He attempted to explain the behavior of prices and the state of economic activity during such periods, which we would term short-run cyclical fluctuations. His explanation is monetary, focusing on interest rate behavior as the source of economic instability: "the peculiar behavior of the rate of interest during transition periods is largely responsible for the crises and depressions in which price movements end."[22]

Economic fluctuations, according to Fisher, occur because the rate of interest fails to respond quickly enough to price changes. In brief, Fisher's conception of the business cycle may be described as follows: Assume that prices are rising. Because of rising prices and widening profit margins, businesses increase their borrowings at commercial banks. Hence deposit money, M', expands. As these funds are spent, prices rise further, enabling profits to continue to increase and still more borrowing to take place. The

---

[22] Fisher, *op. cit.*, p. 56.

cost of borrowing increases, but more slowly than prices. Disturbances in V, V', and the Q's also take place. Because of the apparent good times, increased spending occurs that is not financed solely by increased borrowing. Hence, V and V' increase. Output also rises. Some unemployed workers are drawn into the productive process but the size of population, the rate of invention and the efficiency of labor "pretty definitely limit the amount of trade that can reasonably be carried on."[23] Thus the Q's can only increase to a limited extent and the primary effects of the rising M', V, and V' will be felt in prices.

This type of expansion cannot continue indefinitely, however. As the boom continues, banks will begin to run short of reserves. As a result, the increase of deposit money will stop and the cost of borrowing continue to increase. Profits relative to the cost of borrowing will decrease, and borrowing will diminish. In addition, firms that borrowed heavily will find themselves unable to renew their loans at former rates of interest. Some firms may fail and so precipitate a financial panic. With this loss of business confidence, the cycle will reverse itself.

There is a continuing contraction of loans and deposits. The velocity of money decreases. People become very concerned with "solvency" and refrain from spending. All of this leads to a decline in prices. Interest rate adjustments lag behind the decline of prices. Output tends to diminish somewhat and a depression of trade occurs. Prices continue to fall until rates of interest diminish sufficiently. By the time this happens, however, weak firms will have been forced out of business. Once interest rates are low enough for borrowers to be in a position to resume borrowing, prices will stop falling and the previously described upward movement will begin anew.

From a present-day vantage point, the two greatest defects of this cycle model are its overemphasis on the rate of interest as an economic determinant and the assumption that prices are not only flexible in an upward direction but also in a downward direction. If the response of business borrowing to interest rate adjustments is negligible, as many contemporary economists contend (see Chapter 19), then the lag of interest rates to price changes can no longer be considered the modus operandi of successive cyclical expansions and contractions. Furthermore, on the downward side of the cycle, it is possible that businesses might generally refuse to accept lower prices in the face of decreased demand. They have the alternative of reducing output (the Q's) and employment. In such a case, the decrease in Q's may not merely be temporary as Fisher contended; therefore, the cycle may not be self-correcting.

Summary and evaluation. Irving Fisher was one of the most important early twentieth-century formulators of monetary theory. His principal and

---

[23] *Ibid.*, p. 62.

lasting contribution is probably his statement of the equation of exchange, a tool of economic analysis that is used by economists of almost all shades of theoretical leanings. In addition, his statement of the quantity theory of money was succinct and carefully qualified. Rephrased so as to make money stock variations a principal cause of variations in gross national product, rather than simply prices, his statement of the quantity theory is viewed by some economists as a rough but relatively valid and current theory of income and output determination. Incidentally, Fisher was one of the first economists to attempt to verify his hypotheses statistically. Close to one-quarter of his book, *The Purchasing Power of Money*, is devoted to an empirical verification of his views.

Fisher will probably not be remembered for his description of cyclical disturbances. He seems to have overemphasized the importance of interest rate variations. Although he stresses the fact that cycles differ markedly, his analysis of the causes of cyclical disturbances seems to rely too much on a unidirectional sequence of events. In this he does not differ substantially from other early twentieth-century economists, like Ralph Hawtrey, who also developed theories of the cycle. Present day economists prefer to stress the interrelationship of these critical variables.

Knut Wicksell (1851–1926)

Like Irving Fisher, Knut Wicksell was a quantity theorist concerned primarily with the relation between money stock, expenditure, price, and interest rate variations as sources of economic disturbance. He believed that changes in the quantity of money (which he defined as currency) would lead to variations in the demand for goods and services and consequently to price and expenditure change. Thus, he argued that "the result of the increase in the quantity of money is a rise in the demand for commodities, and a fall in their supply, with the consequence that all prices rise continuously—until cash balances stand once again in their normal relation to the level of prices."[24]

Changes in the quantity of money are not in themselves the sole cause of economic disturbances, however. Wicksell felt that the source of changes in money, supply, expenditures, prices, and economic fluctuation lay in discrepancies between market and natural rates of interest. So long as these two rates are equal there will be no change in the price level. When the market rate of interest is less than the natural rate, however, then cumulative price inflation will occur until such time as the two rates are equal. On the other hand, when the market rate is above the natural rate, then a cumulative price deflation will take place until such time as the two rates again coincide.

What is meant by the "natural" and "market" rates of interest? The

---

[24] Knut Wicksell, *Interest and Prices*, translated by R. F. Kahn (London: 1936), p. 41.

natural rate of interest is much the same as what economists call the marginal efficiency of capital or investment; it is *the expected yield on newly created capital. The market rate of interest* is the *rate charged by banks.* Should the natural rate be above the market rate, profit margins will be high, and the demand for capital goods strong. Prices would increase. However, should the natural rate be less than the market rate, profit margins will be low, the demand for capital goods weak, and prices will decrease.

Wicksell thought that a discrepancy between these interest rates could set off cyclical disturbances. Thus, commercial bank behavior can be one cause of a variance between the rates. For example, Wicksell indicates that banks

raise the rate when their gold stocks are threatened with depletion or their current obligations are so great that their disparity in relation to their gold holdings is regarded as dangerous, or, still more, where both of these things occur together, as is often the case. They lower their rates of interest under the reverse conditions: increased gold holdings or diminished commitments, or both.[25]

Conversely, *a fall in the market rate of interest as banks lower their rates* may lead to the following sequence of events:

In the first place saving will be discouraged and for that reason there will be an increased demand for goods and services for present consumption. In the second place, the profit opportunities of entrepreneurs will thus be increased and the demand for goods and services, as well as for raw materials already in the market for future production, will evidently increase to the same extent as it had previously been held in check by the higher rate of interest. Owing to the increased income thus accruing to the workers, landowners, and the owners of raw materials, etc., the prices of consumption goods will begin to rise, the more so as the factors of production previously available are now withdrawn for the purposes of future production. Equilibrium in the market for goods and services will therefore be disturbed. As against an increased demand in two directions there will be an unchanged or even diminished supply, which must result in an increase in wages (rent) and, directly or indirectly, in prices.

. . . we are entitled to assume that all production forces are already fully employed, so that the increased monetary demand principally takes the form of rivalry between employers for labour, raw materials and natural facilities, etc., which consequently leads to an increase in their price, and indirectly, owing to the increased money income of labour and landlords and the increased demand for commodities, to a rise in the price of all consumption goods in addition to that which arises from diminished savings.[26]

Thus, according to Wicksell, an increased supply of money and decreased market rates of interest mean increased demand for consumption and capital goods, and, in a full employment economy, increased prices. This rise in prices will continue so long as banks can continue to lend and keep the market rate beneath the natural rate. Wicksell, however, did not believe that

---

[25] Knut Wicksell, *Lectures on Political Economy*, vol. II (New York: The Macmillan Company, 1936), p. 204.
[26] *Ibid.*, pp. 194–95.

this type of fluctuation would continue to be cumulative. Instead, he felt that the economic system contained forces that tended to eliminate the differences between the natural and monetary rates of interest, self-corrective forces.

A rise in prices exerts its influence . . . on the demands of the monetary circulation. The quantity of coins and notes circulating in the hands of the public is usually much larger than the available reserves of the banks. It follows that quite a small rise in prices may bring about a very significant contraction of the banks' reserves.[27]

A loss of reserves, of course, means a reduction in the lending ability of the banking system. If bank solvency is threatened, banks will raise their lending rates. Once they approach the "natural" rate, the cumulative process of price inflation will stop.

On the other hand, a rise in the market rate above the natural rate, caused by a loss of bank reserves, for example, will cause this process to work in reverse. There will be decreased consumption and capital good demands, reduced profit opportunities, and a reduction in prices. This process will continue until a return flow of reserves to the banking system takes place, permitting banks to reduce their lending rates. "It is thus confidently to be expected that the Bank rate, or more generally the money rate of interest, will always coincide *eventually* with the natural capital rate, or rather that it is always *tending* to coincide with an ever-changing natural rate."[28]

This discussion has explained Wicksell's theory of how changes in market rates can set off economic disturbances. It should not be assumed, however, that market rate changes were viewed by Wicksell as the principal initiating force behind business fluctuations. Actually, he thought that the difference between the money and natural rates was usually caused first by a change in the natural rate, and then by the typical slowness of the banking system to adjust its lending rates.

In other words, the difference between the actual loan and normal rates, which we have already designated as a major cause of fluctuations in commodity prices, arises less frequently because the loan rate changes spontaneously whilst the normal or real rate remains unchanged but on the contrary because the normal rate rises or falls whilst the loan rate remains unchanged or only tardily follows it.[29]

Anything tending to change the expected return on new capital will cause changes in this natural rate. If the prospects for production improve, possibly because of technological advance, then the natural rate rises, and, with the lag of bank rates, a boom takes place. If, however, business expectations worsen or if few innovations occur, then the natural rate falls and we have "bad times."

---

[27] Wicksell, *Interest and Prices*, pp. 113–14.
[28] *Ibid.*, p. 117.
[29] Wicksell, *Lectures on Political Economy*, p. 205.

Assuming this theory to be correct, is there some appropriate economic policy that would eliminate discrepancies between the market and natural rates of interest, and accordingly economic fluctuations? Wicksell thought that an appropriate central bank policy could do the job. "The only possibility of a rational control of the price level must lie in . . . the proper regulation of the interest policy of the banks."[30] Ideally, he argues, a "spontaneous raising or lowering of the discount rate should in the long run have a more powerful influence on prices than any other cause."[31]

Summary and Evaluation. Wicksell was a quantity theorist. His analysis, however, was not restricted to a mere treatment of a direct relation between money and prices. Instead, he developed a dynamic theory designed to explain price and business fluctuations. He stressed interaction among many variables. Those forces which determine the market and natural rates of interest can set off discrepancies between each other and, accordingly, a price level change. A continued difference between these rates means either boom or bust, depending on whether the natural rate is higher or lower than the market rate. Thus, pressures on bank reserve positions could bring to a halt either cumulative price inflation or deflation. As a principle of economic policy, he advocated the use of central bank action to regulate bank lending rates.

The principal shortcomings of this analysis are fairly obvious. Wicksell assumed a full employment economy. As a result, cyclical changes necessarily meant price rather than output changes. He also assumed that prices were equally flexible upward and downward. In these respects he made the typical early twentieth-century assumptions (see our earlier discussion of Irving Fisher). Also, like other monetary theorists of his period, he may have overemphasized the importance of the interest rate as a determinant of economic activity.

The Cambridge School

While Irving Fisher in the United States was developing the equation of exchange, stressing the relation between M, V, P, and Q, various English economists were developing alternative equations. These economists are usually called members of the "Cambridge School," and the equations they developed are known as cash-balance equations.[32]

The main difference in approach between Fisher and the members of the Cambridge School is that Fisher related the money stock to total expendi-

---

[30] *Ibid.*, p. 216.
[31] *Ibid.*
[32] D. H. Robertson, Alfred Marshall, A. C. Pigou, and John Maynard Keynes are usually identified with the Cambridge School. Leon Walras on the continent also made significant contributions to the cash-balance approach.

tures (PQ) through the velocity of circulation, whereas the Cambridge School related the money stock to total expenditures through the demand for money. This alternative approach caused the Cambridge economists to stress the reasons for *holding* money, whereas Fisher stressed the reasons for *spending* money. Actually, as we shall see, the velocity of money and the demand for it are simply reciprocals of each other.

The Cash-Balance Equation. There are many different formulations of the Cambridge equations. The most frequently cited version is as follows:

$$M = KRP \qquad\qquad [17-7]$$

where M is the amount of money in circulation at a moment of time; R, the real national output of goods and services per unit of time; P, the price of R; and K, the proportion of RP that the community wishes to keep enough money to purchase.[33] The equation "can be read as follows: In a stable community the quantity of money in existence is also that which people wish to hold, having regard to the level of output, its price level, and their preferences as regards the form in which they hold their resources."[34]

This equation is closely related to the various equations discussed earlier. Consider equation 17–4, $MV = PQ$, in which PQ refers to gross national product. The PQ of this equation may be equated with the RP of the Cambridge cash-balance equation cited above. It has the same meaning in both cases as long as our time period is a year. Thus, equation 17–7 may be rewritten as $M = KPQ$, and equation 17–4 may be restated as $M = PQ/V$. Then, since $PQ/V = KPQ$, it follows algebraically that $K = 1/V$. In other words, K and V are simply the reciprocal of one another; the demand for money to hold and the velocity of circulation of money are the inverse of each other. Assume for example, that the money supply, M, is used four times in the course of a year to purchase PQ. This is just another way of saying that in the course of a year, people, on the average, held an amount of money equal to one-fourth of the value of their expenditures on PQ.

Stating the relationship between money and PQ in this manner enables us to focus on the motivations for demanding money to hold. Alfred Marshall, for example, stressed this when he reasoned:

The total value of a country's currency, multiplied into the average number of times of its changing hands for business purposes in a year, is of course equal to the total amount of business transacted in that country by direct payments of currency in that year. But this identical statement does not indicate the causes that govern the rapidity of circulation of currency: to discover them we must look to the amounts of purchasing power which the people of that country elect to keep in the form of currency . . . *changes in the rapidity of circulation*

[33] D. H. Robertson, *Lectures on Economic Principles*, vol. III (London: Staples Press, 1959), Chapter 1.
[34] *Ibid.*, p. 18.

of money are themselves incidental to changes in the amount of ready purchasing power which the people of a country find it advantageous to keep in their holding.[35]

What are the factors that determine the relative demand for money, K? They are actually much the same as the forces that determine Fisher's V. Dennis Robertson divides them into five groups:

1. Factors connected with business habits—the frequency and regularity with which payments are made, and so forth;
2. Factors connected with the structure of industry—in particular how far the production and sale of output are split up into stages in the hands of different firms between whom payments have to be made for the transfer of goods in process or in store;
3. The general conditions of social and business life, and hence the degree of certainty and confidence with which consumers and producers are making their plans . . . ;
4. The state of development of the markets for existing capital goods—land, houses, etc., and of paper titles thereto: this works both ways,—such things need money to exchange them with, but some of them are also partial substitutes for money;
5. The rate of return obtainable by employing resources otherwise than by tying them up in the form of money.[36]

The cash-balance equation as a tool of analysis. Given changes in any of the five groups of factors above, forces are set in motion that will lead to a change in K, the demand for money, and consequently to changes in any or all of the other three magnitudes in the cash-balance equation. For example, assume that adverse expectations concerning the business outlook lead to an increase in the demand for money relative to expenditures. In the absence of money stock increases there will be a decrease in spendings, and hence a drop in gross national product (RP). This occurs because the only way in which people can increase their money holdings in such a situation is to refrain from making expenditures. Thus the demand for goods and services decreases. There are fewer sales, incomes decrease, and people discover that they are not really able to increase their money holdings. Some individuals will have increased their holdings, but only at the expense of others. In the aggregate, therefore, it is not possible for the community as a whole to acquire additional money holdings unless the monetary authority is willing to supply more.

An almost identical description of events can be made using the Fisher velocity approach. Here, however, we start by saying that people reduce the velocity of circulation of money because of adverse expectations concerning the business outlook. Reduced spending of money means less demand for goods and services, and hence less gross national product (PQ). While

[35] Alfred Marshall, *Money, Credit and Commerce* (London: Macmillan and Company, 1923), p. 43. Italics are mine.
[36] Robertson, *Lectures on Economic Principles*, pp. 20–21.

both the "velocity" and "cash-balance" approaches are equally valid, the latter is generally considered more satisfactory because, as the last quote from Alfred Marshall implies, the cash-balance equation relates more directly to individual motivation. In addition, the cash-balance equation fits more conveniently into the perspective of the economist's basic concepts of supply and demand.

Summary and evaluation. The monetary theory of the Cambridge economists was organized around the cash-balance equation. This equation, like the equation of exchange, provides us with a convenient framework within which changes in macroeconomic behavior may be analyzed. By emphasizing the relationship between the K and RP, the Cambridge economists called attention to the motives for holding money.

The influence of the Cambridge School on contemporary thought has been substantial. The emphasis on the demand for money by the two groupings of current economists, the "Keynesians" and the "Chicago School Quantity Theorists," indicates the importance of the Cambridge contributions.[37]

CONCLUSION

This chapter has briefly traced the development of monetary theory since the sixteenth century. Economists have long recognized a relationship between money and economic activity and contemporary theory, imperfect as it is, represents a continuation of earlier theories. The relationship between money and prices was first stressed in the sixteenth century. In the seventeenth and eighteenth centuries a fuller understanding of the relations between money, velocity, economic activity, and trade developed. In the nineteenth century, a period of comparatively high employment levels, there were few advances in monetary theory. The early twentieth century was witness to significant theoretical developments, however. Alternative analytical approaches to theory were formulated and comprehensive theories of the cycle were developed. These theories proved inadequate as an explanation of the depression thirties, however, and economists searched for new approaches. This is discussed in Chapters 18 to 21. It should be born in mind, as the contemporary framework of analysis is studied in the next few chapters, that this, too, will eventually be improved by new tentative hypotheses.

---

[37] In a way it is unfortunate that members of a discipline like economics must be pigeonholed by such appellations as the "Chicago School," "Keynesian," "Cambridge School," "Quantity Theorist," "Harvard economist," "Marxist," etc. These names are convenient handles but all too often they tend to obscure both the differences between people who are members of the same group as well as the similarities of the differing groups. This type of obscurantism tends to stand in the way of economic communication and hypothesis testing.

Supplementary Readings

PRE-TWENTIETH CENTURY

Law, John. *Money and Trade Considered.* 1705.

Locke, John. *Consequences of the Lowering of Interests and Raising the Value of Money.* 1692.

——. *Further Considerations Concerning Raising the Value of Money.* 1696.

Mill, John Stuart. *Principles of Political Economy.* Ashley Edition. London, Longmans, Green, 1909, Book III, Chapters 7–13.

Mints, Lloyd W. *A History of Banking Theory.* Chicago, University of Chicago Press, 1945, Chapter 4.

Monroe, Arthur E. *Early Economic Thought.* Cambridge, Mass., Harvard University Press, 1924, Selections 6 and 11.

Spengler, Joseph J. "Richard Cantillon: First of the Moderns." *Journal of Political Economy* (1954).

Sraffa, Piero. *The Works and Correspondence of David Ricardo.* Cambridge, Eng., Cambridge University Press, 1951, Volumes 1 and 3.

Thornton, Henry. *An Enquiry into the Nature and Effects of the Paper Credit of Great Britain.* 1802, Chapters 8, 10, and 11.

Vickers, Douglas. *Studies in the Theory of Money, 1690–1776.* Philadelphia, Chilton, 1959.

EARLY TWENTIETH CENTURY

Fisher and the Transactions Approach

Fisher, Irving. *The Purchasing Power of Money.* New York, Macmillan, 1911, Chapters 1–6, 8.

The Cambridge School and the Cash-Balances Approach

Marshall, A. *Money, Credit, and Commerce.* London, Macmillan, 1923, pp. 38–50.

Pigou, A. C. "The Value of Money." In American Economic Association, *Readings in Monetary Theory,* Homewood, Ill., Irwin, 1951, pp. 162–83.

Robertson, D. H. *Lectures on Economic Principles.* London, Staple Press, 1959, Volume 3, pp. 9–30.

Keynes, J. M. *A Tract on Monetary Reform.* New York, Harcourt, Brace & World, 1923, Chapters 1–4.

The Swedish School

Wicksell, Knut. *Interest and Prices.* Translated by R. F. Kahn, New York, Macmillan, 1936, Introduction, Preface, and Chapters 5–9.

——. *Lectures on Political Economy.* New York, Macmillan, 1935, Volume 2, pp. 127–228.

Myrdal, Gunnar. *Monetary Equilibrium.* London, Saunders, 1939.

Chapter 18

Concepts of National Income Analysis

INTRODUCTION

Chapter 17 traced the historical development of monetary theory up through the early part of the twentieth century. The theories developed in this period proved inadequate as an explanation of continued depression in the 1930's, however. Most of the economists of the 1920's and early 1930's accepted Say's law, that production creates its own demand, for example. In addition they assumed that there was upward and downward flexibility of wages and prices. Given these assumptions, it followed that conditions of less than full employment could not continue for long. When goods and services are produced, they create income equal to the value of production, and all this income, according to Say's law, must be spent. If consumers do not spend all their income, then that portion which is saved will eventually be channeled to investors in plant and equipment. Thus the demand for and supply of goods must always tend to be equal. Price and wage variations would not affect this conclusion. When prices rise, demand will be sufficient to take goods off the market, since wages are also rising. On the other hand, demand will be sufficient to take all goods off the market when wages are falling because with falling wages businesses will have decreasing costs and will thus be able to lower prices. Lower prices will stimulate demand and thereby eliminate any threat of a glut of goods on the market.

These may have been plausible assumptions for the economic world of the nineteenth century, but the depression of the thirties clearly pointed to fallacies that made them inadequate for our modern economy. The number of unemployed people in Western countries in the thirties and the overall duration of unemployment proved conclusively that the depression was anything but a temporary dislocation from long-run full employment. John Maynard Keynes in his *General Theory of Employment, Interest, and Money* flatly denied the validity of Say's law, arguing that "effective demand associated with full employment is a special case."[1] In addition, it

---

[1] John Maynard Keynes, *The General Theory of Employment, Interest, and Money* (New York: Harcourt, Brace & World, 1936), p. 28.

was demonstrated that there are institutional rigidities (administered prices and labor unions) that often prevent downward movements in wages and prices. This disproved another fundamental assumption of Say's law, that prices were fully flexible downward.

The abandonment of Say's law and early twentieth-century monetary theories was termed the "Keynesian Revolution." This revolution took place at both levels of theory: as *hypothesis* and as *framework of analysis*. We are going to study the developments at the second level, what contemporary economists label the "Keynesian Income–Expenditure Framework." This approach is an outgrowth of Keynes' *General Theory of Employment, Interest, and Money*. The theory presented here, however, is actually the contemporary refinement of Keynes' theory as developed by J. R. Hicks, Oscar Lange, Franco Modigliani, Alvin Hansen, Don Patinkin, Lloyd Metzler, Abba Lerner, and many other economists.[2]

This contemporary income–expenditure framework of analysis, which emphasizes the role of money in the economy, is studied in some detail in the two chapters which follow. The purpose of this chapter is to lay the groundwork for the succeeding chapters. The income–expenditure framework of analysis is designed to explain the factors that determine the economic well-being of the nation. The measure that economists use to assess economic performance is gross national product. When gross national product indicates that output and employment are high and increasing, it is generally taken to mean that we have an advancing economy, one in which standards of living are increasing and people are better off than before. Thus, in order to understand the principles governing economic performance, we must first understand the uses and limitations of this measure of performance, gross national product.

GROSS NATIONAL PRODUCT

The Market Value of All Goods and Services

By gross national product we mean the market value of all final goods and services produced in an economy within some specified period of time, usually a year. Gross national product (GNP) is not a measure of the total *number* of units of output, only of their *value*. If the value of the production is increasing and the prices of the individual units of output remain constant, then we can say that the number of units of output produced has increased and that the economy is therefore more productive than formerly and has more goods and services to distribute to the population.

This conception of gross national product as the total market value of

---

[2] See the list of supplementary readings at the end of Chapter 20 for specific references.

goods and services produced in a year's time may also be expressed in symbols:

$$GNP = PQ$$
$$= \Sigma p_1 q_1 + p_2 q_2 + p_3 q_3 + p_4 q_4 \ldots + p_n q_n \qquad [18\text{--}1]$$

p_1 represents the price of product number 1; q_1 is the number of units of product number 1 that were produced in the economy. Similarly p_2, p_3, p_4, and p_n represent the prices of the second, third, fourth, and so on up to the nth product produced; q_2, q_3, q_4, and q_n are the respective quantities of these products produced. Gross national product is thus the sum of the price of each good or service multiplied by the amount produced. GNP has both a price and a quantity element and may increase or decrease as a result of a change in price or output. For this reason we stated that when GNP increases, economic performance is thought to improve also, barring a price increase. Thus, *GNP may only be used as a measure of performance if prices neither increase nor decrease.* Prices change constantly, however. Column 1 of Table 18–1 shows that GNP was $125.8 billion in 1941 and $624.0 billion in 1964. This means that the *value* of all goods and services increased more than five times in the twenty-three year period. This does not mean, however, that *productivity* in the economy increased more than five times, because as column 4 shows, prices doubled. Therefore, the economy was only about twice as productive in 1964 as it was in 1941. Hence, *GNP must be adjusted for price change in order to be used as a measure of performance.*

To arrive at a value of gross national product that reflects only output change over time, we divide the dollar figures for GNP of a given year (often called current dollars) by the price index for that year (often called price deflator).[3] The resultant figure tells us what the output for the given year would have cost had the prices of the output remained unchanged from some particular year in the past. This figure is termed the "real" gross national product, or the GNP in constant dollars. When the real GNP figures for different years are compared, as in Table 18–1, the difference in the figures is attributable to real output change. Here it can be seen that price changes substantially alter the apparent performance record of our economy. Output during the depression 1930's dropped markedly from the 1929 level, for example, but not by as much as GNP in current dollars, which is distorted by price change. Similarly, although

---

[3] Division gives us this result because if $GNP = PQ$, then $Q = GNP/P$. Since GNP and P are known, Q can be determined. Some texts treat the subject of index number construction more extensively. See W. H. Steiner, E. Shapiro, and E. Solomon, *Money and Banking* (New York: Henry Holt and Company, 1958), pp. 392–401. Our purpose here is simply to develop the significance and limitations of GNP as a measure of economic performance. For a discussion of some of the limitations to the accuracy of real output measures based upon price indexes see John J. Klein, "Price-Level and Money-Denomination Movements," *Journal of Political Economy* (1960), p. 369.

TABLE 18-1. UNITED STATES GROSS NATIONAL PRODUCT, REAL GROSS
NATIONAL PRODUCT, AND IMPLICIT PRICE DEFLATOR, 1929–1964

YEAR	GROSS NATIONAL PRODUCT (IN BILLIONS OF CURRENT DOLLARS)	REAL GROSS NATIONAL PRODUCT, 1954 (IN BILLIONS OF CONSTANT DOLLARS*)	IMPLICIT PRICE DEFLATOR (1954 = 100)
1929	104.4	181.8	57.4
1930	91.1	164.5	55.4
1931	76.3	153.0	49.9
1932	58.5	130.1	44.9
1933	56.0	126.6	44.2
1934	65.0	138.5	46.9
1935	72.5	152.9	47.4
1936	82.7	173.3	47.7
1937	90.8	183.5	49.5
1938	85.2	175.1	48.7
1939	91.1	189.3	48.1
1940	100.6	205.8	48.9
1941	125.8	238.1	52.9
1942	159.1	263.4*	60.4*
1943	192.5	275.8*	69.8*
1944	211.4	270.7*	78.1*
1945	213.6	258.6*	82.6*
1946	210.7	282.5	74.6
1947	234.3	282.3	83.0
1948	259.4	293.1	88.5
1949	258.1	292.7	88.2
1950	284.6	318.1	89.5
1951	329.0	341.8	96.2
1952	347.0	353.5	98.1
1953	365.4	369.0	99.0
1954	363.1	363.1	100.0
1955	397.5	392.7	101.2
1956	419.2	400.9	104.6
1957	442.8	408.6	108.4
1958	444.5	401.3	110.8
1959	482.7	428.6	112.6
1960	502.6	439.9	114.3
1961	518.2	447.7	115.7
1962	554.9	474.8	116.9
1963	585.1	492.9	118.5
1964	624.0†	520.0†	120.0†

Source: 1929–55: U.S. Department of Commerce, Office of Business Economics, *U.S. Income and Output*, Supplement, 1958, pp. 118, 119, 220, 221; 1955–56: *Federal Reserve Bulletin*, October, 1961, pp. 1240–41; June, 1964, p. 778.

* Estimated by the author. See John J. Klein, "Price-Level and Money-Denomination Movements," *Journal of Political Economy* (1960). The implicit price deflator is estimated by dividing column 1 by author's estimate of the price level in column 3.

† Estimated by the author.

output has increased almost continuously in the last two and one-half decades, it has not increased by as much as current GNP dollars because prices have also increased.

GNP and the Time Period: Stock and Flow Concepts

GNP is a measure of the value of output *over a period of time*. This is what economists call a *flow* concept. A flow is simply something that is measured over a given period of time. Thus, when we say that the economy produced $624 billion worth of goods and services in the year 1964, for example, we are not saying that at any moment of time in 1964 there were $624 billion worth of goods and services available in the economy, but rather that the total value of goods and services produced during the year amounted to $624 billion.

GNP is also used to express a *rate* of output, instead of an *amount* of output. It could be said, for example, that in the third quarter of 1964 production was at the rate of $624 billion per year. This does not mean that $624 billion in goods and services were actually produced, but rather that the economy might be expected to produce that amount in goods and services over the year if production continued at the same pace as in the third quarter of the year. Thus in the illustration only one-fourth of the $624 was actually produced in the time period measured. To arrive at the estimated annual rate, we multiply the amount produced by the number of quarters in the year, four.

The concept of the rate of production is important in terms of economic policy considerations. Economic events move quickly. If the rate of output diminishes during one part of a year, it is important that the appropriate offsetting policy action be taken without delay. There is not usually sufficient time to permit a full year to pass in order to compare the different outputs for successive years. In the meantime the whole economic situation may have worsened to a serious degree. Thus we study shorter time periods in order to be able to predict the future rate of production more accurately.

We have said that GNP is a flow concept. As such, it may be contrasted with *stock* concepts. A stock of something is simply a quantity existing at a moment of time. Measures such as the supply of money, liquid wealth, and non-liquid wealth are stock measures. Table 2–1 for, example, showed us that the total stock of near money holdings of the nonbank public on March 30, 1964, was $683.3 billion.[4]

---

[4] Sometimes stock measures are stated as averages over time rather than as totals at a moment of time. Thus, if we were to add up the end-of-the-month liquid-wealth holdings of the nonbank public for thirteen consecutive months starting with December 31, 1963, and ending with December 31, 1964, and divide the sum by thirteen, we would have the average liquid-wealth holdings of the nonbank public for the year 1964. This figure would be the amount of liquid wealth that people had, on the average, *at any moment of time during the year 1964.*

The importance of the distinction between stocks and flows cannot be overemphasized. Critical errors of analysis are often made because this distinction is not understood. Income and the amount of money on hand are often confused, for example. A person may receive money payments over the year totaling $12,000. His income, in other words, is $12,000; this is a flow concept. What happens to his money holdings at the end of one year compared with what happens at the end of the next, a stock concept, depends only in part on the size of his income. A $12,000 income after deductions does mean that $12,000 in money was received by the income recipient, but if he makes no payments out of those receipts, then his money *stock* increases by $12,000. On the other hand, if he purchases $12,000 in goods and services, there is no change in money balances over the year. This illustrates an important relationship between stocks and flows: *a flow, other things being equal, will result in a stock change equal to the flow.*

This also holds true for GNP. If the economy in a given year produces $300 billion in final goods and only $275 billion are consumed, then there is an addition of $25 billion to the amount of real wealth in the economy. Thus the difference in the end-of-year stock of wealth figures for two consecutive years is equal to the value of the goods produced but not consumed during the year. This difference is termed *saving*. On the other hand, if an economy consumes more goods than it produces, then there is a reduction of real wealth and this difference is termed *dissaving*. These differences represent the connecting links between the flow (value of output) and the stock (real wealth) in the economy.

ALTERNATIVE MEASURES OF GNP: PRODUCT AND INCOME

The Identity of Income and Product

Equation 18–1 demonstrated that GNP has both a price and an output element. Thus

$$GNP = PQ \qquad [18\text{–}1]$$

GNP, may also be interpreted as a measure of the nation's expenditures on its total product or as a measure of its income. In the first instance the emphasis is placed upon the expenditures that are made on particular types of goods and services. The U.S. Department of Commerce, for example, calculates GNP as the sum of expenditures on consumption, investment, and government goods and services. Also included is the difference between the value of our production for export and our imports of goods and services. All of this may be expressed in symbols as follows:

$$Y = C + I + G + (X - M) \qquad [18\text{–}2]$$

TABLE 18-2. GROSS NATIONAL PRODUCT, 1963
(IN BILLIONS OF CURRENT DOLLARS)

Personal consumption expenditures (C)		
Durable goods	51.5	
Nondurable goods	167.1	
Services	154.5	
Total		373.1
Gross private domestic investment (I)		
New construction		
Residential, nonfarm	25.0	
Other	21.6	
Total	46.6	
Producers durable equipment	30.9	
Change in business inventories	4.7	
Total		82.3*
Net exports of goods and services (X − M)		
Exports	30.7	
Imports	−26.2	
Total		4.5*
Government purchases of goods and services (G)		
Federal	66.3	
State and local	58.6	
Total		125.1*
Gross national product		585.1*

Source: *Federal Reserve Bulletin*, June, 1964, p. 778.
* Differences in totals are due to rounding.

where Y is gross national product, C is expenditures by households on consumer goods and services, I is expenditures on investment goods, G is government expenditures on goods and services, X is exports of goods and services, and M is imports of goods and services.[5]

Gross national product may also be a measure of income. Incomes are earned in the process of producing the goods and services upon which expenditures are made. Individuals receive wages and salaries in exchange for their productive efforts that help the economy produce the desired goods and services. After taxes and other adjustments, individuals are left with personal disposable income, the amount of income that each man is actually able to spend or save over a year's time. Businesses have profits after selling their output, meeting their costs of production, and paying taxes. Government collects the taxes for their income. Thus, the total value of the output is distributed to producers in these forms. This may be expressed in symbols as follows:[6]

$$Y = Y_d + S_b + T \qquad [18-3]$$

[5] From this point on, in accord with general practice, we shall refer to gross national product as Y.

[6] It should be emphasized that the symbols in the equations are for the most part drawn directly from the term they represent. For example, T stands for taxes, S_p for personal saving, etc.

TABLE 18–3. GROSS NATIONAL PRODUCT AS INCOME, 1963
(IN BILLIONS OF CURRENT DOLLARS)

Disposable personal income (Y_d)		
Personal consumption expenditures (C)	373.1	
Personal saving (S_p)	29.3	
Total		402.4
Disposable business corporate income (S_b)		
Corporate profits and inventory valuation		
Adjustment	51.1	
Dividends	−17.8	
Profits tax liability	−24.4	
Total	8.9	
Capital consumption allowances	51.6	
Total		60.5*
Government taxes (T)		
Personal tax and nontax payments		
Federal	50.9	
State and local	9.6	
Total	60.5	
Corporate profits tax liability	24.4	
Indirect business tax and nontax liability	56.6	
Contributions for social insurance	27.2	
Government transfer payments	−34.6	
Net interest paid by government	−8.4	
Subsidies less current surplus of government enterprise	−0.7	
Total	125.0	
Statistical discrepancy	−3.0	
Gross national product as income		585.1*

Source: Adapted from *Federal Reserve Bulletin*, June, 1964, pp. 778–79.
* Differences in totals are due to rounding.

where Y is gross national income or product, Y_d is personal disposable income, S_b is business income, and T is federal, state, and local government tax receipts. The total value of output must always be distributed as income in one of these forms. Therefore, since

$$Y = C + I + G + (X - M) \qquad [18\text{-}2]$$

and

$$Y = Y_d + S_b + T \qquad [18\text{-}3]$$

it follows that

$$C + I + G + (X - M) = Y_d + S_b + T \qquad [18\text{-}4]$$

This equation can be simplified still further when we consider how individuals dispose of disposable income. They either spend it or save it. Thus

$$Y_d = C + S_p \qquad [18\text{-}5]$$

where S_p is personal saving. Substituting equation 18–5 for Y_d in equation 18–4 we get

$$C + I + G + (X - M) = C + S_p + S_b + T \qquad [18\text{-}6]$$

C is the same on both sides of the equation. Therefore

$$I + G + (X - M) = S_p + S_b + T \qquad [18\text{--}7]$$

This equation must always hold true for the past performance of an economy because of the exact equality of income and product. When product is produced, its value is distributed as income to its producers. Tables 18–2 to 18–4 demonstrate this by giving the component measures of

TABLE 18–4. DISPOSABLE PERSONAL INCOME, 1963
(IN BILLIONS OF CURRENT DOLLARS)

Compensation of employees			
Wages and salaries			
Private	253.0		
Military	11.0		
Government civilian	48.3		
Total		312.3	
Supplements to wages and salaries		28.0	
Total			340.4*
Proprietors' income			
Business and professional	37.7		
Farm	12.8		
Total		50.5	
Rental income of persons		12.1	
Net interest		24.1	
Government transfer payments		34.6	
Net interest paid by government		8.4	
Dividends		17.8	
Business transfer payments		2.3	
Personal tax and nontax payments			
Federal	−50.9		
State and local	−9.6		
Total		−60.5	
Contributions for social insurance		−27.2	
Disposable personal income (Y_d)		402.4*	

Source: Adapted from *Federal Reserve Bulletin*, June, 1964, pp. 778–79.
* Differences in totals are due to rounding.

gross national product and gross national income for a recent year, 1963. These tables will not be discussed in detail; they are included merely to show how the equations given relate to our actual income statistics.

THE FINANCING
OF GROSS NATIONAL PRODUCT

In the preceding discussion it has been established that PQ, Y, $C + I + G + (X - M)$, and $Y_d + S_b + T$ are equivalent. No mention has been made of the financing of these magnitudes, however. Obviously money is the medium used when Y is purchased. As indicated in Chapter 17, when the average amount of money in the economy during a specified period of time, such as a year, M, is multiplied by the number of times it is spent on final goods and services, V, the product is a measure of the value of the expenditures on final goods and services produced. That product, of course, is Y.

Hence it follows that

$$Y = C + I + G + (X - M) = Y_d + S_b + T = PQ = MV \quad [18\text{--}8]$$

Each section of this equation is simply a different way of looking at the same thing, Y. The significance of equations 18–1 through 18–8 for income determination will be more fully developed in the chapters which follow.

SUMMARY

Gross national product is the market value of all final goods and services produced in the economy within some specified period of time. Since Y is counted in current market values, it must be deflated by an appropriate price index before it may be utilized as a measure of real output value over time, and in this respect it is a flow concept. Incomes are paid when product is produced. Consequently, Y may be viewed as either a measure of the economy's income or as the expenditure on product. Y is financed through the use of money.

The following two chapters develop a model showing how gross national product, Y, is determined in a relatively industrialized economy like the United States. Succeeding chapters on economy policy will then consider alternative economic policies that may be used to bring about stability in the flow and growth of Y.

Supplementary Reading

Hawtrey, R. G. "Money and Index Numbers," reprinted in F. A. Lutz and Lloyd W. Mints, eds., *Readings in Monetary Theory*, Philadelphia, Blakiston, 1951.

Data Sources

U.S. Department of Commerce, Office of Business Economics. *U.S. Income and Output*. Washington, D.C., U.S. Government Printing Office, 1958.
———. *Survey of Current Business*. July, 1964.
National Bureau of Economic Research. *A Critique of United States Income and Product Accounts*, Studies in Income and Wealth. Vol. 22, Princeton, N.J., Princeton University Press, 1958.

Chapter 19

A Model of Income Determination, Part I

Monetary theory seeks to explain the role of monetary supply and demand flows in the determination of economic activity. Contemporary economists recognize, however, that there are many variables in addition to money that help determine income and output. Thus today monetary theory is an integral part of macroeconomic theory. To appreciate the importance of money, therefore, we must understand how money works with and is affected by these other variables.

This chapter and the next are concerned with contemporary macroeconomic theory. Specifically, we shall examine the factors that cause change in our measure of economic performance, gross national product. The most important sources of economic change will be isolated on a graphic analytical framework that will help us interpret income determination by depicting the interaction of these variables visually. This abstraction from reality is a type of economic model. Despite the fact that it is an abstraction, however, our economic model will be fairly rigorous so that the complexities of the economy may be realistically described. The development of the model is divided into two sections. This chapter will examine the determination of the factors in equation 18–6: $C + I + G + (X - M) = C + S_p + S_b + T$.[1] Chapter 20 then adds monetary supply and demand to the model and shows how the model may be used to interpret the interaction of various economic forces.

INTRODUCTION TO THE MODEL

In essence, contemporary income theory argues that the interaction of demand and supply forces determines the level of economic activity. When demand is less than supply, stocks of goods accumulate and businesses are forced to reduce Y, aggregate output. If prices do not subsequently de-

---

[1] A brief listing of all symbols used in these chapters will be found at the end of Chapter 21.

cline when supply exceeds demand, then all of the drop in gross national product is in real output. On the other hand, when the demand for goods and services exceeds the supply, the stock of goods declines, business expectations improve, and businesses are induced to increase output. Hence gross national product increases. Should the economy already be operating at full employment capacity, however, all the increase in Y will be in prices; the value of output will grow but not the real amount of output. Thus, the only time that Y will not change is when there is neither a shortage nor an excess of demand relative to output, when demand equals supply.

These are the essentials of modern income analysis. The demand for goods relative to the supply is of crucial significance and businesses respond to differences between demand and supply by adjusting aggregate output. This does not explain the fundamental sources of income and output change, however. For this we must examine the components of demand in more detail.

Equation 18–6 offers us some insight into the sources of demand determination. We have said that this equation is always accurate for past performance. Thus, when we say that the sum of C, I, G, and $(X - M)$ must equal the sum of C, S_p, S_b, and T, we are speaking after the fact; we are discussing what has occurred. This is what economists call *ex post* analysis.

Since investment, saving, and expenditure *plans* are made independently and by different individuals, there is no reason why the *planned* magnitudes should be equivalent. Thus the two sides of our equation may differ when the magnitudes of the variables represent plans that look to the future. The total amount of planned expenditures of businesses, of governing bodies, and of exporters and importers may differ, therefore, from the total amount of planned personal saving, expected business profits, and expected government tax receipts. When we say that the sum of the *plans* for C, I, G, and $(X - M)$ may differ from the plans for C, S_p, S_b, and T, we are speaking before the fact; we are looking ahead to what has not yet occurred. This is what economists call *ex ante* analysis.

When the plans for the magnitudes in equation 18–6 *are* equal, then the economy may be said to be in equilibrium; there are no forces at work tending to change income and output. Aggregate demand and supply will be equal. Businesses will produce just enough goods to meet anticipated demands.

Therefore, it is the plans for C, I, G, $(X - M)$, S_p, S_b, and T that are sources of income determination. The remainder of this chapter examines each of these magnitudes in some detail and then places them in our model of income determination.

PERSONAL SAVING
AND CONSUMPTION DEMAND

It will be recalled from Chapter 18 that individuals dispose of personal disposable income either by spending it or by saving it. Thus a decision to save may also be looked upon as a decision not to make a consumption expenditure. Hence

$$Y_d = C + S_p \qquad [18\text{--}5]$$

where Y_d is personal disposable income, C is consumption demand, and S_p is personal saving. Changes in decisions to save and spend lead to changes in spending and, therefore, changes in gross national product. Since consumption spending is quantitatively the single most important component of Y, the determination of consumption and saving behavior should be studied carefully. In the following discussion we examine those variables that economists consider most likely to influence consumption and saving.

Disposable personal income

The principal determinant of personal saving and consumption demand is generally believed to be the level of disposable personal income. The logic of this view is quite simple: increased incomes enhance the spending ability of individuals; with more to spend individuals tend to raise their standards of living, saving just a portion of the increased income. Decreased incomes decrease the spending ability of individuals. People are forced to reduce their actual spending, but the reduction will not usually be by as much as the decrease in income, because people typically attempt to maintain their prior living standards under such conditions. This analysis applies not only to an individual but to the aggregate of individuals as well. For example, income and output may increase without actually raising the income of anyone already working. This is what happens when more people are employed. As the unemployed are drawn into the working force, their disposable incomes rise and they increase their expenditures and saving. Whether the increased incomes are of those already working or of the newly employed, the economy still feels the impact of the consumption expenditure and saving increases.

This contention seems to be supported by the data given in Table 19–1 and Figure 19–1. Here we see that consumption appears to be closely related to Y and Y_d change.[2] When gross national product and disposable personal income rise, consumption also increases. When they decline, consumption declines. During the depression of the 1930's, for example, Y, Y_d, and C all decreased, although consumption as a percentage of Y and Y_d actually increased. This is evidence for the theory that with decreased incomes people generally try to maintain their customary level of expenditures.

As incomes increased after 1933, C also increased but not proportionately by as much as Y and Y_d. The reason for this appears to have been the in-

---

[2] The relationship between S_p and Y_d is not shown, since according to equation 18–5 S_p is simply the difference between C and Y_d.

TABLE 19–1. GROSS NATIONAL PRODUCT AND ITS COMPONENTS, 1929–1963

	GNP AND ITS COMPONENTS (IN BILLIONS OF DOLLARS)						COMPONENTS OF GNP AS PERCENTAGES OF GNP*				
YEAR	GNP	C	I	G	$(X - M)$	Y_d	C	I	G	$(X - M)$	$\dfrac{C}{Y_d}$
1929	104.4	79.0	16.2	8.5	0.8	83.1	75.7	15.5	8.1	0.8	95.1
1930	91.1	71.0	10.3	9.1	0.7	74.4	77.9	11.3	10.0	0.8	95.4
1931	76.3	61.3	5.5	9.2	0.2	63.8	80.3	7.2	12.1	0.3	96.1
1932	58.5	49.3	0.9	8.1	0.2	48.7	84.3	1.5	13.9	0.3	101.2
1933	56.0	46.4	1.4	8.0	0.2	45.7	82.9	2.5	14.3	0.4	101.5
1934	65.0	51.9	2.9	9.8	0.4	52.0	79.9	4.5	15.1	0.6	99.8
1935	72.5	56.3	6.3	10.0	−0.1	58.3	77.7	8.7	13.8	−0.1	96.6
1936	82.7	62.6	8.4	11.8	−0.1	66.2	75.7	10.2	14.3	−0.1	94.6
1937	90.8	67.3	11.7	11.7	0.1	71.0	74.1	12.9	12.9	0.1	94.8
1938	85.2	64.6	6.7	12.8	1.1	65.7	75.8	7.9	15.0	1.3	98.3
1939	91.1	67.6	9.3	13.3	0.9	70.4	74.2	10.2	14.6	1.0	96.0
1940	100.6	71.9	13.2	14.1	1.5	76.1	71.4	13.1	14.0	1.5	94.5
1941	125.8	81.9	18.1	24.8	1.1	93.0	65.1	14.4	19.7	0.9	88.1
1942	159.1	89.7	9.9	59.7	−0.2	117.5	56.4	6.2	37.5	−0.1	76.3
1943	192.5	100.5	5.6	88.6	−2.2	133.5	52.2	2.9	46.0	−1.1	75.2
1944	211.4	109.8	7.1	96.5	−2.1	146.8	52.0	3.4	45.7	−1.0	74.8
1945	213.6	121.7	10.4	82.9	−1.4	150.4	57.0	4.9	38.8	−0.7	80.9
1946	210.7	147.1	28.1	30.5	4.9	160.6	69.9	13.3	14.5	2.3	91.6
1947	234.3	165.4	31.5	28.4	9.0	170.1	70.6	13.4	12.1	3.8	97.2
1948	259.4	178.3	43.1	34.5	3.5	189.3	68.7	16.6	13.3	1.4	94.2
1949	258.1	181.2	33.0	40.2	3.8	189.7	70.2	12.8	15.6	1.5	95.5
1950	284.6	195.0	50.0	39.0	0.6	207.7	68.5	17.6	13.7	0.2	93.9
1951	329.0	209.8	56.3	60.5	2.4	227.5	63.8	17.1	18.4	0.7	92.2
1952	347.0	219.8	49.9	76.0	1.3	238.7	63.3	14.4	21.9	0.4	92.1
1953	365.4	232.6	50.3	82.8	−0.4	252.5	63.7	13.8	22.7	0.1	92.2
1954	363.1	238.0	48.9	75.3	1.0	256.9	65.6	13.5	20.7	0.3	92.6
1955	397.5	256.9	63.8	75.6	1.1	274.5	64.7	16.1	19.0	0.3	93.6
1956	419.2	269.9	67.4	79.0	2.9	292.9	64.4	16.1	18.9	0.7	92.1
1957	442.8	285.2	66.1	86.5	4.9	308.8	64.4	14.9	19.5	1.1	92.4
1958	444.5	293.2	56.6	93.5	1.2	317.9	66.0	12.7	21.0	0.3	92.2
1959	482.7	313.5	72.7	97.2	−0.8	337.1	65.0	15.1	20.1	−0.2	93.0
1960	503.4	328.5	72.4	99.7	2.9	349.4	65.3	14.4	19.8	0.6	94.0
1961	518.7	338.1	69.3	107.4	4.0	363.3	65.2	13.4	20.7	0.8	93.0
1962	553.9	356.7	76.6	117.3	3.8	382.9	64.2	13.8	21.2	0.7	93.2
1963	585.1	373.1	82.3	125.1	4.5	402.4	63.8	14.0	21.4	0.8	92.7

Source: Office of Business Economics, U.S. Department of Commerce, *U.S. Income and Output*, 1958; *Survey of Current Business*, July, 1963; *Federal Reserve Bulletin*, June, 1964, pp. 778–79.

* Figures may not add to 100.0 because of rounding.

crease in the income tax rate which occurred in the 1930's and continued into the war years.

World War II brought sharp income increases. Consumption did not rise proportionately, however. Increased taxes and the general unavailability of major consumer durable goods such as automobiles and major household appliances restricted consumption expenditures. Immediately after the war, Y decreased but consumption expenditures rose, for government tax rates

FIGURE 19-1. Gross national product, consumption expenditures, and personal disposable income, 1929-1963.

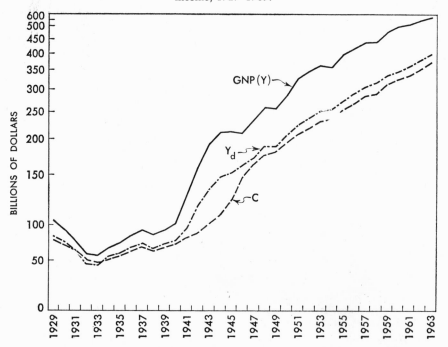

Source: Office of Business Economics, U.S. Department of Commerce, *U.S. Income and Output*, 1958; *Survey of Current Business*, July, 1963; *Federal Reserve Bulletin*, June, 1964, pp. 778-79.

had decreased and disposable income had increased. Through the last part of the 1940's consumption expenditures moved along with gross national product and disposable personal income.

Since 1950, changes in C have continued to parallel Y and Y_d changes, but at a lower level than in the late 1940's. Part of the reason for this may be that the pent-up demand for consumer goods and services that had accumulated during the depression and war years was, for the most part, satisfied in the latter half of the 1940's, thereby enabling people to lower their consumption rate and increase their rate of saving in the fifties and sixties. In general, however, the movement in Y, Y_d, and C has been upward, although years of recession have witnessed a slight reduction in the amount of income and consumption expenditure increase in comparison with more prosperous times.

Thus the relationship between Y, Y_d, and C appears to have been fairly close over time. This supports the view that income is an important determinant of consumption demand and spending. It should be noted, however, that consumption is directly determined by Y_d rather than Y because the full amount of Y is not available to the spender. The causation, in other words, runs from Y to Y_d and then to C.

Wealth as a Source of Consumption and Saving Change

The volume of liquid wealth may also exert an influence on consumption demand and personal saving. At any given level of personal disposable income, the greater the volume of liquid wealth, the greater the demand for consumption goods and services. The logic on which this assertion is based is that more liquid wealth means more command over goods and services and less need to save out of current income to meet unforeseen contingencies. The lower the level of liquid wealth, the less ability individuals have to make high-level consumption expenditures and the greater the need to save.

The total volume of liquid wealth is influenced by saving out of personal disposable income. Thus, when a person saves and does not spend, his liquid wealth holdings increase. Initially, as disposable income exceeds consumption expenditures, money receipts will exceed money expenditures and liquid wealth holdings in the form of money balances will increase. Subsequently, however, the saver may decide to keep his increased liquid wealth holdings in another form. Thus he may choose to increase his holdings of savings deposits, government securities, corporate stocks, privately issued bonds, or insurance policies. As these forms of wealth increase in volume while holdings of physical wealth remain unchanged, it becomes more and more likely that the rate of expenditure on consumption goods and services will increase and that the saving rate, S_p, will decrease. The ability to meet future expenditures, both foreseen and unanticipated, will have increased, and consequently, there will be less need to maintain the same saving rate as at a lower level of liquid wealth.

The situation is different when consumption expenditures exceed disposable income and S_p is negative; dissaving occurs then. An excess of expenditures over income can only be financed by borrowing or drawing down liquid wealth holdings. Thus the ability to make future needed expenditures and meet unforeseen contingencies will be reduced, and to recoup these holdings will necessitate a reduction in expenditures.

Empirical evidence tends to support this analysis. "As a general rule, the saving rate for individual households appears to vary inversely with the ratio of liquid assets to income, and the influence of liquid assets on saving tends to diminish as the level of income rises."[3]

So far the discussion of the influence of liquid wealth on expenditures and saving has made no mention of prices. We have assumed that prices are constant. What happens if prices vary? Assume, for example, there is an increase in the price level. When this occurs, there is a corresponding decrease in the purchasing power of most forms of liquid wealth; about the only forms of liquid wealth that will increase in value are stocks, the price of which usually fluctuates along with the general price level. Other forms of liquid wealth usually have a fixed nominal value. Thus $1,000 in money or savings deposits continues to be $1,000 regardless of price level change; a bond with a maturity value of $1,000 will continue to have that same maturity value, although the market price of the bond will probably decline. The decreased purchasing power of bonds and the availability of favorable alternative financial investments, such as corporate stocks, generally leads to a decline in the price of bonds that have already been issued. On balance, with a price level increase the purchasing power of liquid wealth tends to decrease.

What influence will this have on consumption expenditures? Since the real purchasing power of liquid wealth generally decreases with an increase in the price level, people feel that there is a need to recoup the ability to meet unanticipated expenditures. One way of doing this is to increase saving out of income. Consequently, consumption expenditures fall and saving rises.

Liquid wealth and the real value of liquid wealth have been introduced as possible sources of influence on consumption demand. *Real wealth* should also be considered. The amount of physical goods in the economy may also help to determine consumption expenditures on consumer durable goods. The more physical goods are owned, presumably, the less the need for additional units of them, and hence the lower the expenditures on them.

This only applies if the average age of physical goods is constant over time, however, for it is also true that the greater the average age of physical goods, the more likely there is to be an extensive demand for these goods, regardless of the total volume of real wealth then extant. The increasing age of the stock of consumer durables during the depression and World War II is at least part of the explanation for the strong postwar consumer demand for durables, which occurred despite the fact that there was a large amount of physical goods in American households. Overall, we find in the U.S. economy that the average age of real wealth owned by individuals is not constant, because there is a tendency for consumer expenditures on durable goods to fall off in recession and to increase in more prosperous periods.

---

[3] Robert Ferber, "Research on Household Behavior," *American Economic Review* (1962), p. 37.

$1000 (.04) = 4 000$
$4000 (8\pounds) = \frac{4 000}{1 500}$

The Rate of Interest

The rate of interest affects consumption demand in several ways. For example, an increase in the rate of interest may usually be expected to lead to an increase in the rate of saving and, other things being equal, to a decrease in consumption spending. Since interest is paid to savers to compensate them for giving up current consumption, the higher the interest return, the more people are induced to save. Conversely, the lower the interest return, the less saving occurs.

The relationship between the rate of interest and consumption demand should also be considered from the borrower's point of view. The individual who finds that he may borrow a given amount of money at a reduced interest cost may be induced to borrow more and so increase his spending. Similarly, when banks extend their loans because of increased excess reserves and leave their lending rates unchanged, credit conditions are easier. Borrowers who previously did not qualify for loans may now be able to borrow. When they do, their spendings will increase.

Changes in the interest rate and consumption demand may also move in the same direction, however. Those people who only feel it necessary to get a specific dollar interest yield on their financial investments will save less if interest rates increase, since less savings will give the same total dollar yield. Hence consumption demand may increase. For example, a person who wants $30 in interest income needs $1,000 in savings when the interest rate is 3 percent but only $500 in savings when the interest rate is 6 percent.

There are still other possibilities. A rise in the rate of interest paid on newly issued securities relative to that paid on already existing securities will cause the market price on the old securities to decline. If a potential bond purchaser is to be induced to buy an old security instead of a new security, then he must be offered an *effective yield* on the old security that is comparable to that of the new security. Assume, for example, that an old bond has a par value of $1,000 and a 3 percent rate of return, while a comparable new security yields 4 percent. The price of the old security must drop in order to meet this competition. To give the investor an effective 4 percent return on his investment when the dollar yield on the old bond is $30, the seller must ask himself: $30 is 4 percent of what size financial investment?

$$(x)(.04) = \$30$$

or

$$(\$750)(.04) = \$30$$

Thus, the price of old bonds declines during periods of generally rising interest rates. This means that the volume of liquid wealth in the form of old securities has declined and that, accordingly, an increase in saving and a decrease in consumption demand has been induced. In general, economists *believe* that interest rate increases tend to increase saving and lower consumption, and that interest rate decreases have the reverse effect. Quantitatively, however, it is difficult to make a reasonably accurate prediction as to the potential effects of interest rate changes on the rate of saving and consumption expenditures. This has led many economists to the conclusion that there are many variables at work here and that interest rate changes are difficult to disentangle from them as causal forces affecting consumption and saving.

Additional Explanations of Personal Saving and Consumption

In addition to the factors previously mentioned, other factors such as age, education, distribution of income, and price expectations are often mentioned as determinants of consumption demand and saving. It is often argued, for example, that the older the population, the less the need for consumer durable goods. Furthermore, the lower the level of education, the less income people may be expected to earn, and the lower their spending will be. In addition, the greater the proportion of income going to high-income groups, the less the tendency to spend on consumption. Because of standards of living that are already high, those with large incomes tend to save more and spend a smaller fraction of additions to their income than do those with lower incomes. Finally, the greater the expectation that prices will increase, the greater the apparent need to buy before prices actually rise, since there is no point in allowing the purchasing power of income to deteriorate.

These are just a few of the other determinants that economists take into consideration in their explanations of consumer spending and saving. The explanation of spending behavior is a complicated affair. Many of the problems are not even touched upon here. For example, consumption behavior seems to be differently affected by income changes over a short period of time than over a long period of time. Economists have offered numerous explanations for this paradox, but none of them appear completely satisfactory.

An Equation for Personal Saving

Having examined separately a number of determinants of saving and consumption, we must now attempt to describe in some way the combined effect of these various factors on consumption and saving behavior. Selecting those determinants that seem most relevant on the basis of empirical study and careful a priori reasoning, we have Y_d, personal disposable income; i, rate of interest; W, liquid wealth; and X, all the other factors that may influence C and S_p. Putting this into equation form, we get

$$S_p = f(Y_d, i, W, X) \qquad [19\text{--}1]$$

and, since $Y_d = C + S_p$ (equation 18-5), then, substituting, we have

$$Y_d = C + f(Y_d, i, W, X); \quad C = Y_d - f(Y_d, i, W, X) \qquad [19\text{-}2]$$

These equations tell us that consumption demand and personal saving are f, a function of (determined by) personal disposable income, liquid wealth, rate of interest, and other relevant variables. If X remains constant, we may assume that the *saving* rate increases with a rise in personal disposable income, a drop in liquid wealth, and a rise in rate of interest. Thus the relation between saving, disposable income, and rate of interest is direct, whereas the relationship between saving and liquid wealth is inverse. On the other hand, *consumption* rises with an increase in disposable income, an increase

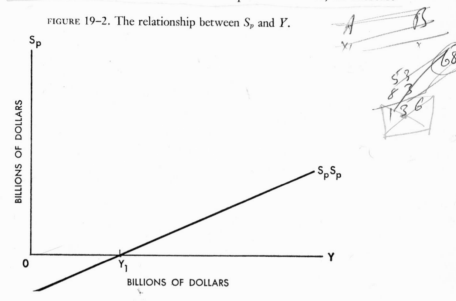

FIGURE 19-2. The relationship between S_p and Y.

in liquid wealth, and a drop in rate of interest. Thus the relation between consumption, disposable income, and liquid wealth is direct, whereas the relationship between consumption and rate of interest is inverse.

In developing a diagrammatical representation of Y changes, we shall concentrate on the saving equation 19-1 rather than the consumption equation 19-2 in order to keep the analysis comparatively simple. In a sense, the analysis illustrates consumption determinants too, however, for C and its determinants may be derived readily from equation 19-1. Once we determine S_p, we can easily compute C from $C = Y_d - S_p$. This also means that we can deal with equation 18-7, $I + G + (X - M) = S_p + S_b + T$, instead of equation 18-6, $C + I + G + (X - M) = C + S_p + S_b + T$. C is identical on both sides of the equation and thus cancels out.

The relationship between the variables of equation 19-1 may be illustrated diagrammatically as follows: Planned personal saving at any level of Y is measured along the vertical axis in Figure 19-2; Y is measured along the horizontal axis. Y, rather than Y_d, is written along the horizontal axis because, ultimately, a model of income determination must be designed to explain changes in Y. Thus in Figure 19–2 *the line* S_pS_p *shows the relationship between* S_p *and* Y. This line records the total amount of personal saving that people plan to keep at various levels of Y. The greater the level of Y, the greater the volume of personal saving that people feel it necessary to keep. Thus at any point above an output of Y_1 people want to save. At any level of output below that there will be dissaving; people will tend to spend more on consumption goods than they receive in income.

The line S_pS_p also shows the relationship between change in personal saving and change in gross national product. Let the symbol delta, Δ, refer to a small change. By moving from any point on the line S_pS_p to another we can observe the change in S_p that is induced by a change in Y. Thus, the ratio $\Delta S_p/\Delta Y$ is a measure of how changes in Y induce changes in S_p. In terms of the diagram, it is also a measure of the slope of the line S_pS_p, which we have drawn as a straight line to keep the analysis simple. The slope of the line is less than one (less than 45°). This reflects the desire of the public both to save and to spend when a change in Y occurs; thus, as Y increases, the amount of saving also increases, but by less than the increase in Y. The remainder of the change in Y goes into consumption expenditures, government tax collections, and business income.

This last point requires some further explanation. It will be recalled that Y_d is the direct determinant of C and S_p, but not Y. The ratio of a change in personal saving induced by a change in personal disposable income is $\Delta S_p/\Delta Y_d$; this is called the *marginal propensity to save*. The remainder of any change in Y_d goes into consumption change. The ratio of the change in consumption expenditures induced by the change in personal disposable income is $\Delta C/\Delta Y_d$, which is called the *marginal propensity to consume*. It should be noted, however, that the marginal propensity to save, $\Delta S_p/\Delta Y_d$, differs from $\Delta S_p/\Delta Y$. As gross national product increases, personal disposable income increases but so do business earnings and government tax collections. In our economy, the tax structure is geared to the level of income and output. The higher Y becomes, the greater the amount of taxes collected by the government. For these reasons the marginal propensity to save must differ from the ratio of the change in personal saving to a change in gross national product. The marginal propensity to save, $\Delta S_p/\Delta Y_d$, must be *greater* than the ratio $\Delta S_p/\Delta Y$. Assume, for example, that 80 percent of changes in Y go into a Y_d change, 10 percent into a change in business income, and 10 percent into a change in government tax collections. Assume further that the marginal propensity to save is .20. Given these conditions, an increase of $50 billion in Y will become a $40 billion increase in Y_d, a $5 billion increase in government tax collections, and a $5 billion increase in business income. In turn, the $40 billion rise in Y_d results in a $32 billion increase in consumption expenditures and an $8 billion rise in personal saving, S_p. In other words, for every dollar change in Y there will be a 16 percent change in S_p. Thus the ratio of S_p to Y is .16, in contrast to the marginal propensity to save of .20.

What about the other determinants of consumption and personal saving?

How do they fit into this diagram? Since a two-dimensional diagram can only show the relationship between two variables along any one given line such as S_pS_p, the other variables must be assumed to be fixed. If other variables do change, however, then the position of the line S_pS_p must change to show the relationship between S_p and Y, given the new values of the other variables. Thus in terms of this diagram S_pS_p will move upward if, at any given level of Y, there is a decrease in liquid wealth or a rise in the rate of interest. In addition, anything that would cause X to change would also lead to a change in S_pS_p.

Business Saving and Taxes Added to Personal Saving

We have said that when the total of the plans for $S_p + S_b + T$ differs from the total of the plans for $I + G + (X - M)$, economic change occurs. What do the totals of the plans for S_p, S_b, and T look like at any given level of gross national product? This relationship is depicted in Figure 19–3.

The tax line, TT, shows the relationship between the tax receipts at all levels of government and the level of gross national product. This line is drawn sloping upward and to the right, since the various governmental bodies collect more taxes as incomes increase. For the sake of simplicity, we have assumed that the governmental tax collections are a constant proportion of Y changes. The position of the line TT is determined by the actions of the legislatures, of course. Thus it is unlike S_pS_p in that it is not directly influenced by economic variables such as Y_d, i, and W. The legislatures are influenced by economic conditions indirectly, of course.

T may be defined as follows:

$$T = f(Y,Z) \qquad\qquad [19\text{--}3]$$

This equation tells us that T, the total of government tax collections, is a function of Y, the level of gross national product, and Z, a general variable standing for all those forces that cause the legislature to change the tax rate. As already indicated, in Figure 19–3 the relationship between T and Y is assumed to be positive.

In Figure 19–3 S_bS_b, the business saving line, shows the relationship between the level of business disposable income, S_b (sometimes called business saving), and gross national product.[4] This relationship is positive, for businesses expect to have higher earnings as the level of income in the economy rises. For the sake of simplicity we have assumed that the relationship between changes in the amount of business disposable income and Y are always proportionate. Thus the equation for S_b is

$$S_b = f(Y,U) \qquad\qquad [19\text{--}4]$$

---

[4] The data published by the U.S. Department of Commerce for business disposable income covers only corporate enterprise. The earnings of unincorporated enterprise are included in personal disposable income.

Thus business disposable income is a function of Y and U, which stands for any forces tending to change S_b at any given level of Y.

Forces included in U are government business taxes, corporate dividend policies, and capital consumption allowances. Decreases in business taxes, legally permissible higher capital consumption allowances, and reduced dividend rates will all tend to raise S_bS_b. Hence business disposable income may be increased at all levels of Y. As before, however, a given line such as S_bS_b in Figure 19–3 assumes other factors to be fixed. Assuming that all other determinants of S_p, S_b, and T other than Y are fixed, we may depict the combined impact of the three lines S_pS_p, S_bS_b, and TT. This is represented

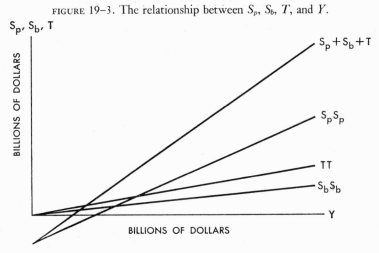

FIGURE 19–3. The relationship between S_p, S_b, T, and Y.

by line $S_p + S_b + T$, which shows the expected total of S_p, S_b, and T at various levels of Y. The relationship is positive, with a slope of less than one but greater than zero.

Shifts in the $S_p + S_b + T$ Line

A shift in S_pS_p attributable to W and i changes will usually cause the entire line $S_p + S_b + T$ to shift by the same amount. Shifts in the S_bS_b and TT line, however, may not move $S_p + S_b + T$ by the same amount, since these changes affect the level of personal disposable income. For example, if the distribution of gross national product changes as income rises, so that a greater proportion goes into business disposable income and taxes, the net effect will be a reduction in personal disposable income. Personal saving will also be affected; at any given level of Y there will be a downward turn of S_pS_p. As a result, the total line $S_p + S_b + T$ will turn up somewhat, but not by as much as the upward turn of TT and S_bS_b. This is illustrated in Figure 19–4. We assume an increase in tax rates. S_bS_b and TT are added together to simplify our analysis. The solid lines represent the original positions of $S_bS_b + TT$, S_pS_p, and $S_p + S_b + T$. The distance between the old $S_p + S_b + T$ and the new total line is equal to the difference between the upturn in $S_bS_b + TT$ and the downturn in S_pS_p.

FIGURE 19–4. The relationship between S_pS_p, $S_bS_b + TT$, and changes in the tax rate.

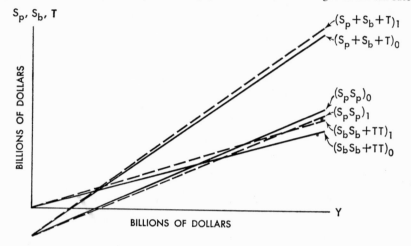

Summary of Forces Affecting the $S_p + S_b + T$ Line

The $S_p + S_b + T$ line will shift whenever determinants of S_p, S_b, and T, other than Y, change. Thus

1. S_pS_p, and hence $S_p + S_b + T$, will fluctuate inversely with movements of liquid wealth.[5] It will rise with a decrease in individual holdings of the components of liquid wealth—the stock of money, time deposits, savings and loan share accounts, U.S. government securities, corporate stocks, bonds, and life insurance policies. Conversely, S_pS_p, and hence $S_p + S_b + T$, will fall with an increase in those liquid wealth holdings.

2. S_pS_p, and hence $S_p + S_b + T$, vary directly with price level changes because of the change in the purchasing power of liquid wealth. On the other hand, S_pS_p and $S_p + S_b + T$ vary inversely to price expectations.

3. S_pS_p, and hence $S_p + S_b + T$, vary directly with the interest rate.

4. S_pS_p falls whenever the tax rate is increased, but $S_p + S_b + T$ rises. The upturn in $S_p + S_b + T$ is less than the increase in TT, however. Conversely,

---

[5] That is, at any given level of income, personal saving will increase with a drop in liquid wealth. This ignores the fact discussed earlier that as saving takes place liquid wealth will increase. What happens is that liquid wealth accumulates as saving occurs and this subsequently will enable S_pS_p, the *rate* of saving, to fall and consumption to increase at all levels of income.

a tax rate cut causes a downward turn in $S_p + S_b + T$ that is less than the decrease in TT.

5. S_pS_p varies inversely with changes in business disposable income. $S_p + S_b + T$, however, moves in the same direction as business disposable income changes. Hence the change in $S_p + S_b + T$ is less than the change in S_bS_b.

6. TT changes with legislative action that alter the tax rate. $S_p + S_b + T$ varies as described above in 4.

7. S_bS_b varies inversely with changes in the rates of taxes on business and corporate dividend payments but directly with capital consumption allowances.

INVESTMENT BEHAVIOR

The Importance of Investment

A major role in bringing about economic prosperity is usually ascribed to investment expenditures. A high level of expenditure on plant and equipment, increasing inventories, and residential construction is generally considered to be a sign of a healthy and growing economy. For instance, an increase in the amount of productive plant and equipment enhances the output capabilities of the work force, and thus enables any given amount of labor to produce more goods for the economy. Higher output should lead to higher consumption levels and a higher standard of living. Even if there is no increase in the amount of plant and equipment, the maintenance of a given amount by means of capital replacement may have similar beneficial effects on the economy, since old plant and equipment is normally replaced by new, higher quality products.

Investment expenditures do not exhibit the same stability relative to gross national product as consumption expenditures. Table 19–1 and Figure 19–5, for example, show that investment expenditure as a percentage of gross national product has varied in recent decades from a low of 1.5 percent in 1932 to a high of 17.6 percent in 1950. Similarly, the volume of investment expenditure went from a low of $900 million in 1932 to a high in 1963 of $82.3 billion. Year-to-year variations in I are substantial.

Other data suggest that investment expenditure change may well be a source of income and output change, which in turn may induce a change in the amount of consumption expenditures. As can be seen in Table 19–2, the years of investment expenditure decline are often the years when consumption slowly increases. From 1948 to 1949, I dropped by $10.1 billion and consumption rose by $2.9 billion; from 1953 to 1954, I fell $1.4 billion, while C increased $5.4 billion. More recently, from 1957 to 1958, I dropped by $9.5 billion and, from 1960 to 1961, by $3.1 billion; during those same years *C* rose by $8 billion and $9.6 billion respectively. On the other hand, when *I* increased markedly in 1950, 1955, and 1959, there were also very sharp rises in *C*. These last three statistics are of particular significance in terms of the consumption–investment relation, because in those years government expenditure changes were small. Consequently, the relationship between *C* and *I* is more visible.

In short, the association between *C* and *I* is by no means neat, historically. Changes in *C* and *I* are clearly not proportionate, and as a consequence the

FIGURE 19–5. Investment and government expenditures for the United States, 1929–1963.

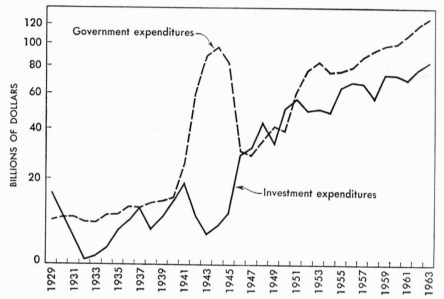

Source: Office of Business Economics, U.S. Department of Commerce, *U.S. Income and Output*, 1958; *Survey of Current Business*, July, 1963; *Federal Reserve Bulletin*, June, 1964, pp. 778–79.

relationship between *I* and *Y* change is not smooth over time. The effects of changes in tax receipts and business income must be considered. Changes in the other determinants of *C* and S_p may also occur. Thus it is the overall effect of the interaction between $S_p + S_b + T$ and $I + G + (X - M)$ that must be examined.

At present, however, we are concerned with investment demand as a source of economic change. The *importance* of *I* change to economic progress and income change is clear, but how do economists explain the fluctuations in investment behavior itself? This is the crucial question. For instance, from the perspective of economic policy, if it is felt that *I* is the variable that should be manipulated, then our analysis must provide clues as

TABLE 19–2. INVESTMENT, CONSUMPTION, GOVERNMENT EXPENDITURE, AND GROSS NATIONAL PRODUCT CHANGES FROM THE PRECEDING YEAR FOR THE UNITED STATES, 1948–1963

(IN BILLIONS OF DOLLARS)

YEAR	INVESTMENT CHANGE	CONSUMPTION CHANGE	GOVERNMENT EXPENDITURE CHANGE	$(X - M)$ CHANGE	GNP CHANGE
1948	+11.6	+12.9	+6.1	−5.5	+25.1
1949	−10.1	+2.9	+5.7	+0.3	−1.3
1950	+17.0	+13.8	−1.2	−3.2	+26.5
1951	+6.3	+14.8	+21.5	+1.8	+44.4
1952	−6.4	+10.0	+16.0	−1.1	+18.0
1953	+0.4	+12.8	+6.8	−1.7	+18.4
1954	−1.4	+5.4	−7.5	+1.6	−2.3
1955	+15.9	+18.9	+0.3	+0.1	+34.4
1956	+3.6	+13.0	+3.4	+1.8	+21.7
1957	−1.3	+15.3	+7.5	+2.0	+23.6
1958	−9.5	+8.0	+7.0	−3.7	+1.7
1959	+15.1	+20.3	+3.7	−2.0	+38.2
1960	−0.3	+15.0	+2.5	+3.7	+20.7
1961	−3.1	+9.6	+7.7	+1.1	+15.3
1962	+7.3	+18.6	+9.9	−0.2	+35.2
1963	+5.7	+16.4	+7.8	+0.7	+31.2

Source: Derived from Table 19–1. The total of the I, C, G, and $(X - M)$ changes may not be equal to the GNP change because of the rounding in Table 19–1.

to just what are the ultimate determinants of I, so that they may be properly manipulated to bring about the desired I change.

The Determinants of Investment Expenditure

In the following discussion the investment line actually describes the behavior of gross private domestic investment. The analysis does not concern itself with the components of gross private domestic investment, however, but rather with the determinants of total investment expenditures. A separate analysis could be made of the various types of investment expenditures, but economists typically refrain from doing so in order to keep their economic models relatively simple and free of the complexities that a plethora of variables would place upon them. As a consequence, we shall be concerned only with the determinants of the aggregate I. Hence for the most part our analysis assumes that the behavior of most forms of investment is comparable to that of investment in capital assets, especially productive plant and equipment.

It is generally thought that investment is determined by the marginal efficiency of investment and the rate of interest. *The marginal efficiency of investment is the after-tax expected rate of return on investment.* It is calculated as a percentage of the outlay cost of the investment. Suppose, for example, that a firm expects to increase its annual sales by $50,000 from the sale of a product they could make on a new machine. Then imagine that the annual increase in costs (principally labor and materials) of producing the additional sales is $25,000 and that the total cost of the new machine is $100,000. Given this situation, the expected rate of return as a percentage of the cost of investment, assuming that the firm is in a 50 percent tax bracket, is as follows:

$$\text{Rate of return} = \frac{\text{Change in sales} - \text{change in costs} - \text{change in taxes}}{\text{Cost of machine}}$$

$$= \frac{\$50,000 - 25,000 - .50(50,000 - 25,000)}{100,000} = \frac{12,500}{100,000} = 12\tfrac{1}{2} \text{ percent}$$

Firms are continually considering alternative investments in plant and equipment. Some potential investments will yield a high rate of return, others a low rate. What determines the cutoff point when the investment no longer appears profitable? In general terms this point is reached when the *marginal efficiency of investment is equal to the cost of getting the funds to finance the investment* project. This "cost of funds" is, of course, the interest rate.[6] Thus in the previous example if the cost of getting the funds to buy the new machine is 10 percent, it would pay for the firm to go into the project yielding 12.5 percent because total profits will be increased by the 2.5 percent spread. It will not pay the firm to make investments that yield less than 10 percent, however, because their interest costs would exceed their expected profits.

Conceptually we may visualize the relationship between the marginal efficiency of investment and the amount of desired investment for the economy as is shown in Figure 19–6. Line *II* is called the investment demand schedule. Investment demand is measured along the horizontal axis, and the marginal efficiency of investment along the vertical axis. Line *II* shows that the nature of the relationship is inverse. It assumes this shape because alternative investment projects are ranked in order of their desirability, that is, in order of their marginal efficiency of investment. All projects to the left of I_1, for example, yield in excess of 8 percent. Projects between I_1 and I_2 yield between 8 and 4 percent. We assume that firms in the economy would most like to invest in projects with a high yield. It is unlikely that they would give priority to investment in a low-yield project unless it were somehow required for business survival (in which case its yield must, in an ultimate sense, be very high, indeed). In the aggregate, however, this latter consideration is not likely to be particularly important in determining overall investment demand.

---

[6] Students of corporation finance and capital budgeting will recognize that for purposes of pedagogical simplification I am treating the cost of funds (or capital) as a constant interest cost rather than as a rising schedule. I have also used a rather oversimplified method of calculating the marginal efficiency of investment.

Now let us approach the topic in terms of the rate of interest on the vertical axis. If the interest cost is 8 percent, then business and individuals will plan to make investment expenditures only to the extent of I_1 billions of dollars. Additional investment expenditure is not apt to take place because the interest cost of getting the funds to invest in real plant and equipment would be greater than the expected return of the investment.

Given this investment schedule, changes in investment expenditure will take place only when there are variations in the rate of interest. If the

FIGURE 19–6. The investment demand schedule.

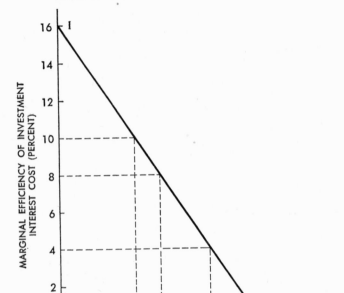

INVESTMENT DEMAND (I)
IN BILLIONS OF DOLLARS

interest rate should rise to 10 percent, for example, investment plans would drop from I_1 to I_0. Many projects that were considered profitable at 8 percent interest costs are no longer so and must be dropped from consideration. On the other hand, a drop in interest costs to 4 percent should lead to a rise in investment expenditures to I_2. There are now more projects that yield in excess of the interest costs, and hence there is a rise in investment expenditures.

On the basis of this line of reasoning, interest costs are clearly an important factor in determining the amount of investment in the economy. If interest rates are important, then such determinants of interest rates as bank lending practices, central bank monetary policy, fiscal policy, the money supply, and money demand become equally significant in determining the amount of investment demand, and hence the overall level of expenditures and gross national product.

Some economists argue, however, that interest rates are not important determinants of investment. Investment is not responsive to interest rate changes. It has been said, for example, that "remarks about the interest inelasticity of investment have been well substantiated by different types of empirical investigation."[7] Or that "Since the late 1930's there has been a general tendency to suppose that investment is relatively insensitive to the interest rate."[8]

On the other hand, recent studies tend to support the more traditional view, which was presented earlier.

The inelasticity of the marginal efficiency function is said to be confirmed by empirical observation and explained by theory. This is clearly a powerful team to contest. But the empirical evidence has recently been questioned. And the theoretical arguments which purport to explain why the function is relatively inelastic appear to be less than watertight.[9]

And again:

In order of statistical significance, variations in yields on industrial funds, on Treasury bills, and on government bonds appear to have an effect on manufacturers' fixed investment, but only with a one-year lag. The explanation offered for the relationship is that considerable time elapses between initial planning and carrying out of investment, and that interest rates serve as indices of credit availability.[10]

Thus evidence concerning the influence of interest rates on investment is contradictory. For the purposes of our analysis in this text, however, we shall treat investment as a function of the rate of interest. As the analysis in subsequent chapters will demonstrate, the model of income determination we are developing can cope with a situation where investment is either responsive or completely nonresponsive to interest rate changes.

Other influences on investment demand are taken into account by the marginal-efficiency-of-investment concept. Anything that can cause a change in the marginal efficiency of investment will lead to a change in the amount of investment at any given rate of interest. For example, if there is an increase in the marginal efficiency of investment, this means that for any given amount of investment the expected rate of return will have increased. It also means that at any given interest cost, entrepreneurs will be willing to

---

[7] L. R. Klein, *The Keynesian Revolution* (New York: The Macmillan Co., 1947), p. 65.

[8] J. Duesenberry, *Business Cycles and Economic Growth* (New York: McGraw-Hill Book Co., 1958), p. 49.

[9] Lorie Tarshis, "The Elasticity of the Marginal Efficiency Function," *American Economic Review* (1961), p. 958.

[10] Franz Gehrels and Suzanne Wiggins, "Interest Rates and Manufacturers' Fixed Investment," *American Economic Review* (1957), p. 91.

spend more on investment goods and services than formerly because more projects may now be undertaken profitably.

Figure 19–7 illustrates a shift of this sort. Line II is the original investment schedule. Line $I'I'$ represents the new investment schedule. In terms of investment I_1, this shift increases the return over cost from i_1 to i_2. If the interest cost is originally i and remains unchanged, then the differential

FIGURE 19–7. Changes in the investment demand schedule.

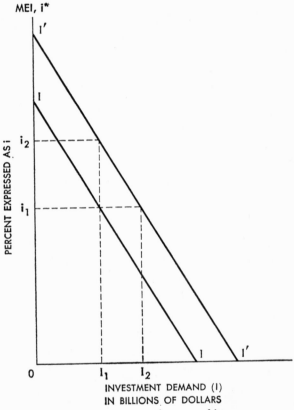

* MEI = marginal efficiency of investment; i = rate of interest.

between the rate of interest and the expected return permits an increase in investment expenditures to take place from I_1 to I_2.

Some of the more important forces that influence the marginal efficiency of investment and hence the investment schedule are (1) income, (2) technology, (3) cost of labor and materials, (4) government tax policies, and (5) business expectations.

The *general level of income*, Y, is an important source of investment change. As income grows, demand for product grows stronger, too. Thus it is likely that businesses will expand their demand for productive plant and equipment in order to tool up to meet anticipated product demand and expected profit margins. The closer a business enterprise operates to full capacity, the more likely it is that there will be investment expenditure increases as final product demand continues to exert a strong pull on the economy. On the other hand, when there is a decline in the economy, there is excess productive capacity, and anticipated final product demand and planned investment expenditures will be low. For instance, as was shown in Table 19–2, the years of greatest investment increase were in periods of prosperity, whereas the largest investment decreases occurred in recessions. This would seem to indicate that investment is dependent upon the level and rate of increase of income. The larger the growth of income, the greater the need for plant and equipment to meet increasing consumption demand needs.

Technological change is another important factor that may function as a source of change in the marginal efficiency of investment. When a cost-saving innovation takes place, the rate of return from investment will increase. For instance, in our previous example on page 323, if a technological advance permits the firm to produce more product, say $60,000 worth, at the same cost of labor and materials and if the price of the machine is the same, then the expected rate of return as a percentage of the cost of investment is

$$\frac{\$60,000 - 25,000 - 17,500}{100,000} = 17.5 \text{ percent}$$

The cost per unit of output will have been reduced, allowing greater production or the same production, but at a lower total cost. Either way the expected rate of return has increased.

Variations in the *cost of labor and materials* will also influence investment demand. If union pressures raise labor cost, for example, then expected costs on investment projects will also rise. As a result, the expected rate of return will diminish. An increase in raw material costs would have the same effect.

Government tax policies are also important. If taxes on business enterprise are decreased, the after-tax profits accruing from any investment project increase, raising the expected rate of return. Similarly, government revision of depreciation schedules and depletion allowances would also affect investment demand. If businesses are allowed to write off the cost of their plant and equipment over a shorter period of time, during any given year while plant and equipment are being depreciated, for example, more funds are available to businesses. This increase in available funds permits businesses to seek additional investment opportunities.

Business expectations of future trends in the economy are of special significance as a determinant of investment demand. In some ways this factor is related to the current level of income and output. If Y is high and rising, expectations will probably be favorable for investment spending. On the other hand, a declining Y may generate adverse expectations and lead to a decline in investment expenditures. Expectations may be influenced by many considerations, however. The prospects of war may lead equipment producers to expect government orders and induce preparations for capacity expansion, for example. Legislative talk of tax revisions may cause businesses to postpone investment outlays until the precise nature of the reforms is known. In this respect, uncertainty and anticipation concerning the future clearly influence investment. Expected increases in the cost of equipment will cause investment expenditures to be made prior to the time they would otherwise have occurred. Similarly, falling stock prices may cause concern about the future and induce investment decreases even in a healthy economy. Although it is impossible to predict what specifically will cause business expectations to change, the factors cited above have a potentially important effect on the economy that should be kept in mind.

In general, the factors that increase expected receipts or reduce expected costs lead to an increase in the marginal efficiency of investment; they cause a shift of the investment demand schedule upward and to the right. The factors that decrease the marginal efficiency of investment cause a shift downward and to the left.

The Investment Demand Equation

We have already explained that investment is determined by the interaction of the rate of interest and the marginal efficiency of investment and that the latter is determined primarily by income, technology, the cost of labor and materials, government tax policies, and business expectations. Of these five forces one is so important that it is often studied separately. That determinant is income. Thus it can be said that investment is determined by i, the rate of interest, Y, gross national product, and U', whch represents the forces other than Y that also help determine the marginal efficiency of investment. In equation form this reads

$$I = f(i, Y, U') \qquad [19\text{--}5]$$

The relationship between interest and investment is inverse. The higher the level of interest costs, the smaller the amount of investment demand becomes; the lower the level of interest costs, the greater the amount of investment demand becomes. The relationship between investment and income is positive, however. The higher the level of income, the greater is the investment demand; the lower the level of income, the lower is the investment demand. When the forces (U') determining the marginal efficiency of investment increase it, investment demand increases; when these forces decrease the marginal efficiency of investment, investment demand decreases.

The relationship between income and investment is shown diagrammatically in Figure 19–8. I, investment demand, is measured on the vertical axis and Y on the horizontal axis. Line II slopes upward and to the right, indicat-

FIGURE 19–8. The relationship between investment and income.

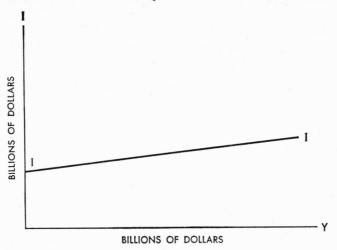

ing that the higher the level of income and output, the greater the investment demand of businesses. It is drawn as a straight line purely for the sake of simplicity.[11]

ADDING GOVERNMENT EXPENDITURES AND THE BALANCE OF TRADE TO THE EQUATION

We have said that when plans for $S_p + S_b + T$ differ from the plans for $I + G + (X - M)$, changes in income will take place. Earlier in this chapter we discussed the relationship between $S_p + S_b + T$ and Y. To complete our discussion we need to show the relationship between $I + G + (X - M)$ and Y.

Line GG in Figure 19–9 shows the relationship between government expenditures and GNP. The line is drawn parallel to the horizontal axis. There is no change in G as Y increases along the horizontal axis because the level of government spending is assumed to be independent of the level of income and output. Instead, as we shall see, the position of line GG is determined by legislative action. An increase in government spending shifts the line upward; a decrease moves it down.

Like tax receipts, government expenditures are determined by legislative action, and legislative action is principally influenced by considerations

---

[11] This investment demand line differs from that in Figures 19–6 and 19–7 where we were concerned with the relationship between investment and the rate of interest. In Figure 19–8 we are simply demonstrating the positive relationship between I and Y, and hence it is assumed that i and U' are fixed. If i increases, then line II in Figure 19–8 must shift down because of the inverse relationship between I and i. If the marginal efficiency of investment decreases, line II must also shift down.

other than the current level of income and employment. During inflation, it is true, there is considerable talk of the need to hold down government expenditures, while in a recession expenditure increases are urged upon the legislature. For the most part, however, federal expenditures on final goods and services are influenced primarily by national defense considerations, and state and local expenditures are determined largely by the need for social goods and services such as highways and schools. Noneconomic variables of this sort seem to play a more important role in determining the level of governmental expenditures than the current level of income and employment do.

FIGURE 19–9. The relationship between I, G, F, and Y.

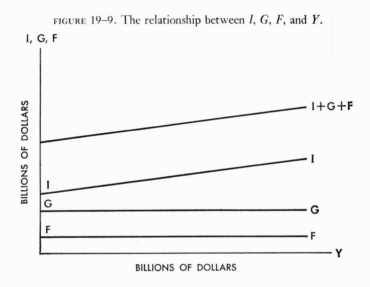

Tables 19–1 and 19–2 and Figure 19–5 show the growth of government expenditures in recent decades. As might be expected, the greatest increase came during World War II, when in 1943 government expenditures, as a percentage of GNP, reached a high of 46 percent. Immediately after the war there was a sharp decline in defense spendings and government spendings as a percentage of GNP, fell back to the levels of the 1930's. During the first five postwar years, government expenditures averaged 13.9 percent of GNP. With the advent of the Korean conflict defense expenditures increased, and in 1953 all government expenditures as a percentage of GNP reached 22.7 percent. Following the Korean conflict there was some reduction in defense spending but not enough to bring government spendings back into their relationship to GNP of the 1930's and late 1940's. Since 1954 this relationship has varied between 18.9 and 21.4 percent. It is federal expenditures that have been somewhat volatile, largely because of variations in our defense needs. In contrast, state and local expenditures in the post-World War II period have grown steadily in volume year in and year out.

Putting these considerations into equation form, we have

$$G = f(Z) \qquad\qquad [19\text{--}6]$$

This equation tells us that G, total government expenditures, is a function of Z, a variable representing those forces that cause legislatures to change government spending. This variable is the same as the Z variable that stood for all the forces that cause the legislature to change the tax rate.

The difference between exports and imports, X — M, is also assumed to be independent of the level of income. Let F be X — M. Line FF in Figure 19–9 represents F, the difference between exports and imports, and illustrates the independence of Y and F. It shifts with changes in the forces that determine the volume of imports and exports. Line FF is above the horizontal axis when exports exceed imports and beneath it when imports exceed exports.

The equation for the difference between exports and imports, F, is

$$F = f(J) \qquad\qquad [19\text{--}7]$$

F is a function of J, a variable representing the forces that cause F to change.

In some ways the assumption that F is independent of the level of income is rather unrealistic; imports do depend on the level of income in one's own country. When income and output levels increase at home, people may be expected to increase their consumption of home-produced goods and services *and* also their consumption of goods produced abroad. Likewise, if incomes decrease at home, the public will probably purchase less of both domestic- and foreign-produced goods and services. Thus if exports remain constant and if the other determinants of imports remain unchanged, F should increase during recession and decrease with the rising incomes of prosperity.

The available data seem to support this line of reasoning. Table 19–3 lists the volume of exports and imports for the post–World War II period. Imports tended to decrease in the recession years of 1949 and 1954, but in other recession years, 1958 and 1961, they only leveled off; they did not fall. Conversely, during prosperous periods imports usually increased. The effects of these various changes in imports upon F, however, are barely discernible because exports did not remain constant.

Just as U.S. imports depend upon national income levels, so do our exports depend upon income levels abroad. If incomes increase abroad, foreigners will demand more of their own goods and also more U.S.-produced goods. Thus, variations in foreign incomes will cause changes in U.S. exports and in F. This seems to cancel out any inverse relationship between F and Y in the United States that arises from the positive relationship between imports and Y.

Furthermore, American imports and exports do not operate independently of one another. When U.S. imports increase because of U.S. income increases, U.S. exports eventually increase also, because an increased demand for foreign goods by U.S. citizens induces other nations to increase their production. As this happens, income and output abroad increase, enabling foreigners to demand more American goods. This leads to increased U.S. exports and incomes. Thus, the greater the extent to which U.S. purchases are concentrated in countries that in turn make heavy purchases in the United States, the more likely it is that increases in U.S. output will lead to both import and export increases for the United States. For these reasons, it is difficult to establish a definite relationship between F (the difference

TABLE 19–3. EXPORTS, IMPORTS, AND NET
EXPORTS OF GOODS AND SERVICES FOR
THE UNITED STATES, 1946–1963
(IN BILLIONS OF DOLLARS)

YEAR	EXPORTS	IMPORTS	NET EXPORTS
1946	12.8	7.9	4.9
1947	17.9	8.9	9.0
1948	14.5	11.0	3.5
1949	14.0	10.2	3.8
1950	13.1	12.5	0.6
1951	17.9	15.5	2.4
1952	17.4	16.1	1.3
1953	16.6	17.0	−0.4
1954	17.5	16.5	1.0
1955	19.4	18.3	1.1
1956	23.1	20.2	2.9
1957	26.2	21.3	4.9
1958	22.7	21.5	1.2
1959	22.9	23.6	−0.8
1960	26.4	23.5	2.9
1961	27.3	23.3	4.0
1962	28.4	25.2	3.2
1963	30.7	27.2	3.5

Source: Office of Business Economics, U.S. Department of Commerce, *U.S. Income and Output*, 1958; *Survey of Current Business*, 1959–64.

between exports and imports) and the level of output in the United States. If exports change as discussed above, then it is equally possible that there will be either a direct or an inverse relationship between F and Y.

Relative prices between countries and official trade policies are some of the other factors that affect the position of line FF. If prices in the United States decline relative to those abroad, both U.S. citizens and foreigners will demand more U.S. goods. The relative drop in U.S. prices induces a greater demand for U.S. goods. On the other hand, if prices in the United States rise relative to those abroad, there will be a shift to the less expensive goods produced outside the United States.

Changes in national trade policies will also affect the shape of the *FF* line. If the United States were to impose more trade restrictions and thus make it more difficult for Americans to buy abroad, imports would decline and, other things being equal, the *FF* line would rise. Other things, of course, do not always remain the same. Thus if we were to make it more difficult for Americans to import, other nations would probably retaliate and restrict their imports from the United States. On the other hand, trade-relaxing arrangements such as the Trade Agreements Act of 1934 and the Trade Expansion Act of 1962 can lead to an increase in international trade and a corresponding rise in both exports and imports.

The $I + G + F$ *Line*

The line $I + G + F$ in Figure 19-9 represents the sum of the three separate lines *II*, *GG*, and *FF*. It is drawn parallel to *II* because investment is the only variable that changes with income and output. This line will shift upward with upward movements in any of the lines that represent its components and downward with downward movements in the component lines. The component lines in turn will shift when changes occur in their determinants other than Y.

INCOME DETERMINATION

Figure 19–10 shows how the $S_p + S_b + T$ and $I + G + F$ lines interact to determine the income levels in the economy. In drawing these lines we are assuming, of course, that the determinants of each of these lines (and consequently of Y) other than those listed are fixed.

Given lines $S_p + S_b + T$ and $(I + G + F)_0$, assume that the economy is initially producing at a rate of Y_1 billion dollars per year; at that rate of output, the planned expenditures on $I + G + F$ exceed $S_p + S_b + T$, the planned withdrawals from the income stream. Under these circumstances, a strong force for income change exists; there is excess demand. More goods and services are wanted than are being produced. Inventories of goods are being depleted. Businesses usually respond to this situation by increasing output, which in turn leads to increased incomes, consumption, personal saving, business disposable income, government tax takes, and investment. Thus C, S_p, S_b, T, and I have all increased because each is partly determined by Y. These forces tend to increase income to Y_2.

On the other hand, if the rate of output is Y_3, then the planned income withdrawals, $S_p + S_b + T$, exceed expenditures on $I + G + F$. Not all that is produced by business is sold, and contraction takes place. Only at income level Y_2 will the amount produced in the economy equal the amount demanded. At this point the economy is in equilibrium.

The critical assumption for the preceding analysis is that other things remain the same. In the real world, however, other things are in almost continuous flux. Fortunately, our model of income determination enables us to predict the direction of economic change with some semblance of accuracy in spite of the almost continual variation in real world conditions, since changes in these conditions usually occur slowly and in limited magnitudes.

Any of the forces that lead to a shift of either $S_p + S_b + T$ or $I + G + F$ may lead to a change in Y. The nature of these changes was discussed earlier in this chapter and will be summarized briefly again at its conclusion.

FIGURE 19–10. Income determination.

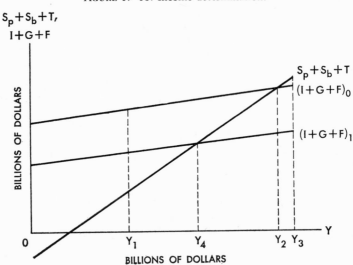

Let us examine one change in detail, however: a decrease in government expenditures. Assume that the economy is initially in equilibrium at Y_2. A decrease in G will then shift the $I + G + F$ line down to $(I + G + F)_1$. Now there is excess supply at Y_2. Investment and consumption spending contract, and actual personal saving, business disposable income, and the government tax receipts decrease also. A new equilibrium income level is reached at Y_4.

Looking a bit more closely at this situation, we see what happens as the government decreases its rate of expenditures. With a smaller demand for output, business must reduce its rate of output or be faced with mounting inventories. With reduced output, employment declines, payments of wages and salaries drop, and personal disposable income decreases. With lower incomes, individuals must reduce their rate of consumption expenditures. People are reluctant to accept a drop in their standard of living, however, and because of this when they reduce their consumption expenditures they will not reduce them by as much as their disposable income has fallen. Consequently their rate of personal saving also falls. Investment by businesses decreases because of reduced orders and lower Y. The induced consumption and investment expenditure decreases will cause income and output to fall even further. Business disposable income also decreases because of inadequate demand and the probability of falling profit margins as businesses produce at substantially less than optimum levels. Finally, government tax collections decrease because they are geared to the level of income. Ultimately, Y will have dropped by some multiple of the reduction in government expenditures.

The overall drop in Y from Y_2 to Y_4 is greater than the drop in government expenditures because of the fact that a drop in Y induces decreases in consumption demand and investment expenditures. Thus there are a series of decreases in Y, C, and I. Each successive decrease, however, is smaller than the preceding one. The fact that people divide their falling incomes between consumption and saving decreases reduces the size of the successive income decreases arising out of the induced consumption expenditure decreases. Similarly, businesses drop their investment expenditures by only a small portion of their income decreases, since they are interested in maintaining their productive capacity.[12]

THE RELATIONSHIP BETWEEN *Y* AND *i*

The income determination process just described assumed one very important variable to be constant: the rate of interest. It will be recalled that both personal saving and investment are a function of interest-rate changes. Thus a different amount of saving and investment takes place at every dif-

---

[12] Economists frequently employ what is called *multiplier analysis* to predict Y changes from changes in government spendings, changes in investment arising out of U' changes, or changes in consumption arising out of W and X changes. This multiplier analysis makes the assumption, however, that there are no rate-of-interest changes. This is a very unrealistic assumption and significantly impairs the usefulness of the comparatively simple multiplier analysis as employed in the classroom.

The concept of the multiplier may be briefly described as follows. Assume that taxes and business disposable income are zero and are not geared to level of income. Further assume that there is no F, and that I and G are fixed amounts. Then the marginal propensity to consume, $\Delta C/\Delta Y_d$, is equal to $\Delta C/\Delta Y$; and $\Delta S_p/\Delta Y_d$ equals $\Delta S_p/\Delta Y$. If this is the case, the ratio of the change in Y to a change in autonomous spending (ΔI or ΔG) will be equal to $1/1 - \Delta C/\Delta Y$. This is known as the *simple spendings multiplier* and can help us predict Y changes from I and G changes. The difference between ΔY and ΔI or ΔG would be induced consumption expenditure change. For example, assume that the marginal propensity to consume is .8. Substituting into the multiplier formula we get $1/1 - .8$ or 5. This tells us that if government expenditures decrease, for example, by \$1 billion, the overall decrease in income induced will be \$5 billion, \$1 billion in the form of reduced government expenditures and \$4 billion in reduced consumption spending. In terms of Figure 19–10, if the slope of the lines were drawn according to these assumptions it would mean that Y_4 is \$5 billion less than Y_2.

FIGURE 19-11. Income determination when the interest rate changes.

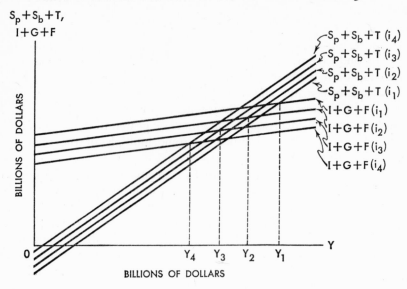

FIGURE 19-12. The relationship between the rate of interest and the equilibrium level of income.

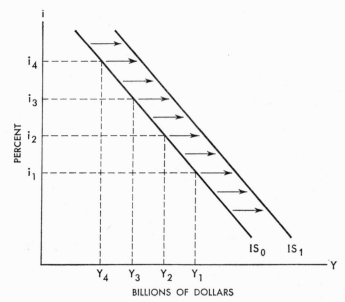

ferent rate of interest, and consequently equilibrium income varies with the interest rate, also.

Figures 19–11 and 19–12 illustrate this relationship. Successively higher interest rates are represented by i_1, i_2, i_3, and i_4 in Figure 19–11. Each higher rate of interest leads to a successively lower $I + G + F$ line. On the other hand, each higher rate of interest leads to a successively higher $S_p + S_b + T$ line and, as a consequence, equilibrium income levels become successively lower. If, for example, the rate of interest is initially i_1, equilibrium income is Y_1. If i is increased to i_3, other things being given, there is excess supply and income and output contract toward Y_3.

The relationship between these alternative rates of interest and the equilibrium income levels that correspond to them is plotted in Figure 19–12 as IS_0. The relationship is inverse; the higher the rate of interest rises, the lower the level of equilibrium income sinks. The line illustrating this relationship is called the *IS line*. At every point on this line, income is in equilibrium, that is, planned $I + G + F$ equals planned $S_p + S_b + T$. This type of equilibrium is frequently called *commodity market equilibrium* because the demand for C, I, G, and F type commodities equals the supply of those products.

The *IS* line is an important link in our model of income determination. Given the personal saving, business disposable income, tax, government spending, and net export functions, the *level of income is determined by the investment function*. Given the marginal efficiency of investment, *the rate of interest determines investment spending*. This further illustrates the economic importance of the rate of interest. Given the *IS* line, there is a different possible level of equilibrium income for every different rate of interest. We cannot determine the actual equilibrium Y until we know the rate of interest and how it is determined, however. This will be taken up in Chapter 20.

SUMMARY OF FORCES AFFECTING *IS*

Bringing together the various functions described in this chapter we are able to illustrate what happens to the *IS* line given various changes in the economy. In general, anything other than i which can cause $I + G + F$ to shift upward or $S_p + S_b + T$ to shift downward will move the position of the *IS* line to the right. For example, in Figure 19–11, all the $I + G + F$ lines will rise with an increase in government spending. Hence equilibrium income, as determined by the intersection of the $S_p + S_b + T$ and $I + G + F$ lines for a particular rate of interest, will be attained at a point farther to the right. This means that there is a new *IS* line to the right of the old one. The line IS_1 in Figure 19–12 illustrates one such possible new location for *IS*. The new position tells us that equilibrium income will now be higher at any given rate of interest. The new income and output will, of course, be some multiple of the government spending increase. Induced expansions of consumption and investment will have occurred.

On the other hand, anything which tends to lower $I + G + F$ or raise $S_p + S_b + T$ shifts *IS* to the left, causing a contraction in Y at any given rate of interest.

More specifically:

1.
$$S_p = f(Y_d, i, W, X) \qquad [19\text{--}1]$$

Given X, S_p varies directly with Y_d (personal disposable income) and i (rate of interest), and inversely with W (liquid wealth). When liquid wealth increases or decreases, IS shifts to the right or left respectively.

2.
$$T = f(Y, Z) \qquad [19\text{--}3]$$

Government taxes are determined by legislative action (Z). Given Z, T (government tax take) varies directly with Y. A change in Z leads to a change in tax rate. If tax rates increase, T increases at all income levels and IS shifts to the left. A decrease in tax rates moves the IS line to the right.

3.
$$S_b = f(Y, U) \qquad [19\text{--}4]$$

Given U, S_b varies directly with Y. A change in U (all those forces other than Y which affect business disposable income) leads to a change in S_b. If, because of U changes, S_b increases at any given income level, IS moves to the left. If S_p decreases at any given income level, IS moves to the right.

4.
$$I = f(i, Y, U') \qquad [19\text{--}5]$$

I (investment demand) varies inversely with i (rate of interest) and directly with Y (level of income). U' stands for the forces that change the marginal efficiency of investment. If these determinants of the marginal efficiency of investment cause it to increase, the IS line moves to the right. Thus a decrease in the costs of production or enhanced profit expectations lead to increases in IS. On the other hand, an increase in the costs of production or worsened profit expectations decrease IS.

5.
$$G = f(Z) \qquad [19\text{--}6]$$

Government expenditures are determined by legislative action (Z). Increases and decreases in G will move IS to the right and left respectively.

6.
$$F = f(J) \qquad [19\text{--}7]$$

IS moves to the right or left with increases or decreases respectively in F (the difference between exports and imports) caused by changes in J (the forces that lead to import and export changes).

Supplementary Readings

See end of Chapter 20.

Chapter 20

A Model of Income Determination, Part II

The preceding chapter demonstrated that, given the commodity market equilibrium line $(IS,)$ there is a different level of equilibrium income for each different rate of interest. Thus, to determine equilibrium income, an equilibrium rate of interest needs to be determined. This chapter adds monetary supply and demand to our contemporary model of income determination and demonstrates how they interact with $I + G + F$ and $S_p + S_b + T$ to establish equilibrium income, Y, and equilibrium interest, i.

THE DEMAND FOR MONEY

People want money for many reasons. Households demand money to purchase goods and services, to hold for future purchases of goods and services, to hold for unforeseen contingencies, to avoid the loss that is possible on other forms of liquid wealth, and to have funds ready to make financial investments when suitable profit opportunities arise. Businesses demand money for the same reasons but are more likely to minimize cash balances in an effort to maximize profits. Governments also demand money, primarily to buy goods and services. It is customary to exclude federal government money holdings from the money stock, however.[1]

Money is not the only asset that can satisfy these motives for holding money. At any point in time, an individual may hold his wealth in the form of money, other liquid assets, or real wealth. Only one of these assets, of course, can serve directly as a medium of exchange in the purchase of goods and services—money itself. Thus a decision to hold money necessarily involves a decision not to hold that amount of wealth in other assets. When a householder or business enterprise decides to increase expenditures, wealth holdings are redistributed from money to goods. This means that the wealth

---

[1] It will be recalled that the money stock consists of currency and demand deposit holdings of the nonbank public. When the government taxes and spends, both the velocity and amount of money held by the nonbank public may vary.

holdings of both the purchaser and the seller of goods will change in composition.

Generally, other things being given, *the demand for money*, and hence the asset composition of total wealth, *is determined by* Y, *the rate of expenditures on gross national product*, i, *the rate of interest, and* W', *total wealth*. Put into equation form we have

$$M_d = f(Y, i, W', X') \qquad [20\text{--}1]$$

where M_d is the demand for money, Y is gross national product, i is the rate of interest, W' is total wealth, and X' represents other variables that may influence the demand for money.

The Relationship Between the Demand for Money and GNP

Other things being given, the relationship between the demand for money and the rate of expenditures is positive. The greater the expenditures are, the more money is needed to make those expenditures. The smaller the rate of spending becomes, the less money is needed. The demand for money, however, will always be a fraction of the rate of expenditures. Since expenditures and income receipts occur over a period of time, the average amount of funds held during a period of time will usually be less than the total amount of expenditures.

If the rate at which funds are received and the rate at which expenditures are made remain unchanged, then the demand for money should remain the same. If expected expenditures increase, however, and the rate of income remains the same, then the amount of money demanded will increase; otherwise the expected expenditure increases will not take place. The additional funds will be acquired by selling security holdings, converting time deposits into money, or borrowing from banks. Should expected expenditures decline, on the other hand, there is less need for money to carry out transactions. Money will grow idle, and there may be an effort by the holders of these idle balances to lend to others, convert demand deposits into time deposits, or make profitable use of the funds in some other way.

Although M_d is directly related to transactions, it should be emphasized that the measure of transactions being used in our analysis is Y, gross national product. As was explained in Chapter 17, total transactions in the economy are greater than gross national product. Money is used to effectuate many types of transactions that do not involve the purchase of newly produced final goods such as the purchase and sale of intermediate goods, the purchase and sale of goods produced in earlier income periods, and the purchase and sale of stocks and bonds. The use of money for these transactions causes a total demand for money that is greater than the amount of gross national product.

The Relationship Between the Demand for Money and the Interest Rate

The *interest rate* employed in our analysis is a *weighted average cost of all methods of financing available in the economy*. The cost of each source of funds is weighted according to its relative importance in financing. Thus, for example, if there were only two sources of funds, 4 percent and 6 percent bonds, and the volume of bonds outstanding in each class was $1 million and $5 million respectively, then the average cost of funds would be

$$\frac{\$40,000 + \$300,000 \text{ (annual interest costs)}}{\$1,000,000 + \$5,000,000 \text{ (total value of bonds)}}$$

or 5⅔ percent.

Actually there are a great many different ways of getting funds in the economy, and each has a cost attached to it. There are the short- and long-term rates of interest on U.S. government securities. There are the interest costs on privately issued industrial, public utility, and railroad bonds. There are the dividend costs to issuers of corporate stocks. In addition, there are the short-term costs of trade credit, of borrowing from commercial banks, of borrowing from consumer finance companies, and of borrowing from sales finance companies. Therefore, to examine the effects of the interest rate on the demand for money, we should really study the whole spectrum of rates. This would necessitate some extremely complex calculations, however. Thus, to simplify our explanation of this relationship we use the average cost of all methods of financing on the assumption that there is some stable functional relationship between the yields of all types of financing instruments.

The relationship between the rate of interest, i, and the demand for money, M_d, as we have defined them for the purposes of this analysis, is inverse. Other things being equal, the lower the rate of interest becomes, the greater the amount of money that is demanded. Conversely, the higher the rate of interest becomes, the less money is demanded.

There are a number of reasons why the demand for money increases as interest rates decline. First, business borrowers demand more funds since the widening spread between the expected return from the use of funds and the cost of getting the funds permits an increase in profitable investment expenditures.

Second, with easier credit, consumers also plan to increase their expenditures and borrowings.

Third, as interest rates decline, lenders become less willing to lend. Interest is regarded by many financial investors as a compensation for risks of investment. Barring price inflation, there is no possibility of loss if funds are held in the form of money other than the sacrifice resulting from not having an interest return on idle funds. Stocks and bonds, however, fluctuate in value. Government bonds and privately issued securities frequently sell beneath par. Thus if bonds are not held to maturity, the holder may sustain a capital loss. Furthermore, some companies are unable to redeem their bonds. Similarly, in the event of liquidation many stockholders do not receive the book value of their stock holdings. All of these risks combine to inhibit lenders from purchasing stocks and bonds. As a consequence, borrowers offer an interest return on bonds and a dividend yield on equities as compensation to the lender for giving up liquidity and certain command over goods and services. Therefore, when interest rates decline, the compensation for the risks of investment is reduced, and the willingness of lenders to lend falls accordingly.

Finally, when interest rates have dropped below a certain point, some speculators may wish to hold more of their funds in the form of money because they expect that interest rates will reverse themselves. By getting into money and out of bonds, for example, they may hope to avoid the capital losses that occur to bond holdings as a result of rising interest rates.

On the other hand, as interest rates rise, the amount of money demanded decreases. Lenders become more willing to sacrifice the safety afforded by idle money balances for the chances of profit afforded by higher interest rates; their willingness to lend increases. Borrowers, however, prefer to pay off debt rather than incur the higher costs of borrowing. Fewer consumers borrow for this reason. Businesses find that the cost of funds has increased relative to expected returns from investment, and business borrowing and investment expenditures both decrease as a consequence. Speculators reduce their demand for money and increase their demand for securities so that they may make capital gains if rates subsequently decline as they expect.

The demand-for-money schedule. This functional relationship between the demand for money and the rate of interest is depicted in Figure 20–1. The rate of interest, i, is measured along the vertical axis, and the demand for money, M_d, is measured along the horizontal axis. The line that is labeled LL represents the amount of money that is desired at varying rates of interest, other things being given. It slopes downward and to the right, showing the inverse relationship between the demand for money and the rate of interest. The position of LL, as will be explained in a moment, depends upon the value of the other determinants of the demand for money, such as gross national product.

As drawn, line LL continues to slope downward and to the right as the rate of interest declines. Frequently, however, this line is shown as becoming parallel to the horizontal axis at some low minimum rate of interest. At this rate, the demand for money becomes perfectly elastic; the yield on securities is so low that it does not pay investors to incur the inconvenience and risk of converting money into securities. The yield may even be so low that it will not cover the broker's fees for the purchase of securities. When such a point is reached, the general expectation will be that interest rates must soon reverse. As a consequence, no matter how much money is available in the economy, all of it will be demanded by the public at the low minimum rate of interest. This concept of a perfectly elastic segment of the demand for money curve is called *the liquidity trap*. It is depicted in Figure 20–1 as the dotted part of the demand-for-money line starting at rate of interest i_1. We have drawn the LL line downward and to the right beyond i_1 because we are building a general model of income determination. The liquidity trap is in many ways a special case, which some economists argue cannot be verified empirically. More will be said of this in Chapter 21.

FIGURE 20–1. The demand-for-money schedule.

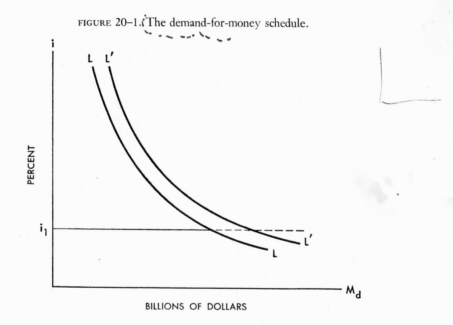

The Relationship Between the Demand for Money
and Total Wealth

The relationship between the demand for money and total wealth is positive also. The greater the volume of wealth becomes, the more demand there is for money. Wealth increases as income and output increase. Thus the demand for all economic goods, including money, increases. In other words, if wealth rises, the demand for all components of wealth should rise also, provided that they are superior goods.[2] Assuming that individuals seek to maintain some optimum distribution among their different types of wealth

---

[2] A "superior good" in this context may be defined as one for which there is an increase in demand as income and wealth increase. An inferior good is one that experiences a decrease in demand as income and wealth increase. Most goods are superior in this sense of the word. Some low-cost goods such as potatoes and bread will be inferior goods, however.

holdings, it follows that if the amount of wealth held in one particular form increases, then this optimum distribution of wealth is disturbed. The situation may be corrected by increasing the amounts held in the other forms of wealth, and people usually attempt to do this by reducing part of their increased holdings in the form that was recently increased. In this manner, the optimum distribution of wealth can be re-established. Similarly, the optimum distribution of wealth can be disturbed by a reduction in the amount of a particular wealth form. When this occurs, there is an increase in the demand for that particular wealth form and a decrease in the demand for other forms.

It follows from the preceding that the demand for money will increase when the desired ratio of money to total wealth is disturbed by an increase in total wealth that is unaccompanied by a proportionate increase in the stock of money. Similarly, the demand for money will decrease when the desired ratio of money to total wealth is disturbed by a decrease in total wealth that is unaccompanied by a proportionate decrease in the stock of money.

Thus, if it is the money stock that increases relative to other wealth forms, then the demand for other forms increase and the demand for money decreases, but not by as much as the total of the money stock increase. On the other hand, if there is a decrease in the money stock relative to other wealth forms, then the demand for other forms decreases and the demand for money increases, but not by as much as the initial money stock decrease.

The significance of total wealth as a determinant of the demand for money should not be overemphasized, however. Economists generally regard i and Y as more important determinants of the demand for money, since these variables can change quickly, whereas the total volume of wealth in the economy is so large that percentage changes in the total are actually very small and occur only over sizable stretches of time. Thus wealth is regarded as a long-run determinant of the demand for money. Liquid wealth, however, does change comparatively quickly. Since the total of liquid wealth, at least that part of it that is in the form of near monies, is only a fraction of total wealth, percentage changes in liquid wealth are thought to be significant as a determinant of both the demand for money and the demand for consumer goods and services.[3]

The Relationship Between the Demand for Money and Other Variables

X' is a variable that represents all the other forces that can influence the demand for money, such as price expectations, future income expectation,

---

[3] It will be recalled that in Chapter 19 W, liquid wealth, was used as a determinant of consumption demand and personal saving.

the desired distribution of the various wealth forms, and the various factors discussed by Irving Fisher and Dennis Robertson (see Table 17–2).

Saying that people expect *prices* to increase is another way of saying that they expect the purchasing power of money to decline. In such a situation, therefore, it pays for them to transfer their funds from money to other assets such as consumer durable goods and equities, for these assets do not normally decrease in price as the price level rises. Instead, their prices accompany the general movement upward in the price level. Thus, with expectations of rising prices, the demand for money decreases. Conversely, expectation of falling *prices* means that people believe that the purchasing power of money will increase. As a consequence they will demand more money, reduce their expenditures, and reduce their holdings of goods that decline in value.

The expectation that future *incomes* will rise simply means that people believe they will be getting more money receipts in the future, thus enhancing their ability to buy goods and services. In anticipation of this, people may decrease their current demand for money and increase their current expenditures. The expectation of decreased incomes, however, means that people feel they will need additional money balances to cover future outlays. Therefore the current demand for money will increase, and the current rate of expenditures will drop.

If the desired *distribution* of wealth changes, then the demand for individual wealth components will also change. For example, in the United States, the number of alternative liquid wealth forms has increased in recent years. The comparatively recent development of such liquid wealth forms as savings and loan association share accounts, pension funds, and credit union share accounts has increased the number of wealth forms competing with money. Similarly, the number of new types of goods and services available each year creates additional uses to which money may be put. The greater the number of goods (liquid and non-liquid) competing with money, the less demand there is to hold money as an asset.

The various forces mentioned by Irving Fisher and Dennis Robertson also affect the demand for money. These are all primarily long-term factors, however. For example, the increased use of installment credit lengthens the period of payment on high-priced commodities. This has reduced the need to accumulate money balances. The more credit is used, the less money is needed. Another closely related factor is the system of payments in the community. The more often and the more regularly people are paid, the less money they need to keep on hand. The more regularly disbursements can be made, the easier it becomes to match receipts and disbursements. Hence there is less need to hold money in reserve for unpredictable expenditures. The increasing use of credit, particularly that variety which involves monthly payments, regularizes expenditures. These are long-term changes, however; institutional changes are only made gradually.

The Demand-for-Money Schedule and Changes
in GNP, Total Wealth, and Other Variables

The demand-for-money line shown in Figure 20–1 depicts how the demand for money varies according to the interest rate, other things being equal. Obviously, however, the other determinants of the demand for money, such as Y, W', and X', do not remain unchanged. Suppose Y increases, for example. This causes the demand for money to increase no matter what the rate of interest. This will cause the LL line to shift to the right to a new position represented by $L'L'$ in Figure 20–1. Suppose, on the other hand, that there is a decrease in income and output. This will lead to a decrease in the demand for money and a shift to the left of the LL line. From this we deduce that there is a whole family of money-demand lines relating the demand for money to the rate of interest. Each line must be representative of the demand for money at different levels of income. Figure 20–2 describes this relationship. Successive LL lines are representative of the demand for money at successively higher levels of income, Y_1, Y_2, Y_3, and Y_4. Each higher level of income leads in turn to a successively greater demand for money, and, consequently, an LL line that is farther to the right. Lower income levels lead to successively lower demands for money and LL lines that are farther to the left.

Changes in W' also lead to changes in LL. Higher wealth levels will raise the demand for money and hence shift LL to the right. Lower wealth levels will lower the demand for money and shift LL to the left. Similarly, to the extent that the forces included in X' operate to increase or decrease the demand for money, LL will shift its position also.

Gross national product, rate of interest, and demand for money are factors that can change rapidly. Total wealth and the forces represented by X', however, usually change gradually. Thus it is relatively accurate to take the family of money-demand lines as a hypothetical representation of the relationship between Y, i, and M_d in the short run. In other words, *given* W' *and* X', M_d *varies directly with* Y *and inversely with* i.

THE INTERACTION OF THE DEMAND
FOR MONEY AND THE SUPPLY OF MONEY

In addition to the demand-for-money lines, Figure 20–2 shows the supply of money schedule MM as developed in Chapter 15. Assuming that income is fixed at Y_1, there is one money demand line and the money supply line, MM. The interaction between these two schedules determines the rate of interest and the actual money stock. Where the two schedules intersect, the demand for money and the supply of money are equal and we have equilibrium in the money market, as at i_1 and M_1. At any other rate of interest there can be no equilibrium since the demand for money and the supply are not equal.

At i_2, for example, given MM and $LL(Y_1)$, there is an *excess supply* of money. The amount of money that can be created exceeds the amount that is demanded. When this occurs, forces are set in motion that tend to reduce the rate of interest. Some lenders are willing to accept lower rates of interest, for example, in order to be able to invest their funds profitably. As interest rates decline, the amount of money demanded increases because some borrowers become more willing to borrow. Similarly, some lenders who are unwilling to lend at these lower interest rates reduce their demand

FIGURE 20-2. The relationship between the demand for money, the income level, and the supply of money.

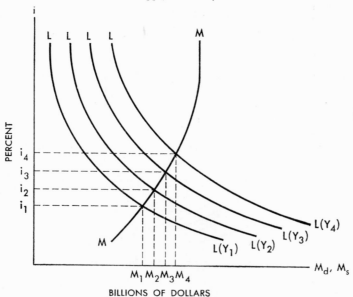

for securities and switch their funds to money instead. The banking system also becomes less willing to make loans and create money at this lower rate of interest. Thus we move down and to the right along the demand schedule and down and to the left along the supply schedule until M_d and M_s are equal at an equilibrium rate of interest, i_1.

On the other hand, at i_1, given MM and $LL(Y_2)$, there is an *excess demand* for money; the amount of money available is deficient to meet the amount demanded. Forces are now set in motion that tend to raise interest rates. Many borrowers may be willing to borrow at interest rates higher than i_1. Thus to insure that they get the funds they feel they need, they will issue securities bearing yields higher than i_1. This, in turn, will induce some holders of funds to reduce their demand for money and to begin lending instead. Other borrowers, unable to pay the higher rates, will stop borrowing. Thus there will be a tendency for the economy to move up and to the left along the demand curve $LL(Y_2)$. At the same time, the higher rate of interest will induce banks to expand their loans and create additional money. This will cause the economy to move up the MM curve. This increase in the amount of money that banks are willing to create and the decrease in the amount demanded brings the demand and supply of money to equilibrium at interest rate i_2 and amount of money M_2.

THE RELATIONSHIP BETWEEN GNP AND THE INTEREST RATE

The preceding discussion assumed a given level of income. The forces that operate to change the rate of interest also work to change the level of

FIGURE 20–3. The relationship between the rate of interest and the level of income.

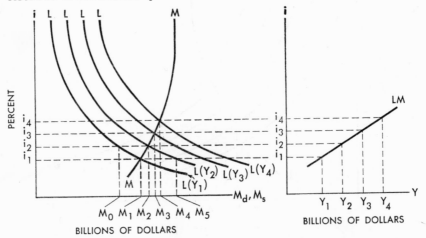

income, however. For example, a decline in the rate of interest, as shown in Chapter 19, expands investment and consumption demands, and consequently it expands Y. It is very unlikely, therefore, that Y will remain stable as i changes. There is a different equilibrium rate of interest equating the demand for money with the supply at every different level of income, Y. Figure 20–3 shows this relationship between the level of income and the rate of interest. The lefthand diagram is an exact replica of Figure 20–2. Equilibrium is reached at interest rates i_1, i_2, i_3, and i_4 when income is at the successively higher income levels Y_1, Y_2, Y_3, and Y_4. The righthand diagram plots the relationship between these alternative income levels and their various equilibrium rates of interest. The relationship is positive, showing that the higher the level of income becomes, the higher the rate of interest that equates the money supply and demand must be. The line depicting this relationship is labeled the *LM* line; at every point on this line, the demand for money is equal to the supply.

At any point to the right of the *LM* curve the demand for money exceeds the supply. For example, if at income level Y_2 the rate of interest is i_1 instead of i_2, then the amount of money demanded is M_5, whereas the amount available is only M_1. This situation should set forces in motion that will tend to raise i and reduce Y. Conversely, at any point to the left of the *LM* curve the supply of money exceeds the demand. For example, if at income level Y_1 the rate of interest is i_2 instead of i_1, then the amount of money demanded is M_0, whereas the amount the banking system is willing to create is M_2. Now forces will tend to lower i and increase Y.

The same forces that determine the position of the money demand lines and the money supply schedule determine the position of the *LM* schedule. Should W' increase or the X' forces operate to increase the demand for money, the family of *LL* lines will shift to the right. This will cause the *LM* schedule to shift to the left. A given rate of interest can now equate the demand and supply of money only at a lower level of income and output. At a given rate of interest, assuming the relation between Y and M_d to be unchanged, an increase in the demand for money decreases the amount of money available for making expenditures. It will be recalled from our earlier discussion that one of the ways in which money holdings may be increased is by reducing the demand for other goods and services.

On the other hand, a decrease in the demand for money caused by W' decreases or X' changes will shift the family of *LL* lines to the left. This will cause the *LM* schedule to shift to the right. Since the demand for money to hold as an asset will have decreased, the amount of money available for making expenditures will have increased. At any given rate of interest, therefore, expenditures should increase.

An increase in the money supply caused by a change in the forces that determine its position will cause the *LM* schedule to shift to the right. Thus at any given rate of interest and income level, the amount of money that can be created will have increased relative to the demand for it, and as a result a higher level of expenditures can be maintained. On the other hand, a movement to the left of the money supply schedule will cause a shift to the left in the *LM* curve.

THE INTERSECTION
OF THE *IS* AND *LM* SCHEDULES

The *LM* schedule, like the *IS* schedule, is an important element in our model of income determination. Chapter 19 established that, given the *IS* line, there is a different possible level of equilibrium income for every different rate of interest. At any level of *GNP* and at any interest rate planned,

$I + G + F$ will equal planned $S_p + S_b + T$. The relationship between Y and i under these conditions is inverse. This chapter has established, however, that given the LM line it is possible, at any level of GNP, to select an interest rate that will equalize the demand for money and the supply of money. The relationship between Y and i under these money market conditions is positive. Given both the IS and LM schedules, we are now in a position to determine how the total demand behind gross national product interacts with monetary supply and demand to determine equilibrium output and an equilibrium interest rate.

FIGURE 20–4. The IS and LM schedules.

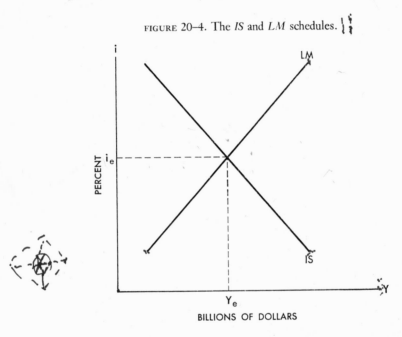

BILLIONS OF DOLLARS

Figure 20–4 plots the intersection of IS and LM lines, other things being given. These lines will intersect at any one point, (i_e, Y_e), which is the only combination of i and Y capable of producing equilibrium in both the money and commodity markets. Only at point i_e, Y_e will the demand for money equal the supply of money, and *ex ante* $I + G + F$ equal *ex ante* $S_p + S_b + T$. As explained earlier, at any point to the right of the LM curve the demand for money exceeds the supply. Conversely, at any point to the left of LM curve the supply of money exceeds the demand. Either of these two situations will set self-corrective forces in motion that will tend to change both Y and i so that the demand for money will equal the supply of money.

Similarly, any points not lying on the IS curve are also points of disequilibrium. At any point to the right of IS, $S_p + S_b + T$ exceeds $I + G + F$; at any point to the left of IS the sum of I, G, and F exceeds the sum of S_p, S_b, and T.[4] Either of these two situations will set self-corrective forces in motion that will tend to bring $S_p + S_b + T$ into equality with $I + G + F$. In the first case, for example, these forces will tend to contract Y, whereas in the second they will tend to expand Y. Chapter 19 examined the forces that cause changes in these saving and spending forces, thereby inducing Y changes. No mention was made of the monetary sources of change, however. The following discussion will explain some of the important interactions between the money market (*LM*) and the commodity market (*IS*) forces that tend to produce equilibrium in both markets, thereby determining Y_e and i_e.

APPLICATIONS OF THE MODEL OF INCOME DETERMINATION

For the purposes of this discussion we will use the model that was developed in Chapters 15, 19, and 20, and we are assuming that the *LM* and *IS* lines of Figure 20–4 are determined by the equations of the model. This means that equilibrium income and equilibrium interest rate are Y_e and i_e respectively. For the sake of simplicity, we are also assuming that wealth changes cannot affect *LM* and *IS* in the short run. The equations used in this model are

1.	$M_s = f(R_0, i, Z_0')$	[15–5]
2.	$M_d = f(Y, i, W_0', X_0')$	[20–1]
3.	$S_p = f(Y_d, i, W_0, X_0)$	[19–1]
4.	$T = f(Y, Z_0)$	[19–3]
5.	$S_b = f(Y, U_0)$	[19–4]
6.	$I = f(i, Y, U_0')$	[19–5]
7.	$G = f(Z_0)$	[19–6]
8.	$F = f(J_0)$	[19–7]
9.	$M_d = M_s$	
10.	$I + G + F = S_p + S_b + T$	

The numbers in brackets on the right indicate where each equation was discussed in the text. There is one difference between the equations discussed in the text and the ones used here for our model. Here, the subscript $_0$ is used to denote forces that are held constant for purposes of simplicity. Other equations creating conditions necessary for equilibrium are included at points 9 and 10.

Equations 1 and 2 determine the nature of the *LM* line. At any point on *LM*, the condition set up in equation 9 is satisfied. Equations 3 through 8 determine the nature of the *IS* line. At any point on *IS*, the condition set up

---

[4] From this point, we shall omit the adjectives "*ex ante*," "planned," "intended," etc., from $I + G + F$ and $S_p + S_b + T$. When we mean "*ex post*," it shall be stated explicitly.

in equation 10 is satisfied. There are ten variables in this system of equations: M_s, M_d, S_p, T, S_b, I, G, F, i, and Y. Everything else is fixed. Two of the variables, G and F, are known because we have arbitrarily assumed that their determinants, Z and J, are constant. Two other variables, Y and i, are also fixed by the two equilibrium conditions in equations 9 and 10; Y and i are determined by the intersection of LM and IS. Y_d, of course, may be derived from Y, S_b, and T.

Effects of an Increase in Government Spending

Let $(LM)_0$ and $(IS)_0$ be the initial LM and IS lines in Figure 20–5. Accordingly, GNP and the rate of interest are in equilibrium at Y_e and i_e. Now

FIGURE 20–5. A shift in *IS*.

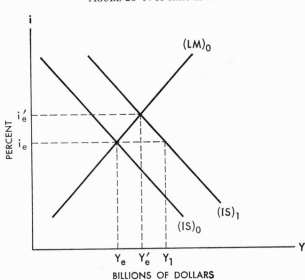

BILLIONS OF DOLLARS

assume that a change occurs. Suppose that as a result of an anti-poverty program federal expenditures increase, and that they are financed through the sale of securities to the nonbank public. Thus G increases because Z has changed through legislative action. In terms of our diagrammatic analysis, the $I + G + F$ line is raised. As a consequence, the IS line shifts to the right by some multiple of the increase in government spending. This shift is represented in Figure 20–5 by the $(IS)_1$ line.[5]

---

[5] Something else has also occurred to change the position of the LM and IS lines. The method of financing the government expenditure increase has lead to an increase in total liquid wealth and its composition. The nonbank public, after the government has spent the borrowed funds, will have as much money as before, but it will now have more government securities, another wealth form. Thus W', W, and X' have changed. This should shift the IS and the LM lines to the right. However, it will be recalled that we have assumed, for the short run, that wealth changes cannot affect the economy.

The shift is a multiple of the change in government expenditures because, as noted in Chapter 19, increased spending in one sector of the economy induces increased incomes, and hence higher levels of spending, in the other sectors. In this case, increased government expenditures should induce increased consumption and investment spending. As a result, the economy is no longer in equilibrium at i_e and Y_e.

To what extent can the increased government expenditures induce an increase in Y? Were it not for money market forces, these expenditures could cause Y to increase to Y_1. Interest rates rise, however, choking off some investment and consumption expenditures that would have taken place had the rate of interest remained the same. (It will be recalled that both investment and consumption are decreasing functions of the rate of interest.)

Interest rates rise because the increased spending that is taking place causes an increase in the demand for money with which to carry on transactions. In terms of Figure 20–3, this is illustrated by the higher demand-for-money lines that accompany higher levels of income. Again, at rate of interest i_e in Figure 20–5, the demand for money must exceed the supply. As the interest rate begins to rise, the amount of money supplied by the banking system also increases. This is represented by a movement up the *MM* line, not a shift in its position. The rate of interest will continue to rise so long as the demand for money increases because of rising incomes. In other words, *rising incomes induce an increased demand for money and a movement up and along the LM schedule.* This movement continues until we arrive at Y_e' and i_e', where both the money and commodity markets are again in equilibrium.

Thus, in general, increased government expenditures induce consumption and investment expenditure increases. As incomes rise, more money is needed to carry on transactions. This induces a rise in the rate of interest, which in turn restrains the potential growth of investment and consumption expenditure.

If, on the other hand, we posit a decrease in government expenditures as a result of a tax surplus and assume that this surplus is being used to retire debt held by the nonbank public, then this process would operate in reverse. The *IS* line would shift to the left, and Y and i would decrease.

In addition, if there were changes in any of the forces behind S_p, T, S_b, I, and F, which were assumed constant, then appropriate *IS* shifts would occur. The process would be almost identical with that just described, except that the initial source of spending change would be different. The position of the *LM* curve would remain unchanged to keep the analysis comparable to that described above.

Effects of an Increase in the Money-Supply Schedule

Assuming an economy at equilibrium at Y_e and i_e, suppose that there is an open-market purchase of U.S. government securities from the nonbank public by the Federal Reserve System. This directly increases the money stock holdings of the nonbank public and R, the reserve base of the banking system. The money supply schedule, MM, must, therefore, shift to the right. As a result, the LM curve in Figure 20–6 must shift from $(LM)_0$ to $(LM)_1$. Points i_e and Y_e are now to the left of $(LM)_1$; the supply of money exceeds the demand. Pressures are set in motion that, in the absence of income changes, will drive the rate of interest down to i_1.

Interest rate decreases affect the commodity market, however. Consumption expenditures increase and personal saving decreases. Investment expenditures rise because of the widening spread between the return expected from investment in plant and the cost of getting funds. As these expenditure in-

FIGURE 20–6. A shift in LM.

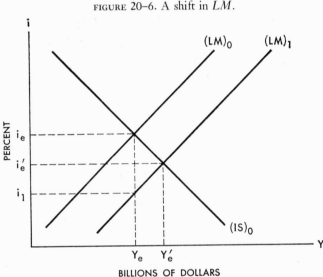

BILLIONS OF DOLLARS

creases take place, income increases, which induces an additional rise in consumption and investment expenditures. Business income and government tax collections rise accordingly.

As income goes up due to the above expenditure increases, the demand for money rises, thereby preventing a fall in the rate of interest to i_1. Instead, i falls to some intermediate level such as i_e'. Equilibrium income rises to Y_e'.

Conversely, a sale of government securities to the nonbank public would result in a shift of the LM line to the left, with a corresponding decrease in Y and an increase in i. The above process would operate in reverse.

Changes in the family of LL curves will produce similar results. Shifts to the right in the LL schedules will cause LM shifts to the left, decreases in income and increases in the interest rate. Shifts to the left in the LL schedules will cause LM shifts to the right, increases in Y, and decreases in i.

An additional factor to be considered in a shift of the LM line is that an increase in MM causes a change in total wealth. Although the nonbank public gives up securities to get money, when the banking system expands money in response to its increased reserves, the total wealth of the nonbank public rises.[6] This leads to an increase in the demand for consumption goods and shifts the *IS* schedule to the right. At the same time, however, there will be an increase in the demand for money, thus restraining forward movement in the *LM* line beyond a certain point. These conclusions concerning the influence of wealth on *IS* only apply if we relax our aforementioned assumptions about wealth.

Summary

The preceding analysis demonstrated how our economic model can be used to interpret the interaction of various economic forces. It should be emphasized that this is a short-term analysis. Nevertheless most forces tending to change *LM* and *IS* may be explained within the context of this model.

THE PROBLEM OF THE PRICE LEVEL

Our analysis to this point has made no mention of price change. Implicitly we have assumed constant prices, which means that when equilibrium income changes as a result of *LM* or *IS* shifts, all of the change in *Y* is shown as a change in *Q*, real output. The assumption of constant prices is comparatively realistic under conditions of less than full employment. Individual prices may change, but as a whole they tend to increase slowly as long as the economy has unemployed productive resources available. Once full employment is achieved, however, it is probable that prices will begin to increase sharply. How do these price fluctuations fit into the workings of our macroeconomic model of the economy?

People want real goods and services; they view their incomes and money holdings in terms of their ability to command real resources. They want a given amount of *Q*, not *PQ*. This means that the position of the *IS* schedule is not directly affected by price level variations, even though it may be affected by changed price expectations.

The *LM* schedule is affected by a change in the price level, however. The demand for money is a demand for real money balances, a demand for a given amount of purchasing power. The supply-of-money schedule, however, merely records the nominal amount of money that the banking system is prepared to create. Thus it is a real money supply schedule only when

---

[6] Some economists would contend at this point that the relevant variable is net worth rather than total or liquid wealth. Thus when an increase in the money stock occurs as a result of borrowing at commercial banks, the net worth of the nonbank public is unchanged. Both assets and liabilities of the nonbank public have increased. See Earl Rolph, *The Theory of Fiscal Economics* (Berkeley, Cal.: University of California Press, 1954).

prices are constant; if prices increase, then the real supply of money drops. For example, assume that the money supply at a given rate of i is $150 billion, given a price index of 100, and that at this time the real money supply is the same as the nominal supply, $150 billion. If all prices increase by 50 percent, however, so that the price index is now 150, then the real money supply only amounts to $100 billion, since $150 billion in nominal money can only buy $100 billion worth of the goods and services it could have purchased at a price index of 100. With the decrease in the real supply of money, the demand for money exceeds the supply, given the same rate of interest, and pressures are set in motion that tend to raise the rate of interest. As this occurs, consumption and investment demand decrease, thereby leading to income and output drops. Thus we find that for every different price level there is a different LM schedule, the schedule for consecutively lower price levels being successively farther to the right. For higher price levels, the LM schedules are successively farther to the left.

Other things being equal, therefore, a rise in the price level is accompanied by a falling real money supply, a rising interest rate, and decreased output. On the other hand, a drop in the price level leads to an increase in the real money supply, and thus a drop in interest rates and a rise in income and output. This may appear paradoxical in light of the fact that in practice output and prices tend to move in the same direction. It must be remembered, however, that we are concerned here with the effects stemming from the price change only. In the real world, prices generally begin rising as product demand increases; that is, IS shifts to the right would induce price increases.

THE PROBLEM
OF THE PRODUCTIVE CAPACITY
OF THE ECONOMY

According to our model, the equilibrium Y_e will be the actual Q the economy will tend to produce, so long as we are at less than full employment. Once full employment is reached, however, any intersection of LM and IS to the right of maximum full employment output cannot be a position of stable equilibrium. In Figure 20-7, for example, Y_f is the maximum output of the economy. Y_e, therefore, where IS and LM intersect, cannot be produced. The demand for real goods, Y_e, exceeds the ability of the economy to produce. Under these circumstances entrepreneurs may raise prices, anticipating greater profits. In an attempt to meet the demand for goods and services, entrepreneurs will also bid labor and other productive resources away from each other. Costs of production will increase. Collectively, however, the most that can happen, since resources are already fully employed, is a redistribution of the composition of output. A greater fraction of total output is produced by those firms that have successfully lured productive resources away from other firms, but the production of the latter firms has dropped. The rise in prices, wages, and costs decreases the real stock of money, causing the equilibrium money market schedule, $(LM)_0$, to shift to the left until it becomes $(LM)_1$, and intersects $(IS)_0$ at full employment output, Y_f.

It can also be argued that an intersection of LM and IS to the left of Y_f is unstable, but only if prices and wages are assumed to be flexible downward. If this situation exists, then the drop in prices caused by entrepreneurs attempting to induce an increase in the demand for their product will shift LM to the right. This will lead to lower interest rates and greater production. Most economists, however, regard the possibility of substantial down-

FIGURE 20–7. The relationship between LM, IS, and the productive capacity of the economy.

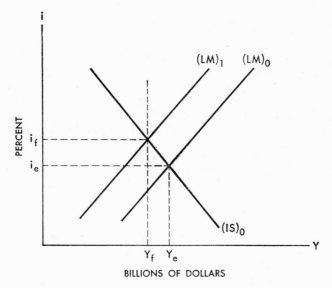

BILLIONS OF DOLLARS

ward price-wage flexibility in the *contemporary American economy* as quite unrealistic.[7] On this basis, an intersection of LM and IS to the left of Y_f may be regarded as a stable, less-than-full-employment equilibrium point.

THE ROLE OF MONEY

The model developed in Chapters 19 and 20 is very general. As will be demonstrated in the next chapter, by making specific assumptions it can be used to illustrate the workings of alternative monetary theories, provided certain specific assumptions are added.

Given the demand for money, the model developed shows that the money supply schedule is important because it fixes the position of money market

---

[7] Downward as well as upward price flexibility is important to theory as logic. This is discussed in Chapter 21.

equilibrium (*LM*) and, through its influence on the rate of interest, helps determine the direction of change in income and output. If one relaxes the short-run assumptions made about the influence of wealth, then the supply of money also affects saving and consumption directly, and thereby helps determine the position of the *IS* line.

Supplementary Readings

American Economic Association. *Readings in the Theory of Income Distribution.* Philadelphia, Blakiston, 1946, pp. 461–76.

———. *Readings in Monetary Theory.* Homewood, Ill., Irwin, 1951, pp. 186–283.

Duesenberry, J. S. *Business Cycles and Economic Growth.* New York, McGraw-Hill, 1958, pp. 49–112.

Ferber, Robert. "Research on Household Behavior." *American Economic Review* (1962), pp. 19–63.

Johnson, Harry. "Monetary Theory and Policy." *American Economic Review* (1962), pp. 335–84.

Keynes, John M. *The General Theory of Employment, Interest, and Money.* New York, Harcourt, Brace & World, 1936.

Metzler, Lloyd A. "Wealth, Saving, and the Rate of Interest." *The Journal of Political Economy* (1951), pp. 93–116.

Patinkin, Don. *Money, Interest, and Prices.* Evanston, Ill., Row, Peterson, 1956.

Chapter 21

Alternative Monetary Theories

Preceding chapters have developed a broad and rigorous model of the macroeconomic determination of income and output. This model was not designed as a comprehensive model of the workings of the American economy, however. It is merely a pedagogical tool intended to depict various economic relationships. Comprehensive models run into many equations, each of which spell out the precise functional relationships between the various factors being studied.[1]

This chapter makes a brief survey of various different contemporary views of the importance of money in the economy. Particular emphasis is placed on the policy implications of the Keynesian theory, the "quantity theory," and the "competing financial asset" theory.[2] In addition, we have included a brief appendix to this chapter which considers contemporary refinements of the logic of monetary theory, in particular Say's Law and the relationship between the demand for money and the price level.

THE KEYNESIAN POSITION ON MONEY

In brief, the basic Keynesian position is that output in the economy is determined by consumption, investment, and government demand for goods and services. Consumption is seen as a function of income, and investment is seen as a function of the rate of interest and the marginal efficiency of investment. In periods of less than full employment, investment demand is relatively interest-inelastic. Government demand is autonomous; that is, it

---

[1] For example, L. R. Klein, R. J. Ball, A. Hazelwood, and P. Vandome in *An Econometric Model of the United Kingdom* (Oxford: Blackwell, 1961) have a model consisting of thirty-seven equations.

[2] It should be stressed that the views presented here as representative of the various groups of monetary theorists are the views of the majority of the members of each group, not the entire group. Thus the Keynesian position presented here is that articulated in the works of Alvin Hansen. Similarly, Milton Friedman has been selected as the spokesman for contemporary quantity theories, whereas some ten or fifteen years ago Lloyd Mints would have been considered the leading exponent of this position. Finally, the views of the "competing financial asset" school are expressed by John Gurley and Edward Shaw, despite the fact that Shaw's views on many matters are those of a quantity theorist.

is determined by the government primarily on noneconomic grounds. The rate of interest is determined by monetary supply and demand forces. The supply of money is autonomous, being determined by the monetary authorities. The demand for money is a function of income and the rate of interest, becoming perfectly elastic at some low rate of interest. Since consumption is determined by the level of income and output, and since the investment schedule is relatively interest-inelastic, it follows that the economy will not be affected significantly by money stock changes, at least during periods of less than full employment.[3] Consequently, Keynesians feel that fiscal policy should be the principal means of influencing total demand and total output in the economy.

There are four principal differences between the Keynesian position and the model that was presented in Chapters 19 and 20: (1) Keynesians do not agree that interest rate changes are a source of consumption and saving change; (2) they do not agree that the money supply is a function of the interest rate; (3) they do not believe that investment is responsive to the interest rate, at least during periods of less than full employment; and (4) they are convinced that at low rates of interest there is a liquidity trap. These disagreements result in *IS* and *LM* schedules that have a different look from those of Chapters 19 and 20. First, the Keynesian *IS* line will become vertical, or perfectly inelastic, showing that savings and investment do not respond at all to interest rate changes. Second, the *LM* becomes perfectly horizontal at some low rate of interest, showing that all of the money stock is demanded. The solid lines *LM* and *IS* in Figure 21–1 illustrate these views graphically.

Important policy implications may be drawn from this Keynesian position. First, if the *IS* schedule is interest-inelastic, then money stock changes are unimportant, since there is only one possible level of equilibrium income, which is dictated by the position of the *IS* schedule. In Figure 21–1, for example, that income level is at Y_e. Second, fiscal policy, changes in government spending and taxation, become important. An increase in government spending, for example, will shift the *IS* line to the right by a multiple of the change in government expenditures. The change in income and output will be determined by the shift in the *IS* line.

A more moderate Keynesian position would concede that investment demand is responsive to some degree to interest rate changes, particularly as firms approach capacity output. Under these circumstances, moderates believe that the *IS* line slopes downward and to the right, as in the broken line $(IS)_1$, of Figure 21–1. Money supply changes still have no effect, but only so long as the *IS* line intersects the *LM* in its liquidity trap section. The higher the income and the output of the economy become, however, the more likely it is that the *IS* curve will be interest-elastic and thus will not

[3] See Alvin H. Hansen, *Monetary Theory and Fiscal Policy* (New York: McGraw-Hill, 1949), Chapters 4 and 5, for a concise statement of this position.

intersect the *LM* curve in the area of the liquidity trap.[4] Under these circumstances, money supply changes can have an economic effect; an increase in the money supply may shift the *LM* line to a new position at $(LM)_1$. Given the $(IS)_1$ line, this will lead to interest-rate decreases, investment-expenditure increases, and hence increased consumption expenditures. A restrictive monetary policy, on the other hand, would shift the *LM* line from $(LM)_1$ to $(LM)_0$. This would lead to increases in the rate of interest and, consequently, decreases in investment and consumption expenditure.

Fiscal measures, unaccompanied by money stock changes, under these more moderate Keynesian views, would be affected by money market con-

FIGURE 21–1. The Keynesian *IS* and *LM* schedules.

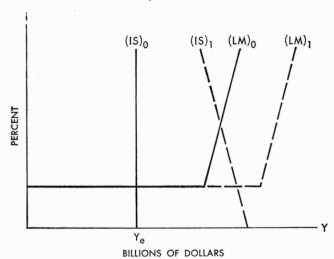

BILLIONS OF DOLLARS

siderations when *IS* intersects *LM* in its upward rising section. Increased government expenditures would cause some interest rate increases, thereby dampening investment expenditures. However, government spending increases financed by an increase in the stock of money would lead to simultaneous shifts to the right in *IS* and *LM*. Thus, money stock increases would reinforce the effects of the increased government spending on income and output.

THE CONTEMPORARY QUANTITY THEORY POSITION ON MONEY

Contemporary quantity theorists, unlike their neoclassical predecessors, no longer focus on the relationship between money and prices in their

---

[4] See Hansen, *op. cit.,* pp. 79–80.

analysis. They no longer assume that full employment is the normal state of the economy. Instead, today they stress the relation between money and income and in this respect their views are comparable to those of Keynesian economists. In many other respects, however, their views differ, and it is these differences that make the money supply, on the whole, a more important variable for the quantity theorist than for his Keynesian counterpart.

To many economists, the central thesis of the contemporary quantity theory of money is that it

is in the first instance a theory of the *demand* for money. It is not a theory of output, or of money income, or of the price level. Any statement about these variables requires combining the quantity theory with some specifications about the conditions of supply of money and perhaps about other variables as well.[5]

In some ways, this definition is not completely in the quantity theory tradition. Early quantity theorists frequently discussed the relationship between money and prices; other recent quantity theorists, like Lloyd Mints, related money to income. The money supply, to these economists, was the crucial variable because they assumed that the demand for money was stable. The statement just cited places the emphasis on the demand for money, rather than on the economic policy variable, the money supply. Therefore, a more complete statement of the quantity theory might be that *the quantity theory of money argues that there is a predictable relationship between money stock changes and gross national product changes. This follows from the fact that the supply of money is determined independently of the demand for money and that the demand for money is stable relative to its determinants.* Actually, however, no matter which statement of the quantity theory one prefers, the demand for money is an important variable.

According to the quantity theorist, the demand for money and its opposite, velocity, have a stable functional relationship with their determinants. To the quantity theorist, the forces that affect the demand for money are much the same as those discussed earlier—income, wealth, and rate of interest. Thus, the demand for money is not a constant for the quantity theorist. He merely states that there is a predictable relationship between the demand for money and its determinants.

What is the difference between the quantity theorist and the Keynesian economist? *First,* the quantity theorist regards the demand for money as more stable relative to expenditures than the marginal propensity to consume ($\Delta C / \Delta Y_d$). It will be recalled from Chapter 19 that the slope of the $S_p S_p$ line is determined by the marginal propensity to save, $\Delta S_p / \Delta Y_d$. The slope of the $S_p S_p$ line, in turn, determines the position of the *IS* line. In essence, therefore, the quantity theorist argues that $\Delta S_p / \Delta Y_d$ and *IS* are comparatively unstable. As a result, he feels that although the income expenditure models are useful

---

[5] Milton Friedman, "The Quantity Theory of Money: A Restatement," in *Studies in the Quantity Theory of Money*, Milton Friedman, ed. (Chicago: University of Chicago Press, 1956), p. 4.

for demonstrating economic relationships and for indicating the direction of movements in income, they are not useful for formulating accurate quantitative predictions of gross national product. As an alternative, the quantity theorist proposes that the economist approach the matter by working from money stock changes to changes in gross national product, since velocity exhibits some regularity of behavior. As Figure 21–2 indicates, money supply changes and gross national product changes seem to correspond quite closely to each other over time.

FIGURE 21–2. Gross national product and the money supply in the United States.

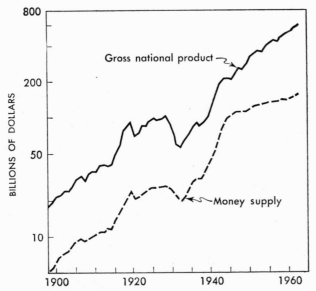

Source: Board of Governors of the Federal Reserve System, *Historical Chart Book* (1964), p. 66.

In addition, recent empirical work of quantity theorists tends to support the view that velocity possesses greater stability than the marginal propensity to save.[6] On the other hand, Keynesian economists contend that the tests made of their models have been performed only on the simplest and crudest versions, rather than on the more sophisticated econometric models.[7]

A *second* area of disagreement between quantity and Keynesian economists has to do with the liquidity trap. Whereas almost all Keynesians believe that it exists at least during periods of deep depression and low interest rates, most quantity theorists question its existence. One early study by

---

[6] Milton Friedman and David Meiselman, "The Relative Stability of Monetary Velocity and the Investment Multiplier in the United States, 1897–1958," in Commission on Money and Credit, *Stabilization Policies*, (Englewood Cliffs, N.J.: Prentice-Hall, 1963).
[7] L. R. Klein, "The Friedman-Becker Illusion," *Journal of Political Economy* (1958). pp. 539–45.

James Tobin was designed to test the hypothesis that the demand for cash balances is elastic with respect to the rate of interest. The study demonstrated that this thesis appeared to be true for the period 1922–45; it even demonstrated that during the war years the relationship between idle balances and the rate of interest tended to be perfectly elastic.[8] Empirical data for the post–World War II economic world tend to disprove this relationship, however. A more recent study indicates that the amount of money demanded as interest rates decline does not tend to increase relative to the drop in interest rates. In other words, the demand for money does not become interest-elastic.[9]

THE "COMPETING FINANCIAL ASSET" POSITION ON MONEY

The quantity theorist regards money as a financial asset that is uniquely important for income determination. Other economists, however, regard money as only one of a group of competing financial assets. For these economists, the more types of financial assets there are in the economy in addition to money, the less important money is, and the more difficult the task of the monetary authorities becomes.

Considerable space was devoted to the development of this concept in Chapters 5 and 8. There we argued that nonbank financial institutions create forms of liquid wealth that compete with money for a place in the portfolios of individuals. Thus people are confronted with a choice between these alternative forms. The more successful nonbank financial institutions are in inducing people to maintain their liquid-wealth holdings in the form of savings bank deposits, savings and loan association share accounts, or life insurance policies instead of money, the less control monetary authorities may have over the economy. This problem is related to a second problem, which is that during periods of economic boom the operations of these non-bank institutions tend to increase velocity and thus aggravate inflationary trends.

In terms of the model developed in Chapters 19 and 20, this "competing financial asset" theory suggests that W' and X' change as a result of the proliferation of financial assets. To these economists this makes it difficult for the monetary authority to control the position of LM by means of money stock changes. These economists have proposed that monetary controls be extended to the liquid-wealth forms created by nonbank financial intermediaries. Thus, while the quantity theorist has questioned the stability

---

[8] James Tobin, "Liquidity Preference and Monetary Policy," *Review of Economics and Statistics* (1947), pp. 124–31.

[9] Martin Bronfenbrenner and Thomas Mayer, "Liquidity Functions in the American Economy," *Econometrica* (1960), pp. 810–34.

of *IS*, the competing financial asset theorist has questioned the ability of the monetary authority to control *LM*.

In fact, the chief differences between the position of quantity theorists and the position of competing financial asset theorists boil down, for the most part, to differences in the definition of money. Most economists restrict themselves to the orthodox definition of money developed in this text —currency outside banks and demand deposits. Others, like quantity theorist Milton Friedman, also include time deposits at commercial banks. Still others, like competing financial asset theorists Edward Shaw and John Gurley, imply (although they do not explicitly say so) that the central bank should define money as consisting of currency outside banks, demand deposits, time deposits at commercial banks, and the liquid-wealth forms created by the aforementioned nonbank financial intermediaries. Interestingly enough, some recent work seems to indicate that the demand function for money is stable for several different definitions of money.[10] Thus it is possible that these differences of opinion may disappear.

CONCLUSION

Chapters 16 through 21 have been concerned with monetary theory, the study of the influence of monetary supply and demand forces on the economy. We have seen how economists have changed their views on this topic over the years. Bodin, we recall, was primarily concerned with the relationship between money and prices. Eighteenth-century theorists saw a connection between money, velocity, and trade. In the nineteenth and early twentieth centuries most economists worked on the assumption of a full-employment economy, concentrating on problems of pricing and resource allocation, accepting Say's law that production creates its own demand. These views were challenged by the economic events of the 1930's and our contemporary theories were born.

Today, for most economists, monetary theory is an integral part of income–expenditure analysis, which is designed primarily to explain what factors determine income and employment. Thus we developed a contemporary model of income determination, a basic framework that almost any modern economist, whatever his theoretical orientation, can use.

Three different views of the role of money in the economy have been presented in this chapter: the Keynesian view, the quantity-theory view, and the competing-financial-asset view. All three groups are in agreement as to the logical structure of the appropriate analysis—witness the fact that all can and do use versions of the model that was developed here. Almost all of these economists concede that money plays an important role in the econ-

---

[10] Allan H. Meltzer, "The Demand for Money: The Evidence from the Time Series," *Journal of Political Economy* (1963), pp. 219–46.

omy. The differences of opinion that we have discussed in previous pages are in a sense merely a discussion of detail, a matter of how much emphasis should be placed on the role of money. The quantity theorists place more stress on the importance of money as a causal force in the economy than do the Keynesians, and the competing-financial-asset theorists place their stress on a broad spectrum of financial assets, only one of which is money.

Supplementary Readings

Friedman, Milton, ed. *Studies in the Quantity Theory of Money.* Chicago, University of Chicago Press, 1956.

———. "The Demand for Money: Some Theoretical and Empirical Results." *The Journal of Political Economy* (1959), pp. 327–51.

Gurley, J., and E. Shaw. *Money in a Theory of Finance.* Washington, D.C., The Brookings Institution, 1960.

Patinkin, Don. *Money, Interest, and Prices.* Evanston, Ill., Row, Peterson, 1956.

Ritter, Lawrence S. "The Role of Money in Keynesian Theory." In *Banking and Monetary Studies,* D. Carson, ed., Homewood, Ill., Irwin, 1963, pp. 134–50.

Tobin, James, "Money, Capital, and Other Stores of Value." *American Economic Review* (May, 1961), pp. 26–37.

Appendix A

CONTEMPORARY REFINEMENTS OF THE LOGIC OF MONETARY THEORY

Say's Law

Say's law, as previously noted, was an important part of nineteenth- and early twentieth-century monetary theory. The protracted depression of the 1930's, however, and the subsequent development of income-expenditure analysis caused economists to put aside the notion that production creates its own demand. Keynes argued that a situation of a satisfied effective demand and full-employment production is not normal, but unusual. Despite the general abandonment of Say's law, however, certain theoretical aspects of the principle are still widely discussed in economic literature.

In terms of our income–expenditure model, effective demand and full-employment production are equivalent only when the propensity to consume and the inducement to invest are in a particular relationship. This occurs when planned $I + G + F$ equals planned $S_p + S_b + T$ at full employment output. Should IS intersect LM anywhere to the left of full-employment output, that point of intersection dictates less-than-full-employment equilibrium. Figure 21–3 shows a less-than-full-employment intersection of $(LM)_0$ and $(IS)_0$ at Y_e, which lies to the left of full employment output, Y_f.

Some Keynesian theorists would go even further and declare that less-than-full-employment equilibrium is possible even with downward flexibility of wages and prices. It is on this point that much recent monetary theory has focused. Most economists agree that there are institutional rigidities to downward movements in wages and prices. Theory as framework of analysis, however, permits us to discuss downward wage and price movements. Thus the Keynesian argument has been attacked on a purely theoretical level.

It will be recalled from Chapter 20 that there is a different LM schedule for every different price level. As prices decline, the LM schedule shifts to the right. Should the IS schedule be sufficiently elastic so that at a positive rate of interest it can intersect LM at full employment output, then full employment can be reached via price-level declines. Such an intersection is at Y_f in Figure 21–3 when $(IS)_0$ and $(LM)_1$ meet. However, should IS not have sufficient elasticity, then it appears that declining prices and less-than-full-employment equilibrium are compatible. This would occur if full employment output were at Y_f' instead of Y_f.

This assumes, however, that the position of *IS* itself cannot be affected by price-level declines. A. C. Pigou and Don Patinkin have demonstrated that, given unlimited wage–price flexibility, full employment output *must* eventually be reached.[1] In their opinion, the *IS* schedule is affected by changes in "real balances," or changes in real wealth. Thus a drop in the price level increases the real purchasing power of money balances, and hence total real wealth. Given the desire of individuals to maintain some stable relationship between expenditures, real money balances, and real wealth, there will be an increase in the demand for consumption goods and services.

FIGURE 21–3. The relationship between *IS*, *LM*, prices, and output.

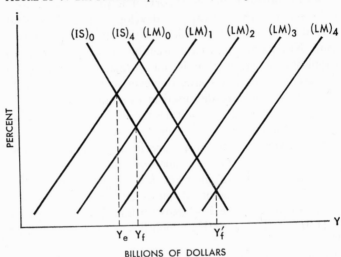

To the extent that businesses are similarly motivated, there will also be an increase in investment expenditures. These changes will cause an upward shift in the $I + G + F$ line and a downward shift in the $S_p + S_b + T$ line. This, in turn, results in a movement to the right in the *IS* line. This process continues so long as prices decline. At some point, therefore, the movement to the right of the *IS* line must lead to an intersection with the *LM* line at a point of full employment output. In Figure 21–3, let *LM* and *IS* initially intersect at less-than-full-employment output Y_e. With decreasing prices, both *LM* and *IS* will shift to the right, eventually reaching full employment when the appropriate schedules are $(IS)_4$ and $(LM)_4$.

This phenomenon is known as the *real balances effect*. Price-level decreases increase real balances, and hence the demand for goods and services.

[1] A. C. Pigou, "Economic Progress in a Stable Environment," *Economica* (1947); and Don Patinkin, *Money, Interest, and Prices* (Evanston, Ill.: Row, Peterson, 1956).

On the other hand, price-level increases result in decreased real balances, and hence reduced demand for goods and services. Thus if prices rise, the *IS* schedule shifts to the left, causing a chance of less-than-full-employment equilibrium, assuming that prices do not reverse themselves with general overproduction.

These contemporary economists accept the real-world possibility of severe depression and less-than-full-employment equilibrium, but they do not go so far as Keynes did. Given downward wage–price flexibility, they believe that full employment must be reached. Given upward wage–price flexibility, less than full employment may also be reached.

Another part of pre-Keynesian monetary economics, closely related to Say's law, was the *classical dichotomy*. According to this theory, the monetary sector of the economy determines the overall price level, whereas the demand and supply of real goods and services is determined by relative prices only. The price level, according to this theory, has no effect on the demand for and supply of real goods and services. The real-balances effect denies the possibility of this dichotomy, for the change in real balances will affect the demand for and supply of goods and services.

How important is the real-balances effect in practice? The real-balances effect is important theoretically as a framework of analysis, but it is generally regarded as a weak force in the real world because it is likely to be swamped by the effects of changing price expectations. It will be recalled that as prices decline, expectations of continued price decreases may lead to decreased spending. The real-balances effect at this point calls for increased spending. Similarly, as prices rise, there may be expectations of further price rises, leading to increased spending rather than the decreased spending called for by the changed real balances. Changes in real balances have an important economic effect only when people expect future prices to remain about the same as current prices.

The Demand for Money and the Price Level

One additional assumption of nineteenth- and early twentieth-century monetary economists was that changes in the price level and the demand for money are proportionate. For example, an increase of 10 percent in the price level should lead to a 10 percent increase in the demand for money, so that people can continue to maintain the same command over real goods and services. Similarly, a 10 percent decrease in the price level should lead to a 10 percent drop in the demand for money.

The real-balance effect does not accept this postulate either. Assuming that all goods, including money, are superior goods, it maintains that a decrease in real balances is caused by a rise in the price level. This, of course, decreases total real wealth and real money holdings relative to other wealth forms. If there is a desire to maintain a given distribution among wealth forms, there will be a decrease in the demand for goods and services and an increase in the demand for real balances. This demand is for an amount of real balances less than the volume held prior to the price-level increase, however. Decreasing the demand for goods and services enables one to recoup his real balances, but if they were completley recovered, the initial distribution among wealth forms would not be recovered. This means that the demand for "nominal" money balances—real balances demanded, multiplied by the price level—increases, but not by so much as to recoup all of the real balances lost through price inflation. Thus the demand for money (nominal balances) has increased less than proportionately to the price level, and has less than unitary elasticity.[2]

---

[2] This discussion is comparable to that given in Chapter 20 in our analysis of the relationship between M_d and W'. There, however, we assumed constant prices. A fuller exposition of these views is to be found in Patinkin's *Money, Interest, and Prices.*

Appendix B

GLOSSARY OF SYMBOLS

The following symbols were introduced in the preceding three chapters:

Y = gross national product

C = consumption expenditures

I = investment expenditures

G = government expenditures

F or $(X - M)$ = net foreign investment (the difference between exports and imports of goods and services)

Y_d = personal disposable income

S_b = business income

T = tax receipts

S_p = personal saving

f = "a function of"

i = rate of interest

W = liquid wealth

X = all other factors that may influence C and S_p

Z = all those forces that cause the legislature to change the tax rate or government spending

U = any forces other than Y that may influence S_b

U' = forces other than Y that help determine the marginal efficiency of investment

J = all the forces that cause F to change

M_d = the demand for money

W' = total wealth

X' = other variables that may influence the demand for money

M_s = the supply of money

R = the reserve base of the commercial banking system

Z' = other variables that may influence the supply of money

PART IV   *Money and Aggregate Economic Policy*

Chapter 22

The Meaning of Economic Policy

I have become aware that anyone's sense of what is good and beautiful must have a somewhat narrow foundation, namely, his circumstances and his particular brand of human nature; and he should not expect the good or the beautiful after his own heart to be greatly prevalent or long maintained in the world.
—George Santayana, *Dominations and Powers*

POLICY DEFINED

An economic policy is a governmental course of action designed to influence the future behavior of the economy. Basically, there are two types of economic policies: microeconomic and macroeconomic. Those policies that are designed to deal with the problems of specific industrial or regional areas of the economy are called *microeconomic policies*. Farm, labor, business regulation, transportation, "pockets of poverty" policies are all microeconomic. *Macroeconomic policies*, on the other hand, deal with the problems of the economy in the aggregate: unemployment, inflation, and growth. In this final section of the text, we shall confine ourselves to the study of macroeconomic policies.

Macroeconomic policy, or *aggregate economic policy*, as it is frequently called, is *any* government course of action designed to attack national economic problems such as unemployment, inflation, and stalled economic growth. Other matters such as the exchange rate and international liquidity may also enter the arena of macroeconomic policy when they affect the national economy.

Three specific types of government action are frequently called upon to deal with these problems. First, there is *monetary policy:* any action taken by the Federal Reserve System to affect the economy through its influence on the money stock and member-bank reserve positions. Second, there is *fiscal policy:* any action taken by the Treasury or Congress to affect the economy through the spending, tax, and debt operations of the federal government. Third, there is *international financial policy:* any action taken by the Federal Reserve, the Treasury, Congress, or the executive branch of the federal government to affect the international monetary position of the United States.

Notice that the two words most frequently used in these definitions are *any action*. An *action* is merely a *means* to an *end*. A *policy* is also a *means* to an *end*. That end is generally considered to be the elimination of basic national economic problems such as unemployment, inflation, and poor economic growth. To the extent that our policies help to correct these problems, they are considered effective. To the extent that they inhibit the correction of these deficiencies in the economy, they are viewed as retarders of economic welfare.

Yet, there are other goals that compete with the elimination of economic want and fear of economic collapse. For example, the freedom for individuals to do as they please so long as they do not harm others physically is usually viewed as a highly desirable political end. If economic policy actions should restrict individual freedom of action and choice, are they then to be regarded as bad, even if they eliminate our pressing economic problems? Should economic policy be permitted to enhance the superior power position of the state, which after all is merely a collection of individuals, relative to the individual members of society?

CHOOSING MEANS AND ENDS

This raises the basic question: how are the ultimate goals of society determined and how are the means to those ends selected?

Economists sometimes contend that it is not their function to deal with such broad social and philosophical questions. It is society's job, they say, to choose the ends. It is the economist's job to indicate what means will best achieve the ends selected by society. He uses economic theory as logic and as a set of substantive hypotheses to rank alternative economic policies in order of their ability to satisfy the ends decided upon by society. The choice between these alternative policies, however, is left to society.

This position of strict impartiality appears illusory. Economics is a social science, dealing with our economic environment and its problems. The economist, like any other scientist, lives in the social and economic environment of his time. He is influenced by the conditions surrounding him. To the extent that his circumstances differ from those of others in society, his thought and behavior patterns will differ. Furthermore, he lives and operates within the context of a given value system. His choice of study, the problems with which he is concerned, the very techniques he employs in scientific investigation are partially influenced by "his circumstances and his particular brand of human nature."[1] Thus the scientist's so-called impartial statement of alternatives can scarcely be called impartial, and it becomes important for the economist and scientist to make his particular value system explicit.

---

[1] George Santayana, *Dominations and Powers* (New York: Scribner, 1951), p. 12.

The economist must also learn to shoulder some social responsibility. He should be willing to make a specific policy recommendation, once he has made his set of values explicit. As a citizen, it is the scientist's duty to instruct his fellow citizens as well as to learn from them. In short, the economist should attempt to shape both the ends and means of national purpose.

How, then, is society to choose the criteria for evaluating economic policy? Several approaches are often used. These usually posit the value judgment that welfare maximization is the ultimate end of policy.

The *first approach* operating on the preceding premise argues that we should *choose that policy which provides more welfare for the members of society than it takes away*. The difficulty with this approach is that it assumes that welfare can be measured. In Part III we said that per capita income is sometimes used as a measure of economic welfare. This measure only provides us with a rough idea of how a hypothetical "average" citizen is faring economically, however. On the other hand, this welfare maximization approach attempts to measure the gains and losses to individuals from particular policy actions. Economists and psychologists are agreed, however, that there is no way of measuring welfare and human satisfaction, and consequently no way of measuring gains and losses in individual satisfaction.

If welfare cannot be measured, is there some other way of evaluating alternative policies? Perhaps individuals themselves could rank various combinations of policies according to the amount of satisfaction produced. This technique also runs into difficulty, however. People are reluctant to reveal their preferences. For example, it is frequently argued that taxes should be based on the benefits received from such social goods as education and highways. The individual who receives little benefit would be taxed the least for the social good and those who most value the good would pay the most taxes. Social goods are generally available, however; they would not be removed by nonpayment of taxes. As a result, those who receive benefit from social goods would attempt to conceal their true preferences. Also, those who need social goods the most are frequently those least able to pay taxes.

A *second approach* argues that in order to maximize welfare we should *choose that policy which produces some gain and no harm*. This approach is, in essence, a policy of inaction. It requires unanimous support for its economic policy, and complete unanimity of opinion is, to all intents and purposes, unattainable in this world.

Since society cannot reach a policy decision on the basis of the two previous approaches, it may do so by means of the *voting process*. Ideally, the voting process should reflect the values of the individual voting members of society and thereby permit society to arrive at a rational social consensus on policy. Unfortunately, even this approach has its difficulties. A democratic majority voting process will lead to a rational social decision only if (1) the values of the members of society are relatively homogeneous, and (2) the value systems of the members of society are single-peaked.

The implications of the first condition are obvious. If people have widely disparate views, and if there is no majority that shares the same views, then no consensus can be reached. Whatever decisions are made will be arrived at on the basis of temporary coalitions of competing groups. Thus whenever there is a realignment of groups within coalitions, previous decisions will be changed. Political chaos results. The Weimar government of Germany in the 1920's, the various French governments of the 1940's and 1950's, and the rapidly changing governments of present-day Latin America are all illustrative of the political situation that exists when the members of society have widely disparate value systems.

The second condition, a single-peaked value system, must also exist before social consensus can be achieved. Assume, for example, that voters are confronted with three policy choices: an extreme left-wing measure, a middle-of-the-road measure, and an extreme right-wing measure. A society that has a relatively homogeneous, single-peaked value system will choose only one of the three alternatives. On the other hand, if the second condition is missing and voters have a double-peaked value system, no consensus is possible. This would occur, in the previous example, if voters preferred either of the extremes to the more moderate middle-of-the-road measure.

Fortunately, both these conditions prevail in the United States. In countries where they do not, policy decisions can be reached by the voting process only on the basis of weak coalitions. If this condition persists, it may so immobilize the government that the only solution may appear to be some form of dictatorship.

SUMMARY AND PREVIEW

Ultimately, our decisions concerning policies and goals must be based on value judgments. In questions of economic and social policy, it is particularly important that we make explicit the modus operandi of the value judgment. Within much of Western society, there is a single-peaked value system and relative homogeneity of values. A social consensus may thus be reached on the basis of the voting process.

When prescribing economic policy, the economist should make his value judgments explicit. To the extent that he can take as given such goals as full employment, stable prices, economic growth, and a favorable balance of payments, he should use the tools of his profession to outline the alternative means available for attaining these goals. In addition, he should take an active part in the decision-making process; he should clearly express his preferences in matters of economic policy.

Succeeding chapters outline alternative monetary, fiscal, and international financial policies. The focus is on the effectiveness of these policies in combating the basic national economic problems of unemployment, inflation, growth, and the need for international financial stability. Where possible, the underlying political bases of the alternative policies are considered.

Supplementary Readings

Arrow, Kenneth J. *Social Choice and Individual Values.* New York, Wiley, 1951.

Musgrave, Richard A. *The Theory of Public Finance.* New York, McGraw-Hill, 1959, Chapters 4–6.

Rothenberg, Jerome. *The Measurement of Social Welfare.* Englewood Cliffs, N.J., Prentice-Hall, 1961, Chapters 1–2, 12–13.

Chapter 23

Alternative Monetary Policies

Monetary policy in the United States is administered and executed by the Federal Reserve System. As you will recall, the capstone to the decision to set up a system of central banking in the United States was the financial panic of 1907. This demonstrated conclusively the inherent defects of the national banking system: the lack of an elastic currency system, the pyramiding of reserves, the inadequate check-clearing facilities, and the overly rigid reserve requirements. The Federal Reserve System had as its original purpose the rectification of these shortcomings. By correcting the inadequacies of the national banking system, it was thought, we could eliminate financial panic forever.

The depression of the 1930's proved otherwise, of course. Various additional monetary reforms were instituted. Federal Deposit Insurance was inaugurated. The Federal Reserve System was given the power to change reserve requirements. Open-market operations became recognized as an important tool of contracyclical economic policy, and currency was no longer redeemable in gold. Because of these reforms of the 1930's and the present viable, adaptive character of the Federal Reserve System, many economists now believe that the economy is depression-proof. Others, however, point to nonbank financial institutions as potential sources of economic difficulty. The dangers of discretionary policies as compared with automatic policies have also been stressed. Debates on how to improve policy, the banking system, and the economy in general are countless. These debates take place in Congress, within the administration, in academic circles, among the lay public, and within the Federal Reserve System itself.

In this chapter we will deal with some of the proposals that have been advanced on how to effect these improvements by changing the goals and strategy of monetary policy.

ECONOMIC GOALS
AND FEDERAL RESERVE POLICY

Present monetary policy, as administered by the Federal Reserve System, recognizes four main goals—(1) full employment, (2) stable prices, (3) economic growth, and (4) a balance in the flow of payments to and from foreign countries. To accomplish these ends the Federal Reserve System relies on general monetary control techniques.

Monetary Controls in Recession

The logic of the control techniques is quite simple, as we pointed out in Chapters 12 and 13. To eliminate unemployment and the accompanying sluggishness in economic growth, the Federal Reserve lowers discount rates,

FIGURE 23-1. Shifts in the *IS* and *LM* schedules caused by monetary and fiscal policy changes.

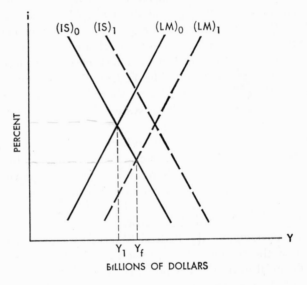

reduces reserve requirements, and purchases U.S. government securities. These policies should result in an increase in the stock of money. In terms of our income-expenditure model and Figure 23-1, the *LM* schedule shifts to the right with an increase in the stock of money. Theoretically, interest rates will then decline, and consumption and investment expenditures will rise. Income and output increase from Y_1 to Y_f. Economic growth is restored through rising investment expenditures; the productive capacity of the economy expands. Unemployment drops as businesses respond to increased demands for goods and services. Recession ends.

Although this appears to be a perfectly logical chain of analysis, it contains several hidden assumptions. If these policies are to work in the prescribed manner, the *IS* schedule must be sufficiently responsive to interest rate changes to intersect an *LM* schedule somewhere close to full employment output, Y_f. If the economy is deeply depressed, however, these conditions are not likely to be met. As a result, many economists recommend stronger policy measures. They suggest fiscal policy measures that will directly increase spending, thereby shifting the *IS* schedule to the right. This type of policy does not rely on indirect influences on consumption and investment spending via interest-rate changes.

Will the suggested monetary techniques for correcting slow growth and recession also promote the other two goals of monetary policy: stable prices and a balanced flow of payments on the international market? To the extent that spending is generated by these money stock increases and directed toward the goods and services produced by depressed industries, little price-level change is to be expected. However, should spending increases occur in industries that are already operating close to capacity, then the increase in the money stock will result in some price inflation. As a result, the real stock of money will decline. Thus, the shift to the right in the *LM* schedule resulting from money stock increases will be offset by a shift to the left in the *LM* schedule arising out of the price-level increase. Interest rate increases may also occur. Thus, an easy-money policy may not be compatible with both price stability and the elimination of unemployment.

Balance in the flow of payments may also be adversely affected by these monetary techniques; this will be discussed in greater detail in Chapters 25 and 26.

Monetary Controls in Inflation

The logic of inflation control techniques is rather straightforward—sell U.S. government securities, raise discount rates, and increase reserve requirements. The result should be a decrease in the stock of money. This would shift the *LM* schedule to the left. Inflation usually occurs during periods of full employment, and investment and consumption expenditure, other things being equal, are likely to be interest-responsive in such periods. As a result, the *LM* shift should induce interest-rate increases, and investment and consumption expenditure decreases. The fall in the demand for goods and services, relative to a stable rate of output, should then stop the increase in prices.

The assumption "other things being equal," however, tends to conceal offsetting forces. Expectations for continued growth in income and prices, for example, may lead to continual increases in demand (shifts to the right in the *IS* schedule). As a result, the Federal Reserve might have to resort to repeated use of its control techniques. Should not fiscal techniques be used directly to reduce the rising demand for goods and services? A reduction in government expenditures or a rise in taxes would shift the *IS* line back to the left, and possibly eliminate price inflation as well.

The use of monetary techniques to stem inflation calls for considerable care. Should money be restricted too severely, the result could be a deficiency of demand relative to the productive capacity of the economy. In terms of our income–expenditure model, if the *LM* is shifted to an intersection with the *IS* at some point to the left of full employment output, less-than-full-employment equilibrium may result. Thus, anti-inflationary techniques are not always compatible with the full employment goal of economic policy.

If a monetary policy is too restrictive it may also discourage needed investment expenditure in new plant and equipment. By decreasing this investment, a restrictive monetary policy can also impede economic growth.

How effective are these policy techniques in controlling inflation if the source of inflation is an increase in costs rather than an increase in the demand for goods and services? Assume, for example, that unions have been successful in securing wage increases. Firms will pass some of the increased costs on to consumers in the form of higher prices. This is a factor that may lead to recesssion. Higher prices mean reduced real purchasing power of money balances (*LM* shifts to the left), and induced rises in interest rates. Consumption and investment expenditures may fall off as a result and these reduced expenditures will mean less employment and output. Clearly, under such circumstances a restrictive monetary policy would be disastrous. Reductions in the money stock would shift the *LM* schedule further to the left. Thus, it is extremely important for the Federal Reserve System to determine carefully whether the cause of inflation is demand or cost increases.

An anti-inflationary monetary policy will help to eliminate an unfavorable balance of payments, however. This is considered in Chapters 25 and 26.

SPECIFIC POLICY PROPOSALS

The preceding analysis has emphasized the difficulties inherent in policy implementation. The evidence suggests, however, that by careful use of our present monetary techniques the Federal Reserve System can (1) reverse mild recessions, (2) help induce economic recovery, and (3) check a rise in prices.

Many modern critics of monetary policy, however, feel that this is not enough, that under the present system of controls we may well find ourselves unable to cope with future depressions and inflations. Other critics argue that the discretionary use of power by the Federal Reserve System is a principal source of economic instability. These economists urge that appropriate automatic guidelines be set up for the implementation of monetary policy techniques. For the rest of this chapter we will study the two proposals for monetary reform that have created the most controversy in recent years.

Financial Intermediary Control

According to the "competing financial asset" position developed in Chapter 21, money is regarded as only one of a group of competing financial assets. The liquid assets that are created by nonbank financial intermediaries have steadily been increasing in dollar volume relative to the stock of money. The economic control techniques of the Federal Reserve System operate in the first instance only upon commercial banks, however. Nonbank financial institutions are regulated, but by agencies whose principal function is to safeguard the claims of the depositors and account holders. In recognition of these changes in our financial system, proposals have been made to expand economic control techniques to include the financial activities of the nonbank financial intermediaries. These controls, it is reasoned, may be either an extension of existing Federal Reserve controls or an entirely new system.

These proposals are all primarily concerned with offsetting the velocity effects of nonbank financial intermediary operations. As you will recall, these institutions create liquid wealth when they tap the idle funds of savers. The funds come to the financial institutions in the form of demand deposits. These deposits are then loaned to borrowers and the borrowers spend these funds for goods and services. Thus velocity, the turnover of the money supply, is increased.

As in commercial banks, the ratio of cash assets to liabilities and capital accounts created by nonbank financial institutions is fractional. There are required reserve ratios for nonbank financial institutions, but they are usually quite low, and, unlike commercial banks, often include such assets as U.S. government securities. These reserve requirements are not normally adjusted in a contracyclical manner; they remain fixed. Thus in periods of restrictive monetary policy nonbank financial intermediaries may continue to expand their lending activity and enhance their competitive position vis-à-vis commercial banks. This occurs, of course, only if the nonbank institutions are successful in their efforts to induce people to change the composition of their liquid-wealth holdings. A switch from demand and time deposits at commercial banks to savings and loan association share accounts, time deposits at mutual savings banks, or life insurance policies must take place.

If, as proposed, monetary controls were extended to cover nonbank financial intermediaries, the Federal Reserve or some other regulatory agency would be able to manipulate the reserve base of all financial institutions.

One specific proposal sometimes advocated is to *extend the legal reserve requirement to nonbank financial intermediaries.* Table 23–1 shows that nonbank financial intermediaries are operating with actual reserves that are far below those required for commercial banks, although recent member bank reserve requirement decreases have tended to narrow the gap somewhat.

Considerable adjustments would be called for if nonbank financial intermediaries were to have exactly the same reserve requirements as commercial banks, however. Nonbank financial intermediaries would be forced to liquidate large volumes of earning assets and this could have deflationary

TABLE 23–1. THE AVERAGE RESERVE REQUIREMENT FOR MEMBER BANKS AND THE ACTUAL RATIO OF CASH ASSETS TO SELECTED LIABILITIES AND CAPITAL ACCOUNTS FOR VARIOUS NONBANK FINANCIAL INTERMEDIARIES, 1954–1964

| | RESERVE REQUIREMENT FOR MEMBER BANKS* | ACTUAL RESERVE RATIO† | | |
YEAR		Savings and loan associations	Mutual savings banks	Private life insurance companies
1954	13.7	7.3	3.8	5.2
1955	13.1	6.2	3.5	5.1
1956	13.0	5.7	3.3	5.3
1957	12.7	5.0	2.8	5.3
1958	12.0	5.4	2.6	5.3
1959	11.5	4.0	2.3	5.4
1960	11.4	4.3	2.5	5.4
1961	11.1	4.7	2.3	5.6
1962	10.9	4.9	2.4	5.6
1963	10.2	4.4	2.0	6.7
1964	9.9	3.7	1.7	6.8

Source: Computed from various issues of the *Federal Reserve Bulletin*, 1955–64; and Institute of Life Insurance, *Life Insurance Fact Book*, 1963. All data as of June 30.

* The average reserve requirement was calculated in the following manner: Σ (country bank demand deposits) (country bank reserve requirement) + (reserve city demand deposits) (reserve city reserve requirement) + (central reserve city demand deposits) (central reserve city reserve requirement) + (all time deposits at commercial member banks) (time deposit reserve requirement) ÷ Σ all member bank demand deposits + all member bank time deposits.

† Calculated as the ratio of cash assets to savings accounts, time deposits, and 80 percent of total assets for savings and loan associations, mutual savings banks, and private life insurance companies, respectively.

repercussions. One alternative to this proposal might be to reduce commercial bank reserve requirements to the level of the actual reserve ratios of the nonbank financial intermediaries. This would expand commercial bank lending capacity; it would also probably call for the sale of government securities by the Federal Reserve to mop up excess reserves.

Assuming that a satisfactory transition to contracyclical regulation of nonbank financial institutions could be accomplished, would the new con-

trols eliminate undesired changes in velocity as a source of economic instability? Not entirely. As you will recall, commercial banks are able, to
some extent, to reshuffle the asset composition of their portfolios from U.S.
government securities to loans. Nonbank financial intermediaries have this
same ability. This could affect velocity within the context of a given Federal Reserve policy. However, this technique has definite limits. Should
financial institutions divest themselves of too many U.S. government securities, the safety and solvency of their assets becomes threatened, since, unlike
loans, government securities are almost riskless if held to maturity.

Automatic Monetary Policy

Our present use of monetary controls is discretionary. Deliberate decisions are made by the monetary authorities to use their powers in a particular way to offset economic disturbances. The proposal to expand monetary
controls to cover nonbank financial intermediaries would expand discretionary monetary policy. The presumption of discretionary policy advocates is that the discretionary authorities, in a free society, can be counted
on to act skillfully in their use of powers, without usurping individual
freedom.

Other economists are not so optimistic. Their argument is on two levels.
One deals with political philosophy, the other with empirical economics.

Those who quarrel with discretionary monetary policy on *political*
grounds are opposed to all types of discretionary government policies. Their
political position is typically that of the nineteenth-century liberal who
wanted freedom from government interference. Individuals should be free
to go their own way, he felt, so long as they did not interfere with the
rights of others to do likewise. Present-day critics view extensive regulation
of the economy by the government as a hindrance to individual free choice
and initiative. The American productive process is largely based upon free
product and resource markets. Interfere too much with these processes, and
you restrict individual freedom of action and set up authorities who coerce
rather than act in response to the social consensus. Even the implementation
of a social consensus decision must be carefully watched, lest there be a
tyranny of the majority. The advocates of this position, however, do not
mean that free enterprise and individual freedom of action should be left
entirely unrestricted. They are not saying that political anarchy is a superior
form of government. Instead, they seek a rule of law to implement the
liberal philosophy, rules that authorities cannot change at their discretion.

Stability in the value of money and the lessening of economic fluctuations
are important policy goals to all economists. They guarantee the individual
an opportunity to have control over his own economic decisions. He is not
free to do so when inflation reduces the purchasing power of money or
when inadequate demand leads to lack of employment. Some type of regula-

tion is needed. But what type will best preserve political liberty and economic freedom of action? Authorities or rules? The "liberal" economists suggest the latter.

Rules have the merit of being simple and easily understandable. The realities of our economic and political world may make such simple rules impractical, however. We have a plurality of goals that are occasionally in conflict with one another. As demonstrated earlier, price stability and full employment are not always compatible. A "rule" to impose price stability on the economy may lead to unemployment. A "rule" to maintain full employment may lead to rising prices. A discretionary authority may solve this dilemma. If the goals are not in conflict, there may be conflict among several means of arriving at the goals. Discretionary decisions have to be made concerning what the correct "package" of means is and when it should be implemented. As one economist has recently argued, "The nature of economic progress, the plurality of goals, the pluralility of authorities, the plurality of tools, all of these operate to make impracticable the conduct of monetary management in conformity with a 'rule.' "[1]

Those who advocate "rules" instead of "authorities" do so on the basis of *economic empiricism*, too. The principal economic basis for advocating rules instead of authorities is that, in the past, monetary authorities have often made the wrong policy decisions. This was particularly true during the 1930's and 1940's. Recently, the record has been better. To some economists, however, the present improved performance record does not alter the picture. They remember how the wrong policy decisions of the past intensified monetary instability; in their view discretionary policy remains a continuing source of economic instability. As a solution they propose automatic monetary policies and various other banking reforms.

One such reform that is frequently proposed is the elimination of fractional reserve banking and the creation of *100 percent reserve banking*. Commercial banks would be required to maintain reserves equal in value to 100 percent of their demand deposit liabilities. Thus they could no longer be lenders of funds, unless they were themselves permitted to issue stocks and bonds on a large scale. In effect, this proposal would eliminate commercial banking as we know it today.[2]

Our experiences during the early 1930's gave rise to this proposal for 100 percent reserves. Bank reserves were (and are today) only a fraction of deposit liabilities. Banks were unable to redeem their deposit liabilities. There were widespread bank failures. Perverse decreases in the stock of money occurred. A 100 percent reserve system would remove a major source of

---

[1] Jacob Viner, "The Necessary and the Desirable Range of Discretion To Be Allowed to a Monetary Authority," in Leland B. Yeager, *In Search of a Monetary Constitution* (Cambridge, Mass.: Harvard University Press, 1962), p. 273.

[2] For a discussion of how to institute this policy change, see George Tolley, "100 Per Cent Reserve Banking," in Leland B. Yeager, *In Search of a Monetary Constitution,* pp. 275–304.

economic instability; people would know that their deposits could be immediately converted into currency at any time.

Deposit insurance produces almost the same degree of confidence as would 100 percent reserves, however, and with far less revamping of our financial institutions. For this reason, most economists have considered the 100 percent reserve proposal impractical. The Federal Deposit Insurance Corporation, established in 1935, assures the safety of bank deposit liabilities. In addition, it is generally felt that 100 percent money proposals are not politically feasible. Such a proposal would encounter widespread opposition from both professional bankers and borrowers.

The 100 percent money proposal is frequently an assumption behind rules suggested for an automatic monetary policy. It is not, however, an indispensable ingredient of an automatic policy.

In past decades, the most widely acclaimed rule for automatic monetary action has been what is known as the *stabilization of the price level*. Henry Simons and Lloyd Mints are the architects of this rule. They suggested that the rule instruct the central bank to buy government securities whenever the price index fell beneath some particular level. The resultant increase in the stock of money would decrease the deflationary forces at work in the economy. Mints and Simons hoped "that the announced policy, when implemented by annual additions to the stock of money, would result in an autonomous maintenance of a high average level of output and an absence of serious movements in the price index."[3] On the other hand, during periods of rising prices they suggested that the central bank be instructed to sell government securities once the price level rose above some particular level. The decrease in the stock of money was expected to put downward pressures on the price level. Mints and Simons recognized the limitations of their system, however: "If price-level stabilization is a poor system, it is still, from a liberal viewpoint, infinitely better than no system at all."[4]

The promised advantages of this policy lie in the fact that it corresponds to the most understandable meaning of the concept of monetary stability, and it affords the opportunity for prompt and ample action to offset disturbances. However, from this latter fact also arises a possible drawback. Of necessity, discretionary control over the extent of open market operations would be given to the monetary agency, and the lag in effect might conceivably cause an unwanted magnification of autonomous developments.[5]

One of the chief economic advantages of a monetary policy involving a rule such as that recommended by Mints and Simons is its automatism. Hence, it is called an "automatic" monetary policy. Once the rule-deter-

---

[3] Lloyd W. Mints, *Monetary Policy for a Competitive Society* (New York: McGraw-Hill, 1951), p. 225.

[4] Henry Simons, *Economic Policy for a Free Society* (Chicago: University of Chicago Press, 1948), p. 174.

[5] Mints, *Monetary Policy for a Competitive Society*, pp. 224–25.

mined conditions for action are met, the monetary authority must follow appropriate corrective techniques. Thus, there is no delay resulting from the deliberations and hesitations of a discretionary monetary authority. Some discretionary lag would remain, of course, but action should still be prompter with the rule than without it.

In addition to the stable prices rule, Mints and Simons also considered "increasing the stock of money at a rate roughly equivalent to the rate of increase in the volume of transactions."[6] By stabilizing the money supply, it was thought that perverse variations in money would be eliminated as a source of economic instability. Velocity changes could still cause instability, of course. Thus they felt that the stable price level rule was superior on this score: "A price-index rule . . . defines . . . appropriate measures for dealing with velocity changes."[7]

Recently, however, various *stable money growth* rules have been re-examined by Milton Friedman, Clark Warburton, Edward Shaw, James Angell, and others. Of the proposed variants of this rule, that of Milton Friedman has received the most attention among professional economists.

The stable money growth rule recommended by Friedman states:

Instruct the System to use its open market powers to produce a 4 percent per year rate of growth in the total of currency held by the public and adjusted deposits in commercial banks. The System should be instructed to keep the rate of growth as steady as it can week by week and month by month and to introduce no seasonal movement in the money stock.[8]

The proposed policy changes would remove from the Federal Reserve System the burden of determining discretionary contracyclical monetary policy. For Friedman and other quantity theorists there is a close relationship between changes in the money supply and changes in economic activity. Empirically,

The rate of change of the money supply shows well-marked cycles that match closely those in economic activity in general and precede the latter by a long interval. On the average, the rate of change of the money supply has reached its peak nearly sixteen months before the peak in general business and has reached its trough over the twelve months before the trough in general business.[9]

If this relationship is so steady, then possibly the Federal Reserve, instead of stabilizing the growth of the money supply, should change the rate of growth of the money supply so as to attain a predetermined rate of eco-

[6] *Ibid.*, p. 123.

[7] Henry Simons, "Rules Versus Authorities in Monetary Policy," reprinted in American Economic Association, *Readings in Monetary Theory* (Homewood, Ill.: Irwin, 1951), p. 355.

[8] Milton Friedman, *A Program for Monetary Stability* (New York: Fordham University Press, 1960), p. 100.

[9] Milton Friedman, "The Supply of Money and Changes in Prices and Output," in Joint Economic Committee, *The Relationship of Prices to Economic Stability and Growth: Compendium*, Document No. 23734 (Washington, D.C.: 1958), pp. 249–50.

nomic activity. This might be an equally acceptable rule as stable monetary growth were it not for the qualification "on the average" in Friedman's empirical work.

This is highly consistent behavior as such observations go and sufficient to pin down the *average* lead within a rather narrow range. But it is highly variable behavior for the individual episode with which policy must be concerned . . . monetary changes have their effect only after a considerable lag and over a long period and . . . the lag is rather variable.[10]

It is the *variable lag*, for Friedman, that makes discretionary monetary policy impractical and rules out the advisability of the Federal Reserve's manipulating variations in the rate of growth of the money stock. Why? Because we cannot predict precisely when a change in the rate of growth in the money stock will have its economic effects. It is entirely possible that a step-up of the rate of growth of the money supply taken during a recession could first make its effects felt during a subsequent boom. Similarly, a decrease in the rate of growth of money during an inflation may take effect in the subsequent recession, thereby aggravating the current crisis. Thus changes in the money stock remain a source of economic instability.

It should be noted, however, that the policy recommendation is not for a stable money supply, but rather for stable *growth* in the money supply. The reason for providing for a steady increase in the money supply is simple. As income and output expand with economic growth, more money is needed to carry on the increasing volume of transactions. If the money supply is not permitted to expand, price deflation can occur unless there is a velocity offset. This could lead to general unemployment.

Many contemporary economists disagree with Friedman's policy recommendations and empirical results. They contend that the lag in monetary policy (and fiscal policy as well) is short enough for a change in policy to have a stabilizing influence on income and output. J. M. Culbertson, for example, states:

The broad record of experience seems to me to support the view that anti-cyclical monetary, debt-management, and fiscal adjustments can be counted on to have their predominant direct effects within three to six months, soon enough that if they are undertaken moderately early in a cyclical phase they will not be destabilizing.[11]

Albert Ando and E. Cary Brown, in an empirical study, also reach conclusions different from Friedman's:

Our conclusion is that it [monetary policy] works neither so slowly as Friedman thinks, nor as quickly and surely as the Federal Reserve itself seems to believe. We find that the effect of monetary policy on the flow of expenditures is far from overwhelming, though it exists and is of a magnitude worth exploiting in

[10] Milton Friedman, *A Program for Monetary Stability*, pp. 87–88.
[11] J. M. Culbertson, "Friedman on the Lag in Effect of Monetary Policy," *The Journal of Political Economy* (1960), p. 621.

the interests of economic stability. We also find that though the *full* results of policy changes on the flow of expenditures may be a long time coming, nevertheless the chain of effects is spread out over a fairly wide interval. This means that *some* effect comes reasonably quickly and that the effects build up over time so that some substantial stabilizing power results after a lapse of time of the order of six or nine months.[12]

These disparate results should not be taken as the basis for despair of arriving at wise policy choices among discretionary and automatic monetary policy proposals. Rather the controversies mentioned here, and in an earlier chapter on alternative monetary theories, are the outward manifestations of a healthy scientific discipline. The process of setting up alternative hypotheses and policy prescriptions is all part of seeking to understand more fully the nature of the world in which we live. In many respects, the more that we learn about this world and about economics, the more we recognize the complexity of apparently simple phenomena. When we investigate problems, instead of solving them we frequently find new questions to be answered.

Supplementary Readings

On financial asset policy proposals
Gurley, J. G., and Edward Shaw. "Financial Intermediaries and the Saving-Investment Process." *Journal of Finance* (1956), pp. 257–76.

On automatic monetary policy
Friedman, Milton. *A Program for Monetary Stability*. New York, Fordham University Press, 1960.
Mints, Lloyd W. *Monetary Policy for a Competitive Society*. New York, McGraw-Hill, 1950.
Shaw, Edward. "Money Supply and Stable Economic Growth." In American Assembly, *United States Monetary Policy*, New York, Columbia University Press, 1958, pp. 49–71.
Simons, Henry. *Economic Policy for a Free Society*. Chicago, University of Chicago Press, 1948.

---

[12] Albert Ando, E. Cary Brown, Robert M. Solow, and John Kareken, "Lags in Fiscal and Monetary Policy," in Commission on Money and Credit, *Stabilization Policies* (Englewood Cliffs, N.J.: Prentice-Hall, 1963), p. 2.

Chapter 24

Alternative Fiscal Policies

Fiscal policy posits the same goals as monetary policy: full employment, price stabilization, economic growth, and a balance in the flow of international payments. Fiscal policy is both discretionary and automatic, however, whereas monetary policy today is wholly discretionary. The instruments of fiscal policy are the tax, government expenditure, and the debt management practices of the Congress and the Administration.

This chapter considers the tax and spending instruments of fiscal policy as they are used to help stabilize the economy. Some mention is also made of the relationship between fiscal policy and economic growth. Debt management practices, already discussed in Chapter 14, are not examined here, because debt management and Federal Reserve policy instruments are fairly well coordinated. This is important, of course. It will be recalled that discretionary management of the debt by the Treasury is capable of exerting a powerful influence on commercial bank reserve positions. Hence the need for coordination between Federal Reserve and Treasury policies with regard to debt management.

FISCAL POLICY AND ECONOMIC STABILITY

Fiscal Policy in Recession

Variation in government expenditures is one way in which fiscal policy can be used to cure a recession. Let us assume that there is an increase in government expenditures. Further assume that Federal tax collections are constant and that there has been a balanced budget prior to the present situation. Under circumstances such as these, increased government expenditures will directly raise the level of spending in the economy. To the extent that consumption and investment-expenditure increases are induced by a rise in income resulting from new government spending, the total rise in the level of income will be some multiple of the government expenditure increase. If the increase in government spending is not accompanied by an increase in the stock of money, however, there will be some rise in interest rates and some dampening of the potential rise in income and output. Interest rates increase because increased spending means increased demand for money relative to the supply. In our income-expenditure model this assumes that the *IS* schedule intersects the rising portion of the *LM* schedule.

If the recession were severe, it would probably be best to finance the additional government expenditures by increasing the money supply. This would shift both *IS* and *LM* to the right, monetary forces reinforcing the increase in government expenditures.

On the other hand, in a mild recession, when unemployment is not particularly high, there is a danger that an increase in government spending may result in price inflation. A shifted *IS* may intersect *LM* to the right of full employment output. For this reason, money supply increases should not be permitted to reinforce government spending increases during mild recessions. A decision to correct a minor downward cyclical disturbance by increasing government expenditures can be self-defeating unless financed through the least inflationary channel, borrowing from the nonbank public. Full employment and stable prices are not necessarily compatible goals.

Fiscal policy can also combat a recession by *decreasing government tax collections*. In an economy with a balanced budget, a decrease in government personal tax collections will lead to an increase in disposable income, and in consumption spending. If business taxes are also lowered, the resultant increase in business-retained earnings should stimulate business investment expenditures. These additional consumption and investment expenditures will lead to a rise in income and output that is a multiple of the decrease in government tax collections. Thus decreased tax collections, like increased government expenditures, can lead to increased income and output.

Decreased government tax collections may also have money market effects. The way a deficit is financed, whether expenditure- or tax-induced, will lead to changes in the stock of money if securities are sold to either the central bank or the commercial banks.

There is at least one important *difference between decreased tax collections and increased government spending* as tools for promoting economic recovery. Increased government expenditures directly cause increased spending, whereas tax decreases cause increased spending indirectly. Assume, for example, that the marginal propensity to consume is .80. An increase of $1 billion in government spending directly increases gross national product by that amount. Subsequently, the marginal propensity to consume comes into play, and, barring money market effects, there will be $800 million, $640 million, etc., increases in the level of income. A decrease of $1 billion in government tax collections, however, will not directly affect spending in this manner. Instead, disposable income is increased by the amount of the tax decrease, $1 billion. This then induces $800 million, $640 million, etc., increases in the level of income. The difference in the effects of these two policies is in the initial effect of the $1 billion of government spending increase on the gross national product. A billion-dollar rise in spending has a greater overall effect on the economy than a billion-dollar decrease in tax collections. Thus *Government spending changes are more potent than tax changes as a contracyclical policy instrument*. Government spending increases are also more likely to cause price inflation than tax decreases. As a curative for a mild recession, therefore, a decrease in taxes seems preferable to an increase in government spending.

Fiscal Policy for Inflation

During periods of full employment and rising prices, the instruments of fiscal policy may be used in the opposite way to offset inflation. *Government expenditures may be reduced or government tax collections increased.* If this occurs, then at a given level of income planned $I + G + F$ becomes less than planned $S_p + S_b + T$. The *IS* line shifts to the left. This will lead to a reduction of income and output amounting to some multiple of the reduction in government spending or the increase in tax collections. If the decrease in government spending or the rise in tax collections occur without any change in the money supply, interest rates will also decline (unless, of course, price rises continue through the period of declining income).

Government spending decreases directly reduce income and thereby induce consumption and investment-expenditure decreases. Raising taxes reduces disposable income and thereby induces consumption and investment-expenditure decreases also. The government spending decrease exerts a more powerful downward influence on income, however, than a comparable dollar increase in tax collections.

The degree of inflation present in the economy should dictate which anti-inflationary fiscal measure would be appropriate. For a runaway inflation, the reduction in government spending might be more desirable because of its swifter and greater impact. For a mild inflation, on the other hand, the less depressive effects of a tax increase seem preferable. In either case, aggregate demand should not be allowed to fall so sharply as to cause less than full employment equilibrium.

Anti-inflationary fiscal measures can also have an important effect on the money supply. A drop in government spending or an increase in taxes may lead to a Treasury surplus, for example. If these funds are held idle or are used to retire government securities held by the central banks, the money supply is decreased. This, in turn, sets up forces that keep interest rates high (the *LM* shifts to the left), reinforcing the effects of the increasing government surplus on income. Chapter 14 treated the mechanics of tax surpluses in some detail.

Effects of Changes in Tax Rates

The relationship between discretionary spending policy and a stabilizing tax structure. In the preceding analysis we assumed that government tax changes were accomplished without reference to the tax structure of the nation. Our approach assumed that the government could deliberately vary the *amount* of its tax collections to help stabilize the economy. No mention was made as to *how* the tax collections would be varied, however. In point of fact, the *amount* of tax collections, as indicated in earlier chapters, varies automatically with the level of income. As gross national product increases, the amount of government tax collections increases; as gross national product decreases, tax collections decrease.

Assume, for example, that there is a proportional income tax of 20 percent. For the sake of simplicity, imagine this tax rate to be geared to gross national product. Under these circumstances, for every $1 billion dollar change in gross national product, there will be a $200 million change in tax collections. Thus *the nature of the tax structure itself tends to dampen whatever phase of the cycle is current.* For this reason our federal tax system is frequently called an *automatic stabilizer.* Changes in government tax collections occur automatically, without the need for discretionary action by Congress or the President.

The income-expenditure model developed in Chapters 19–21 assumed a tax structure that was geared to the level of income. Under this model, the Federal actions affecting equilibrium income are changes in government spending and changes in the "tax rate." The *IS* line does not necessarily shift with changes in the amount of tax collections, as was assumed earlier in this chapter. Only when the amount of tax collections changes as a result of changes in the tax rate will the *IS* curve shift.

How much of a change in government expenditures is needed to change aggregate economic activity by a given amount when tax collections are not fixed but geared to the level of income? More than with the fixed tax collections! Assume, for example, that the government wants to increase disposable income by $1 billion directly. Ignoring the effects on business income, and the induced effects on consumption and investment, we find that only a $1 billion increase in spending is needed. If taxes are stated in fixed amounts, a $1 billion increase in government spending will induce an equivalent increase in disposable income throughout the economy. If taxes are stated in proportion to personal income, however, at a uniform rate of 20 per cent, then a $1 billion increase in government spending will cause disposable income to rise by only $800 million; $200 million will come back to the government in the form of taxes. Thus with a proportional personal income tax government spending will have to be increased by $1.25 billion in order to produce a $1 billion increase in disposable income. Similarly, in reverse, a reduction of $1.25 billion in government spending is needed to cause a $1 billion decrease in disposable income.[1]

A change in the tax rate. What happens when tax rates are changed? In

---

[1] If $\Delta Y_d = \Delta G - .2\Delta G$, *then* $\Delta G = \dfrac{\Delta Y_d}{.8}$ and $\Delta G = \dfrac{1 \text{ billion}}{.8} = 1.25$ billion.

terms of the analysis discussed in Chapter 19, an increase in the tax rate will turn the $S_p + S_b + T$ line up and to the left, leading to a turn of the *IS* line that is down and to the left. This shift is from $(IS)_0$ to $(IS)_1$ in Figure 24–1. Notice that the *IS* lines intersect the upward sloping part of *LM*. We assume that there has been no change in the stock of money resulting from a tax surplus. The result of an increase in the tax rate is thus a decrease in disposable income, which induces reductions in consumption and invest-ment expenditure. Equilibrium income is reduced from Y_e to Y_e', with a drop in the interest rate from i_e to i_e'. If, prior to the tax rate change, there was full employment and rising prices, the increase in the tax rate would

FIGURE 24–1. Effects of a change in the tax rate.

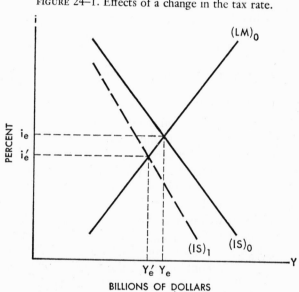

BILLIONS OF DOLLARS

reverse the increase in prices, halting the shifts in *LM* to the left that were probably taking place. If the tax increase is properly planned, the resultant equilibrium income, Y_e', should also be full employment income and output.

Lowering the tax rate should have reverse effects. If no money stock changes result from a deficit, and if Y_e is full-employment output and the initial *IS* line is $(IS)_1$, then a decrease in the tax rate will push the line from $(IS)_1$ to $(IS)_0$. This leads to increased disposable income and induces increases in consumption and investment spending. Equilibrium comes up from Y_e' to Y_e, and the rate of interest rises from i_e' to i_e.

Like government spending changes, tax-rate changes must be carefully planned. Many offsets are possible. For example, a tax cut designed to stabilize the economy could lead people to believe that the government anticipated a severe recession. As a result, expectations for the economic future would worsen. In anticipation of declining incomes, personal saving would increase and business investment plans would be postponed or scaled down. Clearly these events could more than offset the desirable effects of a tax cut. On the other hand, a tax cut or increased government spending may lead people to believe that the government is willing to do almost anything to offset a possible recession. As a result, they may come to assume that severe recession is impossible; the government will take care of everything. Spending plans, instead of being revised downward, will thus be revised upward. In the aggregate, this increase in demand may overshoot the full employment point and cause price inflation.

Another reason for careful government planning of contracyclical fiscal policy is that it can have a serious impact on the money market. As previously noted, the stock of money can fluctuate with surpluses and deficits. Therefore, debt management should attempt to complement tax and spending changes.

FISCAL POLICY AND ECONOMIC GROWTH

Poorly planned fiscal policy can also inhibit economic growth. For example, during periods of inflation appropriate contracyclical fiscal policy calls for an increase in tax rates. If the tax increase is imposed on business, the expected after-tax rate of return from investment projects is thereby reduced. In the absence of offsetting reductions in the cost of funds (interest rate), investment expenditures will decline. A decrease in investment expenditures may lead to real plant and equipment production decreases as well. Thus economic growth is retarded, for to raise the productive capacity of the economy, there must be an expansion of real investment.

With this in mind, some have argued that during inflation and full employment the appropriate contracyclical fiscal policy would be to increase taxes on consumers rather than to raise taxes on business. This, it is suggested, would restrain consumption demand and possibly cause a redistribution of output from consumer to producer goods. Thus we could simultaneously help stem inflation and increase the productive capacity of the economy. A complementary monetary policy would be to keep interest rates high for consumers by means of selective credit controls, and low on long-term credit to encourage business expansion.

During a recession, on the other hand, there is normally no conflict between stabilization and growth policies. Increased government expenditures and decreased tax rates promote expansion in both demand and growth.

FISCAL POLICY
AND THE BALANCE OF PAYMENTS

The contracyclical timing of government spending and taxes also damages our balance of payments. This must also be borne in mind. Taxes and spending can be manipulated so as to influence the balance of payments favorably as well. Some discussion of this point is found in Chapters 25 and 26.

PROBLEMS OF DISCRETIONARY FISCAL POLICY

Our analysis points toward discretionary decreases in government spending and increases in tax rates during periods of full employment and rising prices and the reverse of these policies during recession. These policies are not easy to implement, however. Many of the problems that plague monetary policy also affect fiscal policy in this regard. We have already pointed out the dangers of overshooting the full employment mark when using anti-recessionary fiscal policy. There are also problems of allocation and lag.

The Allocation Problem

When the government spends funds, it can alter the structure of national production by creating a demand for specific goods and services. Business responds by producing those goods and services. On the other hand, tax measures affect disposable income of consumers and businesses; a change in disposable income leads to changed investment and consumption demands for specific goods and services. In this way tax and spending policies are comparable in their impact on production. There is this difference, however. Tax measures permit the private sector of the economy to determine what goods are to be produced. If one values an economy in which individual free choice determines the allocation of resources, then a contracyclical tax policy is to be preferred to a contracyclical spending policy. Of course, the government must undertake those projects (e.g., defense, public education, highways, and social security) that have been approved by a social consensus. The doctrine of individual choice simply suggests that there should be a minimum of interference with the allocation of resources chosen by the free market for privately produced goods, *and* by social consensus for social goods.

The Lag Problem

The problem of lags can also affect fiscal policy. There are three main lags in economic policy: (1) the lag between the time when economic action becomes necessary and the time this need is recognized, (2) the lag between the recognition of the need and the remedial action, and (3) the lag between the action and the time when the effects of the action are felt in the economy.

The first lag occurs in the same degree for both discretionary monetary policy and for fiscal policy. The second lag, however, is much longer for fiscal policy than for monetary policy. Monetary action can quickly be taken by the Board of Governors, but discretionary fiscal action usually involves an Act of Congress, and the legislative wheels grind slowly. Our most recent personal income tax cut was first proposed in the spring of 1962 and not passed until the spring of 1964.

In some matters, discretionary response to need can be swift. The Administration, so long as it operates within the confines of the budget passed by Congress, can speed up or decrease the rate of government expenditures by simply issuing an order. The increase in the rate of defense expenditures ordered in the latter part of 1957 and early 1958, for example, helped to overcome the 1957–58 recession. An overall change in government spending or tax rates, however, requires an Act of Congress.

The third lag, the lag between the action and the time when the effects of the action are felt in the economy, lasts either six to nine months or twelve to sixteen months for monetary policy. The lag is considerably shorter in tax matters. The effects of tax action are usually felt within the first six months.[2] Changes in government expenditures, however—public works projects, for example—take time to plan. If already planned, contracts introduce a delay. "The steps in appropriation, allocation of funds, bidding, contract award, and construction are of such length that only a small fraction of construction can be expected within a year from the initiation of a program."[3] Even the previously mentioned changes in the rate of defense spending "take a considerable period before they register themselves in output . . . Aircraft contracts, for example, change output by only 20 percent of the contract by the end of six months, 55 percent by the end of three quarters, and are nearly fully reflected in output change by the end of a year."[4]

The length of these government spending lags is of such a nature as to suggest that changes in government spending are not really a suitable means of economic stabilization, at least for mild recessions and short-lived inflations. For such problems discretionary taxes or monetary policy actions appear to be more appropriate. However, as noted above, the lag between recognition of the need and the action is usually very long for tax measures. In addition, while tax cuts are always politically palatable, peacetime tax increases are almost impossible to get through Congress. This means that, in practice, tax changes can seldom be used to correct peacetime inflation.

FISCAL POLICY AS AN AUTOMATIC STABILIZER

Automatic fiscal action is at least a partial solution to this dilemma; it helps stabilize the economy without direct action by government authori-

---

[2] Albert Ando, E. Cary Brown, Robert M. Solow, and John Kareken, "Lags in Fiscal and Monetary Policy," in Commission on Money and Credit, *Stabilization Policies* (Englewood Cliffs, N.J.: Prentice-Hall, 1963), p. 2.
[3] *Ibid.*, p. 11.   [4] *Ibid.*, p. 11.

ties, thus eliminating the first two lags. The third lag is of comparatively short duration. In this regard, automatic fiscal policy appears to be superior to both discretionary fiscal and discretionary monetary policy. There is no automatic monetary policy.

There are two principal types of automatic fiscal stabilizers at work, (1) the Federal income tax system and (2) the social security program.

The Federal Income Tax

We have already mentioned that as incomes increase, government tax collections rise, thereby restricting the growth in disposable personal and business income. Actually, our personal income tax is progressively scaled. As incomes rise, the tax collections increase more than proportionately to the growth in income. Thus disposable income becomes an increasingly smaller percentage of gross national product as the latter rises. This helps restrain inflationary forces in the economy. On the other hand, as incomes fall, government tax collections decrease more than proportionately to the decline in income. People move into lower tax brackets and disposable income becomes a greater fraction of gross national product. This helps reduce the severity of an economic downturn.

The Social Security Program

The second type of automatic fiscal stabilizer is the social security program. As income and employment drop, employee contributions to social security decline and increasing amounts of unemployment compensation are paid to the unemployed. This tends to maintain disposable income and thereby lessens the impact of recession. As economic recovery gets under way, unemployment drops, unemployment compensation decreases, and social security tax collections increase. This in turn helps to prevent a recovery from becoming a boom.

Automatic Stabilizers and Less-Than-Full-Employment Equilibrium

To the extent that automatic stabilizers dampen upward and downward movements in the economy, they seem to be an effective means of combating both inflation and deflation. There is also a possibility that they may dampen recovery, however. Gross national product and full employment output expand over time. With a progressive income tax structure, people move into higher income tax brackets as gross national product increases. Thus the average income tax rate increases. This means that at higher levels of income and output more of an effort is needed to keep the economy at full employment output. For example, a $1 billion increase in government expenditures directly increases disposable income by $1 billion when taxes are unchanged, by $800 million when the average income tax rate is 20 percent, and by only $700 million when the average income tax rate drifts up with economic growth to 30 percent. Thus, larger injections of government spending are needed to keep the economy at full employment as the average tax rate climbs.

It is possible that occasional downward revisions of the tax-rate structure might solve this problem. This was one of the arguments behind the 1964 tax reduction. There is one drawback, however. *Lowering the tax-rate structure makes the economy more subject to volatile upward and downward movements in economic activity.* Government control of the economy is weakened. As consumption and investment expenditures increase because of a favorable business outlook, the accompanying increase in government tax collections at the new lower tax rate may not be enough to thwart inflation. Similarly, in a recession the accompanying decrease in government tax collections will be less than the decrease under higher tax rates. Thus a lower tax-rate structure may not be able to cushion decreases in disposable income, either.

SUMMARY AND EVALUATION OF FISCAL POLICY

Discretionary fiscal policy is subject to long lags arising from the slowness in the legislative and administrative decision-making process. Discretionary monetary policy works much faster in this respect. Once tax changes have been made, however, discretionary tax policy operates more rapidly than monetary policy. Automatic fiscal policy can be very helpful in stabilizing the economy, but possibly at the expense of high employment levels. Periodic downward adjustments in tax rates may be the solution.

As was the case with monetary policy, conclusions concerning the potential effectiveness of fiscal policy are mixed. For a deep depression there is no problem: raise government expenditures and cut taxes. For a runaway inflation lower government expenditures and increase taxes. Of course, if a wise economic policy were followed in the first place, we would not get into deep depressions or runaway inflations. The problem arises when mild inflations or recessions occur. Particular care must be taken, for example, in the discretionary use of both monetary and fiscal policy measures when the economy is close to full employment. Because of lags we are in danger of aggravating ensuing phases of economic fluctuations.

In practice, there has been little use of discretionary fiscal policy by Congress since the end of World War II. Congress and the President have seldom deliberately changed government expenditures for purposes of economic stabilization. Government expenditure changes are usually prompted by changing national defense commitments and pressing community needs. Tax cuts have not usually been thought of as anti-recessionary legislation, either. There have been three principal tax cuts in the last two decades. The tax cuts of 1949 and 1954 were fortunately executed in the midst of recessions, but were not planned as a means of pulling the economy out of a slump. The 1964 tax cut, however, was officially justified as a means of increasing spending and reducing unemployment, although this legislation was passed during a period of recovery rather than of recession.

Supplementary Reading
Ando, Albert, E. Cary Brown, Robert M. Solow, and John Kareken. "Lags in Fiscal and Monetary Policy." In Commission on Money and Credit, *Stabilization Policies,* Englewood Cliffs, N.J., Prentice-Hall, 1963, pp. 1–163.

Chapter 25

Exchange Rates
and the Balance-of-Payments Problem

GROSS NATIONAL PRODUCT
AND THE BALANCE OF TRADE

An economy does not function in isolation from the rest of the world; the domestic economic policies of one nation influence economic behavior in other countries, and vice versa. Recession or inflation in one country may have international repercussions.

For example, rising incomes in one nation often lead to increases in the exports of other countries, for as disposable incomes increase, the demand for both domestic *and* foreign goods and services increases. This induces expansion of production abroad. On the other hand, a decline in disposable income at home causes a reduction in the demand for both domestic and foreign goods. This, in turn, can lead to decreased incomes abroad.

The United States is a large nation and most of its production is designed for the domestic market. Exports usually amount to only about 5 percent of the American gross national product. For this reason, the United States is not as likely to be materially affected by economic conditions abroad, except insofar as changes in foreign economic conditions influence American expectations concerning the vigor of the domestic economy.

Imports also represent a small percentage of our gross national product. In dollar volume, however, they are large; total imports for the year 1963 were valued at $26.2 billion.[1] For many small countries exports to the United States are a major source of their gross national product. To this extent the condition of the U.S. economy may well have an important direct effect on the prosperity of these smaller countries.

Goods and services sold abroad are a part of gross national product. They also give rise to a flow of payments into the exporting country. Imports do not directly contribute to gross national product, but they do give rise to a flow of payments out of the importing country. The annual difference in

---

[1] *Federal Reserve Bulletin*, April, 1964, p. 506.

value between a country's imports and exports is termed its *balance of trade*. If exports are greater than imports, the balance of trade is considered positive. If the value of exports is less than that of imports, the balance of trade is negative. As was shown earlier in Tables 19–1 and 19–3, the balance of trade for the United States has almost always been positive. The payments owed the United States have usually been greater than the payments it owes other nations for the purchase of goods and services. Presumably, this should put the United States in a strong position in the international economy.

Generally this is the case, but in the late 1950's and into the first half of the 1960's the United States has experienced some balance-of-payments difficulties. The balance of trade constitutes only a portion of the balance of payments. Other types of international financial transactions are included in this figure in addition to those in real goods and services. It is these other transactions that have been the source of balance-of-payments difficulties for the United States.

THE BALANCE OF PAYMENTS

Definition

A nation's balance of payments is a record of the various payments it has made to foreigners and the payments it has received from them over a period of time. The record of the balance of payments is not to be confused with a balance sheet, however. The balance of payments records the *flow* of international payments and receipts; a balance sheet shows a financial position at a moment of time; it is a *stock* concept.

Actually the balance of payments is always in balance over time. Receipts must equal expenditures. The difficulties in the balance of payments arise from the manner in which balance is achieved. A country has a balance of payments *deficit* when its *current* payments are in excess of its *current* receipts. To make up the difference and achieve balance, the debtor country can draw on its previously accumulated balances of foreign monies, borrow foreign monies, or export gold to meet the demands of creditor nations. A country that does not meet its obligations in gold will cover its deficit by transferring to its creditors claims on some internationally accepted money such as the American dollar.

On the other hand, there is a balance of payments *surplus* when current receipts are in excess of current payments. To make up the difference, foreign countries can follow the same policies: borrow, dip into accumulated balances of foreign monies, or ship gold.

The U.S. dollar stands in a unique position relative to foreign monies in that it serves as international money. Transactions between countries all over the world are settled by the use of dollar deposits. This creates a strong demand for dollars. As a result, when the U.S. balance of payments is in deficit, foreign governments will frequently choose to accumulate claims to dollars rather than demand gold.[2] For example, the balance-of-payments deficit of the United States in 1963 was $3.301 billion, yet the actual U.S. loss of gold was only $461 million. Most of the remaining $2.84 billion was made up by the sale of $702 million of convertible, nonmarketable securities abroad and the accumulation of $1.58 billion in demand deposit claims. This buildup of claims against American money enhances the international economic position of the creditor countries.

The U.S. Balance of Payments

Table 25-1 shows the United States balance of payments for 1963. Most of the items listed are self-explanatory. U.S. receipts on *goods and services* refers to the value of our exports. U.S. payments on goods and services covers the value of our imports. The difference between the two is termed our balance of trade, and was a positive item in the U.S. balance of payments in 1963. *Remittances and pensions* consist primarily of emigrant remittances. This is the term used to describe the currency outflow arising when emigrants in the United States send money to friends and relatives abroad. *U.S. government grants and capital flows* include U.S. military and economic grants-in-aid and long-term loans to foreign governments. This item alone is more than equal to the U.S. balance of payments deficits. A large part of these funds find their way back into the United States, however, in the form of merchandise receipts. *Private capital flows* include principally the purchase of plant and equipment facilities abroad by American businesses and the purchase of foreign-issued securities. These five broad categories resulted in a $3.301 billion deficit in the U.S. balance of payments in 1963. The balancing items were a gold outflow, a sale of convertible nonmarketable securities, and an accumulation of short-term claims against American money. In addition, some countries helped the American situation by making advance repayments on U.S. government loans, as well as advance payments on military imports from the United States.

Most of the balancing items are listed as receipts because they show how foreign governments choose to spend the excess of current U.S. payments

---

[2] It should be noted that even when nations take gold in payment from debtor countries, there is seldom an actual physical transfer of gold from one country to another. For example, many countries have gold "earmarked" for them in the vaults of the Federal Reserve Bank of New York. If the United States owes funds to creditor countries, they may buy gold from the United States Treasury and have it "earmarked" in their name. If others are in debt to the United States, they may sell us some of their "earmarked" gold. In any case, the gold physically remains in the Federal Reserve Bank of New York. This is done because shipping gold from country to country is costly and involves some risk.

over receipts. These items are largely self-explanatory. The reason for listing the $461 million gold outflow as a receipt, however, is not so readily apparent. When U.S. current payments exceed receipts, the creditor countries, as already indicated, may choose to demand gold. The United States must then give up some of its gold holdings in "payment" of its debt. How is this accomplished? Assume, for example, that the deficit of the United

TABLE 25–1. THE UNITED STATES BALANCE OF PAYMENTS, 1963
(IN MILLIONS OF DOLLARS)

ITEM	U.S. RECEIPTS	U.S. PAYMENTS	NET BALANCE
Goods and services			
Merchandise	21,902	16,962	
Military sales	632	2,880	
Investment income	4,565	1,196	
Other	4,504	5,080	
Total	31,603	26,118	5,485
Remittances and pension		812	−812
U.S. Government grants and capital flows, net		3,789	−3,789
Private capital flows			
Direct investments		1,799	
Long-term capital		1,641	
Foreign investments in U.S.	387		
U.S. short-term capital		642	
Foreign short-term capital	5		
Total	392	4,082	−3,690
Errors and omissions		495	−495
Total Net Balance			−3,301
Advance repayments on U.S. Government loans	325		
Advances on U.S. military exports	359		
Sales of nonconvertible nonmarketable securities		43	
Sales of convertible nonmarketable securities	702		
Change in short-term liabilities	1,580		
Change in U.S. monetary reserve assets			
IMF position	30		
Convertible currencies		113	
Gold	461		
Total	3,457	156	3,301

Source: *Federal Reserve Bulletin*, April, 1964, p. 537.

States vis-à-vis Country X is $50 million. When Country X demands gold, it does so by using the $50 million in accumulated claims to "buy" gold from the United States. The gold outflow, therefore, is considered an export from the United States, which "receives" $50 million from the sale of gold. In effect, Country X gives us its IOU's on our currency in exchange for gold and we record the receipt of these IOU's as a receipt of that amount in dollars. Gold flows thereby act to balance the flow of payments.

Table 25–2 shows that in the early post–World War II period, the United States had a surplus balance of payments. The productive facilities of European countries had been devastated by the war and the United States was the only country large enough and sufficiently industrialized to meet the European demands for new plants and equipment. European countries were faced with a "shortage" of dollars, however, because of the lack of U.S. demand for European goods. To solve this problem the United States

TABLE 25–2. SELECTED ITEMS IN THE U.S. BALANCE OF PAYMENTS, 1947–1963

(IN MILLIONS OF DOLLARS)

YEAR	BALANCE ON GOODS AND SERVICES	GOVERNMENT GRANTS AND CAPITAL OUTFLOW	PRIVATE Direct investments	PRIVATE Long-term portfolio	PRIVATE Short-term portfolio	OVERALL BALANCE*
1947	11,529	−6,415†	−749	−49	−189	4,567
1948	6,440	−5,361	−721	−69	−116	1,005
1949	6,149	−5,854	−660	−80	187	175
1950	1,779	−3,935	−621	−495	−149	−3,580
1951	3,671	−3,496	−508	−437	−103	−305
1952	2,226	−2,809	−852	−214	−94	−1,046
1953	386	−2,542	−735	185	167	−2,152
1954	1,828	−2,061	−667	−320	−635	−1,550
1955	2,009	−2,627	−823	−241	−191	−1,145
1956	3,967	−2,841	−1,951	−603	−517	−935
1957	5,729	−3,233	−2,442	−859	−276	520
1958	2,206	−3,131	−1,181	−1,444	−311	−3,529
1959	134	−3,040	−1,372	−926	−77	−3,743
1960	3,769	−3,405	−1,694	−850	−1,348	−3,881
1961	5,444	−4,056	−1,598	−1,011	−1,541	−2,370
1962	4,826	−4,281	−1,557	−1,209	−507	−2,186
1963	5,485	−4,532	−1,799	−1,641	−642	−1,958

Source: *Economic Report of the President*, 1964, pp. 297–98; and *Federal Reserve Bulletin*, April, 1964, p. 537.

* Calculated as the sum of changes in U.S. gold and convertible currencies and short-term liabilities to foreigners. Calculated in this manner, the overall balance differs from the net balance of Table 25–1.

† Minus numbers are payments.

helped provide funds for needy countries by means of unilateral gifts. The Marshall Plan was an early example of such assistance. As Table 25–2 shows, economic aid played a very important role in reducing foreign balance-of-payments deficits in the early postwar years. In 1947, for example, the American balance of trade was $11.5 billion. In the absence of offsetting forces, this would have led to an $11.5 billion balance-of-payments surplus. The actual surplus for that year amounted to only $4.6 billion, however. Government grants and capital outflows accounted for $6.4 billion, almost the entire difference between the balance-of-trade surplus and the balance-of-payments surplus. This government aid enabled other countries to buy goods and services in the United States.

As the rest of the world gradually recovered from the aftereffects of World War II, the dollar shortage gradually diminished. Foreign economies, aided by U.S. economic assistance, were able to resume the production of an ever wider variety of goods and services. As a consequence, people in the United States began to purchase more goods abroad. This occurred to such a degree that our imports grew more rapidly than our exports, cutting down the size of our balance-of-trade surplus. At the same time U.S. government grants, which had dropped by two-thirds through the year 1954, began to increase; both economic aid and military expenditures abroad rose. Most of these expenditures were directed toward less developed nations as part of our cold-war strategy. Britain, Germany, France, and other developed nations of the West that we assisted immediately after World War II no longer need economic aid. The United States continues to make military expenditures in these countries, however, because we have deemed it necessary to maintain a large military establishment overseas. These grants and military expenditures, combined with a decreased trade surplus, have contributed to the balance-of-payments deficits of the late 1950's and early to mid-1960's.

An additional factor contributing to the deficit has been the sharp increase in private capital outflows since 1956. Private direct investment and long-term security purchases abroad have been running two to three times their pre-1956 levels. Expanded foreign markets and greater political stability abroad have tended to expand these long-term financial outlays. Higher interest rates abroad on long-term securities have also stimulated overseas investment. From time to time higher foreign short-term interest rates have also increased the outflow of short-term funds.

Balance-of-Payments Equilibrium

A country that continually has a balance-of-payments surplus or deficit clearly does not have a balance-of-payments equilibrium and so must make adjustments to correct the situation. When a country has a continuing surplus, it means that other countries are short of funds with which to buy goods and services in the surplus country. Therefore, the surplus country must make adjustments to provide foreigners with additional funds, or the deficit countries will be forced to cut down on their expenditures in the surplus country. Thus, when the United States had a balance-of-payments surplus after World War II, it provided other nations with funds in the form of grants-in-aid. More recently, other countries with surpluses, such as Germany, have found different solutions to the problem. Germany revalued its currency upward, for example. Deficit nations, on the other hand, must either cut back on payments or stimulate surplus nations to increase their expenditures. One common solution for the deficit nation is currency devaluation; Britain did this in 1949. In other cases, a change in the interest-rate structure can also help to achieve a balance-of-payments equilibrium.

Thus, in general, continual surpluses dictate the need for an increase in payments or a decrease in receipts; continual deficits require a decrease in payments or an increase in receipts. If the measures taken to achieve these goals are successful, a balance-of-payments equilibrium will be achieved and there will be only a minimal fluctuation in the balancing items of gold flows and short-term claims.

The following chapter examines specific solutions to international balance-of-payments difficulties. We will begin this discussion by explaining the connection between the balance of payments and the exchange rate. To this point no mention has been made of the fact that different countries employ different monetary units of account. This, as we shall see, creates important balance-of-payments problems.

THE EXCHANGE RATE

Introduction

Each country has its own monetary unit of account. Thus prices and money in the United States are added up in terms of the dollar; the unit of account in France is the franc; in Japan, the yen; and in Germany, the Deutsche mark. Within the boundaries of each nation, each currency circulates freely. In international trade, however, it does not, for there is no single international unit of account. Although dollars are often used to settle international transactions, importers and exporters usually need specific currencies to carry on their transactions. For example, United States exporters receive claims against foreign money in payment for their goods, but they need American currency to meet their internal obligations. Conversely, importers need foreign monies to buy goods abroad. Consequently these merchants make use of the foreign exchange market where different types of currencies may be obtained. This market consists of the banks, brokers, and agents who deal in the purchase and sale of foreign exchange (foreign currency).

The principal suppliers of foreign currency in this market are exporters and those who sell securities abroad; the principal demanders of foreign currency are importers and buyers of foreign securities. The *price* at which foreign and domestic currency is exchanged is called the *exchange rate*. It records how much of one country's currency is needed in exchange for a given amount of another country's currency. For example, the exchange rate between the American dollar and the German Deutsche mark during recent years has been approximately one Deutsche mark = $.25. From the

American point of view, this means that one dollar equals four Deutsche marks.[3]

The Relationship Between the Exchange Rate and the Balance of Payments

We have said that the demand for a country's currency depends on the total value of its exports, the inflow of remittances and pensions, the inflow of foreign government capital, and the inflow of private foreign capital funds. On the other hand, the supply of a nation's currency depends on the total value of its imports, the outflow of remittances and pensions, the outflow of government funds, and the outflow of private capital funds.

Thus, at a given rate of exchange, should the demand for a nation's currency exceed its supply, there is a balance-of-payments surplus. On the other hand, at a given exchange rate, should the supply exceed the demand, there is a balance-of-payments deficit. Should the exchange rate change, however, the amounts of a nation's currency demanded and supplied will also change, and so will the balance of payments. Not only does the exchange rate give us the price of one country's currency relative to foreign currency, but it also tells us how much foreign goods and services cost in terms of one's own currency.

For example, if a German product costs 12 Deutsche marks, then, with an exchange rate of $1 = 4 Deutsche marks, the cost in dollars of the German product is $3. Should the exchange rate change to $1 = 5 Deutsche marks, the dollar price of the German good is reduced to $2.40. This should lead to an increase in the U.S. demand for the commodity. In addition, it should cause an increase in the total amount of American money supplied as foreign exchange. This assumes, however, that the American demand for the German good is *price-elastic*—that the amount of the German product demanded expands more than proportionately to the decrease in the price of the product to Americans. For example, if at a price of $1, ten units of product are demanded, then at a price of $.50 per unit the amount demanded would expand to more than twenty units, leading to expenditures in excess of $10.

A drop in the exchange rate also works in the opposite direction. If the exchange rate falls to $1 = 3 Deutsche marks, the price of the good to Americans is increased.[4] This will cause a decrease in the amount demanded.

---

[3] We use the term "exchange rate" here as if there were only one rate of exchange between two different national currencies. Actually there are a number of different rates. For example, there is the *cable rate*, the *thirty-day rate*, and the *sixty-day rate*. Generally, the rate will be higher the sooner one wants foreign monies. If a government has established a fixed ratio between its currency and that of other countries, then these various exchange rates will be very close to the official rate.

[4] By a fall in the exchange rate we mean a decrease in the amount of a foreign currency that a unit of another given currency can command. For the other country, however, this situation is viewed as a rise in the exchange rate because its currency can now command more units of the depreciated foreign currency.

If the American demand for the product is price-elastic, total expenditures on the product will decrease and the amount of American currency supplied in the foreign exchange market will also decrease. Hence, *the quantity of a country's currency supplied in the foreign exchange market will tend to increase with increases in the exchange rate.* This statement however, assumes (1) that the demand for foreign goods is elastic, and (2) that other things remain equal. This is illustrated in Figure 25–1 by that part of the *SS* curve sloping upward and to the right.

FIGURE 25–1. A hypothetical supply and demand for dollars in the foreign exchange market.

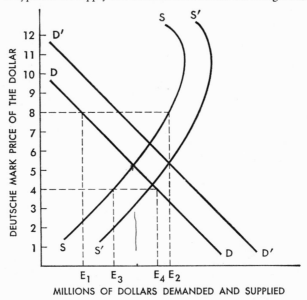

Conversely, should the demand for foreign goods and services be price inelastic, then, as the exchange rate rises, the total volume of currency supplied decreases. When the demand for a product is price-inelastic, the amount of the product demanded expands less than proportionately to a decrease in the price of that product. Hence there would be an increase in the number of units sold but a decrease in total expenditures. In the foreign exchange market, expenditures on imports are part of the supply of a nation's currency. When an import is price inelastic, therefore, the supply of currency slopes upward and to the left as a result of decreased expenditures on foreign goods and services. This decreased supply of currency is shown in the backward bending part of the *SS* curve in Figure 25–1.

The demand schedule for a country's currency slopes downward and to the right, as is shown by *DD* in Figure 25–1. The demand for a country's currency is equal to the total payments other countries are willing to make. Thus, other things being equal, the lower the exchange rate, the lower the price of a country's exports and the greater the amount of its currency demanded. Assume, for example, that an American product costs $1. When the exchange rate is $1 = 4 Deutsche marks, the cost of the American product to a German buyer is 4 Deutsche marks. Should the exchange rate fall to $1 = 3 Deutsche marks, then the price of the good to a German falls to 3 Deutsche marks. This lower price will probably induce Germans to purchase more of the American product. In order to purchase more of this product, however, additional American money is needed, since the dollar price of the product remains unchanged. The change in the exchange rate simply reflects a change in the Deutsche mark price. For this reason, other things being equal, the demand for a country's currency will almost always slope downward and to the right in terms of the demand curve in Figure 25–1.[5]

Figure 25–1 shows hypothetical demand and supply schedules for American dollars. For the sake of simplicity we have assumed a two-country universe, Germany and the United States, in which Germany represents the rest of the world with which the United States trades. On the vertical axis we can measure the Deutsche mark price of the dollar. The number of dollars demanded and supplied at varying exchange rates is measured on the horizontal axis.

The balance-of-payments surplus or deficit is really the difference between the demand and supply schedules, *DD* and *SS*. For example, in terms of our hypothetical supply and demand schedule, if the exchange rate is $1 = 8 Deutsche marks, we know that the supply of American dollars exceeds the demand for American dollars in the foreign exchange market. American payments exceed receipts, causing a balance-of-payments deficit equal to $E_2 - E_1$ million. On the other hand, when the exchange rate is $1 = 4 Deutsche marks, the demand for American dollars exceeds the supply. American receipts exceed payments and there is a balance-of-trade surplus equal to $E_4 - E_3$ million. For there to be no balance-of-payments deficit or surplus, the exchange rate must be $1 = 5+ Deutsche marks. This rate will bring equilibrium to the balance of payments, since it is at this point that the demand and supply schedules intersect.

The Position of the Foreign Exchange Demand and Supply Schedules

The position of the *DD* and *SS* curves in Figure 25–1 depends on a series of given factors. *First* is the *level of domestic income*. As incomes increase,

---

[5] If the German demand for American goods in this illustration had been price-inelastic, the demand curve for American dollars would still have sloped downward and to the right. For price-inelastic goods, Germans would be giving up less of their own currency to get American dollars if the value of the mark were raised. The total number of dollars demanded would still increase with a decrease in the exchange rate. This is so because the dollar price of the American goods would be unchanged by the revaluation of the mark. Therefore, as they seek to purchase more American goods, Germans would need more American dollars.

the demand for home-produced *and* foreign goods and services increases, also. Therefore, if income in the United States should increase, the demand for foreign goods would increase, and accordingly the supply of American dollars in the foreign exchange market would grow. In terms of Figure 25–1, the *SS* line would shift to the right, as is illustrated by *S'S'*. At any given exchange rate, this would mean that the supply of currency has increased relative to the demand. Thus any deficit existing prior to the income increase has widened, and any surplus existing prior to income increase has narrowed.

Conversely, a decrease in domestic income reduces the demand for foreign goods and services. The supply of the currency decreases, deficits narrow, and surpluses widen.

Second, incomes abroad affect the position of the demand for currency. Increased incomes abroad mean that other nations demand both more domestic-produced goods and more foreign goods. For example, an increase in German gross national product induces an increase in the demand for American goods. To get more American goods, however, the Germans need more American dollars. Thus the *DD* line shifts to the right, becoming *D'D'*. If, prior to the German income change, there had been a deficit U.S. balance of payments, this deficit would now have narrowed.

Third, prices at home relative to those abroad affect both the demand for and supply of currency in the foreign exchange market. Suppose that prices in the United States decline relative to those in Germany. This makes the American products more attractive than the comparable German products. Both Americans and Germans demand more American goods and fewer German goods. The result is a decrease in the supply of American currency entering the foreign exchange market (a shift to the left in *SS*) and an increase in the demand for American currency by Germans (a shift to the right in *DD*). This improves the American balance-of-payments situation unless the elasticities are unfavorable. On the other hand, a rise in prices in the United States relative to those in Germany will increase the supply of American dollars in the foreign exchange market and decrease the demand for American dollars. More German products and fewer American products are demanded; the American balance of payments situation worsens.

Fourth, interest rates at home relative to those abroad influence the demand for and supply of currency in the foreign exchange market. Should interest rates decline in the United States relative to those in Germany, the demand for dollars will decline and the supply will increase. The decline in U.S. interest rates makes German securities more attractive as a financial investment. As a consequence, Germans demand fewer American securities, and hence less U.S. money. Americans also purchase fewer of their own securities and increase their purchases of German securities, thereby further increasing the supply of American dollars on the foreign exchange market. Conversely, a rise in U.S. interest rates relative to those abroad will increase the demand for American dollars and decrease the supply.

And fifth, expectations are an important determinant of both the demand for and supply of currency. Suppose that the domestic political stability of a country becomes threatened. As a rule this situation will cause a capital flight to take place. The inhabitants of this country will try to transfer their currency holdings into the currency of a nation with greater stability. At the same time, foreign demands for the goods, services, and securities of the troubled nation will diminish. This will cause *DD* to shift to the left and *SS* to the right. The balance-of-payments situation worsens.

Expectations concerning future exchange rates are also important. If, for example, it looks as though the exchange rate will increase, then it pays to postpone purchases abroad until one's own currency is actually able to command more foreign money. Such a delay causes a shift to the left in the *SS* curve. At the same time, foreign nations try to get into the currency that is soon to be appreciated; they prefer to buy goods, services, and securities prior to the change in the exchange rate. This causes a shift to the right in the *DD* curve. Reverse movements will occur when the expectation is that the exchange rate will drop.

SUMMARY

This chapter has examined some of the monetary effects of a nation's international balance of payments. It has explained the relationship between the balance of payments and the exchange rate. A nation's balance of payments is in deficit when, at a given exchange rate, the demand for its currency is less than the supply in the foreign exchange market. Conversely, there is a surplus balance of payments when the demand for a country's currency is greater than its supply in the foreign exchange market. A major part of the following chapter is devoted to various solutions to balance-of-payments difficulties.

Supplementary Readings
Haberler, Gottfried. *A Survey of International Trade Theory*. Princeton, N.J., Princeton University Special Papers in International Economics, 1961.
Holmes, Alan R. *The New York Foreign Exchange Market*. New York, The Federal Reserve Bank of New York, 1959.

Chapter 26

Alternative International
Economic Policies

The preceding chapter examined the relationship between the balance of payments and the exchange rates. Alternative solutions to balance-of-payments problems are considered in this chapter. In addition we briefly examine the problem of international liquidity.

POLICIES
FOR THE BALANCE-OF-PAYMENTS PROBLEM

Adjustments under Flexible Exchange Rates

One way to establish a balance-of-payments equilibrium is by means of a *freely flexible exchange rate*. When the exchange rate is above the equilibrium level, the supply of currency exceeds the demand, and there is a balance-of-payments deficit. If the government permits its exchange rate to fluctuate freely in response to market forces, however, the exchange rate will decline in response to this deficit. The price of domestic goods will then drop relative to foreign goods and the purchase of domestic goods and services will increase accordingly. This causes the amount of currency demanded to increase and the amount of currency supplied to decrease. Hence the balance of payments deficit decreases.

On the other hand, should the exchange rate be below the equilibrium level, the demand for money exceeds the supply in the foreign exchange market and there is a balance-of-payments surplus. The currency that is in relatively short supply can be expected to increase in value relative to other currencies. This will increase the price of domestic goods relative to foreign goods. Citizens of the surplus country, induced by the increased value of their currency abroad, will step up foreign purchases and decrease domestic purchases. Conversely, citizens of other countries will decrease their purchases abroad and increase their domestic purchases. Thus the amount of the surplus country's currency demanded decreases and the amount of its currency supplied increases. In this fashion the balance-of-payments surplus decreases.

If a country allows its exchange rates to fluctuate freely, payments equilibrium will be quickly established and chronic balance-of-payments deficits and surpluses will be eliminated. Proponents of this view believe that an international policy of this sort will permit a nation to design its monetary and fiscal policies with purely internal problems in mind. No longer need there be a conflict between policies for internal and external economic stability. For example, interest rates are often decreased by the monetary authorities as a means of stimulating the economy during a recession. This domestic policy often endangers balance-of-payments stability, however. As was shown in Chapter 25, a decline in domestic rates relative to those abroad will tend to expand a balance-of-payments deficit. Thus the monetary authority is forced to choose between continuing to keep interest rates low to stimulate economic recovery or raising them to eliminate the balance-of-payments deficit.

Fiscal stabilization policies face the same dilemma. Anti-recessionary fiscal policies could well involve both a decrease in taxes and an increase in government spending. This would lead to much-needed increases in income and output, but it would also conflict with balance-of-payments stability. Rising incomes lead to increased purchase of goods and services abroad, and as previously noted the supply of currency widens relative to the demand for it in the foreign exchange market. Thus the balance-of-payments deficit is increased.

Permitting exchange rates to fluctuate freely can eliminate this conflict between internal and external objectives. No surplus or deficit in the balance of payments can long continue because changes in the exchange rate induce changes in the amounts of currency demanded and supplied in the foreign exchange market. Thus the demand for currency and the supply tend to balance each other.

In spite of these advantages there is strong opposition to the use of flexible exchange rates as an international monetary system. In fact, monetary authorities themselves are usually opposed to such an arrangement. Most countries prefer to fix the value of their currency in relation to the currencies of other nations because they fear that flexible exchange rates would leave the determination of the exchange rate to speculators rather than to free-market demand and supply forces.

With freely fluctuating exchange rates, if speculators expect the rates to decline, for example, they can force the decline by switching to a more valuable currency. Since a decline in the exchange rate decreases the ability of a currency to command other currencies in exchange, it pays the speculator to sell a currency before it depreciates. He simultaneously purchases other currencies. This action increases the supply relative to the demand for the depreciating currency, however, thereby providing the force needed to drive the exchange rate down.

When will the actions of the speculator actually tend to be destabilizing? Precisely when the internal conditions of a country warrant a continuing depreciation in the exchange rate. This is most likely to occur if domestic monetary and fiscal policies are causing continuing price rises relative to price levels abroad. Thus it is chiefly domestic price inflation that triggers currency speculation that is destabilizing in terms of exchange-rate determination, rather than the flexible exchange rates themselves.

In sharp contrast, when exchange-rate movements appear to be temporary, the actions of the speculator may actually have a stabilizing influence. If the exchange rate has temporarily declined and speculators expect it to return to old levels, they will buy more of the depreciated currency because they expect to make a profit by selling the currency after it has returned to higher levels. This added demand for currency when it is depreciated will push exchange rates up.

Most countries are anxious to guard against the possibly destabilizing effects of speculative currency manipulation nonetheless, and consequently they keep firm control of the value of their currency in the foreign exchange market. This effectively prevents flexible exchange rates from becoming a feasible international economic policy.

Adjustments under the Gold Standard

Many countries describe the value of their currencies in terms of gold. The dollar, for example, is defined by an act of Congress as being equal to $\frac{1}{35}$ ounce of gold. This presumably puts the United States on the gold standard. The following discussion describes how balance-of-payments adjustments *should* take place under the gold standard. That they do *not* take place in this manner in the real world arises from the fact that countries are unwilling to accept the internal consequences of the gold standard.

Under the gold standard each country defines its money in terms of gold; governments should be prepared to exchange gold for currency and vice versa on demand. In addition, variations in the supply of gold should be permitted to affect the stock of money. The relationship of each unit of account to gold establishes the exchange rates between the different units of account. For example, if the dollar is worth $\frac{1}{35}$ ounce of gold and the Deutsche mark $\frac{1}{140}$ ounce of gold, then the exchange rate between the two currencies is $1 = 4 Deutsche marks; the dollar is worth four times as much gold as the Deutsche mark.

How would a balance-of-payments adjustment take place under such a gold standard? For the sake of simplicity let us assume that there are only two currencies to deal with, the dollar and the Deutsche mark, which represents the unit of account for the rest of the world. Let us further assume that initially there is a balance-of-payments equilibrium. Now imagine that the American preferences for foreign goods and services increase. This leads to an increase in the demand for foreign goods and an increase in the supply of dollars in the foreign exchange market. The United States now has a balance-of-payments *deficit*. Since the U.S. government is unwilling to decrease the gold content of the dollar, it cannot permit the exchange rate to decrease. Therefore, the U.S. must *lose gold* to the rest of the world. To protect itself against a loss of gold, the central bank in the United States is expected to *raise interest rates*. Other countries, in turn, decrease their interest rates in response to the gold inflow. As noted in Chapter 25, this change in interest rates would tend to improve the balance of payments for the deficit country.

This loss of gold reduces commercial bank reserves in the United States and causes some contraction in deposit money to take place. Deflationary forces are activated in the U.S. economy. At the same time, in other countries the gold inflow increases reserves, and banks with the additional lending capacity expand loans. The lower interest rates abroad encourage foreigners to borrow more at home. In the United States, however, borrowing has become more expensive. Businesses must put a stop to capital expansion in plant and equipment because the margin between expected returns from investment and the cost of funds has narrowed. As a result, employment decreases in the United States.

If prices are flexible in the United States, there also will be *downward pressure on the price level*. At the level of prices prior to the gold outflow, the demand for goods is now less than the supply. With prices flexible downward, however, any loss of employment in the United States will be temporary. In time declining prices will *stimulate demand for home-produced goods* both by Americans and by foreigners. Americans will also purchase fewer goods and services abroad. Thus the real demand for goods relative to the supply will tend to be maintained.

Abroad, however, the situation is the reverse. Lower interest rates have encouraged increased borrowing, expenditures on capital goods have risen, and income and output have increased. Since the rest of the world may be close to full employment, very little of the increased demand can be satisfied. As a consequence, there is upward pressure on prices abroad. Thus the price level in the United States has decreased relative to prices abroad. This, in turn, leads to an *increase in the demand for American currency and a decrease in its supply*. Conversely, the demand for the Deutsche mark (the unit of account we have posited for the rest of the world) decreases and its supply increases. In this fashion, the *balance-of-payments deficit* for the United States is *wiped out*.

This process makes the important assumption that there is downward price flexibility, which assures full employment. It will be recalled from our theoretical analysis in Part III that this was a typical nineteenth- and early twentieth-century economic assumption that has proven unrealistic in the twentieth-century world. We now know that it is possible to have less-than-full-employment equilibrium. The flaw in the gold standard mechanism for adjusting balance-of-payments differences is that it ignored this possibility.

Assume that prices and wages are not flexible downward. This assumption means that to achieve a balance-of-payments equilibrium changes would have to be made in income, output, or employment. If prices do not decline in the United States as gold flows out, the money stock declines and interest rates rise. As a consequence, income, output, and employment must fall. Decreases in income lead to a decrease in the demand for foreign goods. This, in turn, means that the supply of American dollars in the foreign exchange market decreases. So long as the deficit remains, however, gold will continue to flow out and domestic income and output will continue to drop. Once income has dropped sufficiently, the supply of American currency will again become equal to the demand. At this point, the balance-of-payments deficit ends. Internal stability has been sacrificed for external stability.

Adherence to the gold standard prevents national monetary authorities from exercising sufficient control over the domestic level of employment and prices. With price rigidity, deficits tend to lead to unemployment, and surpluses, during periods of full employment, tend to lead to inflation. Thus internal price and employment stability are often sacrificed for balance-of-payments stability.

This was roughly the state of affairs prior to World War I for those countries on the gold standard. Monetary authorities at the time were chiefly concerned with protecting their reserves. As gold flowed out, they increased interest rates; as gold flowed in, they decreased interest rates. Following World War I, however, central banks gradually became more and more interested in maintaining domestic equilibrium. Countries went off the rigid type of gold standard described here to improve domestic stability. Hence, although most economies of the Western world still maintain some fiction of a gold standard externally, most currencies are not convertible into gold internally. Even those countries that do not define their money in terms of gold frequently attempt to maintain a stable rate of exchange beween their currency and the American dollar or the British pound sterling which are still based on gold.

This adherence to the semblance of a gold standard in international trade creates difficulties in the contemporary economic world. We do not permit exchange rates to fluctuate freely so as to correct balance-of-payment difficulties. We do not permit an automatically functioning gold standard to correct for balance-of-payments difficulties, either. How, then, do contemporary economies make adjustments in their balance of payments?

Adjustments under Fixed Exchange Rates

The gold standard is one type of system that depends on fixed exchange rates. No nation follows the rules of the gold standard, however. As a result, monetary authorities must make many *ad hoc* adjustments to maintain stable exchange rates and a balance-of-payments equilibrium. Let us use the United States as an example.

The relation between gold and the U.S. economy. Internally gold has little significance for the U.S. economy. The average citizen has not been able to redeem his coin, currency, and check money for the money metal gold since 1933. Today the only important function that gold performs internally is to act as a reserve for the Federal Reserve banks; for every dollar in member bank reserve and Federal Reserve note liabilities, the Federal Reserve banks must hold twenty-five cents in gold certificate assets. Even this requirement can be suspended by the Board of Governors of the Federal Reserve System, however.

TABLE 26–1. THE BALANCE OF PAYMENTS AND NET GOLD PURCHASES OR SALES BY THE UNITED STATES, 1956–1963 (IN MILLIONS OF DOLLARS)

YEAR	BALANCE OF PAYMENTS	NET GOLD PURCHASES OR SALES
1956	−935	280
1957	520	772
1958	−3,529	−2,294
1959	−3,743	−1,041
1960	−3,881	−1,669
1961	−2,370	−820
1962	−2,186	−833
1963	−1,958	−392

Source: Balance of payments: see Table 25–2; net gold purchases or sales: *Federal Reserve Bulletin*, May, 1964, p. 648.

Gold is chiefly important to the United States as a source of international reserves. By defining the dollar as being equal to $\frac{1}{35}$ ounce of gold, the United States has obligated itself to turn over $\frac{1}{35}$ ounce of gold to foreign monetary authorities in exchange for every U.S. dollar they have accumulated. Since the volume of dollar claims to gold increases with a balance-of-payments deficit and decreases with a balance-of-payments surplus, gold flows are likely to increase with deficits and decrease with surpluses in the U.S. balance of payments.

Table 26–1 lists the balance of payments and the net gold flows for the United States from 1956 to 1963. Notice that the years of largest deficits were also those of the heaviest gold outflows. The one year of balance-of-payments surplus, 1957, had a net gold inflow.

Because of continuing balance-of-payments deficits, the United States has had continual gold outflows in recent years. The net effect has been to reduce the gold stock of the United States from $21.8 billion at the end of

1955 to $15.6 billion at the end of 1963. The United States still had 37 percent of the noncommunist world's gold in 1963, but this was significantly less than the 58 percent it held at the end of 1955.[1]

U.S. adjustments to the balance-of-payments deficit. There are a number of ways in which a country can reduce a balance-of-payments deficit. Most of these involve stimulating the demand for its currency and discouraging increases in the supply in the foreign exchange market. Among the most commonly used techniques are (1) to depress domestic income levels, (2) to reduce the internal price level, (3) to lower the exchange rate (devaluation), (4) to permit the loss of gold reserves and other international reserves to continue, (5) to raise internal interest rates, (6) to reduce government expenditures abroad, (7) to impose trade and exchange controls, (8) to induce one's citizens to buy fewer goods and securities abroad, (9) to induce foreign nations to purchase more goods and securities, and (10) to set up special arrangements with the central banks of other countries. Most of these policies can be used in reverse when there is a balance-of-payments surplus.

The first four of these remedies are not palatable to the United States in its present deficit position. To *depress domestic income and price levels* would sacrifice internal stability. The best that can be done on this score is to prevent price inflation. A *reduction in the exchange rate* is not politically feasible; both Democrats and Republicans are firmly committed to keeping the dollar freely interchangeable with gold at $35 an ounce. This commitment was made to reduce speculation on the dollar and to permit the dollar to continue to serve as an international medium of exchange. Other countries have not been so reluctant to change their exchange rates, however. Britain underwent a substantial devaluation of the pound in 1949. Germany, which in recent years has had a surplus balance of payments, revalued her currency upward in 1961. This was done in part to relieve the United States of some of its balance-of-payments difficulties. It should be pointed out that if the United States were to devalue (lower the exchange rate), other countries could retaliate by also reducing their exchange rates. This latter action could cancel out any beneficial effects of U.S. devaluation. The fourth remedy, to *permit the continued loss of international reserves,* would not serve to correct the excess of supply over demand for American currency in the foreign exchange market. It would merely permit the deficit to continue and eventually the loss of gold would require more remedial action in the absence of a change in the exchange rate.

The other approaches listed above have proven more feasible; varieties of these policies have been followed by the United States. *Monetary policy has been directed toward discouraging short-term capital outflows.* The Federal Reserve System has abandoned its "bills only" policy in an effort to *keep* long-term interest rates low and *short-term rates relatively high.* By buying

---

[1] *Federal Reserve Bulletin,* May, 1961, p. 624, and May, 1964, p. 646.

long-term securities, the Federal Reserve provides funds needed to stimulate an economy operating at less than full employment. By selling short-term securities, it keeps short-term rates high, thereby inducing individuals and businesses with temporarily idle funds to purchase short-term securities in the United States rather than abroad. The Federal Reserve also increased the discount rate in July, 1963, as a further step toward relieving the balance-of-payments deficit. It was hoped that this action would not depress the economy internally.

Again in November, 1964, the discount rate was increased. The aim then was to counter a British rise in the short-term rate from 5 to 7 percent. Britain had increased its rate in order to reduce pressure on the pound resulting from an adverse balance of trade and payments. The American action was designed principally to prevent an increased flow of U.S. dollars to Britain pursuant to a widened spread of interest rates in Britain's favor.

Another means of reducing a balance-of-payments deficit has been the *direct entry of the U.S. Treasury and the Federal Reserve into the foreign exchange market as buyers and sellers*. The Treasury entered the market in 1961 and the Federal Reserve System in 1962. All purchases of foreign currency are carried on by the special manager for foreign currency of the Federal Reserve Bank of New York. By using its sizable foreign exchange holdings, the Federal Reserve can buy back dollars that are held by foreigners, thereby reducing the chance of a gold outflow.

The federal government has also taken *fiscal action* to correct its balance-of-trade deficit. The *rate of military expenditures* abroad has been reduced, for example. Some American military installations in other countries have been closed and regulations regarding whether military dependents may live abroad have been tightened. Our allies have been encouraged to increase their armament purchases from the United States. In addition, the U.S. Treasury has increased the supply of short-term U.S. government securities, thereby further pushing short-term rates upward.

Trade and exchange controls can also be used to decrease a balance-of-payments deficit. Tariffs and import restrictions are trade controls. An increase in tariffs raises the price of foreign goods and services to importers. This decreases the demand for foreign goods and services, reduces the supply of the importing country's currency on the foreign exchange market, and reduces its balance-of-payments deficit. Import quotas also restrict the supply of a country's currency. Under import quotas, only a given amount of foreign goods can be imported, regardless of the demand for the product. Exchange controls work somewhat differently. They restrict the use that nationals and foreigners may make of funds acquired in trade. For example, a foreign nation may be required to spend a given portion of its exchange receipts in the importing country, or the exporters of the country with the controls may be forced to sell their receipts of foreign currency at an official rate to their government in exchange for domestic currency.

The United States government does not endorse such trade and exchange controls as a means of adjusting the balance-of-payments deficit. It is officially and ideologically committed to the removal of trade barriers. It favors a free flow of goods, services, and funds throughout the world. To Americans, the economic common sense of such a policy is obvious; if other countries can be persuaded to reduce their barriers, then foreign demand for American goods, services, and securities will expand, thereby increasing the demand for American currency and decreasing the national balance-of-payments deficit.

The position of the United States on this matter, however, is somewhat ambivalent. On the one hand, it has taken the *lead in reducing barriers* to encourage the free flow of goods and funds between nations. On the other hand, it has also *adopted restraints* that amount to barriers. In 1961, for example, the United States reduced the duty-free exemption for returning tourists to $100 per person. In effect, this raised the price of foreign goods to American tourists and caused the demand for foreign goods and the supply of American dollars going abroad to decrease. In 1964 the United States enacted a restrictive measure called an interest-equalization tax. The tax applies to all Americans who purchase new or outstanding foreign securities (Canadian securities are exempted) maturing in more than three years. The tax is designed to reduce the interest differential between American and foreign securities so as to decrease the supply of American currency in the foreign exchange market. In spite of these apparent contradictions United States policy is still primarily to encourage international trade by eliminating trade and exchange controls.

Aside from the previously mentioned interest-rate changes, tourist import restrictions, interest-equalization tax, and decreased rate of military expenditures, little was done directly through 1964 to curb the domestic demand for foreign goods, services, and securities, or to stimulate the foreign demand for domestic production and securities. Some effort was made to require recipients of American foreign aid to spend these funds in the United States. The cut in the 1963 corporation income tax was primarily directed toward internal tax reform and stability, but may well have contributed to increases in foreign investment in the United States in 1963 and 1964.

In any case, the *main line of defense* against the deficit has been *monetary*. The action taken has been primarily of two types: (1) efforts have been made to *maintain high short-term interest rates*, and (2) *special arrangements have been set up with the central banks of other countries*. Under the latter heading, foreign governments have been persuaded to make prepayments on U.S. loans and military purchases in the United States. This gives only temporary relief to the balance-of-payments deficit, however. A more important feature of our financial arrangements with other countries has been the lessening of speculation on the dollar by the use of devices such as *swap arrangements* and the *Gold Pool*.

In general, a *swap*, in this sense of the word, is an arrangement whereby a central bank agrees to exchange its currency for another currency for a limited period of time, usually not in excess of six months. This enables a country that is experiencing a temporary balance-of-payments deficit to use the foreign currency it acquires in a swap to buy back its own currency in the foreign exchange market and thus reduce the possibility that expanding foreign claims will result in a gold outflow. When we buy up our own currency in this fashion, the demand for dollars expands and the supply of other currencies in the foreign exchange market increases. Speculators who had counted on a deterioration in the price of the dollar relative to other currencies are thus disappointed.

The Federal Reserve System presently has arrangements with the Bank of France, the Bank of England, the Netherlands Bank, the National Bank of Belgium, the Bank for International Settlements, the Swiss National Bank, the German Federal Bank, the Bank of Italy, the Austrian National Bank, the Bank of Sweden, and the Bank of Japan. Swap arrangements have been particularly helpful in relieving the pressure on the U.S. balance of payments caused by short-term capital flows. In addition, the fact that the Federal Reserve and the Treasury may purchase foreign exchange directly stabilizes expectations concerning the rate of exchange. When President Kennedy was assassinated in November, 1963, for example, the Federal Reserve Bank of New York immediately offered to exchange foreign currency for dollars. This demonstrated that the Federal Reserve System was willing to support the dollar in the foreign exchange market, that there would be a continuation of current U.S. economic policies. It helped prevent widespread panic sales of dollars in the foreign exchange market.

The *Gold Pool* is an arrangement whereby various central banks operate in the London gold market to stabilize the price of gold. In the absence of efforts to stabilize the price of gold, speculation could conceivably cause serious fluctuation in the gold market. In the fall of 1960, for example, when the continuing U.S. balance-of-payments deficit led to an expectation of a decrease in the gold content of the dollar, many speculators rushed to get out of dollars and into gold. As a consequence, the dollar price of gold in the London market began to hover around $40 an ounce instead of close to $35 an ounce, since the Gold Pool was not in operation at that time. American pledges of maintaining its exchange rate, however, tended to stabilize expectations.

Since 1961, the Gold Pool has been in operation. By selling and buying gold, defensively, it stabilizes the world price of gold and minimizes the effects of private speculation. The Gold Pool also buys newly produced gold for distribution to its central bank participants.[2]

It is difficult to determine the overall effectiveness of these techniques in eliminating the U.S. balance-of-payments deficit. The deficit has decreased

---

[2] For a more detailed account of the operations of the Gold Pool see Charles A. Coombs, "Treasury and Federal Reserve Foreign Exchange Operations and the Gold Pool," *Monthly Review*, Federal Reserve Bank of New York, (March, 1964), pp. 47–56.

since its 1960 high, yet at the time of this writing one cannot say whether the decrease has been due to U.S. policies or to changed conditions abroad. Europe has had price inflation in recent years, whereas the United States has enjoyed comparative price stability. This has tended to increase the demand for American goods and hence the demand for American currency. At the same time, this factor has tended to decrease the supply of American currency by reducing U.S. demand for imports. This force may operate to end the U.S. balance-of-payments deficit. If it does end, we may again have a surplus as we did after World War II. Should this occur, the problem may become one of reducing a European balance-of-payments deficit and an American balance-of-payments surplus. This is not generally expected to occur, since direct American long-term corporate investments abroad are expanding.

THE PROBLEM OF INTERNATIONAL LIQUIDITY

The term "international liquidity" refers to the distribution and quantity of the gold reserves and foreign exchange holdings of all the countries of the world. Just as in our domestic economy commercial banks need more reserves in order to create the additional money needed for a growing economy, so in the world as a whole more gold reserves and foreign exchange are needed to carry on the increase of international trade. International liquidity is provided principally through gold production or deficits in the U.S. balance of payments. As already noted in our preceding discussion, American deficits cannot continue indefinitely. Even if they could, world trade has expanded more rapidly than the total supply of gold and dollars. To many economists this means that there is now a shortage of international liquidity. How is additional international liquidity to be provided?

A number of solutions suggest themselves. First, the major trading nations of the world could go on a freely fluctuating exchange rate. As noted earlier, however, most countries fear currency speculation and therefore prefer to keep firm control over their currency in the foreign exchange market. Second, the United States could increase the dollar price of gold. Such a devaluation of the dollar is politically inexpedient, however. In addition, while devaluation by the United States would set up forces to correct the U.S. balance-of-payments deficits, other countries could retaliate by also devaluing their currency. While this would help international liquidity, it would complicate balance-of-payments adjustments. For these reasons most proposals concentrate on improving international monetary cooperation by means of devices such as swap arrangements and the Gold Pool, which help channel gold into central banks and away from the hands of private speculators.

The International Monetary Fund is one international financial institution that is designed to help provide international liquidity. The Fund seeks to promote free trade, to stabilize exchange rates at equilibrium levels, and to sell foreign currencies to countries experiencing deficits in their balance of payments. There are 102 members in the International Monetary Fund. Each member nation is assigned a quota of gold and currency that it must contribute to the fund. The quota also indicates the extent to which a member nation may buy foreign currency from the Fund when it has a deficit balance of payments. Until 1958 the resources of the Fund amounted to only $9 billion. The apparent increasing need for international liquidity led to an expansion of quotas in 1959, when the resources of the Fund were increased to $14 billion. This caused the quota of the United States to rise from $2.75 billion to $4.125 billion. Hence the United States may now draw on the Fund up to $5.2 billion in foreign currency. International Monetary Fund resources were again increased in 1961 and 1962. The Fund can now borrow up to $6 billion from various industrial nations when other nations that are short of reserves are making substantial drawings.

Some economists feel that these swap arrangements and improvements of the International Monetary Fund are still inadequate for meeting liquidity needs over the long run. Various alternative proposals that seem radical, at least to international bankers, have been made. Robert Triffin, for example, urges that the International Monetary Fund be strengthened so that it is comparable to a central world bank. According to Triffin's plan, all nations would turn over to a reorganized Fund their holdings of national currencies in exchange for new reserves—deposits with the Fund. Thus international reserves would then consist only of gold and deposits with the Fund. Reserves would expand as the Fund made loans to member nations and thus enhance the ability of member nations to trade in an expanding world economy. Actually, the reorganized Fund would operate in much the same way that the Federal Reserve System does when it expands Federal Reserve credit, which expands member bank reserves and thus increases their lending ability. Triffin does not propose unlimited expansion of international liquidity, of course; he would limit expansion to 3 or 4 percent a year, just enough to cover the need for additional international money as trade expands.

The principal objection to plans of this nature is political. Nations would have to comply with the international financial policies of the Fund. It seems most unlikely that nations that are still accustomed to thinking in terms of "the defense of the national interest" will comply, as a group, to the supranational Fund. If there is a problem of international liquidity, then it is more likely that compensating adjustments will evolve slowly, as they have in the past.

Supplementary Readings
Aliber, Robert Z. "The Adequacy of International Liquidity." In Commission on Money and Credit, *Monetary Management*, Englewood Cliffs, N.J., Prentice-Hall, 1963.

Harris, Seymour E., ed. *The Dollar in Crisis*. New York, Harcourt, Brace & World, 1961.

Kindleberger, Charles P. "Flexible Exchange Rates." In Commission on Money and Credit, *Monetary Management*, Englewood Cliffs, N.J., Prentice-Hall. 1963.

Lutz, Friedrich A. *The Problem of International Liquidity and the Multiple Currency Standard*. Essays in International Finance, No. 41. Princeton, N.J., Princeton University Press, 1963.

Triffin, Robert. *Gold and the Dollar Crisis*. New Haven, Yale University Press, 1960.

Index

Page numbers in italics refer to tables and figures.

Loans (continued)
  by nonbank financial institutions,
    118
  by nonbank institutions, *59*
  unsecured, 64
Lock-in effect, 68, 74
Locke, John, 273 fn., 273–74, 295
Lutz, Friedrich A., 305, 426

Macroeconomic policy, 374
Macroeconomic theory, 269, 306
Malestroit, 272
Margin requirements, 236–37, *238*
Marginal-efficiency-of-investment con-
  cept, 325, *326*, 327–28
Marginal propensity to consume, 316
Marginal propensity to save, 316
Marketable securities. *See* Government
  securities
Marshall, Alfred, 272, 291 fn., 293 fn.,
  294, 295
Marshall Plan, 406
Marxists, 294 fn.
Mayer, Thomas, 364 fn.
Meerman, Jacob P., 131 fn.
Meigs, A. J., 234 fn.
Meiselman, David, 363 fn.
Mellon, W. J., 99
Meltzer, Allan H., 365 fn.
Member banks, 31
  capital requirements for, 33–34
  number of, *32*
  par collection requirement for, 34–35
  qualifications to be met by, 33–35
  reserve requirements for, 35
Metzler, Lloyd, 297, 358
Mill, John Stuart, 279–81, 295
Mint Act of 1792, 127
Mints, Lloyd W., 275 fn., 295, 305, 359
  fn., 387–88, 390
Modigliani, Franco, 297
Monetary controls
  contracyclical use of, 222–24
  evaluation of, 222, *223*, 224–34
  and Federal Reserve credit, 224–27
  of Federal Reserve System, 182–87
  general, 182, 187–208, 209–22
  problems in use of, 231–34
  restrictive, 227, 228
  of the Treasury, 240–48
Monetary liabilities, 258, 261
Monetary policy, 374. *See also* Monetary controls; Monetary theory
  automatic, 385–90

criticism of, 382
discretionary, 385–90
goals of, 379–80
during inflation, 381–82
and nonbank financial intermediaries,
  383–85
during recession, 380–81
variable lag in, 389
Monetary standards
  bimetallic, 123–25
  Congressional adjustment of, 127
  gold, 122, 124–25, 126, 127
  internal paper, 122
  paper, 125, 127
  silver, 124, 125
Monetary theory, 269–70
  competing financial asset concept of,
    364–65
  in the eighteenth century, 274–76
  history of, 271–72
  Keynesian, 359–61
  and macroeconomic theory, 306
  in the nineteenth century, 277–81
  quantity, 361–64
  in the seventeenth century, 273–76
  in the sixteenth century, 272–73
  of supply, 262–66
  in the twentieth century, 281–94,
    296–97
Money. *See also* Currency; Demand
  deposits
  changes in stock of, *15*, 117, 258
  and commercial banking system,
    251–53
  created by banks, 26–27, 76–78, 80–83
  definition of, 2
  demand for, 339–46, 369–70
  demand deposit, 9–10
  as financial asset, 364–65
  function of, 1
  as liquid wealth, 8, 9–10
  as medium of exchange, 4
  Mill's definition of, 280
  Mill's quantity theory of, 280–81
  need for stability in, 2–4
  owners of, 9
  purchasing power of, 2–4
  quantity theory of, 280–81, 284, 361–
    64
  stable growth rules for, 388–89
  as standard of deferred payments, 5
  as store of value, 5
  supply of, 262–66, 346–48

B 6
C 7
D 8
E 9
F 0
G 1
H 2
I 3
J 4